Merit Pay

Merit Pay

A Strategic Approach to Linking Pay to Performance

Third Edition

By

Steven E. Williams

Jon M. Werner

And

Robert L. Heneman

emerald PUBLISHING

United Kingdom – North America – Japan
India – Malaysia – China

Emerald Publishing Limited, Floor 5, Northspring, 21-23 Wellington Street,
Leeds LS1 4DL

Third edition 2026

Cover photo: iStock/AndreyPopov/kasmasov/cnythzl

Reprints and permissions service
Contact: www.copyright.com

British Library Cataloguing in Publication Data
A catalogue record for this book is available from the British Library

ISBN: 978-1-80686-702-8 (Print hardback)
ISBN: 978-1-80686-704-2 (Print paperback)
ISBN: 978-1-80686-701-1 (Online)
ISBN: 978-1-80686-703-5 (Epub)

Typeset by TNQ Tech
Cover design by TNQ Tech
Index created by TNQ Tech
Printed and bound by CPI Group (UK) Ltd, Croydon, CR0 4YY

In memory of

my mother, Phyllis Williams
and
my father, William Edward Williams (SEW)

my father, Donald Sebastian Werner (JMW)

my mother, Jane R. Heneman
and
my father, Herbert G. Heneman, Jr.
(RLH)

CONTENTS

About the Authors .... *ix*

Preface .... *xi*

Acknowledgments .... *xvii*

1. Introduction and Overview *1*

PART I: ASSESSMENT OF THE DESIRABILITY AND FEASIBILITY OF MERIT PAY

2. Pay for Performance *27*
3. Diagnosing Situational Characteristics *75*

PART II: DEVELOPMENT AND ADMINISTRATION OF A MERIT PAY PLAN

4. Measuring Performance *123*
5. Establishing Pay Increases *175*
6. Merit Pay Administration *209*

PART III: EVALUATION OF RELEVANT OUTCOMES

7. Evaluating Merit Pay Outcomes *253*

References *305*

Index..*353*

ABOUT THE AUTHORS

Steven E. Williams has been an adjunct faculty member at several universities in Southern California and Missouri S&T, where he has taught courses is industrial and organizational psychology, human resource management, and statistics. In addition, he has been a management consultant specializing in compensation, employee selection, and applied statistical methods. He earned his PhD in Industrial & Organizational from Alliant International University, USA.

Jon M. Werner is an Emeritus Professor of Management at the University of Wisconsin-Whitewater, USA. He is co-author of *Merit Pay: Linking pay to performance in a changing world, second edition* (with Robert Heneman), as well as *Human resource development/Talent development, eighth edition.* He obtained his PhD in Organizational Behavior from Michigan State University, USA.

Robert L. Heneman is a Professor of Management, retired at the Ohio State University, USA. He is author of numerous books and publications concerning compensation, with a focus on merit pay. He obtained his PhD in Labor and Industrial Relations from Michigan State University, USA.

PREFACE

Purpose

This book was originally written to bring together a summary of the current knowledge on merit pay and to further advance understanding of this type of incentive pay plan. When the writing of the first edition was begun in 1989, there were no books devoted exclusively to the subject of merit pay. Thus, this book was written to fill a void in the compensation literature. Since then, merit pay remains a frequently used method of incentive compensation, and research into the merit pay process continues to grow. However, other forms of incentive pay, such as gainsharing, continue to receive attention, as evidenced by the number of books and articles on this topic in the popular press. In response to the frequent use of merit pay in organizations and the growing body of research, a book-length treatment of merit pay was needed. What we hope to do with this latest edition, beyond updating, is to link merit pay with the many changes going on in total compensation or "reward management" (Fulmer & Li, 2022; R. Heneman, 2001a, 2002, Perkins & Jones, 2020). We will argue that, even among all the challenges and changes that organizations currently face, there is still "merit" in appropriately conceived and implemented merit pay plans (Bartol, 2023; Bates, 2003c; Werner, 2021).

Perspectives

Current knowledge on merit pay is approached from three perspectives. First, we have tried to present a balanced view. Many articles on merit pay in business magazines and journals take a strong, almost emotional stance either for or against merit pay. This book strives for more balance by presenting both sides of the merit pay argument and evaluating these arguments in the context of available research. The book examines the conditions needed for merit pay to work without necessarily taking a side for or against merit pay.

Second, merit pay has been approached from an interdisciplinary perspective. Generally, the treatment of merit pay in academic journals has been somewhat parochial. The conclusions you draw about merit pay may depend on the journal you are reading and the academic discipline it represents. This book, however, draws upon articles from a variety of social science disciplines, including economics, industrial relations, public administration, management, and psychology in an attempt to provide the reader with a more comprehensive understanding of merit pay.

Third, in presenting recommendations for merit pay policy and practice, we have relied primarily on theory and research, rather than organizational practice. It is our belief that sound policy and practice are best drawn from theory and research, rather than from current practice at other organizations. While organizational practices are used to illustrate various points in the book, it is noted when these practices appear to conflict with theory and research.

To emphasize the importance of theory and research, we begin rather than end the book with a chapter on merit pay theory. It is our belief that the reader should understand the underlying rationale for merit pay *before* learning the mechanics of merit pay plans. Also, findings from empirical studies on merit pay are interspersed throughout the book, rather than relegating these findings to one chapter. Our hope is that by weaving research findings throughout the book, the reader will be encouraged to view research as crucial, ongoing input for managing the merit pay process, rather than as a side issue.

Audience

Our goal in writing this book was to serve three audiences: students, practitioners, and researchers. For students, this book can be used as a supplemental reader in a compensation class, or it can be used along with other books for an advanced topics class in human resource management. For practitioners, this book can be used as a reference guide, summarizing the empirical studies on issues arising in the design, administration, and evaluation of merit pay plans. Finally, for researchers, this book is useful as a review of the issues that have been investigated in merit pay research. In particular, our hope is that this book will encourage human resource researchers to expand the scope of performance appraisal/performance management research to include the context in which ratings take place.

Organization

The book begins with an introduction to the concept of merit pay. In the introduction, merit pay is defined and contrasted with other forms of incentive pay. The chapter ends with a model to guide the reader through the remainder of the book. The book is divided into three parts, based on the model.

The first part deals with assessing the desirability and feasibility of implementing a merit pay plan. This is accomplished through a chapter on theory and research and a chapter on diagnosing situational characteristics.

The second part of the book presents the processes used to develop and administer a merit pay plan. Included in the second part are three chapters on measuring performance, establishing pay increases based on measured performance, and administering a merit pay plan once pay increases are linked to performance.

The third and final part of the book describes anticipated outcomes associated with merit pay, methods to evaluate merit pay plans, and studies that have evaluated actual outcomes of merit pay plans compared to anticipated outcomes.

Third Edition

The world of work has changed considerably since the second edition was published. Advances in technology, changes in job design, alternate forms of work processes, and differences in workforce demographics account for many of these changes. In addition, compensation (in general) and merit pay (in particular) also have experienced changes based on these trends and events. The third edition addresses how these occurrences have introduced new theory and research impacting merit pay plans. Below are a few examples.

- *Recession of 2008.* In December of 2007, the US economy saw the beginning of an economic crisis—the housing market collapsed, fueled by low interest rates, easy credit, insufficient regulation, and toxic subprime mortgages. The recession spawned difficult decisions in compensation, such as merit pay budgets. Some firms decreased the amount of merit-pay increases as part of a total compensation reduction (Yoon & Sengupta, 2023). Conversely, other organizations maintained or increased merit pay inducements to offset reducing other forms of compensation, e.g., base pay, benefits (Yoon & Sengupta, 2023). Chapters 3 and 5 speak more to this matter.

- *Generational differences in the workplace.* For the first time in history, five generations or cohorts coexist in the current workplace. They are as follows:
  - *Traditionalists,* a.k.a. *the Silent Generation*: 2% of workforce (born 1925–1945)
  - *Baby Boomers*: 25% of workforce (born 1946–1964)
  - *Generation X*: 33% of workforce (born 1965–1980)
  - *Millennials, a.k.a. Generation Y*: 35% of workforce (born 1981–2000)
  - *Generation Z*: 5% of workforce (born since 2001)

    The age-gap of employees in the present workforce suggests that generational differences in needs, values, and preferences must be reexamined since the last edition. This version does just that, for example, younger workers (Generations Y and Z) react to performance feedback differently from their older counterparts (Traditionalist, Baby Boomers, and Generation X). Younger employees perceive feedback as future advise, while older workers perceive feedback as means of making a difference now (Wang et al., 2015). Differences here have implications for reliable and valid performance ratings, which appear in Chapter 4.
- *Covid-19 pandemic.* In the first quarter of 2020, the Covid-19 pandemic gripped the entire planet. Kniffin et al. (2021) completed a comprehensive study that focused on, and predicted, changes in work practices (e.g., working from home and virtual work teams) based on the pandemic. Time will tell whether or not said changes will be short-lived or last a long time. Several of these changes have implications for merit-pay practices (See Chapter 4 for more details). For example,
  - How will managers adjust to rating working from home (WFH) employee performance? Will this arrangement affect measurement reliability and/or validity?
  - If most, if not all, work behavior is confined to virtual work teams, will supervisors have sufficient exposure to fairly assess performance?
- *Job design and technology.* Since the inception of the internet and World Wide Web in the 1990s, employees began working from home (WFH). The next two decades saw a rapid increase in this work arrangement. Monikers, such as, remote work, and telecommunicating became commonplace. Then, the pandemic occurred, accelerating the WFH trend and galvanizing its permanence in the workplace. For merit pay, several implications have originated, for example, performance appraisal of remote worker (Murphy, 2021)

and geographical differences in determining merit pay increases (Gupta & Dev, 2020). Chapters 4 and 5 investigate these notions.

- *Work teams.* The use of work teams has dramatically changed since the second edition. Advances in teleconferencing and virtual teams have produced several implications for aspects in merit pay. Employees no longer have to be present in the same room, resulting in more efficiency. However, reduced exposure to employee's team behavior may contaminate performance ratings. In addition, new methods in dual (individual/team performance appraisal systems (Tatum, 2018) will be addressed in this edition (Chapter 4).
- *Strategic compensation/Merit pay.* Since the last edition, the scope of compensation (in general) and merit pay (in particular) has increased strategically in organizations. Strategic compensation focuses on pay policies and practices as they affect all organizational units over the short- and long-term. For example, merit pay research and practice has been compartmentalized for many years in addressing only individual performance and motivation in the short-term. Today, the results of merit pay consider other HR functions (e.g., candidate recruitment and employee retention) in the short- and long-term. The reader will see more on strategic compensation and how it interacts with performance management – Chapters 2–4.
- *Performance management.* In the last version, the idea of linking performance standards to an organization's strategic mission was introduced. In this edition, we expound on that connection, under its popular title of performance management. Performance management is a system of linking goals and strategies of the organization with the goals and activities of all organizational units. The implication here is that expanding rating standards from individual ratings to organizational units improves validity. An important aspect of performance management is a comprehensive measurement system that integrates and assesses the output (links) of all organizational units and provides a single metric of firm success. Moreover, the measurement system can also include the evaluation of individual goals and behaviors. As mentioned above, there is a symbiotic relationship between strategic compensation and performance, which will be explained in Chapter 4.
- *Advances in research design and statistical procedures.* In the third version of merit pay, recent advances in research design and statistical methods offer more clarity in understanding merit pay processes and outcomes. For example, meta-analysis creates additional credibility in demonstrating the relationship between

merit increases and past performance (Chapter 2) and merit increases and future performance (Chapter 7). In addition, meta-analysis also shows how internal and external validity can be improved for evaluating merit pay outcomes (Chapter 7). Several research studies in the third edition contain newer, more sophisticated research techniques to improve our understanding of the complexity in merit pay processes and inconsistencies in merit pay research (e.g., structural equation modeling (SEM) and multilevel analysis).

In summary, while much has changed in the compensation world since the second edition, merit pay remains popular—with perhaps as many as 90% of US firms using it (Nyberg et al., 2016; Trevor, 2017)—despite its controversial nature. The timeliness of this edition could not be better, occurring on the heels of major events and trends. We believe readers will benefit from over 230 new references added to the third edition (910 total references). Moreover, this edition provides study questions and case studies to increase student understanding of concepts, principles, and applications. Finally, in selected areas of the book, we added a new feature: Current events in merit pay. These events look at novel and controversial topics that we hope leave readers with thoughts to ponder. While much of the research and examples in this book come from North America, in this edition more international research and examples have been located and included (e.g., Kuvaas & Ding, 2025).

ACKNOWLEDGMENTS

We benefited greatly from many people who graciously gave their time and expertise in helping write this book. We would like to acknowledge and thank them for their contributions. For the first edition, many individuals reviewed the outline and/or individual chapters: John Blackburn, Lee Dyer, Charles Fay, Norman Handshear, Herbert Heneman III, Daniel Mitchell, Vida Scarpello, and Kenneth Wexley. Other individuals reviewed the entire manuscript: John Fossum, Edward Lawler III, Steve Mangum, Peter Riffel, Craig Schneier, Dow Scott, and Tony Townsend. John Wanous challenged me (Robert Heneman) to do more than simply report the current state of affairs with merit pay. Joan Evans did an outstanding job at translating my scrawl into an organized and presentable product.

For the third edition, we thank Cathy Sellars and Grace Harley for helping us get this work into print. We couldn't have done it without you!

We hope that all of the people acknowledged here will see their influence on the final product. We remain solely responsible, however, for any errors or omissions.

Finally, we would like to say some special thanks. Steve thanks his wife, Jan Farley, for her endless support. Steve wants to thank Jon Werner and Rob Heneman for the opportunity to contribute to this edition. Jon thanks his wife, Barbara Ann Werner (yes, like the Beach Boys classic!) for her ongoing support for another revision project, and his mother, Dorothy, for being his lifelong supporter. Rob thanks his wife, Renée Brausch Heneman, for her contributions to the initial writing of this book. Both Jon and Steve say, "thanks Rob!"

Steve E. Williams
Jon M. Werner
Robert L. Heneman

"The worker deserves his wages." (Luke 10:7)

CHAPTER 1

INTRODUCTION AND OVERVIEW

In this chapter, we introduce the concept of merit pay using several approaches. First, we describe our first encounters with merit pay. The questions that were raised by these experiences will be used to illustrate some of the topics to be covered in this book. We also illustrate some of the topics by describing tough decisions managers face when using merit pay. Second, we provide a more formal description of what merit pay is and what merit pay is not. This will give you an idea of the boundaries of merit pay and, in turn, what you can expect to see covered in the book. Third, we present a model of the merit pay process. This model is included to show the major steps that are involved in managing merit pay, and to preview the chapters of the book in the order in which they will be presented.

First Encounters with Merit Pay

All three of us had first encounters with merit pay that left us puzzled, to say the least. First, we will tell you what happened to us, and the questions that these experiences raised. We will then link these questions to concepts covered in this book. Perhaps some of the questions raised by our experiences will be similar to your own.

Williams: My introduction to merit pay occurred as an undergraduate at San Diego State University while I was completing a course on compensation administration. I was intrigued with all aspects of the topic—theory, research, and practice. After graduation, I landed a position as a compensation

Merit Pay, pages 1–24

doi:10.1108/978-1-80686-701-120263001

analyst, where I had the opportunity to practice salary administration. During my third year as an analyst, I realized I preferred research and headed back to college to pursue a graduate degree. I had persistent questions about merit pay. What is the actual relationship between pay and performance? (This is addressed in Chapter 2). Is there a discernible improvement in employee performance after a person receives a merit raise? (Chapter 5 covers this). How much satisfaction do employees experience with various levels of merit increases? (This is addressed in Chapter 7). After graduating with a master's degree in industrial and organizational psychology, I returned to human resource management (HRM) for several years, conducting applied research in employee selection and practicing compensation. Eventually, I decided to pursue a doctorate in industrial and organizational psychology with the hope of expanding my career opportunities. I started teaching HRM courses and completing a few projects as an independent consultant. A client requested that I research merit pay efficacy and develop a plan based on my findings. My research led me to the following conclusions: (a) I still had nagging questions about merit pay and (b) empirical research on the topic was scarce. I then continued my research on merit pay beyond the completion of that consulting gig. All of my collected activity led to the topic of my doctoral dissertation—a meta-analytic review of performance-based pay (PBP) (Williams, 2010, discussed in Chapters 2 and 7). In addition, I also formed a collegial relationship with the authors of the first two editions (e.g., Williams & Werner, 2022). What I did not foresee was the opportunity of contributing to the third edition of this book!

Werner: The topic of my doctoral dissertation was performance appraisal (discussed in Chapter 4). I was using supervisors at my university as the sample for my study, and so was asked to join a campus task force that was studying merit pay issues. Given that this was a large, public university, there were a number of challenges to paying employees based on their level of performance: modest budget increases, reactions from employees (and their employee associations), ever-shifting priorities or "urgent" needs, and so on. One supervisor was especially critical of the whole merit pay process. He said something to the effect that "I have 15 employees. Last year, my merit pay budget was $1,000. The difference between how I can reward my top performers and everyone else comes out to pennies a pay period." The implication here was the manner in which merit pay had been implemented in this organization was ineffective, that is, that the *differences* in how people were rewarded based on this process were so small that employees were not motivated to achieve high-level performance. If anything, the implication was that the merit pay process was causing more problems that it was doing good. As you will see, problems of implementation and administration remain vexing areas for many merit pay efforts (Adamovic, 2023; Bellavari & Allen, 1995).

Heneman: After working for about 5 months in a job many years ago, I was pulled aside by my immediate supervisor at work one day. He told me my performance had been pretty good so far, and as a result, he was going to give me a 5% merit increase. I told him I was pleased with his assessment of my performance, but I wasn't sure what a merit increase was. He explained to me that it was an increase in my salary based on my performance. Needless to say, I was thrilled with a salary increase and walked away with a favorable first impression of merit pay.

This favorable first impression was soon replaced, however, with a number of questions. A few hours after talking with my supervisor, I ran into several other people in jobs similar to mine. It turned out they had also received 5% merit increases. They had been informed by their supervisors that this 5% increase was a market adjustment to make their salaries comparable to increasing salaries being paid by our competitors for similar jobs. After talking with these people and thinking further about the notion of merit pay, I was confused and had a number of questions. These questions, along with chapter references that point out where the questions are discussed in the book, are presented below.

1. Why was my salary increase based on my performance, rather than the time I had put in on the job? It turned out that my supervisor had a theory on how to motivate employees. His theory had to do with paying people on the basis of performance, rather than other factors such as seniority. Theories concerning pay-for-performance are presented in Chapter 2.
2. Why was I given a merit increase, when others in the organization received a cost-of-living allowance instead? In this particular organization, increases for unionized employees were given on the basis of increases in the cost of living, while increases for nonunion employees were given on the basis of performance. As shown in Chapter 3, the types of salary increases granted depend upon the organization, type of job, and situation.
3. Was I paid for my performance, or was it a market adjustment? I was really stumped here. At first, I thought I had been misled by my supervisor. He told me I was paid for my performance, when in reality I was paid for a change in the market that affected everyone and for which everyone was compensated. Years later, it dawned on me that maybe performance-based and market-based pay are related to one another. That is, maybe market adjustments were granted only to those employees with adequate performance levels. To the extent that this was the case, maybe I was not misled by my supervisor after all. Issues surrounding what does and does not constitute performance under merit pay are covered in Chapter 4.

4. Why was I given a 5% increase rather than, say, a 4 or 6% increase? Why this specific amount and not another? Many organizations have formal guidelines that spell out the amount that employees can receive for various performance levels. Guidelines such as these are discussed in Chapter 5.
5. Why wasn't the "real" reason for my salary increase clearly spelled out to me? Organizations have various policies when it comes to the communication of pay information, and supervisors follow these policies to greater or lesser degrees. The formation of and adherence to these policies are discussed in Chapter 6.
6. What did my supervisor expect from me in return for the pay increase? At first, I thought the answer was obvious: I must maintain or improve my performance. After talking with my coworkers, however, I realized that what he expected was for me to remain with the organization. Now, I believe that merit increases are granted for both performance and retention purposes, as well as for other reasons such as employee satisfaction. The returns managers expect for merit pay, including these and others, are discussed in Chapter 7.

Tough Managerial Decisions

Many managers in the United States are required by their organizations to make merit pay decisions. They are asked to evaluate the performance of their subordinates and decide on the size of pay increases their subordinates will receive for their performance. At first blush, this process may seem fairly straightforward and simple. It is not. Even seasoned managers will tell you that tough decisions are required of managers under a merit pay plan.

Following are some comments that represent the tough decisions man-agers wrestle with, along with chapter references that point out where these decisions are addressed in the book:

- *"Why should I give different-sized raises to my subordinates? If I do give different-sized raises, won't my people think they are being treated unfairly, be less likely to cooperate with one another, lose interest in their work, and be less motivated? Given these potential problems, why can't I simply give everyone the same raise under the merit pay plan?"* These concerns are held by many managers and are discussed in Chapter 2. This chapter presents evidence in theory, research, and practice to support paying people different amounts to reflect differences in performance.

- *"Our organization is about to take over a company that has a different product line than the companies in our current organization. My boss proposes that we extend our merit pay plan to include this new company. Does it make sense to use merit pay for employees of this soon-to-be-acquired company? Do I need to convince my boss that merit pay is not appropriate in this case?"* Although merit pay is frequently used, it is not appropriate in all situations. The issues concerning when and where merit pay should be used are addressed in Chapter 3.
- *"Every few years, the Human Resources department distributes a new form that we are expected to use in evaluating the performance of our subordinates. Nothing seems to change, though. Everyone gripes about the forms, especially at the end of the year when we use these forms to make merit pay decisions. What can be done to improve our performance appraisal system? What can I do as a manager to better evaluate my subordinates?"* A critical factor in the success of a merit pay plan is the development of a sound method to measure employee performance. Characteristics of good performance measures and ways to improve the evaluation of employee performance are described in Chapter 4.
- *"I need to submit a budget for merit increases next year. How much will I need to motivate my employees? What do I need to consider in coming up with a budget figure? Is it possible to set up pay increases that will motivate my people more, but cost the organization less?"* Not only are tough decisions required regarding employee performance and merit pay, but tough financial decisions are required as well. Guidelines for establishing pay increases are covered in Chapter 5.
- *"Money does not seem to be the issue with our merit pay plan. Our budget seems adequate. But even though the money is there, people still complain about their merit pay increases, saying that what they got is not fair. What can I do to ensure that my merit pay decisions are seen as fair?"* A number of steps have been identified that managers can take to ensure that merit pay decisions are viewed as fair and just by employees. These steps are described in Chapter 6.
- *"Everyone has an opinion about merit pay. That makes sense, given that we are dealing with people's pocketbooks. When all is said and done, though, is merit pay really worth the time, money, and effort?"* Merit pay *can* and *does* work, but not under all circumstances. As described in Chapter 7, evaluation studies to date have reported mixed success for merit pay plans. Given the limited amount of research on the success of merit pay plans, the book concludes with a strong recommendation that organizations must evaluate the effectiveness of their own plans. Procedures for doing so are presented in Chapter 7. It is not appropriate to make blanket statements about the effectiveness of

merit pay. Organizations are best advised to avoid operating on the basis of blanket proclamations concerning merit pay (or any other management practice, for that matter). Instead, they should review the evidence, implement a plan of action, and evaluate the effectiveness of the plan. This is the recommended model, described later in Chapter 1, that is followed throughout the book.

Description of Merit Pay

In this section, we define merit pay, describe its history and importance, illustrate the various types of merit pay, and contrast merit pay with other forms of pay. These characteristics are described to show how merit pay fits in with other human resource practices.

Merit Pay Defined

At a general level, merit pay is one of many forms of compensation provided by an organization for services rendered by its employees. Merit pay has to do with compensation decisions, rather than other HRM decisions, such as talent acquisition (staffing) or talent development (training and development). Therefore, the term "merit pay" should not be confused with the term "merit system." A merit system is a term used in the public sector to describe hiring and promotion decisions rather than compensation decisions, based on the competence or performance of employees (Greiner et al., 1975).

At a more specific level, merit pay is a particular form of compensation known as incentive pay. Under incentive pay plans, of which merit pay is one type, pay is allocated on the basis of performance. A key characteristic of merit pay is that compensation is provided for *performance,* rather than other factors, such as the worth of the job to the employer or an employee's need for a certain form of income (e.g., retirement).

At a very specific level, merit pay can be defined as individual pay increases based on the rated performance of individual employees in a previous time period (Heneman, 1990). Under this specific definition, salary increases are granted on the basis of a subjective judgment of employee performance in a previous period of time. Two terms that are related to merit pay are "pay-for-performance" and "variable pay." Pay-for-performance is often used to refer to any incentive plan that links employee pay to some measure of performance (Wiscombe, 2001). Thus, pay-for-performance can include merit pay plans that reward employees based on subjectively rated measures of performance, but could also include systems that seek to emphasize only "quantifiable" items (e.g., sales, billable hours, etc.). Variable compensation, or variable pay programs, provides performance-related awards to employees, but unlike most merit pay plans in use, these awards do *not* get permanently added to an employee's base salary. Variable pay plans may include business incentives, stock ownership, or other special recognition for meeting financial or operating goals. In effect, variable pay must be re-earned each year (Hewitt Associates, 2002). For a discussion of a separate, and even more controversial issue related to employee evaluation and pay, see the boxed insert at the end of the chapter on "forced ranking."

As shown in this chapter, merit pay is one of several different types of incentive pay plans. While a salary increase is based on previous performance, it is intended to motivate increased performance in future time periods. Hence, merit pay can be thought of as a two-stage process, as shown in Figure 1.1. In stage one, pay increases are based on previous performance. In stage two, pay increases are granted to motivate future performance.

In discussing pay-for-performance under merit pay plans, it is important to note which stage is being discussed. For example, Chapter 5 looks at linking pay increases to previous performance (stage one of this process). Chapter 7, which discusses outcomes of merit pay, focuses on pay increases as motivators for future performance (stage two of the merit pay process). As shown throughout the book, attainment of stage one is a necessary but not sufficient condition for the attainment of stage two.

In summary, merit pay refers to compensation decisions, rather than other HRM decisions. It is one form of organizational compensation known as incentive pay. It is a specific type of incentive pay whereby pay increases are granted on the basis of ratings of previous performance. These increases are granted with the hope of motivating future performance.

History of Merit Pay

Although the term merit pay is relatively new, the philosophy of linking pay to performance is not. According to Evans (1970), this philosophy dates back to the Protestant Reformation of the 16th and 17th centuries. During

Figure 1.1

Merit Pay as a Two-Stage Process.

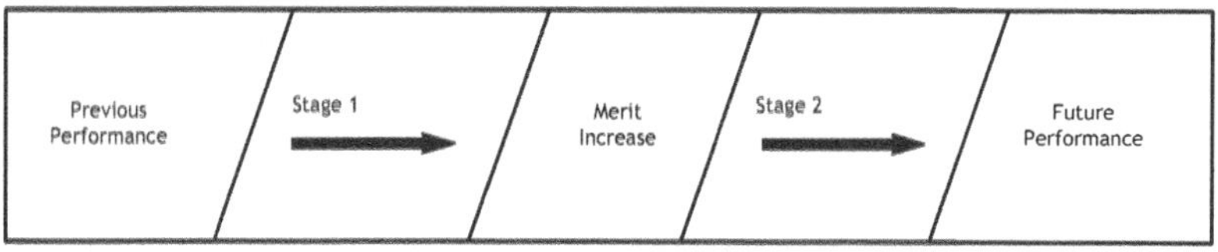

this period, pay was linked to performance in the following way: Hard work was viewed as self-sacrifice in the service of God. Hard work was assessed by the economic success one had. Hence, economic success through hard work was seen as a willingness to serve God. Other writers have traced the rating of employee performance back to the Wei Dynasty in 3rd-century China (Coens & Jenkins, 2000; Murphy & Cleveland, 1991).

Actual merit pay plans appear to have been around since the early 1900s. Schmitt and Klimoski (1991) report that the Larkin Company used merit pay for its supervisors in 1912. Cohen and Murname (1980) estimate that some 40 to 50% of US urban school districts had merit pay plans in the 1920s. The widespread use of merit pay probably accompanied the rapid growth in the use of performance ratings after World War II (Baron et al., 1986; Mitchell et al., 1990). In the 1980s, at least 80% of US organizations had what they called merit pay plans (Peck, 1984; Personnel Policies Forum, 1981; Wyatt Company, 1987).

According to a 2002 Hewitt survey, 90% of the large organizations surveyed had a merit pay plan in place (Hewitt Associates, 2002). This same survey projected 2003 average salary increases from 3.8% for nonunion hourly workers to 4.1% for executives. While other forms of variable pay plans have become popular (e.g., incentives based on group- or organizational-level performance), it would appear that merit pay remains a frequently used methods to link pay to employee performance (Hewitt Associates, 2002; Lowery et al., 2002; St-Onge, 2000). To sum up, the philosophy of pay-for-performance has been around for a long time. However, the translation of this philosophy into formal organizational policy has primarily taken place in the past 80 years.

Importance of Merit Pay

The importance of merit pay to organizations can be illustrated in a variety of ways, including the frequency with which merit pay plans are used, the symbolic nature of these plans, and the evaluated effectiveness of these plans. These three indicators of the importance of merit pay are considered in turn below.

Frequency of Use

One indication of the importance of merit pay is the frequent use of these plans by employers. A number of surveys have been conducted to find out the frequency of use of merit pay plans. The figures reported in these surveys are somewhat approximate because what respondents consider to be merit pay may not be consistent from organization to organization or with the definition in this book. In general, these national surveys suggest that merit pay is probably the most frequently used method of incentive pay.

While merit pay plans are frequently used, the use of these plans is not uniform across industries, between the public and private sector, as well as across countries. As noted above, a survey by Hewitt Associates found that over 90% of large organizations had merit pay plans in place (Hewitt Associates, 2002). Earlier surveys showed that over 80% of private-sector employers have merit pay for at least some of their employees (Peck, 1984; Personnel Policies Forum, 1981; Wyatt Company, 1987). Brown (1990) reported that the use of merit pay in manufacturing varied by industry from a low of 9% in the cotton textiles industry to a high of 63% in the household furniture industry.

A survey of state and local governments indicated that 88% of state governments and 73% of local governments surveyed used merit pay. These percentages were the highest for usage of any of the seven forms of incentive compensation measured (Lewin, 2003). Research suggests considerable efforts in other countries to use performance-related pay plans, including merit pay (see Brown & Heywood, 2002). For example, an Australian survey found that 89.6% of managerial employees, as well as 80.5% of nonmanagerial employees, have merit pay raises added to base pay (Shields, 2002). A survey in Britain found that 64% of the firms surveyed have policies that either support or strongly support the use of merit and individual performance to determine rewards (Poole & Jenkins, 1998). Even in Japan, a country long thought to discourage individual performance-based incentives, survey data suggests that 32% of large Japanese organizations have individual performance-related pay systems in place (cited in Benson & Brown, 2000).

Given a US base rate use of 80–90% in the private sector, there is not likely to be an increase in the use of merit pay in that sector. For state governments, however, there does appear to be an increase in the use of merit pay (cf. Greiner et al., 1975; Lawther et al., 1989; Lewin, 2003). The research featured in Brown and Heywood (2002) suggests an active use of merit pay in other countries as well.

Symbolic Nature of Merit Pay

An important and often overlooked role that merit pay plays is as a symbol of an organization's culture. Merit pay is a large-scale intervention in an organization, not just a simple change in pay policy. It is an important symbol because it signifies a prevailing organizational belief that work is to be rewarded on the basis of performance, rather than on some other basis, such as equality, need, or seniority.

Numerous examples of merit pay as a symbol of culture exist. In the federal government, merit pay is viewed as a symbol of the changing emphasis on the importance of work from time in grade or seniority to performance on the job (Perry & Petrakis, 1988). It has also been viewed by some as a symbol of the government's effort to maintain control over bureaucracy (March & Olson, 1983). At General Motors Corporation, an emphasis on merit pay in the 1980s was seen as a shift in corporate culture from a welfare system, where all people received the same pay increase, to a competitive business, where pay increases were contingent on performance (Schlesinger, 1988). The point of these examples is that merit pay, for better or worse, commands attention from employees in work organizations. As such, it cannot be developed and administered in a haphazard fashion, but instead must be carefully managed.

Overall Effectiveness

A final indicator of the importance of merit pay is the extent to which merit pay plans lead to desirable results. Although there are many ways to view the question, "Are merit pay plans effective?" (presented in detail in Chapter 7), at least one survey indicates that the answer to this question is a tentative and qualified "yes." Peck (1984), in a survey of 521 employers, found that at least some employers under some circumstances see merit pay plans as successful. The results of Peck's survey are shown in Table 1.1.

The details of when and how organizations actually attain successful outcomes are covered throughout this book. For now, these data suggest that merit pay has value for a number of employers. Note that these data from Peck (1984) should be treated as suggestive rather than conclusive, because it is not clear what definition of "success" employers were using when responding to the survey. As shown in Chapter 7, the results of an evaluation of merit pay effectiveness depend on which measure of success is used. Other surveys by the Wyatt Company (1989) and Eskew and Heneman (1996) showed similar results.

Two additional points should be made about the effectiveness of merit pay plans. First, it appears that, on average, the success of merit pay continues to be moderate when other data are considered (Heneman et al., 2002; Williams, 2010). In a survey, senior compensation professionals rated merit pay as "marginally successful" in influencing employee attitudes (pay satisfaction) and behaviors. However, merit pay was most likely to be viewed as effective when employees perceived a link between pay and performance, and when they viewed the system as fair in terms of the process used to administer merit pay (Eskew & Heneman, 1996).

There are, of course, deviations to moderation that should also be considered. What this means is that the potential for success or failure of merit pay in any one setting may be large. The upside returns that are possible with a merit pay plan can be seen in the results of a study of

Table 1.1

Degree of Success of Merit Pay

Industry Category	Degree of Success							
	Very Successful		Moderately Successful		Marginally Successful		Cannot Tell Degree of Success	
	Number	Percent (%)	Number	Percent (%)	Number	Percent (%)	Number	Percent (%)
Manufacturing (*N* = 193)	50	26*	105	54	18	9	20	10
Banking (*N* = 96)	27	28*	50	52	9	9	10	10
Insurance (*N* = 65)	14	22*	40	62	7	11	4	6
Diversified finance (*N* = 9)	3	33*	5	56	—	—	1	11
Total	94	26	200	55	34	9	35	10

Source: Peck (1984). Reprinted by permission.
Note: *Percentages do not add up to 100 because of rounding.

managers in New York City (Allan & Rosenberg, 1986). These managers reported an increase in performance after the implementation of a merit pay plan not only in the first year, but in the second and third years as well. The downside risk associated with merit pay is perhaps best illustrated by a study of federal employees and managers (Pearce et al., 1985). In this study, it was shown that over the course of 48 months after implementation of a merit pay plan, there were no improvements in productivity.

Second, even moderately successful merit pay plans may have considerable monetary value for organizations. Using a procedure known as utility analysis (described in greater detail in Chapter 7), Sterling (1990) reported a potential $3 million return over 3 years for a simulated organization of 157 employees studied by Schwab and Olson (1990). This large monetary return was possible even under the assumption of a moderate relationship between merit pay and subsequent performance. Positive monetary returns were also shown for a moderate pay-for-performance relationship in a study by Sturman et al. (2003).

In summary, the importance of merit pay is reflected in the research on the effectiveness of merit pay. Overall, the success of merit pay appears to be moderate (Williams, 2010). However, it is possible to improve upon this moderate rate of success, as will be shown throughout the book. Finally, even moderately successful merit pay plans can provide large financial returns to organizations.

Merit versus Other Forms of Incentive Pay

Merit pay can easily be confused with other incentive pay plans. The reason for this confusion is that, like merit pay, other incentive plans are also based on the notion of pay for performance. There are, however, some differences between merit pay and other forms of incentive pay that can be used to distinguish among the various plans. The distinctions are important because what works for other incentive plans does not necessarily work for merit pay plans.

Many distinctions have been made between merit pay and other forms of incentive pay (e.g., Johnson et al., 2021; Lawler, 1971; Waldman & Roberts, 1988; Wallace, 1990). First, merit pay is allocated on the basis of actual performance rather than potential performance. Hence, merit pay differs from skill-based pay, which is granted for the acquisition of skills that may contribute to subsequent performance.

Second, merit pay is allocated on the basis of subjective ratings of employee performance, rather than on the basis of more countable indicators of performance such as sales, profit, costs, and time savings. Unlike merit pay, incentive plans like piece-rate pay, sales commissions, profit sharing, and improshare are based on countable indicators of performance, rather than on ratings of performance.

Third, merit pay is granted to individual employees on the basis of individual performance. In contrast, group incentive plans and some gainsharing plans are based on the performance of the entire work group or organization.

Fourth, merit pay is usually based on an overall assessment of long-term performance, rather than on an assessment of performance at one point in time. Overall performance is typically rewarded by a merit increase, while one-time performance may be rewarded with a discretionary bonus (Lowery et al., 2002). So, for example, a counter clerk at a fast-food restaurant might receive a $20 bill from management for the courtesy extended to customers during a particularly busy period. This would be a discretionary bonus. On the other hand, a counter clerk might also receive a 5% increase in weekly pay at the end of the year because they were courteous throughout the year, processed orders quickly and efficiently, was accurate in cash transactions, and so on. This would be an example of a merit increase. The difference, then, between merit pay and a discretionary bonus is that merit pay is based on a formal rating of performance for an extended period of time, while a discretionary bonus is based on a less formal evaluation of one episode of performance.

Although these distinctions are useful in helping to sort out the applicability of policy, practice, and research to merit pay, they are less than perfect and can become blurred from time to time. For example, management by objectives (MBO) is often used in some fashion to measure the performance of supervisors, managers, and professional employees. Using this approach, which will be discussed in Chapter 4, performance assessment is based on quantitative measures of performance such as the number of services provided, tasks accomplished within a certain period of time, and so on. It is tempting to label a pay increase under MBO as something other than merit pay because it uses countable indicators of performance such as the time and number of services. However, in fact, these supposedly objective or countable performance measures are typically based on subjective ratings. The number of services may be measured as the number of successful services and could therefore resemble performance ratings. Given this scenario, a pay increase under MBO appears to be merit pay.

The point is that the difference between merit pay and other incentive plans is a matter of degree rather than an absolute difference. Throughout this book, we make every effort to carefully explain what we consider to be a merit pay plan, and we do consider MBO with pay to be a form of merit pay. The reader is also urged to carefully consider the type of plan described here or elsewhere to assess the applicability of the plan to his or her own circumstances. The distinctions provided here should be of some guidance. Also, as discussed in Chapter 3, merit and other forms of incentive pay should probably be considered as additions to one another rather than alternatives. Organizations such as Pratt and Whitney, Lincoln Electric, and Motorola found that an integrated reward strategy could be more effective than an "all-or-nothing" reward system, in which one and only one incentive plan is used (Heneman, 2001b; Schneier, 1989a).

Although it may not be a preferred strategy, some organizations are able to use only one form of incentive pay. In general, merit pay has two important advantages over other incentive plans. First, the less tangible aspects of employee performance, such as customer service and quality, can be captured with the performance ratings used in merit pay plans. Employers frequently emphasize both of these aspects of performance (Carnevale, 1991; Werner, 1994). Other incentive plans with more objective indicators of performance, such as piece-rate pay, tend to place more emphasis on the tangible aspects of performance such as quantity. Second, merit pay places an emphasis on the performance of the individual. Under group-based incentive plans, individuals may not be motivated to perform at their highest levels because the influence of any one person on group performance may be minimal. One employee may work hard under a group plan, but receive the same pay increase as those who do not work hard. In short, merit pay seems to be most appropriate when there is a concern for the quality of goods or services produced by individual members of an organization.

Types of Merit Pay Plans

Just as there are differences in types of incentive pay plans, so too are there differences in the types of merit pay plans. Distinctions among the various types of merit pay plans can be made along a number of lines (Heneman, 1984b). First, merit pay plans may differ on the standards used to assess performance. Some organizations include seniority and market adjustments as criteria, while others do not. Second, the form that pay takes under various merit pay plans may differ. Under traditional merit pay plans, pay is in the form of a salary increase. Some have proposed alternative forms of compensation, such as benefits. Third, the method used to calculate the merit increase may vary. For example, a merit increase could be calculated as an absolute dollar amount or as a percentage increase in salary. Fourth, the permanency of the increase may vary. Under traditional merit pay plans, the salary increase is a permanent one, with the increase carrying over into the base salary in future evaluation periods. Alternatively, a lump-sum plan could be used when the salary increase is not intended to be permanent. In this case, a salary increase would be granted on a one-time basis and would not be built into base pay.

The extent to which conceptual differences exist in practice is difficult to determine, since there have not been any national surveys that look at these various types of merit plans. There are, however, individual case studies of many of these variations, and they will be examined at various points in the book. The important point to consider is that merit pay plans are not homogeneous. They vary along a number of dimensions, and what works with one plan may not work with another. Throughout the book, we try to spell out when merit pay plan differences are likely to have an impact. When merit pay is discussed as a general concept, we are referring to what seems to be the typical case in merit pay, that is, when a permanent salary increase is granted on the basis of rated performance.

In summary, merit pay is an important form of incentive pay that has been around for at least 80 years. It is probably the most frequently used method of incentive pay, and there are a number of variations of merit pay plans. Overall, merit pay plans have been moderately successful.

A Classification of Merit Pay and Other Incentive Pay Plans

The last two sections attempted to clarify differences *between* merit pay and other incentive pay plans and differences *within* merit pay plans. This section contains a table that classifies merit pay and other incentive pay plans based on dimensions systematically and comprehensively gathered from the compensation literature.

Table 1.2 supplements the previous two sections in three ways. *First,* it contains more dimensions delineating differences in merit pay and other incentive pay plans. *Second,* the structure of the table gives the reader an efficient view for comparing and contrasting said variants. *Third,* each dimension is defined for increased clarity.

There are a few other items the reader should note. *First,* as mentioned above, merit pay and incentive pay fall under various umbrellas. Table 1.2 uses performance-based pay to categorize merit pay and other incentive pay. *Second,* while the dimensions result from a systematic and comprehensive search, they are neither exhaustive nor mutually exclusive. As stated above, the attempt of establishing perfectly clear and distinct boundaries between merit pay and other incentive pay is futile. We, however, believe the previous two sections and the classification table below extend our understanding of merit pay.

Table 1.2

Dimensions Characterizing Merit Pay Plans and Other Incentive Pay Plans

Dimension	Merit Pay	Other Incentive Pay
1. *Addition to base pay* *Definition*: Whether or not performance-based pay (PBP) is added to base salary.	Merit pay is almost always added to base pay. Consecutive years of merit pay distributions create a *compounding-effect* on the organization's total wage bill, something akin to a person receiving compound-interest from a financial investment.	Reward is not generally added to base pay. The absence of this linkage minimizes, if eliminates, a compounding effect, helping in cost-containment. It may constitute an employee's total pay check; that is, employee receives no base pay. For example, a piece-rate pay or sales commission. Sometimes, it reflects a discretionary or one-time bonus for exemplary performance; employee still receives a base salary. For example, a bonus is awarded if a sales quota is fulfilled.
2. *Performance criteria* *Definition*: The method by which individual performance is assessed.	Subjective ratings are used, typically a performance evaluation system. It measures employee behaviors, traits, and/or job results (MBO). Generally, entire job performance is measured. Sometimes, however, assessment may concentrate on a single job dimension, such as, work quality.	A formal or informal evaluation process. It is based on results or outcomes of counting things. Results are usually compared to a standard determined by time motion studies, job analyses, or other economic indicators.
3. *Salary range dependence* *Definition:* Whether or not PBP increases depend on (a) the existence of salary ranges for a job, or group of similar jobs; and (b) an individual's position within a salary range.	Traditionally, merit pay systems are linked to salary ranges with formal minimums and maximums. Individual movement through a salary range typically occurs in fixed intervals and depends on performance appraisal ratings. Because salary ranges have defined maximums, they impose a ceiling on merit pay increases, which may in turn penalize high performing employees. High performers near the top of the salary range, receive lower merit increases than equal performers whose base salaries are situated near the bottom of the salary range or grade. Conversely, other instances exclude a relationship with salary grade placement.	Generally, incentive pay systems do not require salary ranges to be established. Therefore, incentive pay increases (usually lump-sum bonus pay) offer allocators more latitude in the amount to be awarded and when an award may be given. The lack of salary-range consideration reduces, if not eliminates, constraints on PBP increases. There may be one exception here—piece-rate pay. While no formal salary ranges may exist, sometimes payment may be capped to contain costs.

Table 1.2 (Continued)

Dimension	Merit Pay	Other Incentive Pay
4. *Salary level* *Definition*: The degree to which salary levels influence the amount of PBP increase.	Many times, merit-pay increases are based on a percentage of base salary. This practice costs low-paying positions, while benefiting high-paying positions. For example, a merit increase of 4% for a base salary of $40,000 differs substantially from a 4% increase for a base salary of $120,000.	If increases are calculated as a percentage of some base-amount, and if those base amounts widely vary, inequities found in merit pay plans will probably apply to incentive pay systems.
5. *Salary Increase Calculation* *Definition*: The method of calculating PBP increases.	Salary increases based on a merit pay plan are calculated either as a percentage of base salary or an absolute dollar amount.	Some salary increases are based on units produced (piece-rate). Other increases reflect a percentage of sales quota or profit. Other times an absolute dollar amount is awarded for achieving a predetermined goal (e.g., bonus pay).
6. *Evaluation Period* *Definition*: The period of time performance is evaluated.	Performance is usually evaluated for one year, after which payment is awarded. Distribution of award typically occurs on employee's anniversary or a fixed time for all employees (e.g., end of an organization's fiscal year). Evaluation period in not a short period.	Duration of evaluation varies depending on incentive pay plan. Performance assessment may be as short as one day or one week for piece-rate pay. Discretionary bonuses or lump-sum bonuses may range from one month to one year.
7. *Position* *Definition*: The type of position or occupation traditionally associated with a particular PBP.	Traditionally, merit pay has been used with administrative, clerical, and managerial positions. These positions are fluid, multidimensional, and complex. Objective measures hardly exist.	Incentive pay plans are usually reserved for simple, repetitive, routine jobs (e.g., assembly-line workers) and semi-routine positions (e.g., sales). Typically, performance criteria reflect outcome or results. Objective criteria usually exist.
8. *Employment Sector* *Definition*: Whether or not employment resides in the public or private sector.	Merit pay has been used far more in the private sector than in the public sector. The public sector contains more bureaucracy regarding PBP usage than the private sector.	For the same reasons in merit pay plans, incentive pay plans may be affected the same way.

(Continued)

Table 1.2 (Continued)

Dimension	Merit Pay	Other Incentive Pay
9. *Size of Organization* *Definition*: The degree to which the size of the organization affects PBP	The size of organization may affect the amount of merit pay increases. Usually, large organizations have more resources to offer greater PBP increases than small organizations.	The size of organization may affect the amount of merit pay increases. Usually, large organizations have more resources to offer greater PBP increases than small organizations.
10. *Seniority* *Definition*: The degree to which seniority is included in the PBP increase	Sometimes, merit pay increases include seniority. This consideration dilutes the motivational potency of merit pay.	To a lesser degree, incentive pay increases include seniority. Again, this consideration dilutes the motivational potency of incentive pay.
11. *Market Adjustments* *Definition*: The degree to which economic conditions are included in the PBP increase.	Sometimes, merit pay increases include market adjustments (sometimes called cost-of-living adjustment). This consideration dilutes the motivational potency of merit pay.	If incentive pay is added to base pay, its effect will mirror that of merit pay. Again, this consideration dilutes the motivational potency of incentive pay.
12. *Industry* *Definition*: The nature of industry in which PBP is to be used.	Industries predominately with fluid positions use merit pay. Some examples include research, service, financial.	Industries with mostly routine positions utilize incentive pay. Some examples include manufacturing, assembly, produce.
13. *Promotions* *Definition*: Whether or not promotional adjustments are included in the PBP increase.	Sometimes, merit pay increases include promotional adjustments to ensure employee is safely placed in the higher classification. This consideration may not necessary dilutes the motivational potency of merit pay.	Generally, incentive pay is not associated with promotions because incentive pay plans are almost always independent of salary grades.
14. *Combined Reward Systems* *Definition*: Whether or not an individual PBP system is combined with another financial reward system.	Merit pay may be combined with other individually-based, non-merit pay adjustments and group incentive plans.	Incentive pay may be combined with group incentives.
15. *Unionism* *Definition*: The presence or absence of a labor contract.	Merit pay may be severely impacted by a union.	Incentive pay may be severely impacted by a union

A Normative Model of the Merit Pay Process

The normative model of the merit pay process, depicted in Figure 1.2, is intended to show the steps required for creating, using, and evaluating a merit pay plan, and to show how the contents of the remainder of the book have been organized.

At first glance, the concept of merit pay may seem straightforward and a merit pay plan relatively easy to create. However, as pointed out throughout the book, this has not been the experience of most employers. Many difficult decisions have to be made in setting up the plan. Once it has been developed, the implementation and administration steps required to gain adherence to the plan are difficult to enact. After the plan has been implemented, the effectiveness of the plan must be measured and decisions made as to whether to continue or discontinue the plan. Overall, the merit pay process needs to be carefully managed.

Management of the merit pay process consists of establishing three major objectives and pursuing them in the order shown in Figure 1.2. The three major objectives are an assessment of the desirability and feasibility of merit pay, development and administration of the plan, and an evaluation of relevant outcomes. These three objectives, shown in the model, correspond to the three major sections of the book. To achieve each objective, a series of

Figure 1.2

Managing the Merit Pay Process.

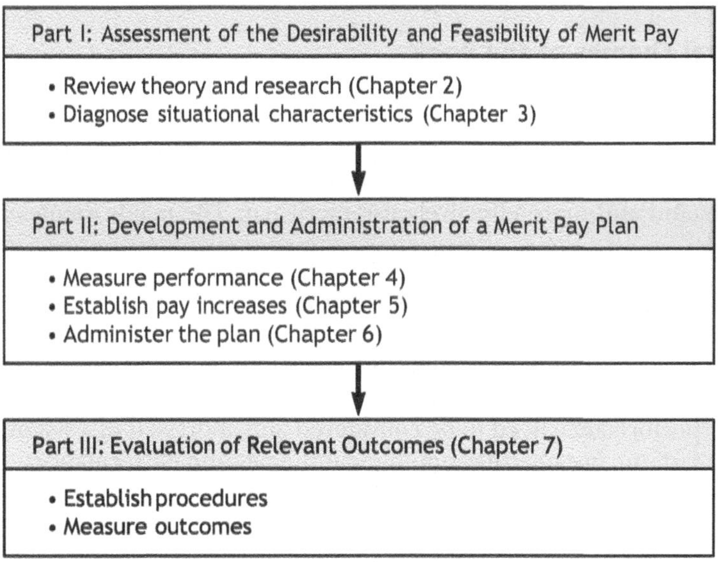

steps or activities needs to be undertaken. The required activities, shown under each objective in the model, correspond to specific, consecutive chapters in the book.

The first part of the book focuses on assessing whether merit pay is feasible or even desirable in a particular organization. To support assessment of *desirability*, a review of the theory and research that underlies merit pay is presented in Chapter 2. To support assessment of the *feasibility* of merit pay, situations where merit pay seems to be warranted are presented in Chapter 3.

The second part of the book addresses issues related to the development and implementation of a merit pay plan after it has been determined that merit pay is desirable and feasible. Activities include the measurement of performance (Chapter 4), linking pay to performance (Chapter 5), and administering the merit pay plan that links pay to performance (Chapter 6).

In the third part of the book, the focus shifts to evaluating the outcomes of merit pay after a plan has been developed and administered (Chapter 7). Activities include procedures that can be used to evaluate merit pay plans, relevant outcomes that should be assessed, and summaries of evaluation studies conducted by other organizations.

This model is normative in that it shows recommended steps for managing a merit pay plan. It is also meant to guide the reader to the appropriate sections of the book. Readers who are considering merit pay for the first time should start with Part I. Readers searching for information on how to establish and administer a plan should focus on Part II. Readers who wish to learn more about how to evaluate a merit pay plan should focus on Part III.

Central Themes of the Book

Three central themes run throughout the book. Although these themes are not used to organize the literature, they are important to consider as they represent the fundamental ideas that need to be examined to better understand and more effectively use merit pay. The major themes are as follows:

1. *Recognize that merit pay needs to be managed.* Although the concept of merit pay is straightforward, it is not simple. Creating a merit pay policy that simply states pay is to be based on performance is likely to lead to disastrous results. Many factors other than pay and performance need to be considered and addressed in a systematic fashion, because they impinge on the pay and performance relationship. Some of these other factors include characteristics of the people making merit pay decisions, characteristics of the people receiving merit increases, organizational conditions, and

environmental conditions such as outside economic forces and the presence of labor organizations (unions). A model is used in the book to provide a systematic way to manage these factors.

2. *Do more with less.* In merit pay plans, a fundamental tension exists between the goals of doing more and doing it with less. Ideally, merit pay should motivate greater performance levels than would occur without merit pay, at a lower cost. A *Newsweek* article (Quinn, 1991) highlighted the popularity of this belief. Merit pay is viewed as offering more for less because pay increases are based on performance, rather than amount of time on the job. Unfortunately, there is often a conflict between the goals of achieving greater performance and reducing cost. For merit pay plans to be effective, a balance must be struck between maximizing performance and minimizing cost. To reach this balance, attention must be given to both motivational and financial considerations.
3. *Understand that the perceived relationship between pay and performance is as important as the actual relationship.* The relationship between pay and performance in a merit pay plan can be examined from differing perspectives. One way to look at merit pay is via the *actual relationship* between performance ratings and salary increases. The actual relationship might, for example, be expressed in the form of a policy statement about the intended relationship between performance and pay. You could also audit the effectiveness of this policy by calculating the statistical relationship between ratings and increases. Another way to look at merit pay is through people's *perceptions* of the relationship between performance and pay. Some may see a positive relationship, others a negative relationship, and others no relationship at all. If merit pay plans are to be effective, the perceived and actual positive relationship between merit pay and performance must be in alignment. You cannot assume that because there is an actual positive relationship between pay and performance that there is also a perception of a positive relationship. Many merit pay plans have failed simply because people within an organization do not see a relationship between pay and performance. An important part of managing the merit pay process is not only to facilitate the actual relationship between pay and performance, but to also ensure that employees see this relationship as well. As was stated to us by a reviewer of this book, "pay matters because of what it means to people." We couldn't agree more!

Little consideration has been given to these three issues in previous writings on merit pay. By understanding and paying close attention to these issues, however, you can better understand merit pay, which, in turn, should help make your merit pay plans more effective.

Summary of Major Points

The major points covered in this chapter are as follows:

1. *Definition.* Merit pay is a form of compensation within the broader category known as incentive pay. Under a merit pay plan, pay increases are granted to individuals on the basis of their rated performance in a previous time period. Pay increases are granted with the hope of motivating future performance.
2. *Importance.* Merit pay remains a popular method of incentive compensation. It is an important symbol of an organization's culture. Its use has been shown to be related to the effectiveness of organizations.
3. *Merit versus other incentives.* Unlike other incentive pay plans, merit pay is most typically based on actual rather than potential performance, subjective ratings of performance rather than countable indicators of performance, individual rather than group performance, and overall rather than one-time performance.
4. *Types of merit pay plans.* Merit pay plans can differ by the performance criteria that are evaluated, the form that merit pay takes, the method used to calculate the increase, and the permanence of the increase.
5. *Management* of *the merit pay process.* The merit pay process needs to be actively managed, rather than left to circumstances. Therefore, care must be taken to assess the desirability and feasibility of a merit pay plan, to develop and administer the merit pay plan, and to evaluate relevant outcomes.
6. *Central themes of the book.* The central themes of the book are as follows: managing merit pay; doing more with less; and understanding that the perceived relationship between pay and performance is as important as the actual relationship.

Conclusions

Merit pay is used extensively in the United States, as well as elsewhere around the world (Benson & Brown, 2000; Brown, 2001; Brown & Heywood, 2002; Poole & Jenkins, 1998). One reason for this frequent use is that organizations hope to do more for less. "More" refers to the improved level of individual performance expected from the good performers due to the merit increases they receive. With across-the-board pay increases, all employees receive the same pay increase. Good performers do not receive any special recognition through larger pay increases; they receive the same increase as everyone else.

"Less" refers to the potentially lower fixed costs under a merit pay plan compared to an across-the-board pay plan. The budget needed to fund merit increases just for good performers is less than the budget needed to fund merit increases for all employees at the same level as the good performers. A survey by the Institute of Management and Administration (IOMA) asked HR professionals how they were "holding the line" on compensation costs. The number one answer provided was to reduce or eliminate merit pay, at least for the short term. This was mentioned by 22% of respondents. However, the second most popular means of controlling compensation costs was to institute a pay-for-performance plan that differentiated between high and low performers (IOMA, 2006). An article in *HR Magazine* provided examples of how this might work (Bates, 2003c).

Another reason for the popularity of merit pay is the method of performance measurement. By using ratings, rather than more countable indicators of employee performance such as the number of goods produced or services provided, less tangible aspects of employee performance, such as quality, can be rewarded. To compete in tough product or service markets, quality is as important or more important than quantity. Through the use of merit pay, employers can, in effect, promote the importance of these less tangible aspects of performance.

While merit pay plans are frequently used to lower costs and motivate performance, their actual success in reaching these goals is mixed (Bates, 2003c). While merit pay seems to work in some situations, it does not work in others. What seems increasingly evident, however, is that merit pay needs to be aligned with the business strategies of the organization, and also be viewed as a part of an overall or "strategic reward management" system (Heneman, 2001a, 2002). In the remainder of the book, we seek to spell out under what circumstances merit pay is likely to have the intended effect.

For merit pay to work, the process of linking pay to performance ratings must also be carefully managed, as shown in Figure 1.2. If the merit pay process cannot be carefully managed, for whatever reason, it is actually better to use a "peanut butter" approach to granting pay increases. Using this approach, every employee is given the same pay increase, just as peanut butter is spread evenly across toast. An explicit, across-the-board pay increase approach like this is probably less offensive to employees and less likely to lead to adverse reactions than a poorly managed merit pay plan that does not actually succeed in awarding pay for performance (Brown, 2001).

Forced Ranking

One of the more controversial management practices in the past three decades is the use of forced rankings to evaluate employees. Ranking employees against other employees, rather than against a fixed or predetermined performance standard, is not new, yet the increasing use of forced rankings, especially among larger organizations, has generated considerable discussion, and even ill will and lawsuits from some disgruntled employees (Bates, 2003b). It has been variously called forced distribution, differentiation, top grading, the vitality curve, and "rank and yank" (Meisler, 2003). As many as 20% of Fortune 1,000 companies use some variation of it (Bates, 2003b). Forced ranking was popularized by General Electric, especially by its former CEO, Jack Welch. Other companies said to be using some variation of forced ranking include 3M, Texas Instruments, Microsoft, and Hewlett-Packard (Meisler, 2003). Both Ford Motor Company and Goodyear discontinued their use of forced rankings, after lawsuits were filed claiming that the rankings discriminated against older workers (Bates, 2003b).

Some organizations are providing more lucrative merit pay raises to those ranked at the top, average raises to those in the middle, and low raises (or none at all) to those at the bottom. In some cases, organizations target those ranked at the bottom for improvement or potential dismissal. It is this last prospect that has led such practices to be labeled as a "Darwinian struggle" in the workplace (Meisler, 2003), or as Clark (2003) stated, "It's survival of the fittest as companies tighten the screws on employee performance reviews" (p. 31). It is interesting to note how few companies identified by Meisler (2003) wished to speak publicly about their practices concerning forced rankings. We discuss this more fully in Chapter 4.

Study Questions

1. In this chapter, the authors attempt to define merit pay, incentive pay, and pay for performance. In your own words, define, compare and contrast these concepts. Why is it so challenging to clearly delineate merit pay and other incentive pay plans?
2. Describe the two-stage model of merit pay. Why is it important in developing a merit pay plan in a firm?
3. How has the history of merit pay impacted its current use? Do you think merit pay is still viable or popular for organizations today? Why or why not?
4. What has been your experience with merit pay? If you have no experience with merit pay, what would it look like to you?
5. Explain the normative model of the merit pay process. How does the model help researchers? How can it assist HR/compensation practitioners?

PART I

ASSESSMENT OF THE DESIRABILITY AND FEASIBILITY OF MERIT PAY

CHAPTER 2

PAY FOR PERFORMANCE

A Review of Theory and Research

The material presented in this chapter can be used to assess the desirability of merit pay. By the end of the chapter, the reader should be familiar with the general requirements and potential benefits and costs associated with merit pay. The first part of the chapter presents various theories that provide the rationale for making pay contingent on performance. The second part of the chapter looks at the extent to which it is possible to link pay to performance. Empirical research shows the actual relationship between pay and performance in a variety of organizational settings where merit pay is used. The third part of the chapter reviews the potential risks or dysfunctional consequences that may be encountered when pay is linked to performance.

Theories Behind Merit Pay

In a national survey, compensation administrators rated the number one objective of compensation systems as being able to tie pay to performance (Peck, 1984). Respondents to the survey indicated that this objective was of greater importance than other important objectives of compensation, including maintaining equitable relationships among jobs, attracting job applicants, and keeping payroll costs competitive. Almost 40 years later, 82% of human resource (HR) leaders from an international survey (n = 820) (Lattice, 2023) conveyed the same sentiment—the link between pay and

Merit Pay, pages 27–73

doi:10.1108/978-1-80686-701-120263002

performance is of utmost importance (de Bara & Test, 2024). Once again, merit pay plans are just one way that organizations seek to link pay to performance, and increasingly organizations are seeking to use an integrated or total reward system to impact individual and organizational performance (Gerhart et al., 2009; Heneman & Schutt, 2003; Jenkins et al., 1998). To understand why pay for performance is given such a high priority in organizations, it is necessary to review a number of relevant theories related to merit pay. These theories show the benefits of paying on the basis of performance and also serve as the underlying rationale for merit pay plans. Finally, these theories show how and why pay based on performance should lead to improved performance.

Theories concerning merit pay come from the fields of psychology and economics. The reason for reviewing both psychological and economic theories is that the similarities and differences between these sets of theories have important implications for merit pay (Kahn & Sherer, 1990). A theme common to both sets of theories is that linking pay to performance should increase performance. A major difference between these sets of theories is their views concerning *why* pay based on performance is likely to lead to better performance. Assumptions about human nature and what motivates people often differ between psychological and economic theories (Herrnstein, 1990; Kaufman, 1989; Tetlock & Goldgeier, 2000; van Raaij, 1999). These differences have implications, which will be referred to throughout the book, for the development, administration, and evaluation of merit pay plans.

Before reviewing each set of theories, it should be noted that these theories were not developed solely to explain merit pay. In fact, these theories look primarily at *pay levels* rather than pay increases. However, under most merit pay plans, pay increases are rolled over into the pay levels received by employees. That is, a pay increase in one year becomes a part of base pay in the next year. Hence, these pay level theories have important implications for merit pay plans.

Psychological Theories

Several theories from psychology suggest that the linking of pay to performance should lead to increased performance. According to these theories, performance is increased because employee motivation is increased when pay and performance are linked. Motivation and ability are generally viewed to be two primary determinants of individual performance (Wright et al., 1995).

Psychological theories differ in explaining why pay-for-performance should be motivational to employees. These different explanations, in turn, have important implications for the design of merit pay systems. In the next pages, these theories, the implications of the theories, and other related research are reviewed.

Expectancy Theory

This theory of employee motivation dates back to at least 1957, when Georgopoulos, Mahoney, and Jones looked at factors related to employee productivity. The first formal model of expectancy theory was developed by Vroom (1964) and has been refined by many authors since then, including Porter and Lawler (1968).

According to expectancy theory, motivation, or the force to act, results from a conscious, decision-making process undertaken by an individual. The decision to act depends upon three sets of perceptions known as expectancy, instrumentality, and valence, which are shown in Fig. 2.1. *Expectancy* refers to the individual's perception that a certain level of effort is required to achieve a certain level of performance. *Instrumentality* is the strength of the belief that a certain level of performance will be associated with various outcomes. *Valence* is the attractiveness of these outcomes to the individual. In making the decision to act, these perceptions are assumed to combine in a multiplicative manner. What th`is means is that if either expectancy, instrumentality, or valence has a value of zero, then motivational force will be zero. An example of the thought process associated with expectancy theory is shown in Fig. 2.2.

Over the years, a substantial body of research has been conducted on expectancy theory. Reviews of this research have been conducted by many authors, including Ambrose and Kulik (1999), Schwab et al. (1979), and Mitchell (1974). In general, these reviews of expectancy theory are supportive of the major components of the theory. Empirical support for expectancy theory tends to be stronger when the theory is focused on the individual, rather than on groups of individuals (Kennedy et al., 1983; Wanous et al., 1983). However, even when expectancy theory is used to predict motivational

Figure 2.1.

Expectancy Theory.

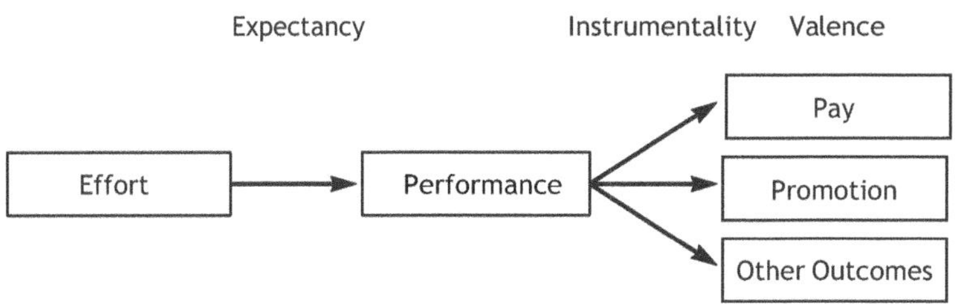

Figure 2.2.

Examples of Employee Thought Processes, as Depicted by Expectancy Theory.

EXPECTANCY	
Question: If I work as hard as possible on this project, how likely is it that I will accomplish what is required?	
Answer 1: " Chances are I will not perform up to the requirements. I just don't have the time or expertise to do it. I'm just not motivated."	Answer 2: " If I work as hard as I can, there is a good chance that I will do a good job. But, I still have to ask myself the next question."

INSTRUMENTALITY	
Question: So what? What's in it for me if I do a good job?	
Answer 1: " Absolutely nothing. Good performance simply is not recognized around here. I'm just not motivated."	Answer 2: " At a minimum, my boss will say thanks for a job well done, and I may get a cash bonus. But, I still have to ask myself the next question."

VALENCE	
Question: How attractive are these outcomes?	
Answer 1: " Praise doesn't mean that much to me, and if the truth were known, I would rather have more leisure time than more pay. I'm just not motivated."	Answer 2: " I would be pleased with the recognition from my boss, and a cash bonus could go toward the boat I have always wanted. All things considered (expectancy, instrumentality, and valence), I am indeed motivated."

force across individuals, rather than predicting motivational force within individuals, there is still moderate empirical support (Schwab et al., 1979).

Expectancy theory has a number of important implications for merit pay plans (Heneman, 1984b; Mount, 1987). In particular, expectancy theory suggests that merit pay is likely to motivate employees when the following conditions are met:

- *Performance must be accurately measured.* If it is not, then employees cannot make the perceived link between effort and performance (expectancy) and performance and rewards (instrumentality).
- *Increased pay must be a valued outcome.* For employees to pursue high levels of performance, the end result of such performance must be attractive or have positive valence. Hence, pay increases must have

greater valence than alternative outcomes such as leisure. If a pay increase is less attractive than leisure, then an employee will feel less motivated to perform when promised a pay increase rather than additional time off the job.

- *The relationship between pay and performance must be clearly defined.* The relationship between performance on the job and pay associated with performance must be clearly spelled out by the organization to ensure that employees perceive performance as instrumental in attaining a pay increase.
- *Opportunities to improve performance must exist.* If an employee does not have the opportunity to increase or improve performance, then it is futile for that employee to expend effort at a task. If opportunity is not present, both expectancy and resultant motivation will not be present. Employees must have the time, equipment, ability, and supervision required to perform a task—which translates into opportunity—before there can be expectations for performance.

In summary, expectancy theory suggests that merit pay is likely to motivate increased performance because performance is instrumental in the attainment of a pay increase. For merit pay to motivate increased performance, performance must be accurately measured, pay must be a valued outcome, pay must be made contingent on performance, and the employee must have the opportunity to have an impact on performance.

Reinforcement Theory

This theory comes in large part from the work on operant conditioning by B. F. Skinner (1953). Reinforcement theory has been extended from laboratory settings to the workplace by a number of authors, including Luthans and colleagues (e.g., Hamner et al., 2015; Luthans & Kreitner, 1975, 1985; Luthans & Stajkovic, 1999). This theory suggests that any behavior, including work performance, is determined by its consequences. Unlike expectancy theory, where attention is given to both antecedents to and consequences of performance, reinforcement theory focuses solely on the *consequences* of performance (Komald, 1986). Hence, in the language of expectancy theory, reinforcement theory provides additional explanation of instrumentality perceptions and is silent on expectancy perceptions.

According to reinforcement theory, the frequency of a behavior is likely to be increased when a valued reward is made contingent upon that behavior. The contingency between the behavior and reward is likely to be strengthened the more clearly the behavior is defined, the closer in time the reward is to the behavior, and the closer in magnitude the reward is to the behavior. If the relationship between a desired behavior and its consequences is not made contingent, then the frequency of the desired behavior may not increase.

The importance of making rewards contingent upon behavior and the careful attention that must be given to these contingencies is illustrated in the following example from a supervisor during a training program. The supervisor warned an employee, "If I catch you coming late to work one more time this year, you will not get a merit raise this year." In making this statement, the supervisor hoped to motivate the person to not be late again. Guess what happened? The person continued to be late to work, but came up with some ingenious ways to avoid getting caught by the supervisor! For the desired outcome to have occurred, merit pay should have been made contingent upon not being late again, rather than on not being caught.

The usefulness of reinforcement theory in industrial settings was covered in earlier reviews of the research (O'Hara et al., 1985; Schneier, 1974). These reviews suggested that when the principles of reinforcement theory are followed, performance is indeed increased as predicted from the theory. These results tend to hold up in both public- and private-sector organizations. It should be noted, however, that most of these studies looked at short-term rather than long-term results, and used fairly straightforward measures of performance, such as quantity. The long-term effects of reinforcers on complex measures of performance such as quality are less well known. It should also be noted that many of the tests of reinforcement theory have used piece rate rather than merit pay.

More recent research on behavioral management or organizational behavior modification provide further support for the use of reinforcement theory in organizational settings (Kim, 2025; Luthans & Stajkovic, 1999; Stajkovic & Luthans, 1997, 2001, 2003). For example, Stajkovic and Luthans (2003) conducted a meta-analysis of 72 studies where money, feedback, and/or social recognition were contingently administered, based upon employee performance. On average, monetary incentives increased employee performance 23%, social recognition 17%, and feedback 10%. When all three reinforcers were used simultaneously, performance increased by 45%. These results are some of the most powerful to date concerning the effectiveness of contingent rewards in organizational settings. While this does not translate directly to most merits plans in current use, it suggests that there is significant *potential* value in efforts to better link employee performance and organizational rewards.

As with expectancy theory, there are also implications for merit pay from reinforcement theory. These implications can be summarized as follows:

- *Performance must be clearly defined.* For desirable rather than undesirable performance to be motivated, a clear distinction must be made between desirable and undesirable performance.
- *Merit increases must be made contingent upon desired performance.* If pay is given for reasons other than desired performance (e.g., seniority), then other behaviors such as retention may be reinforced rather than performance.
- *The size of merit increases should increase with levels of performance.* If one level of merit increase is given out to all performers, then employees will be motivated to achieve only the minimum level of performance needed for an increase.
- *Merit increases should be given out close in time to the desired performance levels.* If performance is reviewed at one time and a salary increase is given out at a later time, then the link between desired performance and pay will be weakened.

In summary, under reinforcement theory, merit pay should motivate increased performance because the monetary consequences of good performance are made known to the employee. For merit pay to lead to better motivation and performance, performance must be clearly defined, merit pay must be made contingent upon desired performance, merit increases should increase in size with increases in performance, and pay increases should be granted close in time to the desired performance.

Equity Theory

A clearly articulated model of equity theory comes from Adams (1965). It is one of several theories of "justice" reviewed by Greenberg (1987b, 2001). Compared to expectancy theory and reinforcement theory, equity theory suggests that motivation not only depends on the pay and performance relationship that the employee experiences, but it also depends on the pay and performance relationship that other employees experience, with whom the person compares him- or herself. Hence, equity theory looks at the role that social comparisons play in motivation.

According to equity theory, employees and employers enter into an exchange relationship. The employer provides outcomes such as monetary and nonmonetary rewards that include pay and verbal praise. In return, the employee provides inputs, which include performance and human capital characteristics like experience and education. When the employee perceives that the ratio of outcomes to inputs is about equal, the employee is likely to be satisfied with the exchange relationship. Under equity theory, a balance of outcomes to inputs is the goal that employees are motivated to achieve.

Figure 2.3.

Making Equity Comparisons.

$$\frac{\text{Outcomes to self}}{\text{Inputs by self}} \quad \text{versus} \quad \frac{\text{Outcomes to others}}{\text{Inputs by self}}$$

In considering the ratio of outcomes to inputs, employees compare themselves to other employees both inside and outside the employing organization. If the employee perceives that the ratio of his or her outcomes to inputs is less than the ratio of outcomes to inputs for others, then the employee may feel underrewarded. If the employee perceives that the ratio of his or her outcomes to inputs is more than the ratio of outcomes to inputs for others, then the employee may feel overrewarded and possibly even guilty. In cases of both under- and overreward, the employee is usually motivated to get the ratio of his or her outcomes to inputs back in line with the ratio of other people's outcomes to inputs.

The process of making the equity comparisons just described is shown in Fig. 2.3. One way that organizations attempt to manage employee beliefs that pay is fair is to set up merit pay plans. By having a merit pay plan, an organization is formally acknowledging that performance is a valued input, which will be rewarded with a corresponding increase in pay. It should be noted, however, that according to equity theory, employees' perceptions of the fairness of merit pay may or may not be in line with the intended fairness of the plan. Sometimes employees may see the plan as not being fair and take actions to correct the situation.

One way that employees can attempt to restore equity perceptions under a merit pay plan is to alter their performance input. If employees feel underrewarded, they may increase the quantity of performance in the hope of receiving larger merit increases. If larger increases are granted, then the employees' outcomes will be increased, which will restore feelings of equity. Also, if underrewarded, employees may decrease the quality of their performance to decrease their inputs. Increasing inputs in the former case and decreasing outcomes in the latter case may restore perceptions of equity. The goal of a merit pay plan is, of course, to provide an equitable relationship between performance and merit increases, so that employees do not have to resort to decreasing their performance.

If employees feel overrewarded, they may decrease the quantity of their performance. The reason for this is that an increase would lead to additional pay, which in turn would create further feelings of overreward and guilt. Alternatively, employees may increase the quality of their performance or some other aspect of performance that they believe will not lead to as large a merit increase. Equity is restored in the case of overreward by decreasing outcomes and increasing inputs. The goal of merit pay is to ensure that the relationship between pay and performance is equitably perceived, so that employees do not have to resort to lowering some aspect of performance to decrease outcomes and restore equity.

The research on equity theory provides moderate support for the theory (Ambrose & Kulik, 1999; Carrell & Dittrich, 1978; Heneman & Schwab, 1979; Miner, 1980; Mowday, 1979). In particular, support seems to be strongest in the form of predictions made about time-based pay plans under laboratory conditions. The evidence is more mixed when incentive plans are examined in field settings (Johnson et al., 2021). Also, while cases of overreward inequity have been reported (e.g., Garland, 1973), it would appear that the threshold for overreward is very high. That is, one must perceive that outcomes are very large indeed before feelings of guilt set in. Miner (1980) argued that the theory sets forth few testable hypotheses, and Schwab (1980) suggested that the methods used to test the hypotheses have not been consistent with the theory. Both of these factors may account for the moderate empirical support for the theory. Research on the notion of equity sensitivity, that is, that some employees are more sensitive to justice issues than others, holds promise that individual differences may also explain past results concerning organizational equity issues (Huseman et al., 1987; Miles et al., 1994; Sauley & Bedeien, 2000).

The following are some implications for merit pay derived from equity theory:

- *Merit pay decisions cannot be made independently of one another.* Merit pay increases received by one employee are likely to have an impact on the equity perceptions and resulting behavior of other employees.
- *Inputs must be clearly defined.* Employees bring many inputs to the workplace. Employers must take care to establish the value of alternative inputs (e.g., performance vs. seniority), so that an accurate assessment of the ratio of outcomes to inputs can be made.
- *Merit pay information must be communicated to employees.* If merit pay plans are not communicated to employees, then employees may make incorrect assessments of the ratio of outcomes to inputs. For example, Lawler (1965) found that managers in various industries tend to overestimate the pay of individuals subordinate to them. If these subordinates contribute less to the organization, managers may feel underrewarded and engage in dysfunctional behaviors. Feelings of equity may be restored if actual pay levels are better communicated. The communication of merit pay is addressed in Chapter 6.
- *The perceived relationship between pay and performance should be viewed to be as important as the actual relationship.* According to equity theory, it

> is the perceived relationship between pay as an outcome and performance as an input that is the determinant of motivation. It cannot be automatically assumed that the perceived relationship is the same as the actual relationship. Information regarding the actual relationship between pay and performance may become distorted as this bit of information passes from policy to practice to individual interpretation. Even well-developed merit plans may not work if not communicated properly. Hence, attention should be given to both the perceived and actual relationship between pay and performance.

In summary, equity theory suggests that merit pay is likely to increase employee motivation if it leads to equitable perceptions by employees. For merit increases to be seen as equitable rather than inequitable, merit pay decisions cannot be viewed in isolation, inputs need to be clearly defined, merit information needs to be communicated to employees, and the perceived relationship between pay and performance needs to be given as much attention as the actual relationship between pay and performance.

Goal-Setting Theory

The theory of goal setting as it relates to incentive pay was first established by Locke (1968). According to goal-setting theory, goals are motivating to employees when they are specific, challenging, and accepted by employees. Goals need to be made specific, as "do your best" or general goals do not give a clear target toward which the employee can direct effort. Goals need to be challenging. Goals that are too easy to attain may suggest to the employee that the goals are not important. However, goals that are too difficult to reach may suggest to the employee that effort to attain them is futile. Goals also need to be accepted by the employee before they can internalize and act upon these goals (Klein et al., 1999). Incentives such as merit pay should contribute to the motivational effects of goal setting in several ways (Locke et al., 1968; Wright, 1989). First, merit pay that is provided for goal attainment may create greater commitment to the goal. Second, merit pay may result in the setting of more difficult goals to earn larger rewards. Third, merit pay may result in the setting of more goals to justify larger merit increases.

Considerable research and support for goal-setting theory has been generated (Bandura & Locke, 2003; Denrell et al., 2025; Locke & Latham, 1990, 2002; Mento et al., 1987; Tubbs, 1986). Goal specificity, difficulty, and acceptance (or commitment) have all been shown to relate to performance in a variety of situations. In contrast, the relationship between incentives and goals is not well understood. There is little empirical research on this relationship, and the research that has been conducted on this topic has some methodological limitations (Wood et al., 1999; Wright, 1989). In one well-designed study, however, Wright (1989) found that incentive pay does increase the level of goals, as well as commitment to those goals. Even the results of this study are somewhat tentative, however, as the study was conducted with undergraduate students, and the magnitude of the results was only moderate.

Given this line of theory and research, some logical extensions can be made to merit pay. Goal-setting theory suggests the following:

- *Merit increases should be contingent on specific, rather than "do your best," goals.* Employees may have very little idea as to what constitutes "do your best" in the eyes of the supervisor or person allocating merit increases. Hence, specific criteria need to be established.
- *Merit increases should be based on goal difficulty as well as goal accomplishment.* If goal difficulty is not factored into rewards, employees may be motivated to set lower goals because they are easier to accomplish and still rewarded.
- *Goals and merit increases should be discussed at the same time.* The limited research suggests that the setting of goals and allocation of rewards serve as additions to rather than substitutes for one another. That is, motivation is greater when goals and rewards are coupled together rather than being treated separately by managers. Hence, they should be discussed at the same time rather than separately.

In summary, goal-setting theory suggests that merit pay increases motivation because merit increases result in the setting of more goals, the setting of more difficult goals, and greater commitment to goals. Adhering to this theory, merit increases should be based on the attainment of specific goals that have been weighted by difficulty. Goals, weights for each goal, and merit increases should all be discussed at the same time to have the desired motivational effect.

Self-Determination Theory (SDT)

This theory proposes that individuals intentionally choose when to exert effort and when not to do so. This decision is a learned behavior from collected human experiences. Over time, people acquire a value system and learned behaviors that motivate them based on satisfying three basic psychological needs for autonomy, competence, and relatedness (Gagné & Deci, 2005). Autotomy refers to the freedom of choosing one's behavior.

Competence focuses on the perception of having mastery and being effective in one's environment. Relatedness refers to the perception of being connected to others.

According to Self-Determination Theory (SDT), or SDT, two types of motivation—autonomous and controlled—result from satisfying these basic needs (Gagné & Deci, 2005). Autonomous motivation is the same as intrinsic motivation; employees feel in control of their motivation and want to perform a task for its own sake. Controlled motivation is based on extrinsic rewards (e.g., pay). The original construction of SDT suggests that only need satisfaction leads to autonomous motivation and positive work outcomes (Gagné & Deci, 2005). However, subsequent refinements to the theory predict that the introduction of fairly distributed financial incentives positively link to autonomous motivation and work performance (Gagné & Forest, 2008; Landry et al., 2017). The reader should note that decisions here are intentional.

Research on SDT show that need satisfaction positively relates to autonomous motivation and employee well-being (Van den Broeck et al., 2010). In another study, Landry et al. (2017) used path analysis, and discovered that fairly distributive financial incentives and bonuses made employee more competent and autonomous, leading to better work outcomes.

Integrating SDT and research, the following implications exist for merit pay:

- *Employees must perceive merit-pay increases are distributed fairly according to performance.* An unfair treatment of merit pay could backfire and have negative consequences on various outcome, such as, retention, and behavior.
- *Employees must perceive they have control over their performance.* This aligns with job holders wanting autonomy in their jobs. Employees with little control over their performance will probably become dissatisfied with their jobs and leave the organization.

In conclusion, SDT proposes that intentionality in satisfying three basic needs for autonomy, competence, and relatedness promotes intrinsic motivation. A modified version of the theory suggests that financial incentives also bring about intrinsic motivation under certain conditions. Overall, SDT suggests need satisfaction, extrinsic motivation, and intrinsic motivation should be considered in concert for optimizing positive work outcomes.

Social Exchange Theory

Social Exchange Theory (SET), or SET, examines social interactions through the lens of costs and rewards (Cropanzano & Mitchell, 2005). Two parties, such as an employee and an employer, enter into an interdependent relationship based on the exchange of different resources. An employee receives extrinsic rewards (pay and benefits) and socioemotional resources in exchange for contributing (through acceptable work performance and commitment) to the employer's objectives and sustainability. Both parties look to maximize rewards and minimize costs. A set of rules, norm of reciprocity, governs the exchange: the actions of one party results in actions by the other party (employee action is implied as obligation to the employer). As long as rewards exceed costs, the relationship between parties will continue. On the other hand, if costs exceed rewards over the long haul, one or both parties will terminate the relationship.

SET has been studied and supported in various organizational situations. Kuvaas et al. (2020) tested the effects of SET on two different pay systems—base pay and variable pay. Using a cross-lagged study over 30 months, the results showed that increases in base pay, but not variable pay, were attributable to social exchange relationships. In another study, Aryee et al. (2002) found a social exchange model explained the mediating effects of trust on workplace outcomes. The researchers found that trust in the organization mediated the relationship between justice (distributive, procedural, interactional) and job satisfaction, turnover intentions, and organizational commitment. In addition, trust in the supervisor mediated interactional justice and work behavior.

Taken together, SET and research provide implications for merit pay.

- *Employees must trust the organization and the supervisor.* This implies that transparency among merit pay policies and procedures must be clear and factual. A combination of procedural, distributive, and interactional justice must be monitored.
- *Employee effort can be maximized if the employer provides expected merit pay increases.* Perceived relationships between pay and performance play a large role here. Employers should ensure merit increases align with employee expectations based on fair and accurate performance measurements.

In summary, SET has been widely researched in the workplace. It shows a successful exchange of resources results in a robust employer-employee relationship with desirable outcomes. An employee gains economic and socioemotional resources, while the employer receives hard and committed workers.

Economic Theories

Another set of theories that address the pay and performance relationship comes from the field of economics. Theories from economics have not received the widespread attention that psychological theories have in the merit pay literature. Nevertheless, they have clear applicability to merit pay and are referenced and discussed at several points in the book.

The economic theories reviewed here are similar to the psychological theories just reviewed in that both sets of theories suggest that individuals direct their efforts toward the maximization of outcomes, such as pay, which will provide the greatest level of satisfaction (Kaufman, 1989). The theories differ from one another, however, in several ways. First, economic theories tend to be directed to the operation of the firm or market, rather than the motivation of individuals within the firm or market. Second, the pay and performance relationship tends to be examined from the employer's rather than the employee's perspective. Third, when economic theories do address the issue of individual rather than organizational performance, as is the case, for example, with efficiency wage theory, they place a greater emphasis on the opportunity costs to the employee that are associated with employment decisions, such as deciding at what level to perform at work. Psychological theories tend to emphasize the attractiveness of outcomes to individuals more than the costs. As a result, economic theories yield a somewhat different set of implications for merit pay than do psychological theories, which in turn leads the reader to a more comprehensive understanding of merit pay.

Marginal Productivity Theory

According to Tobin (1985), this theory can be traced back in the United States to the work of Clark (1889). Under this theory, employers pay employees at the value of their marginal products. What this means is that employers provide higher rates of pay to those employees whose inputs result in higher rates of profit to the organization. In a competitive market, where an employer must minimize costs to remain in business, employers will grant pay increases only up to the point where pay is equal to the input or performance contribution of the employee. Clearly, employers need to carefully define the performance input and pay according to this input to contain labor costs and be competitive in the market.

By paying on the basis of marginal productivity or performance, firms receive three types of benefits (Bishop, 1987). First, this system serves as an incentive to employees to expend greater effort. Second, it tends to attract workers who are willing and able to work hard. Third, it helps diminish the chances of the best performers leaving the organization and the worst performers remaining with the organization. All three of these benefits are in line with maximizing the profits of the organization.

The research on marginal productivity theory suggests that it is extremely doubtful that employers pay exactly at the level where wages equal marginal productivity, even under ideal circumstances (Miller, 2001; Palley, 2001). Frank (1984) found that even in highly competitive industries such as auto and real estate sales, where marginal productivity theory is most applicable, employees are not exactly paid to their marginal products. Bishop (1987) suggests that there are a number of reasons why pay cannot be linked precisely to marginal productivity, including the difficulties involved in measuring performance and the overhead costs involved in doing so.

While the research does not show a one-to-one correspondence between pay and marginal productivity, as would be expected under marginal productivity theory, the theory still has several important implications for merit pay, as follows:

- *Performance must be carefully measured.* To contain costs, performance must be carefully measured to determine the contribution of the employee to the organization, so that employees can be paid in line with their contributions.
- *An upper boundary for merit increases must be established.* The demand for the labor of an employer is derived from the demand in the market for the employer's goods and services. Merit increases, which are in part dependent upon the demand for labor, need to be set at a level consistent with the demand for goods and services.

In summary, marginal productivity theory suggests that pay is issued on the basis of performance to minimize labor costs and remain competitive in the labor market. To do this, attention must be paid to the measurement of performance and to the demand for goods and services. While research indicates that pay and performance are not always directly related, it is a goal that employers work toward. A 2002 survey by Hewitt and Associates indicated that fully 80% of the surveyed organizations included "variable pay" as a major component of their compensation design.

Implicit Contract Theory

Many have heard the phrase "A fair day's pay for a fair day's work." This saying captures the notion of an implicit contract between an employer and employee. In exchange for services provided by the employee, the employer promises to pay the employee. In exchange for pay from the employer, the employee promises to provide services to the employer. In essence, then, an implicit contract is formed between the employer and employee (Holmstrom, 1999; Murdock, 2002).

According to Rosen (1985), the phrase "implicit contracts" was first coined by Gordon (1974). The theory was developed in response to two of the major assumptions sometimes attributed to marginal productivity theory (Nalbantian, 1987). First, some presentations of marginal productivity theory assume that performance is a homogeneous input in work organizations. Second, it is also sometimes assumed that performance, or marginal productivity, can be perfectly measured. Bishop (1987) reviewed these two assumptions and other criticisms of marginal productivity theory.

Implicit contract theory does away with these two assumptions. It suggests that for many jobs, performance varies from person to person. To the extent that employers pay the same wage to all employees, employers may be incurring additional costs by overpaying those who produce the least with an average wage. Implicit contract theory also suggests that it is difficult to measure performance in many jobs. As will be shown in Chapter 4, measures of employee performance may not only capture actual employee performance, but may also capture the effects of other variables that have an impact on the employee's actual performance. For example, sales may be greater for one individual than another not because of a difference in effort, but simply because one individual was assigned a better sales territory. As a consequence of less than perfect measurement, employers may end up overpaying employees for performance results unrelated to their individual efforts. Therefore, to minimize these potential costs, it is to the employer's advantage to set up contracts with individuals in which the relationship between pay and performance is clearly specified rather than assumed.

A common practice for outside sales positions, where the employee is on the road selling goods and services rather than selling in a retail establishment, is to establish sales commissions with "bogeys" (Patten, 1976). Under this incentive arrangement, a contract is clearly established, with pay increases allocated on the basis of sales. But, as you can well imagine, some products sell better than others, and sales are more plentiful in some regions than others. Therefore, sales results are adjusted to reflect the differences in products or regions before pay increases are granted. These adjustments, or bogeys, are made to ensure that pay increases or commissions are issued for performance that is under the direct control of the outside sales representative.

Three reviews of the empirical literature provide some support for the notion of implicit contracts. Bishop (1987) provided evidence suggesting that marginal productivity of employees does indeed vary and is not homogeneous as assumed under classical marginal productivity theory. Rosen (1985) reviews evidence suggesting that marginal revenue product and, in turn, wages are indeed affected by exogenous factors, or elements outside of employees' control. For example, wage rates in manufacturing have been shown to be related to local labor market conditions, but not to aggregate output measures. Additionally, a survey found support for the influence of implicit contracts on wage rigidities among 801 German firms (Franz & Pfeiffer, 2003). The psychological process underlying the formation of implicit contracts has been researched in psychology under the term "psychological contracts" (Rousseau & Ho, 2000).

Taken together, the theory and research behind the concept of implicit contracts suggests the following for merit pay plans:

- *Performance must be measured, not assumed.* If an employer assumes that all employees are equally productive, the employer may end up with payroll costs that are larger than necessary. Poor performers who are being paid an average wage on the basis of equal performance will be overpaid. Therefore, the employer must measure performance to contain costs.
- *Performance ratings should be adjusted for factors outside an employee's control.* Without an adjustment, some employees may end up receiving greater merit increases than they deserve for their individual contributions while other employees may receive less than they deserve for their individual contributions.

In summary, implicit contract theory suggests that merit pay is a form of an implicit contract. This contract is formed by employers to minimize labor costs. Employers must measure the performance of each individual rather than assuming that each person performs at the same level. An employee can then be paid on the basis of his or her actual contribution. Also, to minimize labor costs, the employer must take care to adjust performance ratings for factors outside the employee's control before tying pay to these ratings.

Efficiency Wage Theory

The origin of this theory can be traced back to the work of Salop (1979). In essence, efficiency wage theory suggests that the level of wages determines effort. In general, a premium wage is paid to ensure that employees perform up to their maximum levels (Stiglitz, 1987). The reason to provide a premium wage is because employees have an incentive to perform at less than their maximum level (Nalbantian, 1987). By working less hard than someone else and receiving the same rewards, an individual employee maximizes his or her net returns. That is, employees may attempt to get more for less.

When a wage premium is offered, which could be in the form of a merit increase, employee performance should be improved over what would be expected if a premium were not offered, for a variety of reasons (Katz, 1986; Levine, 1989; Thaler, 1989). First, an employee is less likely to shirk job responsibilities. If an employee shirks his or her duties or, in other words, does not perform his or her assigned duties, the employee is likely to lose his or her job. It will then be difficult for the employee to find a similar job at the same premium rate. Hence, the loss of a job for which an efficiency wage is paid is very costly to the employee. Second, voluntary turnover is likely to be minimized because alternative jobs at premium wages are not readily available in the labor market. Hence, an employee receiving an efficiency wage is unlikely to leave. Third, employees may feel obligated to perform at higher levels in return for the more-than-fair treatment being offered by the employer.

In paying an efficiency wage, an employer bears an additional cost not faced by others in the labor market; namely, the premium wage that is being paid. In a sense, however, it may be worth it because the employer expects to see a return on this investment. In particular, the employer expects to see lower turnover, more qualified applicants, and less shirking. An employer may incur some large wage costs up front in the hope of regaining these costs through better performance in the future. By paying efficiency wages, the employer is able to minimize turnover and thereby reduce the costs associated with turnover. When an individual leaves the organization, it costs the employer money to replace the person because the recruitment and hiring process must be repeated. Also, while the person was employed by the organization, there were costs to the organization to train and pay the person. These costs will not be offset by the services of the person to the organization if the person leaves. Interestingly, Henry Ford paid nearly double the going wage rate back in 1914 and argued, in line with efficiency wage arguments, that raising wages was actually a cost-saving measure (Raff & Summers, 1987).

Another reason that costs may be lower for an efficiency wage employer is that the cost of monitoring and controlling employee performance may be minimized. The employer has, in a sense, an insurance policy by paying efficiency wages. Employees are less likely to shirk their duties because they may not be able to find similar work at such a premium efficiency wage elsewhere in the marketplace. As a result of this high-wage insurance premium protecting against poor performance, employers may not need to assiduously monitor and control employee performance. Employees will monitor their own performance to retain their jobs.

Katz (1986) provided an insightful review and evaluation of the research on efficiency wage theory. There is some support for efficiency wage theory in studies that examine wage differentials among industries. Employers in some industries, such as mining and petroleum (Krueger & Summers, 1988), pay a high wage even after controlling for the effects of union, job, and worker characteristics (Thaler, 1989). Precisely why this interindustry wage effect is present is a subject of debate. Even if this differential is attributable to efficiency wage theory arguments, we do not know which arguments are best supported. More well-controlled studies are needed to test the shirking, turnover, or obligation hypotheses from efficiency wage theory at the level of the individual employee. Some research has provided mixed support for efficiency wage theory predictions (Chen & Edin, 2002; Ewing & Payne, 1999). In a survey of human resource executives, Klaas (1999) found that a number of environmental and strategic HR issues predicted organizational willingness to *lower* rather than raise direct compensation in the face of competitive pressures or labor market opportunities (see also Klaas & Ullman, 1995). We discuss some of these "contingencies" further in Chapter 3.

Although the evidence for efficiency wage theory's positive effect on employee behavior is not large, the theory has the following implications for merit pay:

- *Merit pay levels should be aligned with the competitive market.* In determining the sizes of merit increases, employers should consider increases being offered by their competitors. By doing so, it may be possible to minimize the shirking of job duties and voluntary turnover.
- *Merit increases are particularly important in low-wage organizations.* By offering attractive merit increases as additions to the base wage, it may be possible to provide a premium to high performers in low-wage organizations, thereby minimizing turnover. In high wage organizations, merit increases may be of lesser importance to employees as a premium is already being offered in the form of base pay.
- *Merit pay should lead to better self-monitoring of performance.* The employer may not need to devote as much time to monitoring employee performance because employees are more likely to monitor their own performance. Employees may self-monitor to ensure that they retain efficiency wages.

In summary, efficiency wage theory suggests that pay be set high to obligate employees to fully perform, not shirk their duties, and remain with the organization. When employers pay a premium wage, it is costly for their employees to lose their jobs. One way to establish a premium is on the basis of merit. For merit to be a premium, merit increases would need to be set relative to the competition. The initial investment in a wage premium may be offset later by better performance and lower monitoring costs.

Tournament Theory

Tournament theory suggests that participants in a competition aspire to win the top prize and will expend the necessary effort to be the winner

(Connelly et al., 2014; Lazear & Rosen, 1981. This logic can be applied to employees who compete with others for a chance of "winning the prize," that is, getting a large salary increase for being promoted to a higher position in the organization. Candidates will exert as much effort as they need to optimize their chances of getting the promotion. The theory states that the motivational effect is a function of the salary difference between the pre-promotional level and the post-promotional level. As the differential of the two salaries widens (the salary of the target position exceeds that of the original position), promotional candidates will summon extra effort to win the prize. That is, the greater the differential between the salary of original position and the targeted position, the harder employees will work (Brown et al., 2003; Pfeffer & Langton, 1993; Shaw et al., 2002).

For example, a large governmental contractor advertises a promotional opportunity for a pool of internal candidates in two classifications—software engineer I and software engineer II. The yearly mid-point salaries are $120,000 and $133,000, respectively. The vacant position, software engineer IV, has an annual mid-point salary of $146,000. According to tournament theory, software engineer I has more motivational impact than software engineer II. The salary differential between the lower engineer and the target position is greater ($26,000) than that of the higher software engineer and the target position ($13,000).

Tournament theory has been used to explain why company executives (particularly, CEOs) command exorbitant salaries (Connelly et al., 2014; Lazear & Rosen, 1981; O'Reilly et al., 1988; Rees, 1992). Executives work exceeding hours (expending maximum effort) and assume huge risks navigating an entire organization. Several studies support tournament theory. Using structural equation modeling (SEM), DeVaro (2006) found that tournament strategies yielded more effort in promotions when opportunities constituted highest ranking positions. Gomez-Mejia et al., (2009) showed that employee perception of tournament fairness affected their amount of effort. Henderson and Fredrickson (2001) revealed that greater margins between organizational rankings resulted in more effort of competitors. In two studies, researchers found that greater prizes in tournaments generated more solutions in problem-solving (Boudreau et al., 2011; Terwiesch & Ulrich, 2009; Terwiesch & Xu, 2008).

While this theory generally applies to pay differences in the internal structure of organizations, there are also implications for merit pay:

- *Effort must be clearly linked to performance.* An unclear link might lead to unattended consequences. For example, a hard working employee may grow frustrated with the merit pay system and not work harder, which in turn, may lead to apathy.
- *Performance assessment must perceived as valid and fair.* Nothing will ruin a merit pay plan more than a poorly constructed, performance measure system and the unfair implementation of it. Attention must be given to the construction of any measure system, so that

psychometric properties (reliability and validity) are optimized. In addition, raters must be trained in rating biases and fair treatment of appraising employees.

- *The amount of merit increase must be sufficiently large.* If employees perceive merit increases are insufficient, they will not exert the necessary effort to attain higher performance levels. This can undermine a merit pay plan.

In summary, tournament theory suggests that employees work harder for coveted rewards. The greater the difference between the present position and the higher (future) position, the more effort a person will expend. For merit pay, employees must perceive that their effort will lead to graduated levels of performance. They should also perceive the amount of the merit increase (prize) is sufficient.

Sorting Effects

Sorting effects suggest that individuals sort themselves in and out of organizations based on what is important to them (Lazear, 1986). If an organization pays for performance rather than adhering to bureaucratic rules or maintaining the status quo, individuals who prefer financial rewards will gravitate to, and remain in, such organizations. Indirectly, the theory suggests that employees will also work harder to earn higher pay levels, assuming they see a direct link between their efforts and the rewards they receive. In contrast, people who do not want to exert effort for financial gain will either refrain from joining such a organization or will leave it. In other words, individuals will sort themselves out of the organization. This interaction may produce a more productive workforce if only high performers remain in the organization.

Several studies support the sorting effect. Gerhart and Fang (2014), Hausknecht et al. (2009), Nyberg (2010), and Salamin and Hom (2005) found that top performing employees, who desired and received performance-based pay, stayed in their organizations far longer than low performers who were not concerned about financial incentives. Taken together, theory and research contain inferences for merit pay:

- *Merit pay plans must be highly visible to applicants.* The research here implies highlighting merit pay plans during external recruitments so that the probability of recruiting high performers is optimized.
- *A pro-merit pay culture must be present in the organization.* Employees must perceive bosses distributing merit pay increases are fair and knowledgeable about the system. In addition, merit pay must be highly desirable. Finally, administrative processes and policies for merit pay plans must be fair and transparent (see Chapter 6).

- *Performance ratings (measurement systems) must be reliable and valid.* Employees must feel the measurement system is fair. This implies performance measures must be constructed with sufficient reliability and validity. An employee's decision to remain with the organization may depend on the fairness and accuracy of the appraisal system that determines their merit increase.

In summary, sorting effects explain individual decisions for joining and staying with an organization based on their receiving desirable rewards. Moreover, the theory implies that workers will exert more effort if they see extra motivation links to higher pay levels. Organizations may find that advertising merit pay plans increases the number of recruits, especially in a tight labor market.

Summary of Theories

A variety of theories impact merit pay. These theories are integrated in Fig. 2.4. As shown in this figure, the theories can be summarized using an expectancy theory framework. The arrows leading from various psychological and economic theories to expectancy theory show which components of expectancy theory are related to each theory.

Both efficiency wage theory and goal-setting theory address the issue of expectancy, or the perceived relationship between effort and performance. Efficiency wage theory and SET suggest that if merit pay is provided, employees may feel obligated to exert effort and not shirk their duties. Goal-setting theory and tournament theory suggest that merit pay may lead to increased effort because it may induce the setting of and commitment to more specific and difficult performance goals.

Equity theory, marginal productivity theory, and implicit contracts all address the notion of instrumentality, or perceptions of the relationship between performance and rewards. Equity theory, SET, and SDT suggest that there must be a balance between performance and pay for merit pay to strengthen instrumentality perceptions. Marginal productivity theory indicates that there is, from the organization's perspective, an upper boundary to the amount of merit pay that can be allocated to strengthen the link between pay and performance. Implicit contract theory, sorting effects, and tournament theory indicate that, for instrumentality perceptions to be made, performance must be carefully measured, and the contribution of the individual to the organization needs to be separated out from factors outside the employee's control.

Finally, reinforcement theory and sorting effects are related to both instrumentality perceptions and to the concept of valence, or the perception of the attractiveness of outcomes such as merit pay. Reinforcement

Figure 2.4.

Summary of Psychological and Economic Theories Related to Merit Pay.

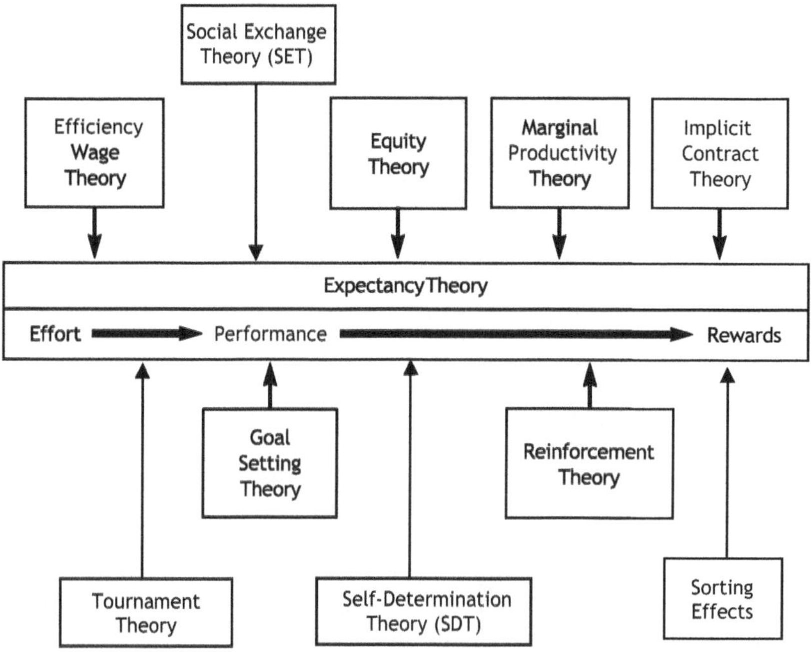

theory suggests that merit needs to be made contingent on performance for there to be instrumentality perceptions. Also, merit increases must be viewed by employees as more attractive than alternative outcomes, such as leisure, to motivate improved performance.

The Pay-for-Performance Relationship

The previous section showed that there are sound reasons, from both economic and psychological perspectives, for an organization to have a policy of paying on the basis of performance. The objective of this section is to review research that looks at the extent to which organizations *actually do* link pay to performance. Having a policy of pay for performance does not guarantee that pay will actually be tied to performance in practice.

In reviewing the pay-for-performance relationship, two points should be kept in mind. The first point is that pay-for-performance can be viewed both in relationship to previous performance, as well as in relation to subsequent performance. For merit pay to lead to subsequent improved performance, it must first be related to previous performance, as discussed in the earlier overview of theories. This chapter reviews studies that examine pay for *previous* performance. In Chapter 7, we deal more fully with pay for subsequent performance.

The second point to bear in mind is that the pay-for-performance relationship can be examined both in terms of actual relationship and in terms of people's perceptions of the relationship. Both the actual and perceived relationship between pay and performance are important to consider if a merit pay plan is to be effective. Sometimes employees' perceptions of the relationship are different than the actual relationship, which can cause problems for managers of merit pay plans. For example, as presented in the discussion of equity theory, employee motivation is a function of perceptions of the ratio of pay to performance, rather than the actual ratio of pay to performance. Because of the importance of this distinction, the studies reviewed here are broken down into actual and perceived relationships.

Actual Relationship Between Pay and Performance

It is indeed possible for organizations to establish an actual link between pay and performance. This is illustrated in Table 2.1.

In the first column, the authors and date of the study are listed. This citation can be used to find the full reference for the study in the reference list at the back of the book. The second column describes the types of jobs or occupations held by the participants in the study. The third column assigns a general label to the type of organization in which the participants worked. Study type, listed in the fourth column, notes whether the study was conducted in a setting where merit pay was actually being used (field), or in a setting where the researchers simulated a situation involving merit pay (laboratory). The fifth column shows the sign linked to the results of the study. A positive sign indicates that there was a positive relationship observed between previous performance and the size of merit increases. That is, as ratings of employee performance increased, merit pay increased as well. A negative sign indicates that as ratings of employee performance increased, merit pay decreased. Significance of the results, shown in the sixth column, indicates the degree of certainty that we can have in the results. The smaller the number in this column, the less likely the reported result is due to chance associated with the selection of the study sample.

In some 40 of 42 studies that looked at the relationship between pay and performance in organizations with merit pay, there was a positive relationship between current merit increases and previous performance. In a small number of the studies, the results were not statistically significant, but this could be due to small sample size. The actual positive relationship between pay and performance appears to be robust. It has been observed in laboratory and field settings, private- and public-sector organizations, service and

Table 2.1

Summary of Studies Showing Relationship Between Merit Increase and Previous Performance

Authors		Participants	Organization	Study Type	Results	
					Sign	Significance ($p<$)
Alexander and Barrett (1982)	4,582	Managers, Scientists, Students	Intl. Research Group	Lab.	+	0.001
Bass (1968)	113	Students	University	Lab.	+	?
Birnbaum (1983)	10	Faculty Members	University	Lab.	+	?
	125	Students	University	Lab.	+	?
Bishop (1987)	456	Professionals	Various Private Sect.	Field	+	0.01
Dreher (1981)	1,414	Employees	Manufacturing Co.	Field	+	0.05
Fossum and Fitch (1985)	20	Students	University	Lab.	+	0.001
	40	Managers & Professionals	Various Private Sect.	Lab.	+	0.001
	42	Managers & Professionals	Various Private Sect.	Lab.	+	0.001
Foster and Lynn (1978)	56	Managers	Various Private Sect.	Lab.	+	?
Gerhart and Milkovich (1989)	5,550	Admin. & Professionals	Diversified Firm	Field	+	0.01
	840	Admin. & Professionals	Diversified Firm	Field	+	0.01
Goodman (1975)	65	Students	University	Lab.	+	0.05
Greene (1973)	62	Managers	Manufacturing Co.	Field	+	0.01
H. Heneman (1973)	68	Managers	Retail Firm	Field	+	0.01
R. Heneman and Cohen (1988)	175	Employees	Manufacturing Co.	Field	+	0.01

(Continued)

Table 2.1 (Continued)

Authors		Participants	Organization	Study Type	Results	
					Sign	Significance (*p*<)
Hills et al. (1988)	1,255	Employees	Transit Authority	Field	+	0.001
Huber et al. (1987)	229	Managers	City Government	Lab.	+	0.001
Ivancevich (1983)	104	Engineers	High-Tech Firm	Field	+	0.01
	66	Scientists	High-Tech Firm	Field	–	n.s.
Johnson and Kasten (1983)	32	Faculty Members	University	Field	+	0.05
Kaun (1984)	144	Faculty Members	University	Field	+	0.01
Koch and Chizmar (1973)	229	Faculty Members	University	Field	–	0.01
Kopelman (1976)	142	Engineers	Tech-Based Co.	Field	+	0.01
	138	Engineers	Tech-Based Co.	Field	+	0.01
	119	Engineers	Tech-Based Co.	Field	+	0.01
Landau and Leventhal (1976)	120	Students	University	Lab.	+	0.01
Leventhal et al. (1972)	120	Students	University	Lab.	+	0.01
	44	Students	University	Lab.	+	?
Magnusen (1987)	40	Faculty Members	University	Field	+	?
Markam (1988)	71	Managers	Manufacturing Co.	Field	+	n.s.
Medoff and Abraham (1980)	2,763	Employees	Manufacturing Co.	Field	+	varied
	2,491	Employees	Manufacturing Co.	Field	+	varied
Medoff and Abraham (1981)	7,078	Managers & Professionals	Manufacturing Co.	Field	+	varied

(Continued)

Table 2.1 (Continued)

Authors		Participants	Organization	Study Type	Results	
					Sign	Significance ($p<$)
Scott et al. (1987)	800	Employees	Transit Authority	Field	+	varied
Sherer et al. (1987)	11	Managers	Hospital	Lab.	+	0.01
Teel (1986)	?	Professionals	Various Private Sect.	Field	+	?
Turban and Jones (1988)	25	Managers	Rehabilitation Center	Field	+	0.05
Vecchio and Terborg (1987)	67	Students	University	Lab.	+	?
Wyatt Company (1987)	1,415	Professionals	Various Private Sect.	Field	+	?

Source: Adapted from R. Heneman (1990). Reprinted with permission.

manufacturing jobs, and at many job levels, as demonstrated by this collection of studies.

The data clearly indicate that it is possible for organizations to successfully implement the concept of pay-for-performance. However, it is just as important to note that theory and practice do not always perfectly coincide with one another. The magnitude of the relationship between pay and performance in these studies is not large. As shown in a previous review (Heneman, 1990) and in many places throughout the book, there are many factors, in addition to previous performance, that influence merit pay. In practice, these other factors result in less than "picture perfect" merit pay plans.

New Techniques, Mounting Evidence

Meta-Analysis

Since the second edition, more sophisticated methods in analyzing data from synthesized studies have been utilized. One such method is meta-analysis. Meta-analysis aggregates a collection of individual research studies of a common topic, calculates an average common metric or statistic across said studies (a correlation for our purpose in assessing the pay-performance relationship) and considers intervening variables (called moderator variables) that may explain mixed results in individual studies. This method constitutes a marked difference from the voting technique Heneman employed above (Heneman, 1990). The traditional voting system yields useable, but limited, information, such as, the direction of the pay-performance relationship (positive or negative correlations) and the probability that the relationship resulted due to random chance associated with the selected study sample. Conversely, meta-analytical techniques provide a plethora of data that can expand our understanding of phenomena in different disciplines, such as, education, sociology, psychology, medicine, and business. Besides the direction of an association and probability value of a random chance result, a meta-analyst can calculate various statistics for understanding the nature of the aggregated studies. They include (a) effect size (ES) of each individual study that reveals both the strength and direction of a relationship, (b) average ES across studies, (c) variance of the ES across studies, and (d) confidence intervals (CI) around the average ES. As the reader can see, the amount of information expressed in meta-analysis creates a powerful research tool for expanding our knowledge of merit pay.

To date, we are familiar with only one meta-analytic study of merit pay plans. Williams (2010) used Hunter and Schmidt's (1990, 2004) psychometric methods of meta-analysis to examine different conditions under which the link between merit pay and performance holds. Table 2.2 is a summary of studies included in the meta-analysis that show a relationship between merit increases and previous performance. The first column shows authors and date of each study in the analysis. Each citation can be used to find the full reference for the study in the reference section at the end of the book. In the second column, the type of performance measure is listed. In every study, ratings of overall performance were used. Ratings assessed at least three performance dimensions: quantity, quality, and timeliness. Some studies included assessments of results or objectives. The reader may remember that ratings measures are a hallmark of merit pay systems. The third column illustrates the study setting—laboratory and field—of the study. One objective for meta-analysis is to examine different effects on the pay-performance relationship. More will be said about this below in Moderator Variables. The fourth column specifies general job classifications of participants in the study. In the fifth column, the size of each sample is shown. The range is 4,458 participants (4,478 – 20). The effect-size statistics (correlations), shown in sixth column, indicate the direction and strength for performance-pay relationships in all 26 individual studies. The seventh column reveals 95% CI for sample effect-sizes. CI provide the probability that merit pay levels influenced performance levels due to random chance or not. A CI containing a sample ES of zero suggests the result occurred due to random chance; no claim can be made that pay links to performance. Conversely, a CI with a high, non-zero correlation suggests that a link between pay and performance is very possible. It also implies that not many other things have a big influence (e.g., seniority) on the pay-performance relationship. A reader versed in statistics will notice the use of CI (CIs) instead of a significance level (p value), which were addressed above in Table 2.1. Among other limitations, a significance level only tells whether or not a sample ES differs from zero. On the other hand, CIs provide much more information. CI indicate *how much* ESs differ from the point of significance and reveal the range of possible ES statistics in the interval. The interested reader is referred to Schmidt and Hunter (2015) for details.

The *average* ES (correlation) across 26 studies is 0.43 with a sample standard deviation of 0.15. The 95% CI of the average ES is 0.37–0.49 and excludes zero, implying, on average, previous performance levels indeed link to merit increases. In other words, the pay-performance relationship *least* likely resulted from random chance. For constituent studies, *all* but one (Gomez-Mejia & Balkin, 1989) has a zero correlation and four (Duckwall, 1986; Gomez-Mejia & Balkin, 1989; Ivancevich, 1983; Markham, 1988) have CIs with zero or a negative figures, suggesting a zero or negative association between pay and performance. A couple of notes are appropriate here. First, meta-analysts do not concern themselves with non-significant results in individual studies. The purpose of meta-analytic studies is to include *all possible* studies no matter a significant outcome or not, so long as studies meet inclusion criteria. The inclusion of all acceptable studies provides a clearer indication (understanding) of the topic under study. This is the

Table 2.2

Studies in Meta-Analysis Showing a Relationship Between Merit Pay and Performance (Williams, 2010)

Study	Performance Measure	Study Setting	Participants	Sample Size (n)	Effect Size Statistic	95% CI
Barkley and York (2003)	Ratings of overall job performance	F	Professors	36	$r = 0.90$	0.81–0.95
Dreher (1981)	Ratings of overall job performance	F	professionals, technical, management	692	$r = 0.36$	0.29–0.42
Duckwall (1986)	Ratings of overall job performance	F	Professors	113	$r = 0.06$	−0.13–0.24
Eisenburger et al. (1999)	Ratings of overall job performance	F	sales support, salespeople	348	$r = 0.25$	0.14–0.35
Fossum and Fitch (1985)	Ratings of overall job performance	L	Students	20	$r = 0.73$	0.42–0.89
Fossum and Fitch (1985)	Ratings of overall job performance	L	line managers	40	$r = 0.71$	0.51–0.84
Fossum and Fitch (1985)	Ratings of overall job performance	L	compensation managers	42	$r = 0.75$	0.58–0.86
Gerhart and Milkovich (1989)	Ratings of overall job performance	F	professional, technical, managers	6,340	$r = 0.30$	0.28–0.32
Gomez-Mejia and Balkin (1989)	Ratings of overall job performance	F	scientists, engineers	175	$r = 0.0$	0.0–0.0
Greene (1973)	Ratings of overall job performance	F	Managers	63	$r = 0.36$	0.12–0.56
Huber et al. (1987)	Ratings of overall job performance	L	Managers	229	$r = 0.57$	0.48–0.65
Ivancevich (1983)	Ratings of overall job performance	F	Engineers	104	$r = 0.24$	0.05–0.41

(Continued)

Table 2.2 (Continued)

Study	Performance Measure	Study Setting	Participants	Sample Size (n)	Effect Size Statistic	95% CI
Ivancevich (1983)	Ratings of overall job performance	F	Scientists	66	$r = 0.16$	−0.09–0.39
Koch and Chizmar (1973)	Ratings of overall job performance	F	Professors	229	$r = 0.81$	0.76–0.85
Kopelman (1976)	Ratings of overall job performance	F	Engineers	107	$r = 0.39$	0.22–0.54
Kopelman (1976)	Ratings of overall job performance	F	Engineers	104	$r = 0.55$	0.40–0.67
Kopelman (1976)	Ratings of overall job performance	F	Engineers	112	$r = 0.60$	0.47–71
Markham (1988)	Ratings of overall job performance	F	managers, professionals	71	$r = 0.19$	−0.05–0.41
Scott et al. (1996)	Ratings of overall job performance	F	professionals, technical, clerical	667	$r = 0.69$	0.65–0.73
St-Onge (2000)	Ratings of overall job performance	F	Students	321	$r = 0.39$	0.29–0.48
Turban and Jones (1988)	Ratings of overall job performance	F	nurses, clerks, OTs	155	$r = 0.67$	0.57–0.75

definition of external validity, which is discussed in Chapter 7. Second, the findings here support Heneman's (1990) findings. Obviously, the major difference between both studies resides in the cumulation technique. A meta-analysis yields more information from which to understand the nature of the actual relationship between pay and performance. Moreover, this method has the capability of addressing and clarifying inconsistent results of individual performance-based pay studies. Therefore, taken together, both studies indicate a robust performance-based pay relationship across different settings, organizations, and various classifications.

From a practical perspective, organizations considering a merit pay plan have more assurance now than in the past that a link between performance and merit pay is possible. However, a strong pay-performance link is only one of many other conditions that must be satisfied to establish a successful merit pay plan. This is the focus of chapter seven.

Moderator Variables in Meta-Analysis

A strength of meta-analysis is the capacity to detect moderator variables. Moderator variables are often included in meta-analyses to investigate whether a particular study characteristic (e.g., organizational size) would change the results of the original study had the moderator variable been included in it. Such an analysis may result, a priori, based on theory or previous research, or it may be accomplished a posteriori, resulting from additional data. In any event, examining moderator effects is a useful tool for studying merit pay plans because of the complexity surrounding them. Below are a few moderator analysis based on the Williams' (2010) study.

Effect of Study Setting. Two meta-analytic studies investigated the moderating effects of study setting—laboratory, work simulation, field—on the pay for performance relationship. The first study (Jenkins et al., 1998) involved incentive pay, whereas the Williams' (2010) study dealt with merit pay. Both researchers found study setting differentially influenced the association between pay and performance. *Why does this matter?* The results above taken separately or jointly come to the same conclusion: study setting makes a difference in the pay-performance relationship; a meta-analysis without considering different study settings (a moderator) would have given an inaccurate conclusion. A similar problem can be seen in organizations. Sometimes, organizations benchmark competitors, looking at ideas, such as a new merit-pay program. As tempting as this practice is, it may not be a good idea. As the reader will see many times in the book, organizations are complex entities—their cultures and practices are difficult to duplicate. Attempting to copy another organization's merit pay plan without considering its context, processes, and policies may be futile; it is highly doubtful that an isolated view of the merit pay plan will yield satisfactory results. This is analogous to the meta-analytic results above. An organization that wants to copy a merit pay plan from another organization must consider the interactions (moderators) between merit pay and other organizational factors.

Effect of Performance Evaluation Intervals. Some authors propose shorter appraisal intervals translate into higher levels of motivation and improved performance (Murphy & Cleveland, 1999; Yang et al., 2023). On the other hand, Heneman and Werner (2005) contend both intervals are desirable for different reasons. Shorter intervals may help rater memory, while longer intervals allow for more exposure of employee performance. These observations prompt interesting questions. First, should varying intervals impact the merit-pay performance relationship? Second, if so, at what point should appraisal intervals affect rater and employee outcomes? Williams (2010) examined the degree to which different performance appraisal intervals influence the relationship of pay and performance. He found that short appraisal intervals (3 months) and long performance periods (12 months) had no effect on the pay-performance relationship. *Why does this matter?* If future research indicates shorter appraisal intervals indeed promote more motivational force, then a moderator analysis may help researchers better trace the components of motivation in merit pay plans. From a practical perspective, shortening assessment intervals, in conjunction with merit pay increases, can possibly optimize employee motivation, and in turn, increase productivity.

Long-term effects on pay-performance relationship. Several authors posit that pay for performance tends to lose motivational potency over time (Belcher & Atchison, 1987; Kohn, 1993a). Empirical research, using conventional methods, showed support for this notion (Guzzo et al., 1985; Rothe, 1978). On the contrary, Schwab and Olson (1990), using a Monte Carlo simulation, found the relationship between merit pay and performance remained equally strong across several performance appraisal intervals. Given mixed methods and results, Williams (2010) also examined the long-term effect of the same relationship. The results showed that the pay-performance correlation in the first year ($r = 0.46$) increased in the second year ($r = 0.57$). According to the Schmidt and Hunter criteria, the increase over two years could be attributable to a real difference in moderator effect. The results here partially match those of Schwab and Olson's Monte Carlo simulation. Both studies rendered comparable first year correlations ($r = 0.46$ vs. $r = 0.43$). However, in the second year, the meta-analytic study (moderator analysis) produced a larger ES ($r = 0.57$) than the computer simulation ($r = 0.45$). This disparity raises an interesting question: Why would an increase occur? Perhaps, employees perceive over time a stronger link between pay and performance as the cumulative effect of merit pay increases become more visible and more meaningful. For example, an employee receives a 3.5% merit increase for two consecutive years. While 3.5% one year may not mean much, the cumulative effect of 3.5% + 3.5% (total of 7%) over two years may be perceived as a strong motivator. *Why does this matter?* As mentioned above, advances in research methods since the second version provide researchers and practitioners new perspectives. New research tools and techniques allow for increments in consistency and accuracy in analyzing complex organizational systems and processes. Conventional methods still remain viable; however, more sophisticated techniques help answer questions that could not have been tackled in the past, as per the moderators presented here. For practitioners, the implications from this moderator analysis suggests that testing a merit system may take longer than one fiscal cycle before valid results may be realized. The mounting evidence here supports that a stronger link between merit pay and performance is possible.

Current Trends in Merit Pay

Merit Pay Research: A Symbiotic Relationship

Science evolves as more sophisticated research methods are developed and new knowledge is acquired. The same holds true for applied science, where research, and practice merge. The study and practice of merit pay represent an applied science. A symbiotic relationship exists between human resource managers and researchers. Applied researchers attempt to solve managerial and organizational problems through theory and research methods. Reciprocally, HR managers look to applied scientists for help in solving these issues. The last section showed the advancement of a research technique (meta-analysis) to better understand the relationship between pay and performance. New research techniques in SEM (Kline, 2023), multilevel analysis (Hox et al., 2017), and multivariate analysis (Meyers et al., 2016) are also available to help applied researchers. A theme we hope to convey is that best practices based on theory and research will be shown throughout this book. Below is an example that exemplifies this theme.

Werner (2021) summarized the last two decades of research in linking merit pay and performance. He highlights the integration of merit pay plans and the larger context of strategic compensation and performance management. Historically, the study of performance-based pay had been rather compartmentalized on the motivational force of money on performance. This view has led to inconsistencies in merit pay research and in practice. A newer paradigm places more weight on (1) aligning merit pay plans with human resource management and organizational objectives, and (2) the internal and external context in which merit pay operates. Certainly, some ideas here are not new, but the *emphasis* on them are, especially considering new research tools cited above. For example, instead of concentrating only on performance motivation, a current (expanded) view of pay for performance includes other compensation objectives—attracting and retaining employees (Fulmer et al., 2023; Martocchio, 2023). Merit pay has the potential to improve employee recruitment and retention, which in turn provides for improved organizational performance (Fulmer et al., 2023).

In summary, this section blends new research methodology and the reality of organizations to show how researchers and practitioners reciprocally can improve the implementation and administration of merit pay systems. The reader will see more of Werner's (2021) findings in Chapters 3 and 4.

Perceived Relationship Between Pay and Performance

In contrast to the numerous studies on the actual relationship between pay and performance, much less research has been conducted on the perceived relationship between pay and performance. In general, the data suggest that a positive perceived relationship does exist under merit pay plans. St-Onge (2000) studied pay-for-performance perceptions in a large manufacturing organization covered by a merit pay plan. Pay-for-performance perceptions were significantly predicted by five variables: (1) the actual increases received, (2) the strength of the pay-for-performance linkage (i.e., the extent to which merit raises in fact correlated with ratings given), (3) the extent to which employees perceived the evaluation process to be procedurally fair, (4) employee trust in the merit pay decision-makers, and (5) employee satisfaction with the outcomes received. Interestingly, the variable with the strongest impact on pay-for-performance perceptions was procedural justice.

Vest et al. (1989) reported an average of 2.6 on a scale with the following parameters: 1 = weak perceived pay-for-performance relationship to 6 = strong perceived pay-for-performance relationship. Todd et al. (1974) reported that there was a significantly greater number of strong than weak perceptions of pay for performance for a sample of accountants. Wisdom and Patzig (1987) found that about 60% of private-sector employees perceived a strong relationship, while only about 40% of public-sector employees saw a strong link. Similar results were reported by Rainey (1979).

Additional studies shed light on these findings. First, Peck (1984) reported that the overall relationship between effort and rewards was weak for a huge, combined sample of merit- and nonmerit-based organizations. This study, along with the ones just mentioned, suggests that pay-for-performance perceptions are stronger in merit-based companies alone than in a combined sample of merit-based and nonmerit-based companies. Logically, this suggests that pay-for-performance perceptions are somewhat stronger in merit-based than nonmerit-based companies.

Second, R. Heneman et al. (1988) found that in a hospital without a formal merit pay plan, the average pay-for-performance relationship was about 2.4 on a scale where 1 = weak pay-for-performance relationship and 6 = strong pay-for-performance relationship. Comparing the perceptions found in the organizations just reviewed, it appears that pay-for-performance perceptions are somewhat stronger in merit-versus nonmerit-based organizations. However, this difference is not large.

Third, Jenkins and Lawler (1981) conducted a study where the organization appears to have shifted from a nonmerit to a merit-based system. Pay-for-performance perceptions decreased during this change by a small and insignificant amount. The results of this study cast some doubt on the notion that pay-for-performance perceptions are necessarily strengthened under a merit pay plan. However, these results are not conclusive. Some factor other than the introduction of a merit pay plan may have been responsible for the lack of a significant change. The study design did not allow for the testing of other factors.

Fourth, Lowery et al. (1996) surveyed employees in a large service organization that had introduced an incentive bonus based on supervisory ratings on performance, that is, a new merit pay plan. In responding to an open-ended question concerning what they liked about the new plan, 31% of the employees stated that they liked the concept of merit pay. Their concerns or dislikes about the merit pay plan centered around implementation issues (e.g., fairness, quality of the goals used to evaluate employee performance, and paperwork issues).

In summary, there appears to be a positive perceived relationship between pay and performance under merit pay plans. These perceptions appear to be stronger in merit-pay-based than in nonmerit-pay-based organizations. However, a shift from a nonmerit-to a merit-based system does not seem to automatically strengthen these perceptions. Given the limited number of studies, and the general comparisons made here, these conclusions are not strongly established.

Potential Pitfalls With Merit Pay

The information presented so far indicates that there is both theoretical and practical substantiation for seeking to link pay to performance with a merit pay plan. Overall, merit pay *can* be a desirable method of pay because of the potential for improved performance. It has also been shown, however, that there are some specific requirements that must be met for merit pay to have the desired end result of improved performance. These requirements are reviewed throughout the book.

The tradeoff between performance and resources is an important factor in determining the overall desirability of merit pay. Merit pay may not be as desirable because of the resources that need to be devoted to creating and implementing the plan (the resources that need to be committed to a merit pay plan are described in Chapters 4, 5, and 6).

Also, in assessing the desirability of merit pay, management must examine the line of arguments that have been made *against* merit pay over the years. In this section, some of the potential risks or pitfalls with merit pay are addressed, including the potential for a decrease in intrinsic motivation, cooperation, self-esteem, and equity. These pitfalls are illustrated in Fig. 2.5 and are discussed in turn.

Figure 2.5.

Problems Believed to be Associated With Merit Pay.

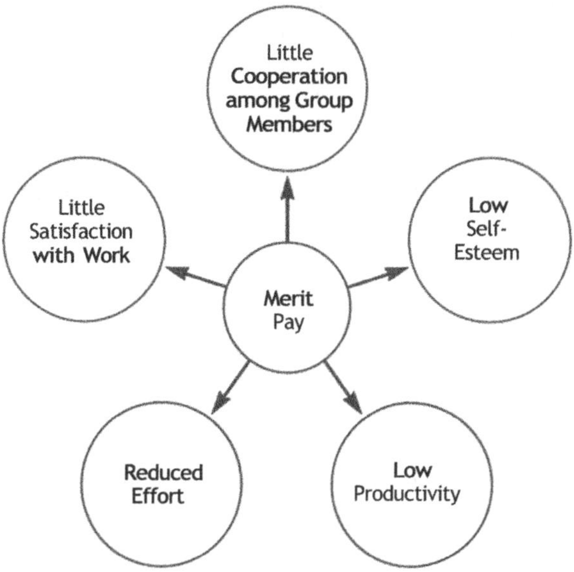

Merit Pay and Intrinsic Motivation

Deci (1972) advanced the argument that when people are paid on the basis of performance, the pay reduces the amount of pleasure or intrinsic motivation they receive from performing the task. That is, by rewarding people for what they already enjoy doing, motivation will decrease. In support of this argument, he conducted a laboratory study in which pay was made contingent upon the completion of an enjoyable task (solving a puzzle). Deci found that the amount of time the participants spent on the puzzle during their free time was actually less for those granted pay on the basis of performance than for those not granted pay on the basis of performance. Thus, the laboratory study supported his argument.

While interesting, Deci's work has been subject to criticism. Dyer and Parker (1975) found that the concept of intrinsic motivation is difficult to define, let alone measure. Given this definitional problem, it is difficult to know when merit pay does or does not affect intrinsic motivation. Even when there appears to be a reasonable measure of intrinsic motivation, empirical studies conducted by other authors do not lend much support to Deci's argument. For example, in a well-designed study by Scott et al. (1988), it was shown that pay-for-performance did not reduce intrinsic motivation. Instead, the trend was for pay-for-performance to increase intrinsic motivation. This study suggests that, at a minimum, merit pay will not reduce intrinsic motivation and, in fact, may actually increase intrinsic motivation. The results of these two studies and others indicate that a decrease in intrinsic motivation does not appear to be a likely outcome of merit pay.

Kohn (1993a, 1993b) resurfaced the decreased intrinsic motivation argument. His argument also does not hold. His conclusions are based primarily upon primary and secondary students in classroom settings, rather than adults in work settings. Pfeffer (1998) raised the argument that rewards decrease intrinsic motivation. Upon careful scrutiny of his arguments, however, there is again little support (see Gerhart & Rynes, 2003).

As mentioned above, advances in research techniques hold promise for clarifying inconsistencies in merit pay research, particularly concerning intrinsic motivation. Two meta-analytic studies show that financial incentives do not erode intrinsic motivation on performance. Jenkins et al. (1998) meta-analyzed 47 correlations between incentive pay and performance in 39 studies. A moderator analysis examined the relationship between pay and task performance (quantity and quality). Tasks coded for intrinsic motivation showed a positive correlation ($r = 0.34$) between incentive pay and task quantity, but not for task quality. Cerasoli et al. (2014) examined the relationship between pay for performance, intrinsic motivation, and performance. Their meta-analysis included 183 individual studies across various settings (e.g., work, school). The researchers found that incentive pay and intrinsic motivation jointly correlated with performance (r = 0.21–0.45). The use of SEM in one-shot studies also show comparable results. Cabanas et al. (2020) applied a three-path sequential mediation model (a form of structure equation modeling) to examine the relationship between pay and intrinsic motivation. The study included 184 human resource consultants. The results show that pay for performance (PFP) positively correlates with intrinsic motivation ($r = 0.24$). Landry et al. (2017) examined if social determination theory could explain why financial incentives would increase intrinsic motivation based on fair distribution of the financial incentive reward. Using SEM, the researchers indeed validated their SDT model and found pay correlated positively with intrinsic motivation ($r = 0.34$). More recently, Chen et al. (2023) examined how cognitive evaluation theory (psychological processes and mechanisms) can help explain the relationship between pay for performance and job performance. Using meta-analysis and path analysis, the results showed that the ES correlation for the pay-performance association was 0.14.

In conclusion, although Deci (1972) argued that pay would decrease intrinsic motivation, a growing body of evidence suggest otherwise. A glance at the results from the different studies above show a robust and positive correlation range (0.14–0.45) between performance-based pay and intrinsic motivation. We refer the interested reader to Velghe et al. (2024) for more detail on this topic. We argue that it is time to put to rest the notion that incentive pay *necessarily* undermines intrinsic motivation.

Merit Pay and Cooperation

Another criticism that has been made is that merit pay decreases cooperation among work group members. That is, individual rewards, such as merit pay, foster conflict rather than cooperation as work group members compete against one another for pay. Conflict arises because the size of most merit pay budgets is fixed. This argument is especially damaging when individuals are dependent on one another for the completion of work. This line of reasoning dates back to at least Whyte (1955) and has been summarized by Pearce (1987).

Over 120 studies have examined the impact of cooperation and competition on performance. These studies have been reviewed by two sets of authors (Cotton & Cook, 1982; Johnson et al., 1981). Although they reviewed the same studies, these two sets of authors reached different conclusions about the desirability of competitive rewards because of differences in the two review procedures used. Also important to note is the fact that these studies do not directly address merit pay. Nevertheless, the findings from these reviews do have implications for merit pay. The implications differ depending on whether you are looking at the Cotton and Cook or the Johnson and colleagues reviews.

A liberal interpretation of the more than 120 studies is offered by Johnson et al. (1981), who conclude that cooperation is superior to competition in increasing productivity. Is this conclusion at odds with the concept of merit pay? If a merit pay plan emphasizes individual goal attainment over group goal attainment, then the answer may be "yes," because productivity may decline. However, this need not be the case. As pointed out by Patten (1976), performance standards can and should be developed to reflect the amount of collaboration individual employees have with their fellow work group members. That is, cooperation can be one of the standards against which individual performance is rated. An example of this can be seen in university settings, where collegiality is sometimes used as one measure of faculty performance. Collegiality might, for example, be rated higher for a faculty member who covered the classes of a colleague who was out sick. In a controlled laboratory experiment where university supervisors were asked to rate secretarial performance, a cooperation dimension was explicitly used as a basis to assign overall performance ratings to a sample of six hypothetical employees (Werner, 1994). Not one supervisor protested the use of cooperation as a dimension to rate individual secretarial performance. Another example of using cooperation as a dimension for assessing individual performance comes from Johnsonville Foods of Wisconsin (Stayer, 1990). In their evaluation form, teamwork is defined by performance standards such as contribution to groups, communication, willingness to work together, and attendance and timeliness. Both employees and their supervisors (coaches) are required to evaluate employee performance using these standards.

A more conservative interpretation of the 120-plus studies is offered by Cotton and Cook (1982). Their review suggests that competition is "healthy" and may be more conducive to productivity increases than cooperation when task interdependence is low, the task is simple, or groups are small (fewer than six people). This conservative assessment suggests that it is not always desirable to use cooperation as a performance standard under merit pay plans. Indeed, under some conditions, competition is to be encouraged.

Although the cooperation/conflict argument has not been addressed directly in the literature on merit pay plans, the indirect evidence suggests that it would be incorrect to conclude that merit pay inevitably causes competition and that, in turn, this competition causes decreased performance. Instead, it seems that management can design merit pay plans that promote either cooperation or competition by setting performance standards accordingly. And, either cooperation or competition can increase performance, depending on the nature of the task. Cooperation is more likely to lead to increased performance when tasks are interdependent, complex, and worked on in large groups. Competition is more likely to improve performance when tasks are independent, simple, and worked on individually or in small groups.

Merit Pay and Self-Esteem

Meyer (1975) criticized merit pay on the grounds that merit pay threatens an employee's self-esteem. He based this assertion on his research at General Electric Company (GE) in the late 1960s. There he found that when employees were asked to evaluate their own performance relative to others, the average self-rating was at the 77th percentile. This rating indicates that, on average, each GE employee felt that they were better than 77% of all other GE employees. By comparison, when managers evaluated these same employees, the average rating was at the 60th percentile. Similar results were obtained in several other studies of employees in various jobs and companies (Meyer, 1975). These distributions of self-ratings are shown in Table 2.3.

The way these results tie in with merit pay is that most employees with inflated self-ratings are disappointed with their merit increases, because they feel the increase is too small a reward for their superior performance. However, in most organizations, merit increases are limited by budget

Table 2.3

Self-Rating Distributions for Several Employee Groups

Self-Ratings	Employee Groups			
	Blue-Collar Group Plant A	Blue-Collar Group Plant B	Engineers in Research Laboratory	Accountants in Several Companies
Top 10%	46%	40%	29%	37%
Top 25%	26%	28%	57%	40%
Top 50%	26%	28%	14%	20%
Bottom 50%	1%	2%	0%	3%
Bottom 25%	0%	0%	0%	0%
Bottom 10%	0%	0%	0%	0%
No response	1%	2%	0%	0%
	100%	100%	100%	100%

Source: Herbert H. Meyer, "The Pay-for-Performance Dilemma." Reprinted, by permission of publisher, from *Organizational Dynamics*, Winter 1975, © 1975 American Management Association, New York. All rights reserved.

constraints. In Meyer's view, the disappointment felt by employees translates into threatened self-esteem. To cope with this threat to self-esteem, employees may work harder to improve their performance; withdraw effort at work in the form of tardiness, absenteeism, and reduction in output; or adjust their unrealistically high opinions of their own performance. According to Meyer (1975), most employees opt for the middle option of withdrawing effort at work.

Conceptual arguments and empirical studies tend to cast doubt on Meyer's (1975) assertions. At a conceptual level, both Patten (1977) and Lawler (1976) argued that organizations could help employees adjust their unrealistic expectations by the manner in which salary increases are allocated and communicated to employees. Lawler (1976) also argued that the threat to self-esteem is more problematic for lower-rather than higher-performing employees. To the extent this is true, it may be that low-rather than high-performing employees leave the organization. This outcome may be desirable, rather than undesirable, for some employers.

Although the exact model of Meyer's (1975) arguments has not been fully tested, the related research is not supportive of Meyer's argument that low self-esteem leads to low performance. As shown by Brockner (1988) in his review of the self-esteem literature, this relationship has not received empirical support. Perhaps this is to be expected when a general trait, like self-esteem, is studied for its effect on specific behaviors at work, like performance (Herman, 1973). Merit pay may, in fact, be related to low self-esteem in isolated cases, but even when it is, it may not lead to negative consequences for the organization such as lower productivity.

Another form of self-esteem has been adopted in this literature—organizationally-based self-esteem (OBSE) (Pierce et al., 1989). OBSE is an employee's perceived worthiness and competency within an organization based on multiple organizational influences (e.g., supervisor and coworker feedback, organizational culture and values) (Pierce et al., 1989). Scott et al. (2008) finds that merit pay increases relate to older employees with high PFP perceptions. In addition, the results also show that the opposite is true—higher OBSE relates to younger employees with low PFP perceptions. Clearly, additional studies investigating the relationship between OBSE and merit pay increases are needed.

Merit Pay and Perceptions of Equity

It has also been argued that merit pay leads to decreased employee perceptions of equity. Two causes, the Matthew Effect and overreward inequity, have been advanced to explain this potential decline in equity.

Matthew Effect

Gabris and Mitchell (1988) borrow a quote from the Apostle Matthew in the Bible (Matthew 13:12): "For to him who has shall more be given, and he shall have abundance, but from him who does not have, even that which he has shall be taken away." They use this quote as an analogy to the alienating impact of merit pay plans on lower-performing employees. According to the Matthew Effect, merit increases are frequent and plentiful for good performers. However, poor to average performers suffer because money is taken from them to pay large merit increases to the good performers. The lower performers perceive inequity because their pay is reduced to reward the better performers. Proponents of the Matthew Effect assert that merit pay is not at all motivational to lower-performing employees. Pursuing this reasoning, merit pay simply motivates those who are already motivated.

While this is an interesting line of reasoning, it has not received much empirical support (Gabris & Mitchell, 1988; Porter et al., 1990). While it does appear that merit increases may be somewhat more motivational to higher-than lower-performing employees, there is no evidence that it is not motivating to average performers. Since the bulk of employees are average performers, this criticism of merit pay has limited applicability to employees other than low performers. Moreover, for low performers, dissatisfaction with merit pay may be advantageous to the employer, if it encourages poor performers to leave the organization and be replaced with better performers. This is in line with the sorting effect, which was described above in theories behind merit pay.

Overreward Inequity

The other argument that asserts a decreased perception of equity due to merit pay plans is the concept of overreward (Adams, 1965). To the extent that high performers receive disproportionately high merit increases compared to low performers, high performers feel guilt and, consequently, withdraw effort. This argument suggests that merit pay may decrease the motivation of high performers. In contrast to the Matthew Effect prediction that lower performers will withdraw effort, overreward inequity argues that it is the higher performers who will withdraw effort.

Empirical research casts doubt on the overreward inequity prediction. In reviewing equity theory research, Miner (1980) suggested that, in a few studies, overreward did produce a withdrawal of effort by high performers. However, he notes that, generally, people have a high threshold for this type of guilt reaction to overpayment. Leventhal (1976) suggested that most studies show that overreward results in more rather than less effort because the so-called overpayed employee may feel indebted to the person who allocated the overpayment. Finally, Schwab (1980) reviewed studies that indicate employees expend greater effort for overpayment, perhaps out of fear of losing their jobs or to bolster self-esteem. These arguments are, of course, consistent with efficiency wage theory. In summary, while we still are not exactly sure why the overreward prediction of reduced effort does not hold, such reduced effort does not seem to occur with much frequency. Gross instances of overreward may produce a reduction in effort. But only organizations that are extravagant in their merit increases need worry about such an effect.

Because of these arguments against merit pay, some have argued that merit pay should not be used (e.g., Coens & Jenkins, 2000; Kohn, 1993a, 1993b; Meyer, 1975). Following Deci, Alfie Kohn argued that merit pay destroys or reduces intrinsic motivation. Others, such as Coens and Jenkins (2000), built on arguments made by W. Edwards Deming (1986, 1994), claiming that individually based merit pay systems are inconsistent with total quality management. We will not attempt an exhaustive response to these critics of merit pay. However, given the empirical evidence related to each of the arguments, outright rejection of merit pay appears to be too strong a conclusion (Heneman, 2001b; Heneman & Gresham, 1998; Lawler, 1976). Instead, it appears that these arguments should be considered as *potential* rather than actual pitfalls associated with merit pay.

They should, of course, be considered in assessing the desirability of merit pay, but should not a priori lead to an outright rejection of the merit pay concept. A brief summary of criticisms of performance-based pay (which includes merit pay) and a rebuttal to each argument is provided by R. Heneman and Gresham (1998). These criticisms and rebuttals are reproduced in Table 2.4.

Summary of Major Points

Below are the key points covered in this chapter.

1. *Reasons for merit pay.* Psychological and economic theories provide the rationale for merit pay. According to these theories, the linking of pay to performance should lead to improved performance because motivation is increased. In turn, this increase in performance helps organizations maximize profits.
2. *Implications of theory.* Both psychological and economic theories have implications for the design and administration of merit pay plans. These implications center around the measurement of performance, the establishment of pay increases, and the linking of

Table 2.4

Criticisms of Performance-Based Pay, With Empirical Response

Criticism	Empirical Rebuttal
• Performance-based pay leads to decreased intrinsic motivation (Deci, 1972; Kohn, 1993a, 1993b).	• Performance-based pay does not decrease intrinsic motivation (Eisenberger & Cameron, 1996; Montemayer, 1994; Podolske, 1996; Scott et al., 1988).
• Individual performance-based pay is inconsistent with total quality management (TQM; Deming, 1986).	• TQM organizations see greater rather than less importance for individual performance-based pay (Knouse, 1995; Risher, 1992).
• Performance-based pay doesn't work with unionized employees.	• About 25% of union contracts have performance-based pay clauses (Heneman et al., 1997).
• Performance-based pay doesn't work in other cultures.	• Performance-based pay has been used in Russia (Gaga & Kaz, 1996), and in Japan (Pollack, 1993).

Source: Heneman, R. L. and Gresham, M. T. (1998). Performance-based pay plans. In J. W. Smither (Ed.), *Performance appraisal: State-of-the-art methods for performance management* (pp. 496–536), Society for Industrial and Organizational Psychology Professional Practice Series. Jossey-Bass. Reprinted by permission of Jossey-Bass, Inc., a subsidiary of John Wiley & Sons.

pay to performance. It takes time, money, and effort to build these features into a merit pay plan.

3. *Pay-for-performance relationship.* Many studies have examined the actual and perceived relationship between pay and previous performance. The results suggest that it is possible to put the theory of merit pay into action. This is seen in a variety of organizational settings where there is a robust relationship (average correlation of $r = 0.43$) between actual performance and pay, when a merit pay plan is in place. Studies that have looked at the perceived relationship between performance and pay also show moderate results in terms of the magnitude of the relationship.
4. *Potential pitfalls with merit pay.* Along with the potential advantages of merit pay, such as improved performance, there are some potential drawbacks. These drawbacks or pitfalls could include decreases in intrinsic motivation, cooperation, self-esteem, satisfaction, and perceived equity. The research that considers these issues does not provide strong support for any one of these arguments. Nevertheless, they should be considered relative to the potential benefits of merit pay when assessing the desirability of a merit pay plan.

Conclusions

The rationale behind merit pay is not the product of idle speculation. Instead, the concept of linking pay to performance is well grounded in theories from economics and psychology. Moreover, the tests of these theories, which have been conducted through empirical research, have for the most part been supportive. In short, the rationale behind merit pay has been well established.

The idea of linking pay to performance under a merit pay plan is grounded in practice as well as in theory and research. As shown in Tables 2.1 and 2.2, organizations have been able to put pay-for-performance into practice. In almost all of the studied organizations, a positive relationship was observed between pay increases and performance ratings. This relationship was observed in a variety of organizational settings, with many different study participants, and in both laboratory and field settings. It is possible to take the theory of pay-for-performance and put it into practice.

Because there is a solid rationale behind merit pay, and because it is possible to put it into practice, merit pay may be a desirable pay policy for many organizations. However, as shown throughout the book, having a merit pay plan does not guarantee that merit pay will lead to the desired result of improved performance. The entire merit pay process must be carefully managed for merit pay to have the desired results. The initial consideration of merit pay *feasibility* is just one step in managing the process. As shown in this chapter, linking actual pay to actual performance ratings does not necessarily guarantee that employees will see the relationship between pay and performance. If employees do not perceive this relationship, then it is doubtful merit pay will lead to the desired result of improved performance.

It should also be recognized that along with the theory that supports the notion of pay for performance, there is also some theory that casts doubt on its potential for positive outcomes. Given the limited amount of research that has been conducted on these alternative theories, however, we believe that it is inappropriate to argue that merit pay should never be used. Also, the limited research that has been conducted does not lend strong support to the arguments made against merit pay. Finally, even when there is some empirical support for a theory that argues against pay for performance, it may be possible to take these potential pitfalls into account in the design and administration of a merit pay plan. For example, if it is believed that merit pay will decrease cooperation, then one aspect of performance that can be both measured and rewarded is cooperation, which should increase rather than decrease cooperation.

The arguments presented here should challenge those who argue that merit pay should never be used. There are some desirable features to merit pay. Unfortunately, there are some organizations that have stopped using or never considered using merit pay because of the counterarguments, which have limited empirical support. Some of these organizations could and should be using merit pay. Also, as discussed in Chapter 3, there are organizations currently using merit pay that should not be, given the circumstances that they face. Merit pay is not appropriate in all situations.

The theories presented here provide a strong starting point for developing a formal organizational policy regarding merit pay. They can be used to create a document spelling out the *intent* of merit pay (e.g., "The intent of this merit pay plan is to reward past performance, in order to motivate future performance ..."), the *standards* that will inform the organization when the intended objectives of the plan have been met (e.g., "It is expected that the quarterly department productivity reports will show improvement throughout the year"), and the *procedures* to be followed to ensure that the standards are met (e.g., setting specific and challenging performance goals, adjusting performance ratings for factors outside the employee's control, and so on). In addition, these theories represent a framework for further research into merit pay, Advances in research methods lend to better support for this theoretical framework. This can provide practitioners with best practices to implement and carry out effective merit pay plans.

Study Questions

1. Why does the perceived relationship between pay and performance play such an important role in merit pay plans? What approaches can compensation decision-makers take to ensure employees' perceptions of the pay-performance relationship are optimized?
2. Refer to Tables 2.1 and 2.2 and answer the following questions:
   A. Several studies are shown on both Tables 2.1 and 2.2. Compare and contrast the data of each study in both tables. Which table gives more conclusive evidence in the pay for performance relationship? Why?
   B. According to Table 2.2, which study in the first column has the strongest pay-performance relationship? Explain how you derived your answer. Which study in the first column has the weakest pay-performance relationship? Why?
   C. Explain the meaning of *p*-values in Table 2.1 and the 95% CI in Table 2.2. How are *p*-values and 95% CI the same? How are they different?
3. Describe each theory of work motivation. How are each of them related to expectancy theory? For each theory, explain how it relates to merit pay. What is the purpose of theories?
4. What is the current state of merit pay's effect on intrinsic motivation? What is the difference between extrinsic motivation and intrinsic motivation?
5. Describe pitfalls of merit pay plans. What can be done to overcome them, if anything?
6. What is meta-analysis? Why is it important for an HR practitioner to have a rudimental familiarity with the concept? Why is it important for an applied researcher?

CHAPTER 3

DIAGNOSING SITUATIONAL CHARACTERISTICS

In the previous chapter, general information was presented to help organizations assess the desirability of merit pay. This chapter addresses the feasibility of using merit pay in specific organizational settings. The objective of the chapter is to describe some of the situations where it may be more advantageous to use a merit pay plan.

To accomplish this objective, settings where merit pay plans are likely to be found are identified, using the limited empirical research available, as well as the logical arguments advanced by various authors. The reasons why merit pay plans are used in some situations and not in others are discussed to diagnose when merit pay is appropriate. However, a word of caution is in order at this point. Many of the arguments are speculative. Much of what has been written has to do with what should be done. There is little research on what is actually done. There is almost no research on how effective merit pay plans are under various organizational conditions. Hence, the arguments presented here need to be considered carefully by the reader.

Guidelines are offered concerning the conditions that are needed for merit pay to be a viable compensation plan. Both monetary and nonmonetary additions to merit pay are reviewed to guide the reader to other sources if merit pay is not considered feasible or in line with the objectives of a particular organization.

Merit Pay, pages 75–119

doi:10.1108/978-1-80686-701-120263003

A Merit Pay Framework

Given the heavy emphasis on pay-for-performance under merit pay plans, it is tempting to focus primary attention on pay and performance in discussing merit pay plans. To do so, however, would be a disservice, ignoring situational characteristics that could hinder or impede the linking of pay to performance. A discussion of the *context* is important for all reward allocation decisions, including merit pay (Freedman & Montanari, 1980; R. Heneman, 1990, 2002; Jackson & Schuler, 1995; Leventhal, 1976).

The importance of considering factors in addition to pay and performance became quite clear in a study of merit pay undertaken with Debra Cohen (R. Heneman & Cohen, 1988). We conducted the study in a Midwest manufacturing firm. Organizational representatives told us that all human resource decisions, including pay increases, were made strictly on the basis of performance, without regard to any other factors. The written policy of the organization regarding pay raises also made this point clear. As you might expect, there was a significant positive relationship between the performance of employees and their pay increases.

We also found, however, that characteristics of the supervisors who granted the pay increases were related to the pay increases received by their employees. Characteristics of the supervisor such as age, seniority, and salary predicted employee pay increases almost half as well as did actual performance levels of employees. What this example illustrates is the need to focus on the context in which merit increases are given. Ignoring contextual characteristics may lead to incorrect assumptions about the reasons for merit increases. In turn, if we are unaware of the actual reasons, then we may have a difficult time managing the merit pay process.

As shown in Figure 3.1, pay-for-performance decisions under merit pay plans are embedded in a rich context. This context includes characteristics of the allocator, recipient, organization, and environment. In this chapter, specific attention will be given to each of these characteristics to help the reader establish the feasibility of merit pay.

The environment consists of factors outside the immediate boundaries of the organization that should be considered in making decisions regarding merit pay. Environmental factors may include the present and anticipated state of the economy, laws and regulations, and the presence or absence of labor organizations. Like organizational characteristics, these environmental conditions can either facilitate or hinder the use of merit pay.

Characteristics of the organization that could have a bearing on merit pay include obvious features, such as the size of the budget, type of organization, and type of work performed. They also include less obvious features, such as the culture of the organization and government subsidies received.

Figure 3.1

Merit Pay Framework.

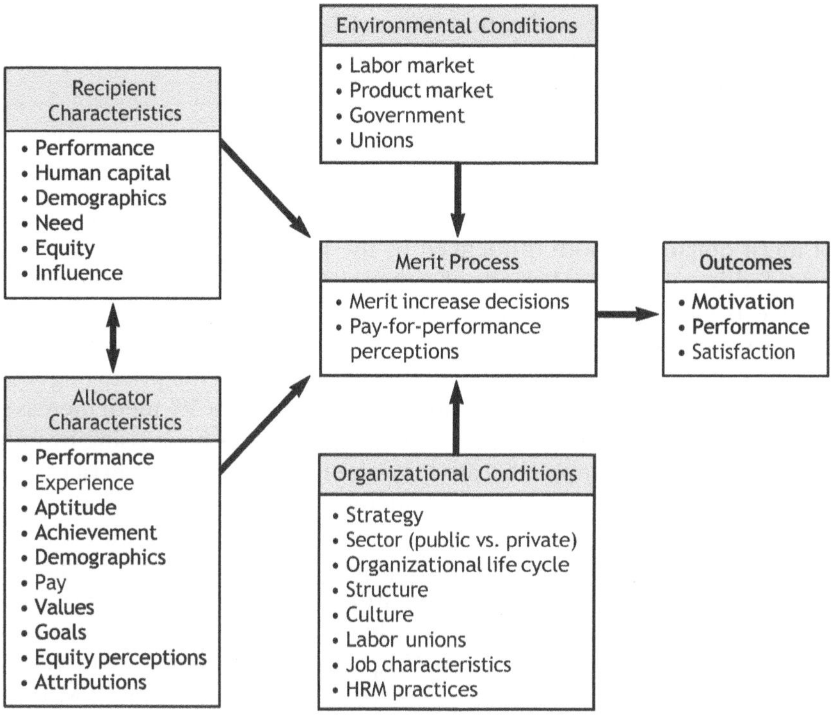

Source: Adapted from R. Heneman (1990). Reprinted with permission.

Both obvious and less obvious organizational features influence the degree to which merit pay plans can be used.

Finally, the feasibility of merit pay may also be determined by the preferences of organizational members. Allocators' and recipients' preferences for merit pay over other forms of pay are also reviewed here.

Economic Considerations

When rewarding employees on the basis of merit, organizations have to contend with sometimes harsh and sometimes favorable economic conditions. The present and anticipated status of economic conditions has a huge influence on the feasibility of merit pay. Economic conditions that must be taken into account occur at both the economy level and at the individual organizational level as well.

Economy-Level Influences

The economy represents the sum total of monetary exchanges for goods and services. These monetary transactions can be categorized by industry, geographic area, and occupation. Several features of the economy have direct bearing on merit pay. These features include the stability of prices, tax rates, and wage and price guidelines.

Price Stability

Money that is available to fund merit increases and the purchasing value of merit dollars are both influenced by the prices of products or services provided by employers. Periods of either rising or declining product and service prices can make the feasibility of merit pay difficult. During inflationary times, when product prices are increasing, the purchasing value or real value of merit increases declines. For example, if the prices of goods and services are rising by 10% and an employee receives a 5% merit increase, the value of the raise is less than it would be had prices been rising by only 4%. The raise has less value because the amount of goods and services that can be purchased is less when price inflation is 10% rather than 4%. As a result, employers might expect that the motivational mileage they can get from merit plans will be altered during periods of inflation. An example comes from a survey conducted by Miller (1979) during a period of double-digit inflation in the United States. Respondents to his survey indicated that not only is motivational impact reduced when merit increases are less than the level of inflation, but motivational clout is also lost even when merit increases are 1–2% *above* the inflation rate.

Another view of inflation with regard to merit pay is that the size of the merit increase is illusory. Employees may think they are getting more when they actually are getting less. That is, employees may only look at the absolute size of their merit increases. During inflationary periods, these raises may be larger in an absolute sense, but less in terms of actual purchasing power. Increases may be larger because, as noted in the earlier discussion of marginal productivity theory in Chapter 2, wages are derived from the demand for goods and services. To the extent that the absolute amount rather than real amount of merit pay is the focus of employee efforts, it could be argued that employees will be more motivated during periods of rising prices. This illusion, however, is probably only short term for some employees. You would expect that most employees would eventually see the real value of their merit increases as reflected in their smaller-than-anticipated baskets of goods and services.

Periods of price stability or deflation also have an influence on the feasibility of merit plans. Cook (1987) pointed out that during tight economic times such as the mid-1980s in the United States, employers did not have much flexibility to adjust product or service prices upward.

As a result, funds for merit increases were limited, as were the sizes of increases in many organizations. In this situation, merit pay may also lose its motivational value. While the purchasing power of merit increases is better in tight economic times, the absolute amount that is available for purchases is limited. Hanson (2020) describes a similar situation. According to a Watson Wyatt survey, nearly half of all companies reduced their salary increase budgets for 2002, but this led to difficulties in attracting and retaining employees with critical skills (Hanson, 2020). This discussion of the stability of prices suggests that it is difficult, if not impossible, to implement a new merit pay plan during periods of high or low price inflation. Also, the discussion suggests that merit pay plans already in place may lose their motivational impact during periods of high or low inflation.

Recessionary conditions also have implications for merit pay increases. During 2007–2009, America experienced "The Great Recession." By December of 2007, a confluence of a housing-market collapse, low interest rates, easy credit, insufficient regulation, and toxic subprime mortgages caused a financial crisis. It resulted in companies laying off many employees and freezing pay structures. In 2008, COLA and merit increases were 2.9% and 3.4%, respectively. The same amounts were predicted for the following year. However, actual compensation in 2009 dipped to 1.2% for COLA and 2.1% for merit pay because of the uncertainty in the economy (WorldatWork, 2009–2010). Even though 2009 saw low inflation, companies offered higher merit increases than COLAs so that employees would remain motivated and inclined to stay with their firms (WorldatWork, 2009–2010); firms placed a greater emphasis on tying pay to performance.

This discussion of the stability of prices, and the economy in general, suggests that it is difficult, if not impossible, to implement a new merit pay plan during periods of very high or low price inflation. Also, the discussion suggests that merit pay plans already in place may lose their motivational impact during periods of high or low inflation. Finally, organizations should plan ahead for anticipated economic conditions. Organizations need to look at the forecasted rates of inflation if a merit pay plan is to be implemented at a future time.

Wage and Price Guidelines

One response to periods of high inflation is for the government to step in and impose mandatory controls or voluntary wage and price guidelines. This was done by the Nixon administration during the early 1970s in response to inflation in the United States. Wage and price guidelines are also sometimes imposed in response to national priorities. For example, controls were imposed in the early 1940s to help the United States war effort during World War II.

When guidelines or controls are imposed, the ability of the employer to grant salary increases on the basis of merit or other factors is again limited. As shown in a survey by Miller (1979), compensation administrators felt that wage and price guidelines detracted from the motivational impact of merit pay, especially when the ceiling for guidelines is below the rate of inflation. Bruce Ellig summarized this point in the Miller (1979) article:

> The federal guidelines become a limiting factor because in many instances the *average* increase must be *less than the rate of inflation*. It becomes a Hobson's choice: Increase the number of "no increases" (thereby lowering the purchasing power and increasing the dissatisfaction of many employees) in order to adequately reward the top performers (and thereby minimize the risk of their leaving), or establish a very narrow range of increases (thereby protecting the purchasing power of most employees but increasing the risk of losing the top performers). (Reprinted, by permission of the publisher, from *Personnel*, July/August 1979, © 1979 American Management Association, New York. All rights reserved).

Tax Rates

Along with the influence of price stability and wage and price guidelines at the economy level, tax rates also need to be considered. Cook (1987) showed one potential consequence of changes in tax rates. Lower marginal tax rates on ordinary income may result in greater purchasing power for merit pay increases. The real value of the increase will be greater to the employee because less of the increase is being held by the government. One might expect, therefore, that the motivational impact of merit increases would have been somewhat greater during the 1980s than the 1970s because, in part, of the lowered marginal tax rates enacted by the Reagan administration in the 1980s.

Another potential consequence of the tax structure has to do with the funding of merit pay plans. If tax breaks are given to employers for one component of the total compensation package (e.g., benefits), then employers may shift their portfolio of compensation funds away from other components of the total compensation package (e.g., direct pay) where the employer does not receive a tax break. For example, an employer might possibly limit the size of the merit budget to put additional money into private pension plans, thereby receiving the tax savings available for qualified pension plans.

Another example of the influence of tax rates is the shifting of merit increases from cash to paper. Such was the case at Primerica, a company that set up an employee stock ownership plan (ESOP) in 1989 for its 1,500 middle managers (Bernstein, 1991). Managers at Primerica were rewarded for good performance with a paper increase in the form of company stock, rather than a traditional merit pay increase in the form of cash. The reason for this shift from cash to paper was to take advantage of the tax savings associated with ESOPs. Under ESOPs, organizations are given tax breaks in return for granting employees ownership in the company via shares of company stock.

Firm-Level Influences

The economic picture at the organizational level also exerts an influence on the desirability of merit pay. Two aspects of the economic picture include government subsidies sometimes received by employers and the adequacy of the merit pay budget.

Government Subsidies

The U. S. government has at times, offered subsidies to employers for helping in matters of national priority. One example from the 1970s is on-the-job training subsidies offered to employers who hired and trained the hard-core unemployed. The hard-core unemployed are workers with limited skills and long durations of unemployment. This subsidy was authorized under the Comprehensive Employment and Training Act (CETA), and later extended by the Job Training and Partnership Act (JTPA). A study by Bishop (1987) showed that employers who received this subsidy tended to grant larger merit increases than those employers who did not receive this subsidy. This result suggests that when employers are subsidized by the government, it may be more feasible to have a merit pay plan. The Bishop study suggests that money that could have gone to special training needs of the hard-core employed may have been used by employers for incentive pay instead. Today, funds to assist unemployed individuals primarily flow to the states through block grants under the Workforce Innovation and Opportunity Act (Employment and Training Administration, 2024).

Adequacy of Budget

Another economic variable at the firm level is the size or adequacy of the budget for merit increases. Even if the economy is cooperative in terms of price inflation, individual organizations need to be of sound financial status to be able to fund merit increases. A study by Miceli and Near (1987) found that satisfaction with pay was greater for middle managers and executives in a government agency with merit pay when perceptions of the adequacy of the budget for merit increases were strong. This result, based on *perceptions* of the budget rather than *actual* budget figures, underscores the importance of factoring in budget considerations when assessing the feasibility of merit pay. Unfortunately, current research offers little direction with regard to this consideration. Research is needed on the impact of actual budgets on merit increase decisions.

Summary

In summary, the feasibility of a merit pay plan depends, in part, on economic considerations at the level of the economy as a whole, as well as at the level of the organization. Economic conditions that are conducive to the use of merit pay plans include stable prices, absence of wage and price guidelines, low marginal tax rates, subsidies from the government, and an adequate merit pay budget.

Institutional Arrangements

Along with economic conditions, another set of conditions that has a bearing on the feasibility of merit pay plans are institutional arrangements, or the policies formed by organizations in response to their business environment. These considerations have to do with the interaction of the organization and environment as shown in Fig. 3.1. In particular, these considerations can be grouped into the following categories, which are covered in turn: business strategy, product or service markets, organizational life cycle, structure of the organization, allocation norms or culture, labor unions, job characteristics, politics, and human resource practices.

Business Strategy

The compensation policy of the organization should be tailored to the strategic mission of the organization in order for the organization to survive, grow, and prosper in its product or service markets. Many tools and methodologies are available for helping organizations to decide upon the appropriate role of incentives in furthering the business strategy (R. Heneman, 2001a, 2002). These include financial, planning, statistical, and organizational effectiveness models (Hurwich, 1986).

Carroll (1987) described an organizational effectiveness model that is relevant to merit pay. Carroll utilized the framework proposed by Miles and

Snow (1978), which suggests that the structure of the organization needs to be congruent with the business strategy for the organization to meet its goals. Carroll's discussion suggests that merit pay is more likely to be appropriate for organizations that pursue a "defender" rather than a "prospector" business strategy. A defender organization is one that is protecting rather than expanding its current product or service markets. Typically, a defender organization is highly structured, with stable tasks. Under these structured and stable conditions, performance measures are somewhat easier to develop and use than under the unstructured and unstable conditions found in organizations pursuing a prospector strategy.

Unstructured and unstable conditions are present in the prospector firm as it seeks to locate and develop new product and service markets. Under these conditions, performance is difficult to define and measure. Since measures of performance are better developed in defender than prospector firms, we are more likely to find merit pay being used successfully in defender rather than prospector firms.

Although not a direct test of Carroll's (1987) arguments, some indirect empirical support was generated in a study by Balkin and Gomez-Mejia (1990). In this study of compensation officials from manufacturing companies, they found that merit pay was more frequently and effectively used by single product manufacturers, rather than diversified manufacturers who carried multiple product lines. One might argue that the strategies of single product carriers are similar to defender firms, while the characteristics of diversified organizations are more like prospector organizations. Regardless of interpretation, however, these data suggest that the desirability of merit pay is related to the strategy of the organization.

Business unit strategies can be generically described in terms of organizations seeking to compete on cost, differentiation, or by employing a focus or niche approach (Glueck, 1976; Porter, 1980). A cost leadership strategy emphasizes efficiency and seeks to offer goods or services for less than competitors offer them. A differentiation strategy seeks to distinguish the organization's products or services from competitors on some attribute other than cost (e.g., higher quality). A focus strategy seeks to serve a particular niche in a market that is unserved (or underserved) by competitors (Mello, 2002).

These generic strategies were expanded by R. Heneman (2001a). Seven business strategies that organizations can follow include:

- Reduce costs
- Improve productivity (e.g., by increasing outputs, decreasing inputs, etc).
- Improve financial capital (e.g., using models such as economic value added, or EVA)

- Emphasize distinctive customer service
- Emphasize the distinctive quality of one's product or service
- Emphasize innovation and time to market
- Emphasize human capital (i.e., view employees as a source of revenue generation, not just as a cost).

Few organizations pursue any of these approaches as a pure business strategy, and instead seek to compete using more than one approach. Kaplan and Norton (1996) popularized a "balanced scorecard" approach that emphasizes four key areas for organizations to monitor: (1) financial (e.g., return on capital invested), (2) customer (e.g., customer loyalty, on-time delivery), (3) internal/business process (e.g., process quality, cycle time), and (4) employee learning and growth (e.g., employee skill development). As you can see, this emphasizes many of the strategies described above. What is significant here is the recommendation that organizations need to weigh or "balance" these various factors to determine overall organizational effectiveness. The weights given to these various areas will differ for different organizations, and may change over time for any given organization (R. Heneman, 2001a). Becker, Huselid, and Ulrich (2001) provided an extension of the balanced scorecard approach to human resource management. What seems most important is that organizations need to find and utilize a business strategy that is difficult for competitors to imitate (Barney, 1997). Reward systems in general, and merit pay plans in particular, need to match the business strategies that the organization is seeking to attain (Mello, 2002; R. Heneman, 2002).

Product or Service Markets

Differences between and within product and service markets appear to have an influence on the use and effectiveness of merit pay. Comparisons have been made between manufacturing and service sectors, high-versus low-technology organizations, and the public versus private sector. These comparisons will be considered in turn.

Manufacturing versus Service

Service-sector organizations, in comparison to manufacturing-sector organizations, tend to have less tangible products, more customer involvement in service output, and consumption of services at the time of production (Jackson, Schuler, & Rivero, 1989). A study by Jackson et al. (1989) indicated that merit pay is used more frequently in the service sector than in the manufacturing sector of the economy. The reason for this finding, according to the authors, is that performance ratings are more readily available in the service sector as a check on the quality of the service provided. More countable indicators of performance, such as number of products (associated with other incentive pay plans like piece-rate systems), are more readily available in the manufacturing sector.

High versus Low Technology

A distinction that is often made, but difficult to define, is between high- and low-technology organizations in manufacturing. According to Milkovich (1987) and Balkin, Markman, and Gomez-Mejia (2000), high-technology firms are those in which innovation and invention are emphasized in the business strategy, a high level of resources is devoted to research and development, competition is worldwide and in short-cycle product markets, and a high percentage of the workforce is comprised of engineers and scientists. Merit pay plans are less likely to be used in high-than low-technology firms for three reasons. First, high-technology firms tend to be less risk-averse and more innovative. Hence, they are less likely to use traditional merit pay plans and more likely to use other innovations in compensation, such as long-term stock option plans. Second, there is some evidence that group incentive plans are more effective than individual incentive plans such as merit pay for engineers and scientists in research and development organizations (Gomez-Mejia & Balkin, 1989). Third, firms making greater use of advanced manufacturing technology are more likely to emphasize external equity issues than firms making less use of such technology (Snell & Dean, 1992). This would presumably entail greater use of wage survey information, rather than merit pay plans, to determine salary increases.

Although we might expect the concept of merit in general to be emphasized more frequently in high-technology firms, Jackson et al. (1989) suggested that this is not always the case. They reported that there was not a statistically significant difference in the use of merit by high-technology and low-technology firms. Hence, this distinction, which is troublesome to define, does not seem to have much bearing in the actual practice of merit pay.

Rather than focusing on high-tech versus low-tech organizations, it would seem to make more sense to focus on tailoring the reward packages that are offered to the particular needs of *technical employees* (Gomez-Mejia, Balkin, & Milkovich, 1990; Hansen, 2002; Risher, 2000).

Public versus Private Sector

An obvious but important difference between these two sectors of the economy is ownership. Although there are some exceptions, in general, ownership of organizations in the public sector is held by the public, and ownership of organizations in the private sector is held by private parties. This difference in ownership has resulted in differences in human resource management practices such as merit pay. In turn, these different HR practices have led to different levels of effectiveness for merit pay. A more detailed explanation of these differences follows.

Several authors have described some of the situational characteristics found more often in the public sector than in the private sector, and which can limit the effectiveness of merit pay plans (Kellough & Selden, 1997; Lewin, 2003; Perry, 1986; Rainey, 1979; Risher, 1997, 1999a, 1999b; Scott, Hills, Markham, & Vest, 1987; Silverman, 1983). These constraints include, among other things, limited merit pay budgets, limited discretion in merit pay decisions, accountability to conflicting constituencies, and a long history of pay based on longevity rather than performance. These limiting situational characteristics and others are shown for government organizations in Figure 3.2.

A survey of HR managers in state agencies found that 34% of respondents reported that their agency had some form of pay-for-performance system in place (Kellough & Selden, 1997). Merit pay plans were used in more than 90% of these agencies, and this was clearly the most frequently used type of incentive plan. Interestingly, 81% of those with merit pay plans agreed with the statement that their agencies should not abandon the concept of merit pay.

In a similar survey of state and local government employees, managers, and officials, Lewin (2003) found a very high usage rate for merit pay and "performance-based pay" (i.e., pay changes based upon achieving individual employee performance goals). Results from this survey are shown in Table 3.1. As noted by Lewin, an employee in one of these government units is about five times as likely to be covered by a merit pay or pay-for-performance plan than by a pay-for-knowledge or bonus plan. Professional (82%) and technical (79%) employees were most likely to be covered by some form of incentive compensation plan, whereas clerical (38%) and manual (34%) employees were least likely to be covered by such plans. When asked what percentage of their total direct compensation they would like to have as incentive compensation, the mean for all groups was 16%. When asked what percentage of total direct compensation they *thought* they were receiving as incentive compensation, the average was 8%. In fact, the actual amount of incentive compensation as a percent of total direct compensation was 6.15 for all employee groups. Strikingly, for a sample of private firms (used by a subsample of government units to set prevailing wage rates), this percentage was 19.2%. Thus, Lewin (2003, p. 611) characterizes present-day usage of incentive compensation in state and local governments as "broad but not deep."

The constraints described above have led to mixed or limited success of merit pay plans in the public versus the private sector. For example, in a

Figure 3.2

Reasons for Merit Pay Failures in Government Organizations.

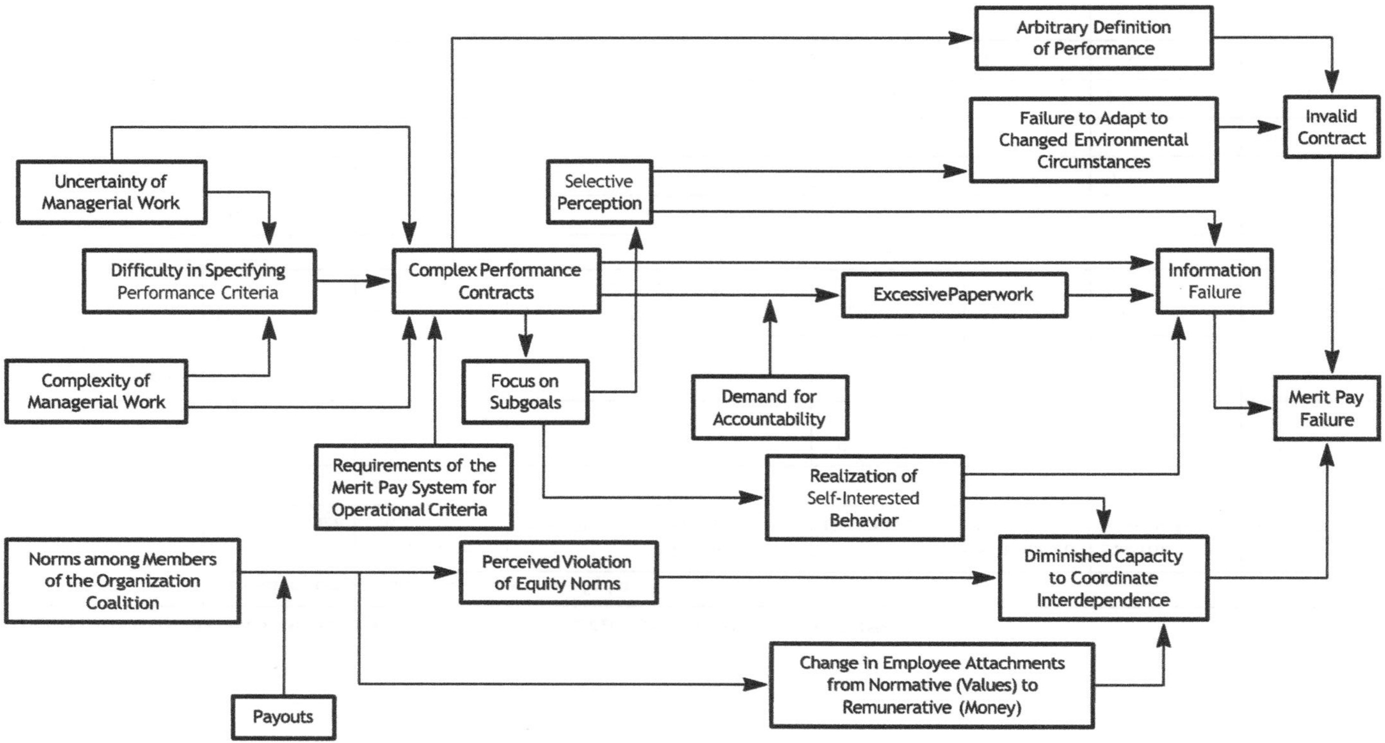

Source: Perry (1986). Reprinted by permission.

Table 3.1

Incentive Compensation Usage in State and Local Governments in 1998

	Incentive compensation usage by type of plan							
	Overall Usage	Perf.-Based Pay	Merit Pay	Productivity Sharing	Gain-Sharing	Skill-Based Pay	Pay-for-Knowledge	Bonus Pay
Level of Government								
State governments ($n = 17$)	94%	82%	88%	18%	29%	41%	12%	12%
Local governments ($n = 284$)	85%	69%	73%	17%	35%	42%	14%	7%
Total governments ($n = 301$)	86%	70%	74%	17%	35%	42%	14%	8%
Employee Group								
Manager	69%	54%	56%	9%	15%	16%	8%	11%
Professional	82%	64%	67%	13%	19%	39%	26%	8%
Technical	79%	63%	64%	15%	17%	51%	21%	12%
Clerical	38%	34%	36%	7%	13%	32%	13%	4%
Operative	58%	51%	42%	26%	41%	44%	8%	6%
Manual	34%	28%	24%	12%	28%	34%	5%	5%
Other service	51%	43%	42%	14%	19%	39%	9%	3%

Source: Lewin (2003). Reprinted with permission.

survey by Wisdom and Patzig (1987), public-sector employees were significantly less likely than private-sector employees to agree with the statement that "If I do my job well, I am likely to get a promotion or a pay raise" (in Chapter 2, this was referred to as the performance–reward expectancy). Also, public-sector employees perceived the effectiveness of merit pay to be lower as well. Both of these findings were statistically significant at the $p < 0.01$ level (the smaller the significance level, the greater the confidence that we can have that the results will be similar for a larger population). In contrast, anecdotal evidence of successful implementation of merit pay plans has been reported at the Federal Aviation Administration (Risher, 1999a), in several city governments (Risher, 1999b), as well as in numerous research laboratories within the U.S. Department of Defense (Burnkrant, 2002; La Police, 2002; Schay, 2002; Shorter, 2002).

While it appears that it is more difficult to link pay to performance in the public sector, the potential returns for doing so may be even greater than in the private sector, as shown in Fig. 3.3. Giles and Barrett (1971), for example, found that pay satisfaction and fairness perceptions increased for each additional dollar allocated to merit increases in the public sector. In contrast, pay satisfaction and fairness perceptions actually declined when allocation of merit pay dollars reached a certain point in the private sector.

Overall, then, it would appear that conditions tend to be less favorable for implementing merit pay in the public than the private sector. While the results of merit plans in the public sector have not been overwhelmingly

Fig. 3.3.

Pay Fairness–Pay Satisfaction Perceptions as a Function of Pay Increase.

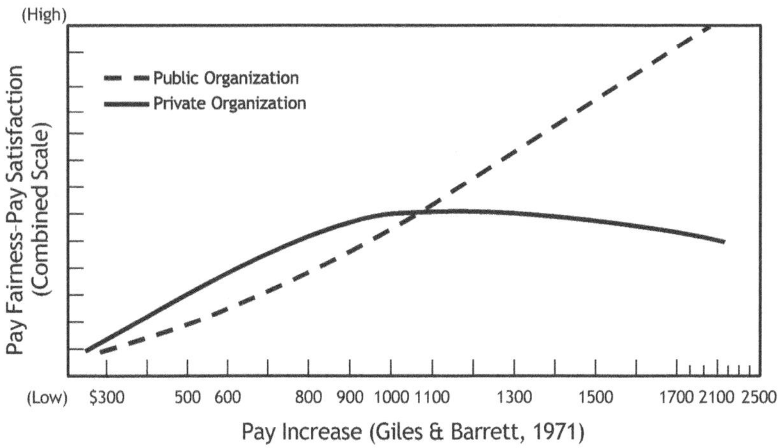

Source: Schuster, Colletti, & Knowles (1973). Reprinted with permission.

positive to date, neither have they been a total disaster (M. Brown, 2001; R. Heneman, 1990; Lewin, 2003; Risher, 1999a, 1999b). Performance-related pay continues to generate controversy in the public sector (Risher, 2002), especially for jobs such as public school teachers (Chamberlin, Wragg, Haynes, & Wragg, 2002). Yet, other studies, reviewed in Chapter 7, show positive results for merit pay in some public-sector organizations. Although perhaps problematic to implement, the potential returns on merit pay plans may be somewhat greater in the public sector than in the private sector.

Current Trends in Merit Pay

Different Industries: What Do We See?

This section looks at trends in performance-based pay for public school teachers and healthcare professionals. While the context in which the positions reside and the systems in which they operate differ, results of them are comparable for several reasons that will be discussed below.

Merit Pay for Teacher Performance in Public Schools. The notion of incentivizing public school teacher is not new. In 1908, merit pay was first implemented in the United States in 1908 in Newton Massachusetts, but it failed to achieve national popularity. From 1960 to 1990, experiments with pay for performance continued, but again, they were abandoned for various reasons, notably because of questionable criterion measures of teacher performance (Ingersoll, 2000). That is, decision makers in education, government, and labor associations could not agree on the best sources of evaluating teacher performance—supervisory appraisals, public feedback, and/or student scores. However, in the early 2000s merit pay for public teachers resurfaced with federal support and fund (Lacey, 2021). In this iteration, student test scores from standardized tests became the default criterion for assessing teacher performance. Today, this practice continues with mixed results and much debate. Below summarizes a few salient points and counterpoints of merit pay for public school teachers (The reader should note that merit pay, as defined here, is a misnomer. It actually resembles incentive pay because student grades are objective. However, authors and researchers in primary and secondary education predominately adhere to this moniker. We also adopt this label for continuity, with the understanding incentive pay and merit pay differ. However, whatever label is used, the result remains the same: educators are attempting to incentivize public school teachers).

Point: Merit pay offers public school teachers an incentive to work hard in improving student scores in standardized tests.

Counterpoint: This proclamation assumes that teachers have control over student scores. This is false. Teachers have limited influence in student test performance. Other influences account for test results: student characteristics; school personnel, policies, and funding.

Point: Test scores are objective, resulting in no rater bias and high validity.

Counterpoint: While test scores may be free of rater bias, the claim of high validity is false. Student test scores result from a confluence of factors. A teacher's contribution is small. (See above) The link between performance and student test scores is tenuous. (See below)

Point: Teacher performance is related (correlated) with student test scores.

Counterpoint: This is empirically false. Results from individual and meta-analytic studies show inconsistent and near zero correlations between teacher performance and student test scores (Pham et al., 2021).

(Continued)

Current Trends in Merit Pay (Continued)

Merit Pay for Healthcare Providers. Before merit-based pay systems, healthcare compensation often relied on different models that did not directly tie payment to performance outcomes (Gettel et al., 2022; Shenoy, 2021). Popular models included (a) Fee-for-Service, (b) Capitation, (c) Salary-based Compensation, (d) Blended Model. In the early 2000s the notion of merit-based incentive payment systems (MIPS) emerged as a way to incentivize healthcare providers. Experts in healthcare recognized the need to align provider compensation with quality of care and patient outcomes rather than simply the volume of services provided (Gettel et al., 2022; Green et al., 2017; Shenoy, 2021). This transition reflects a broader shift towards value-based care, where the focus is on improving the overall value of healthcare by emphasizing quality, patient satisfaction, and cost-effectiveness (Green et al., 2017; Shenoy, 2021).

From its origin, the system was revised several times until 2017 when it was consolidated with other Medicare incentive programs, considered a major milestone in the system's history (Bond et al., 2022). From 2017 to present, many studies followed (Bond et al., 2022). Overall, the results of these studies showed inconsistencies in the relationship between MIPS scores and healthcare process metrics and outcome measures. Green et al. (2017) found that MIPS did increase adherence to incentivized measures, but at the expense of lower quality of care, less satisfied patients and a great risk for overtreatment. In a large study of 80,246 primary care physicians and 3.4 billion patients, Bond et al. (2022), revealed MIPS scores inconsistently related to process metrics and outcome measures. The authors contend MIPS has merit, but the system requires further refinement in its design and implementation to overcome inconsistent results. The reader should note that merit pay, as defined here, broadly represents multiple measures that contain both subjective ratings feedback and objective indicators. From this perspective, ratings represent merit pay, while objective indicators reflect incentive pay.

In conclusion, merit pay plans continue to be used in various industries and positions. The two examples above illustrate this. The overall theme that should be noted here is that performance-based systems tend to work in some contexts, but not others. This is mentioned here and in different sections of the book.

Organizational Life-Cycle

Some authors have argued that the effective use of merit pay depends on the stage in the organization's life cycle (Balkin & Gomez-Mejia, 1987; Seals, 1984). Organizations, as human *systems* typically go through a cycle of life just as humans do. People are born, develop, mature, and eventually die. Collections of people, such as organizations, have life cycles that generally parallel the human stages of development. The typical development of organizations over time involves several phases, including startup, growth, maturity, and decline. Startup is characterized by the small organization with low current profits and a high potential for future profits. The growth phase is characterized by an increase in size from a small-to medium-sized firm with high profitability and high potential. The maturity phase occurs when the organization becomes medium to large in size with high profitability and low potential. The decline stage is characterized by a large-to medium-sized firm with low profits and low potential. Some organizations obviously respond to decline with successful efforts aimed at organizational renewal (Ciavarella, 2001; Miller & Friesen, 1984).

Under this organizational life cycle theory, merit pay would seem to be more appropriate in some phases than others as a reward system. For example, merit pay would not be appropriate during the decline phase, since the organization may be cutting back its resources and, as a result, employee trust may be low and the budget for merit increases limited. Pagano (1985) describes the disastrous results of merit pay during a reduction in force at the U.S. Department of Health and Human Services. Merit pay would also seem to be less appropriate during the startup phase, because more emphasis may be required for long-term incentives to achieve a high potential for profits.

Merit pay would seem to be most appropriate during the growth and maturity phases, when current profitability is high, and merit pay can be used to reinforce and maintain the behaviors contributing to profitability. In support of these ideas, Balkin and Gomez-Mejia (1990) found that the use and effectiveness of merit pay was greater in the growth than in the maturity stages of manufacturing firms.

Balkin and Gomez-Mejia (1984) also present data from a study of high-technology firms that suggest merit pay be given less emphasis in the growth than maturity stage. During the growth stage, innovation is likely to be emphasized, with both merit pay and cash bonuses used to reinforce this emphasis. Yet, for the successful completion of specific projects, cash bonuses might be the incentive of choice. In summary, merit pay would seem to be most applicable in the maturity phase, followed by the growth phase. It would be much less applicable in the startup and decline phases. Past writings have emphasized a more complex, contingency approach to the relationship between organizational life cycle and HRM practices (Jackson & Schuler, 1995; Kozlowski, Chao, Smith, & Hedlund, 1993). We would argue that this same approach be applied to merit pay discussions as well.

Organizational Structure

The way that work is arranged and coordinated in organizations may also influence the degree to which merit pay is used. Jackson et al. (1989) reported that some, but not all, indicators of organizational structure were related to the use of merit pay. For example, Jackson and colleagues found in their study that organizations with "flexible, specialization technologies" used merit pay more frequently than did organizations with "mass production technologies." In the former organizations, work is organized into jobs with wide scope and task diversity. In these types of jobs, not only are employees responsible for performing the work, they also have a voice in how the work is to be done and may be authorized to alter work arrangements as needed. In the latter organizations, work is arranged into simple and repetitive tasks like those found on an assembly line. Perhaps the difference in the use of merit pay is due to the availability of performance measures. You might expect to find countable indicators of performance (which lend themselves to piece rate pay) in mass production organizations. On the other hand, in flexible specialization firms, you might expect to find the more subjective ratings of performance usually associated with merit pay. For example, there was no difference in the use of merit pay between organizations arranged along product lines and those arranged along service lines. There was also no evidence of any differences in the use of merit pay in small versus large organizations.

In another study, C. Brown (1990) expected that merit pay would be used more frequently in smaller organizations because the costs of monitoring employee performance are greater in larger than in smaller organizations. In contrast, his study showed the opposite of what he predicted. Large firms used merit pay more often than small firms. However, this result should not be surprising. Large organizations are more likely to have the resources to meet the requirements of a merit pay plan, as discussed in Chapter 2. Also, while the total costs of monitoring employee performance may be greater in larger firms, the fixed costs per employee are less.

It should also be noted that simply because industries with "flexible specialization technologies" are more likely to have merit pay plans, these merit plans are not guaranteed to be effective. In a study of the Environmental Protection Agency (EPA), which at the time was characterized as flexible in structure, managers were not receptive to a merit pay plan because it was seen as imposing a rigid set of performance standards that threatened the managers' autonomy (Gaertner, Gaertner, & Akinnusi, 1984). This study demonstrated the importance of considering culture as well as structure in assessing the feasibility of merit pay.

Organizational Culture

Another organizational characteristic related to the feasibility of merit pay is the culture of the organization. Culture refers to the shared set of beliefs and values held by members of the organization (Ott, 1989). One would expect that merit pay would work better in organizations in which there is a shared belief that pay increases should be granted on the basis of performance. Also, one would expect that merit pay would work better in organizations where recipients of merit pay share the same belief as the allocators of merit pay in pay-for-performance. As discussed below, not all employees are necessarily in favor of granting pay increases on the basis of merit.

Pay can be allocated in a variety of ways (Kopelman, 1976; Leventhal, 1976). Some of these methods of pay allocation are as follows (Gardner, 1961): birthright, egalitarianism, and competition. *Birthright* refers to pay allocated on the basis of nepotism or some other form of favoritism. *Egalitarianism* refers to pay based on parity, where everyone receives the same pay increase. An example would be a general increase offered to all employees once a year. *Competition* refers to pay allocation on the basis of merit or best performance. Also, the notion of *Marxian justice* could be added to this list, whereby pay is allocated in accordance with people's needs (Greenberg, 1987b; Lerner, 1982). For example, pay increases might be larger for those with a larger number of dependents. Finally, pay could also be allocated according to the principle of *equity* or relative contributions (Birnbaum, 1983; Vecchio & Terborg, 1987). Pay allocated on the basis of equity might include an *adjustment sys*tem, in which persons equally underpaid receive equal raises, or *a relative system,* in which persons with equal merit receive equal percentage raises. As can be seen from this list, the competition model, in which pay is based on performance, is only one of many ways to allocate pay increases.

Empirical studies on these various methods of allocating pay suggest that beliefs in these systems depend on many factors. Alexander and Barrett (1982) provided evidence to suggest that belief in these systems of pay allocation depends on one's nationality. They found that Japanese managers were more likely to follow a merit strategy than were managers in the United States, Austria, Germany, Italy, and the United Kingdom. Managers in these other countries were more likely to evaluate factors other than performance in determining salary increases. Kidder, Bellettirie, and Cohn (1977) provided evidence from the laboratory that suggests that men are more likely to follow a reward strategy of equity, while women are more likely to follow a reward strategy of egalitarianism. Meindl (1989) found that the allocation strategy followed by managers depended on the situation (e.g., task interdependence) and person (e.g., leadership style).

Some recent studies emphasize aligning the organizational culture with a merit pay plan. First, Adamovic (2023) investigated the influence of culture predicting employee preference for reward allocation. Prior research predicted that individualistic and collectivistic individuals prefer different rules assigned to allocation rewards, the former desiring equity allocation (i.e., allocation based on task performance) the latter favoring equality allocation (Hui & Triandis, 2021). However, the results of these studies were inconsistent. Culture values matched preferences in reward allocation. That is, individualistic employees preferred reward allocation based on individual task performance, while collectivistic employees preferred allocated rewards based on extra-role performance (i.e., teamwork, helping others). The study explains inconsistencies in prior research: (a) lack of saliency in distinguishing task and (b) extra-role performance to allocate rewards. Moreover, the results suggest that multinational organizations must exercise extreme sensitivity in the allocation rules of rewards because their workforce often has different cultural orientations and expectations about such allocations.

Second, Sturman et al. (2012) researched the moderating effects of culture and performance-based pay on the curvilinear relationship between performance and turnover. They also examined the moderator effect of culture on the linear relationship between merit-pay and performance. The authors used a non-linear, hierarchical linear model procedure to conduct the analysis from a sample of 4,072 employees from 24 countries. Four cultural dimensions that relate closely to compensation—uncertainty avoidance, power distance, institutional collectivism, performance-orientation—were used to best match the cultures representing the 24 countries. The results show that indeed culture and pay for performance moderated the relationship between performance and turnover. The findings also show that culture also moderated the effects of merit pay-performance association.

Third, Ruffini et al. (2020) examined the implementation of a new pay for performance system in a public sector organization. Previously, the organization experienced lack lustered performance among its employees based on implicit motivation, leading to a negative organizational culture. Soon after the implementation of its performance-based pay system, survey data showed an increase in self-assessed performances and heighted sense of positivity in the workplace. A follow-up showed that the same levels of job performance and affect towards the organization. The study suggests that (a) the use of performance-based pay can lead an organizational change effort and, conversely, (b) strengthen future pay for performance efforts because of a new, positive culture.

The studies reviewed here suggest that not all organizational cultures are supportive of merit pay. For merit pay to be an accepted organizational strategy, the philosophy of pay for performance must be congruent with the present culture of the organization. Although it may be possible to use merit pay as the vehicle to change the culture from, say, one of egalitarianism to one of merit, it could be problematic if not accompanied with other programs of organizational development (Patten, 1977). An example is offered by Kroeck, Avolio, Small, and Einstein (1987), who found that it was possible to shift resource allocation preferences for managers in a laboratory environment when panel discussions were conducted. A more conservative route would be to only use merit pay when the culture is in line with the merit philosophy. At least one study (H. Heneman & Young, 1988) showed that disruption of the social system through merit pay may lead to negative consequences for the organization.

Labor Unions

It is sometimes mistakenly assumed that merit pay is not used at all in unionized settings. In fact, merit pay is used in some unionized settings. For example, at General Motors, the United Auto Workers agreed to a merit pay plan of sorts, as the time span was shortened for automatic pay increases to be received by outstanding performers (Milkovich & Newman, 1987). Under this arrangement, pay increases were granted more frequently to outstanding than to average performers. Another example comes from Boeing Helicopters, where the United Auto Workers agreed to 2% semiannual selective adjustments. These adjustments were made on the basis of performance (Cimini, 1990). Another example comes from Harley-Davidson. Local 175 of the Machinists Union agreed to a merit pay plan for production and maintenance employees at the York, Pennsylvania, assembly plant (Cimini, 1991). While merit pay has been used for some unionized employees, as shown in these examples, it is used less frequently for unionized than nonunionized employees. Earlier surveys conducted by The Conference Board, U.S. Department of Labor, and the Bureau of National Affairs indicated that only between 10 to 16% of unionized employees are eligible for merit pay increases (Balkin, 1989; Mitchell, 1989; Weeks, 1976). Another survey found about 25% of organizations had some form of performance-based pay plan in place (R. Heneman, R. L., Porter, et al., 1997; R. Heneman & Gresham, 1998). Somewhat surprisingly, there was no difference in the rate of usage of merit pay plans between unionized and nonunionized organizations in this survey.

In part, the general absence of merit pay for unionized employees may be attributable to resistance to merit pay plans by some labor unions and union members (Archer, 2000; M. Brown, 2001; Greenhouse, 2000). Unions and other employee organizations may be against merit pay for several reasons. First, it has been suggested that unions may fear that management will use merit pay to take money away from lower level union jobs to reward high-level management officials. For example, this concern was expressed by federal workers in the wake of the firing of striking air traffic controllers by President Ronald Reagan (Wildstrom, 1986). Chrysler workers expressed their dissatisfaction with merit pay for much the same reason. Higher-level salaried employees were given merit increases at roughly the same time that lower-level unionized employees were asked to take a reduction in salary (Naughton, 1990). To prevent pay from being taken from lower-level jobs, unions have sought to standardize wage increase criteria within organizations (Balkin, 1989; Freeman, 1982).

A second and related concern that members of labor unions may have about merit pay is the subjective ratings involved in the process, especially when employees' ratings do not include actual indicators of an employee's contribution to the organization. This concern was voiced by Ray Pasmore, Business Manager of Local 1,466 of the International Brotherhood of Electrical Workers (Alloy, 1988): "If you happen to be an individual that's very good at your job, but you don't happen to have the right kind of personality to where you get along with your supervisor, your raise may show what your supervisor feels about your personality rather than your work" (p. 4). Third, labor unions are political institutions. As pointed out by Freeman (1982), solidarity and organizational strength are likely to be bolstered when workers are paid the same wage increase, rather than different wage increases. Merit pay is viewed by some unions as the imposition of an artificial barrier between workers. Also, as pointed out by Freeman (1982) and Balkin (1989), unions tend to emphasize indirect pay in the form of benefits over direct pay in the form of salary increases. Because labor union members' preferences are more often for benefits over salary increases, labor union officials may bargain more forcefully for benefits than merit pay. The incentive for labor union officials to push for benefits is the need to represent their members' preferences in order to be reelected by these members.

Fourth, the administration of merit pay plans may be troublesome to union members (Barkin, 1948). Given the complexity of administering merit pay plans, as discussed in Chapter 6, it is costly for unions to enforce the agreed-upon terms and conditions of a merit pay plan. For example, the costs of monitoring the extent to which actual employee performance is being measured, rather than nonmerit considerations such as personality, may be very high.

In summary, while merit pay is indeed used in some unionized firms, it is not widespread. There is often union resistance because of the perceived subjectivity of the merit process and the goals of the labor movement. Therefore, merit pay appears to be more challenging to implement in union than nonunion organizations (R. Heneman, R. L., Porter, et al., 1997).

Job Characteristics

As discussed in the next chapter, a major stumbling block to implementing merit pay successfully is the measurement of performance. Some jobs lend themselves better to performance measurement than others. As a result, it is more feasible to link pay increases to performance in some jobs than others. Given the current state of the empirical literature, it is not possible to say precisely which jobs lend themselves better to merit pay. It is possible, however, to sketch out the general characteristics of work that should be factored in when determining the feasibility of merit pay.

Two characteristics of jobs seem to lend themselves to merit pay (Konrad & Pfeffer, 1990; Mohrman, Resnick-West, & Lawler, 1989). First, an employee must be responsible for performing a whole piece of work. What this means is that there must be a distinct start and finish to the product or service being generated by the employee. If this is not the case, it may be difficult to assess what it is that the employee is contributing to the organization. Second, the employee must have the opportunity to have a noticeable impact on performance. In some jobs, employees are given so little autonomy, discretion, or authority in performing their tasks that it is difficult to establish their contributions to the organization.

Both of these conditions seem to be required for merit pay to be feasible. In some jobs, while discrete units of work are being performed, the employee has little discretion in performing the job. For example, on an assembly line, there may be an identifiable part placed repeatedly on the product. However, the speed at which the number of parts are placed is often outside the control of the individual employee and determined by the speed of the assembly line. Hence, if the number of parts placed on the product in a given time period is the performance standard, there will not be enough variability in performance to make a case for merit increases for higher performers.

Perhaps because both discrete units of work and discretion in performance are required, national surveys show that exempt jobs are associated with merit pay much more frequently than nonexempt jobs (e.g., Peck, 1984). According to the federal Fair Labor Standards Act, exempt jobs must, by definition, have an inherent component of discretion over the work to be performed. Nonexempt jobs do not have this job characteristic. In exempt jobs, you are likely to find both the performance of whole units of work, as well as more employee autonomy in the way work is performed. Hence, merit pay is well suited for exempt positions, because both the job characteristics required for an effective merit pay plan are present. It should be noted, however, that even when both conditions are present, performance measurement may still be problematic, as shown in the next chapter. In nonexempt jobs, employees do not have authority to control the way in which work is performed. As a result, merit pay is less suited for nonexempt positions because employees do not have an impact on performance.

A discussion of job characteristics impacting merit pay would not be complete without looking at a popular trend in the workplace—working from home. During the 1990s, organizations were experimenting with employees working from home to help the environment, lessen traffic congestion, and maintain employee wellbeing. Advances in computer technology made this possible, and the Pandemic accelerated levels of employees working off-site. Two arrangements have become popular—hybrid work and remote work. The former includes employees working part of the time in the office and the other from home. The latter allows employees to work home all the time. As of 2024, about 14% of America's workforce works remotely, while about 27% works a hybrid model (WorldatWork, 2024). These percentages will likely increase in the near future and continue an upward trajectory (WorldatWork, 2024). If these projections are accurate, compensation specialists will have to spend more time carefully considering reward systems for hybrid and remote workers. If merit pay is selected as part of total compensation, then the suggestions above for on-site positions apply here too; however, additional attention and consideration is required for reliably and accurately observing and measuring the performance of remote and hybrid workers. This touches on reliability and validity of performance measurement, which is addressed in detail in Chapter 4.

Organizational Politics

In some organizations, or in some positions in organizations, the climate may be so driven by office or workplace "politics" that it is not feasible to use merit pay. In this context, organizational politics refers to deliberate attempts by the allocator to enhance or protect his or her self-interests to the extent of creating inaccurate performance appraisals (Longenecker, Sims, & Gioia, 1987). In these types of situations, it may be impossible to use merit pay because performance is based on political factors rather than performance. For example, ratings and, in turn, merit increases may be more a function of who you know than what you do. Politics may also interfere with merit pay even when performance is being accurately measured. For example, a large merit increase given to a good performer may be attributed by others to favoritism, rather than actual good performance.

While politics in organizations, both actual and perceived, can create problems in organizations and decrease the feasibility of merit pay, it should not be concluded that organizational politics always lead to dysfunctional consequences for organizations. As pointed out by Longenecker et al. (1987) and Ungson and Steers (1983), politics in organizations can sometimes be functional for the organization and may even be encouraged. For example, in a study of managers' perceptions of politics in performance appraisal, Longenecker and colleagues found that some managers viewed it as legitimate to give out lower ratings than a particular employee deserved to "shock" that employee back to higher levels of performance. While this example suggests that politics may be useful from time to time for developmental reasons, it is doubtful that a merit pay plan would be successful in a politically charged environment.

In another study, Tenhiala and Jamsen (2010) found that perception of politics and fairness in implementing a new merit pay system can have varied results. Three governmental organizations (n = 367) that implemented analogous merit pay systems had their employees respond to a survey about their perceptions of politics and fairness with the new systems. A hierarchical moderated regression indicated that perceptions of politics and fairness predicted whether the pay system was perceived effective in achieving its objectives. The results suggest that some forms of politics in performance appraisals (e.g. compression) might be perceived less detrimental than others (e.g. favoritism). In a highly charged political environment, pay system effectiveness varied as a function of the level of distributive justice. Giving employees a voice in the pay system development only mattered in a situation where there was a low level of organizational politics.

As argued by Lawler (1971) and empirically verified by numerous researchers (Ferrin & Dirks, 2003; Parco, Rapoport, & Stein, 2002; Vest et al., 1989), trust is an important component of reward systems. If pay is based on politics but alleged to be based on performance, employees may have less trust in organizational decisionmakers. In such a situation, these employees conceivably could seek employment elsewhere or seek representation by a third party such as a labor organization.

Human Resource Management Practices

Reward systems such as merit pay are only one component of the many human resource management activities undertaken in organizations. Other human resource management activities, such as staffing and training and development, also influence the feasibility of merit pay. In general, the more successful an organization is with other human resource activities, the less merit pay is needed. With success in other areas of human resource management, the base rate of success is high. That is, the ratio of an organization's successful employees to its total employees (i.e., the base rate) is high. When the base rate is already high because of other human resource activities, it is difficult to significantly improve on this situation through merit pay. In other words, in truly excellent organizations, it is difficult to make human resources even more productive. The organization has already hired the best available talent, carefully manages work practices, provides training when needed, and provides a sound pay package. Under these circumstances, it is difficult for merit pay or any other new human resource procedure to improve upon the existing situation.

In the opposite situation, if the base rate is very low, merit pay may not make much of a difference. Under a low base rate, other human resource activities may be so poorly performed that merit pay cannot increase the base rate enough to make up for the poor practices in other areas of human resources.

Hence, merit pay seems most applicable under circumstances where there is a moderate base rate of employee performance. When the base rate is moderate, human resource operations can be improved. At the same time, human resource operations are not so poor that the results of a merit pay plan will be swamped by the ineffectiveness of other human resource procedures. When there is a moderate base rate, other human resource activities play a strong supporting role for merit pay. For example, as shown throughout the book, training in the merit pay process is an essential component to the proper administration of merit pay. In turn, merit pay also supports other human resource management activities. For example, merit pay can be used to reinforce the principles learned in training back on the job.

The notion of high performance work practices, that is, that various HR and other organizational practices can lead to high levels of organizational performance (Becker et al., 2001; Gephart, 1995; Huselid, 1995; Van Buren & Werner, 1996). A major argument in these writings is that such practices need to be *integrated* with one another to form what has been called a high performance work system. While much remains to be learned about such systems (Becker & Huselid, 1998; Singh, Yoo, Park, Chaudhuri, & Sihag, 2024), research to date supports the arguments made above concerning the need for merit pay to fit with (or be integrated with) other HR practices used by the organization.

Summary

In summary, it has been shown that institutional arrangements need to be considered along with economic factors in determining the feasibility of merit pay. Conditions that seem to facilitate or hinder the use of merit pay are shown in Table 3.2.

Table 3.2

Institutional Arrangements Contributing to the Feasibility of Merit Pay

Merit Pay More Feasible Under These Conditions	Merit Pay Less Feasible Under These Conditions
Service sector	Manufacturing sector
Private sector	Public sector
Middle stages of organizational life cycle	Early or late stages of organizational life cycle
Flexible specialization technologies	Mass production technologies
Competitive culture	Egalitarian culture
Nonunionized	Unionized
Low politics	High politics
Moderate base rate	High or low base rate
Well-defined job characteristics	Poorly defined job characteristics
High discretion in work performed performed	Low discretion in work

Preferences for Merit Increases

In addition to considering economic conditions and institutional arrangements, attention should also be given to the preferences of organization members concerning merit increases. Salary increases can, of course, be based on many factors other than performance, including seniority, cost of living, and promotions. Other examples include "comparability adjustments," sometimes granted in an attempt to equalize pay in the public sector relative to the private sector, or "general increases" granted to every current employee of an organization. A merit pay plan would be more feasible when organizational members prefer merit increases over these other options.

As might be expected, merit pay is not always preferred by all organizational members. Over the years, many surveys have been conducted in which organizational members are asked to rank order their preferences for merit pay and other types of pay increases. One such survey is shown in Table 3.3. The figures in this table can be interpreted as follows.

In each of the three studies, participants were asked to indicate the importance of each criterion for merit pay decisions on a scale from 1 = least important to 5 = most important. The mean shown in the table refers to the average numerical score assigned by the participants to each criterion. The higher the mean, the more important the criterion to the participants. The standard deviation (SD) shows the dispersion in values assigned by participants around the mean. In essence, the smaller the SD, the more agreement by study participants on the importance of this criterion. The rank refers to the rank ordering of means from the highest to the lowest. Along with the mean, it is another summary statistic of the importance of each criterion to the participants in the study. The results of this survey and others are reviewed in this section to help assess which organizational members are likely to prefer merit pay. Preferences for merit pay seem to vary by the following categories, which will be discussed in turn: job type and level, merit pay plan characteristics, income and performance, gender, and motivation.

Job Level and Type

Surveys of both managers' and employees' preferences for merit pay have been conducted (M. Brown, 2001; Bureau of National Affairs, 1988; Cable & Judge, 1994; Clugston & Howell, 2000; Dyer & Theriault, 1976; Fossum & Fitch, 1985; Koys, Keaveny, & Allen, 1989; Mahoney, 1964; Nigro, 1981; Pearce & Perry, 1983; Scott et al., 1987). The results of these surveys suggest that managers' preferences for merit pay are generally stronger than employee preferences. In these surveys, managers are more consistent in ranking merit pay as their number one preference than are employees. Hence, preferences for merit pay seems to be related to job level.

Table 3.3

Importance of Pay Increase Decision Criteria: Means, Standard Deviations, and Rank Order

Criterion	Study 1			Study 2			Study 3		
	Mean	SD	Rank	Mean	SD	Rank	Mean	SD	Rank
Level of job performance	4.70	0.66	1	4.93	0.27	1	5.00	0.00	1
Size of salary increase budget	4.30	0.77	2	3.58	1.30	3	4.44	0.80	2
Cost of living increases	4.10	0.73	3	3.88	0.99	2	2.93	1.01	4
Tightness of the labor market for this type of job	4.00	0.65	4	3.53	1.13	5	3.35	1.16	3
Degree of disruption that would occur if the job holder quit	3.90	0.85	5	3.55	1.28	4	2.78	1.38	5
Length of service	3.30	0.86	6	2.93	0.92	6	2.33	1.00	6

Source: Fossum & Fitch (1985). Reprinted with permission. *Note:* Study 1:22 students in undergraduate personnel course and graduate compensation class; study 2:40 full-time professional and managerial employees in MBA personnel class; study 3:42 employees of 21 Midwestern private-sector organizations in personnel and line management positions.

It should be noted, however, that just because managers, on average, prefer merit pay does not necessarily mean that their actual decisions are based solely on merit. Sherer, Schwab, and Heneman (1987) reported a correlation of 0.65 between preferences and actual weights used for performance and other factors in merit pay decisions. A correlation of 0.65 means that about 42% of those who favored merit pay actually made pay decisions on the basis of merit. It should also be noted that just because managers prefer merit pay does not mean that they are in favor of the current system under which they are required to operate. For example, Hyde (1988) reports the results of a study by Clark and Wachtel (1988). In this study of 4,000 federal managers, 90% favored the concept of merit pay; however, 74% felt that their current system was unfair.

Types of jobs are also related to preferences for merit pay. It appears that merit pay preferences are stronger for white-collar than blue-collar employees (Beer & Gery, 1972; Koys et al., 1989). White-collar jobs include technical, professional, and clerical positions, while blue-collar jobs include more traditional manufacturing jobs. In the Koys et al. (1989) study, cost of living was the first-choice preference for blue-collar employees, while merit pay was the first-choice preference for white-collar workers.

Taken together, the results of these two sets of studies suggest that those individuals who are in higher-level, white-collar types of jobs tend to have stronger preferences for merit pay. It should be noted, however, that there are exceptions to the rule. For example, H. Heneman and Young (1988) found that school administrators had unfavorable perceptions about merit pay. The implication of this general finding is that it may be easier to "sell" some parts of an organization on the feasibility and desirability of merit pay than other parts of the organization.

Merit Pay Plan Characteristics

In two interesting empirical studies, it was shown that characteristics of the merit pay plan also have a bearing on an employee's preferences for merit pay. Koys et al. (1989) found that preferences for merit pay were stronger when it was perceived that merit pay did not decrease teamwork. Beer and Gery (1972) reported that preferences for merit pay vary by type of merit pay plan offered. In their sample of white-collar workers, a merit increase based solely on performance was preferred over one that includes both performance and a general increase for all employees. However, both of these merit plans were preferred over a high-risk merit plan where only above-average performers are rewarded. This type of plan is high-risk because no merit increase is granted to anyone rated less than above average. These studies suggest that in surveying organizational members about their preferences for merit increases versus alternative arrangements, considerable care should be taken to specify the type of merit plan in the survey.

You would also expect that preferences for merit pay would be related to perceptions of performance appraisal. Performance appraisal is an essential component of the merit pay process, as discussed in Chapter 4. The research on this issue, however, is mixed. Koys et al. (1989) found that the perceived validity of the appraisal system used to make merit decisions did not have an impact on preferences for merit pay in a university setting. In contrast, Pearce and Perry (1983) found that there was a significant positive relationship between perceptions of a fair and objective appraisal system and preferences for merit pay in federal agencies.

These findings concerning performance appraisal suggest that the present performance appraisal system may not always be an obstacle in the eyes of organizational members when considering the adoption of a merit pay plan. It would be wrong, however, to conclude that the perceived validity of the appraisal system is not important. As will be shown in Chapter 4, the perceived validity of the appraisal system does impact people's reactions to merit pay after such a plan has been implemented.

Income and Performance

Individuals with higher levels of performance (Beer & Gery, 1972) and income (Mahoney, 1964) have been shown to prefer merit pay over alternative increase policies. Perhaps this is because high performers are more likely to receive a raise than low performers under a merit pay plan. Also, high-income employees may favor merit pay because they have sufficient income to rely on should their merit increases be less than adequate. People with larger incomes, from work and/or other outside sources, may be more willing to "risk" pay based on performance ratings because whether they get an increase or not, they still have other sources of income to meet their basic needs. By comparison, someone with a lower income, perhaps without any source of outside income, may be less willing to run the risk of not getting a merit increase because they cannot afford the loss. In short, employees with low incomes may prefer the security of a small increase each year over the gamble of a large increase—or no increase—in any given year. Increases are seldom guaranteed under a merit pay plan.

Gender

There is mixed data concerning the impact of gender on preferences for merit pay. On the one hand, Koys et al. (1989) reported a gender effect in preferences for merit pay, in that more men preferred merit pay than did women. The authors speculate that this may be because women allocators prefer to distribute pay across the board to all employees, rather than on the basis of merit (Majors, 1988). Brenner and Bertsch (1983) found that gender preferences may be moderated by personality. Assertive men preferred pay increases based on merit, while assertive women preferred pay increases based on seniority. In contrast, M. Brown (2001) found that female employees were in general *more* likely than males to support a merit pay plan. It is unclear whether Brown's sample (a large, public-sector research organization in Australia) led to her results being different from previous studies. However, a study of a government-owned nuclear waste facility in the southwestern United States found that males earned more than females in the facility, but that females received higher percentage wage increases over a 2-year period (Harris, Gilbreath, & Sunday, 2002). Finally, a study by Shaw and colleagues found no significant impact of gender on pay level satisfaction, satisfaction with pay raises, or future behavioral intentions for a sample of hospital employees (Shaw, Duffy, Mitra, Lockhart, & Bowler, 2003).

Recent research shows that males tend to receive higher performance ratings and merit pay increases than females in the same positions. Belliveau (2014) found that inexperienced managers (vs. experienced ones) tend to (a) rate men higher in performance than women and (b) distribute greater merit pay increases to men. The results of the study suggests training in gender bias is mandatory for new managers and supervisors. In another study, Kronberg (2020) explored whether gender differences in merit rewards narrowed or remained constant as organizational tenure increased. Data were collected from 2005–2014 of employees from the same firm. The author analyzed longitudinal data with multilevel growth curve models and found no evidence for declining gender effects on pay when employees stay longer; males, though out the entire 14-year period, constantly received higher merit increases than their female counterparts. Finally, Castilla and Bernard (2010) discovered when firms claim to be meritocratic, managers who decide merit pay increases tend to pay males larger increases than females in similar positions. The results here suggests that even when an organization champions meritocracy, it must remain mindful of implicit, gender bias in merit pay.

Suffice it to say that the impact of gender on merit pay preferences remains far from clear at the present time. It appears the same holds true for gender biases in merit pay distributions and performance appraisal ratings, although recent studies seem to suggest that males tend to profit more than females. At the least, the findings in this section imply merit pay designers and stewards must keep vigilant about gender differences.

Motivation

In two studies, employee motivation was examined as a correlate of merit pay preferences. Meyer and Walker (1961) reported that individuals high in achievement motivation preferred merit pay more than those low in achievement motivation. Those who are oriented toward task mastery and accomplishment may prefer merit pay because it provides employees with feedback on how well they are doing.

Beer and Gery (1972) also concluded that merit pay was preferred by individuals high in the need for achievement. They based their conclusion on the finding that employees with high needs for advancement, responsibility, and interesting and challenging work preferred merit pay over those employees low in these needs. Also, they found that people high in the need for security, vacation, and money preferred a general increase for all employees more than employees low in these needs. Beer and Gery reasoned that these latter employees were more concerned with security and therefore preferred a general increase because it was less risky than merit pay. A general increase usually involves less risk because it is granted to all employees regardless of performance. On the other hand, increases under a merit pay plan involve more risk because increases are usually granted only to those employees who perform at or above a certain level.

Pay Plan Types

Research (Cable & Judge, 1994; LeBlanc & Mulvey, 1998) on preferences clearly shows that all employees prefer merit pay to team pay or variable pay.

Summary

The research available on preferences for merit pay is somewhat sparse, disjointed, and often dated. However, it does clearly indicate that not all organizational members prefer merit pay. The limited research suggests that merit pay is more likely to be preferred by those in higher-level, white-collar positions; by those who are male, good performers, and achievement oriented; and by those who like to work in a climate where performance differences are emphasized and teamwork is not diminished. However, when pushed, most employees prefer merit pay to team-based or variable pay. Please note that these are tendencies or generalizations. It is by no means the case that all people who fit this profile will prefer merit pay, or that all people who do not fit this profile will be opposed to merit pay. Nevertheless, organizations need to consider the preferences of their members prior to the implementation of a merit pay plan. Also, merit pay may have an influence on the recruitment of new members to organizations. Individuals with a preference for merit pay may be more likely to be attracted to organizations with a merit pay plan in place.

Alternatives or Additions to Merit Pay

After considering the various environmental constraints, organizational considerations, and employee preferences described above, the reader may conclude that merit pay is not feasible in his or her organization. However, even if merit pay is not an appropriate choice, the reader may still be faced with the difficult prospect of motivating his or her workforce. Alternatively, perhaps the reader will want to combine merit pay with other reward systems.

This section offers readers some alternative motivational programs that can be considered. For those readers who have concluded that merit pay is a viable option for their organization, this section suggests some additions to merit pay. For those who decide against merit pay, this section provides alternatives.

In many organizations, more than one reward system is needed (O'Dell, 1986; Wallace, 1990), and these systems need to be integrated with one another (R. Heneman, 2001a, 2002). Multiple reward systems and the integration of these systems will be addressed here. Readers desiring even more information on other reward strategies will be referred to other sources.

Promotions

Meyer (1987) has forcefully argued that it is very difficult to effectively administer a merit pay plan. He advocates that employees be motivated on the basis of promotions rather than a salary increase based on merit. The reason for using promotions rather than monetary rewards, according to Meyer (1975), is that more objective criteria accompany promotion decisions than pay increase decisions. Also, Meyer asserts that the cutthroat competition associated with merit pay can be avoided if promotions are made on the basis of peer nominations (see Chapter 2 for a look at the notion of competition).

Meyer (1975, 1987) takes a broad view of promotions as a reward. In his view, promotions do not include just the traditional model of technical employees moving up and through the managerial ranks. Instead, Meyer considers the creation of technical career tracks as promotions. Under this approach, employees can continue to move up in the organization without necessarily becoming a manager. Meyer also includes lateral moves in his definition of promotions. Under this type of arrangement, employees are "promoted" when they acquire new skills or different job responsibilities even when this occurs at the same level as their previous job.

Lawler (1976) disagrees that promotions should be substituted for monetary rewards. He suggests that the problems of competition and the subjective criteria associated with some merit pay plans are also likely to be associated with promotion decisions as well. Moreover, he argues that promotions place more emphasis on potential than actual performance. Therefore, if only promotions are used, actual performance may not be taken into account by the organization, and motivation will decline.

Looking at both sets of arguments, it would seem that both monetary and promotion systems are needed in organizations. Merit pay or other monetary pay systems can be used to reward and motivate actual performance. Promotions and/or pay based on the acquisition of new skills (e.g., Lawler, 1981) can be used to reinforce the potential for performance. As a practical matter, organizations may need to place more emphasis on merit pay than on traditional upward promotion systems. Many organizations have been downsizing by eliminating middle-management positions.

Other Monetary Incentive Plans

As indicated in several parts of this chapter, conditions may favor using another type of incentive pay strategy. For example, countable indicators of performance may exist in some jobs and, as a result, *a piece-rate pay plan* may be more appropriate to reinforce continued production. In other organizations, jobs may be highly interdependent, with performance determined more by the overall functioning of the group than by any one individual. Under these circumstances, a group incentive plan may be appropriate. Extensive reviews of the empirical research on piece-rate and group incentive plans can be found in Guzzo and Bondy (1983); Honeywell-Johnson and Dickinson (1999); Jenkins (1986); Jenkins et al. (1998); Katzell, Bienstock, and Faerstein (1977); Locke, Feren, McCaleb, Shaw, and Denny (1980); and Welbourne and Cable (1995). Alternative monetary reward strategies are discussed in O'Dell (1987). Some of the older and newer incentive pay plans reviewed by O'Dell are described in Table 3.4.

In the last two decades, the use of work-teams (work-groups) has increased dramatically. Before the 21st century, about 40% of the U.S. workforce was involved in a work-team (Katzenbach & Smith, 1993). Currently, working in teams increased almost 200% (Garcia-Buades et al., 2019) (The reader should note that even though the frequency of teams has increased dramatically, individual jobs still make up a majority jobs in the American workforce).

Table 3.4

Some Definitions of Nontraditional Reward Practices

Earned time off	Due to exceptional performance, employees are eligible to earn time off from work with pay.
Gain sharing plan	Unit-wide bonus system designed to reward all eligible members for improved performance. Gains are shared with all employees in the unit according to a single predetermined formula or target (several measures may be included in the formula). Examples of common gainsharing plans are Scanlon, Rucker, Improshare, and unit level (other than corporate level) cash profit sharing, but limited to these. If profit sharing is corporate-wide and/ or deferred, consider this practice "profit- sharing plans" (below).
Small group incentives	Similar to gainsharing plans, except that bonuses are based on small-group performance rather than single-formula, unit-wide performance. Formulas and bonuses can vary from group to group within a unit, depending on nature of the work and performance.
Individual incentives	All or part of an individual's pay is tied to individual performance. This would include all standard hour incentive plans, engineered incentives, production incentives, piece rate, etc. *Does not include merit raises or executive compensation packages.*
Lump sum payment/Bonus	Eligible employees are given one-time, lump sum payments or bonuses instead of all or part of a base wage or salary increase. Bonus does not become part of base pay. This is independent of any incentive or gainsharing pay.
Pay-for-knowledge	Hourly or salaried pay, or pay progression, is determined by the number of jobs an employee can do, not the job (s)he actually performed on a given day.
Profit-sharing plans	Annual bonus or share based on company/corporate profit performance. An employee's share could be paid in cash, or deferred into a retirement fund.

Source: O'Dell (1987). Reprinted with permission.

A consequence of increased work-teams suggests a revised look at criteria for deciding suitable incentive plans. Recent scholarly writing and research provide such a framework for linking work-teams and incentive plans (Schweyer, 2021).

Teams are divided into four general categories (listed below) based on two *primary* dimensions - interdependence of team members and team size. Then various *secondary* and *tertiary* characteristics (e.g., complexity of work, communication requirement, and team cohesion) are considered. Then, three types of financial incentives—*team-based*, *hybrid* (combination of team-based and individually-based), *individually-based*—are matched to the four team categories.

Highly-interdependent Teams

Highly-interdependent work, such as, a restaurant crew, rely heavily on members to work with each other to achieve team goals. Research shows that teams engaged in highly interdependent work are best suited for team-based rewards (Lee et al., 2015; Wang & Chen, 2022). Team-based incentives can improve group communication and cohesion, leading to improved performance outcomes (Kwon et al., 2024; Lee et al., 2015).

Loosely Dependent Teams

Loosely dependent teams consist of serially-independent work, such as an assembly line. Team members get their part of the job done and then pass it on to others. Research suggests that efforts to improve communication and team cohesion should not be forced through group measures or incentives. In fact, extra time and effort to optimize team communication and cohesion may actually erode team performance (Khoshsoroor et al., 2019).

Small Teams

Small teams have 10 or fewer members. Research indicates team-based rewards become less effective as the size of the team increases (Powell & Lorenz, 2019). Ten is not fixed, as the maximum size differs depending group characteristics, such, as, the complexity of work and if members previously worked together (Powell & Lorenz, 2019). Furthermore, larger and newer teams with more complex work should consider hybrid incentives (Garbers & Conradt, 2014). Compensation specialists should consider designing their appraisal and feedback process for individual team members and the entire as a whole (Garbers & Conradt, 2014).

Large Teams

Large teams consist 10 or more members. Research evidence indicates that large teams completing complex work should use individual-based incentives, as it motivates each member in optimally performing his or her work (Kozlowski & Bradford, 2013). On the other hands, if a large team is engaged in highly-interdependent work, hybrid incentives may be a better choice (Kozlowski & Bradford, 2013).

The above model is not an exclusive one. Kozlowski & Bradford (2013) and Pearsall et al. (2010) offer comparable models, but with much more detail that is beyond the scope of this book. Moreover, an extensive search of the compensation literature suggests the model above is a reasonable and valid representation of the others.

In many organizations, several incentive pay plans are needed rather than just one. Different plans accomplish different objectives. For example, skill-based pay is used to facilitate the acquisition of new skills, group incentive plans are used to motivate performance of the group, and merit pay is used to motivate individual performance. Although multiple incentive plans are desirable, these plans need to be integrated and coordinated.

Schneier (1989a, 1989b) detailed an integrated reward system, put in place at Pratt and Whitney, known as the Performance Management, Recognition, and Reward System (PMRR). This system used merit increases, bonuses, special cash awards, along with nonmonetary rewards. It was integrated by being tied into and reinforcing the business strategy of the organization.

Pacific Gas and Electric Company (1989) used an integrated incentive plan for its managers. This plan, which was also tied to the strategic mission of the organization, provided incentive pay for corporate, work group, and individual performance. One of the oldest, and perhaps best-known, examples of an integrated incentive plan was at Lincoln Electric Company in Cleveland, Ohio (Eisenberg, 2001; Lincoln, 1951). At Lincoln, incentive pay plans are viewed as a means to manage, and have been in use for over 80 years. Financial rewards are provided for individual and group performance, profits, and employee suggestions (Perry, 1990).

A research study examined the effects of integrating multiple financial incentives on performance. Park & Sturman (2012) examined the relative effects of three different performance-based rewards - merit pay, yearly bonus, and long-term incentive—on individual performance over two years. The authors adopted a two-step, multiple regression procedure from Kahn & Sherer (1990) to predict the association between second-year performance and the three rewards (merit pay, bonus pay, and long-term incentive pay). Moreover, the second-year predictions were expressed as a percentage of the first-year salaries, placing measurements on a common (ratio) scale, so that percent differences between the rewards could be compared as a ratio of each other. The results showed that all performance-based pay systems positively related to future performance, in the following strengths: *Merit pay* had the strongest effect, showing a 1% raise was 27% stronger than the effect of a 1% *bonus*, and the effect of the 1% merit raise was more than 10 times stronger than the effect of 1% in *long-term incentives*. In addition, the effect of a 1% *bonus* was more than 8.5 times stronger than the effects of 1% in *long-term incentives*. The implications of the findings here suggest that adding merit pay increases to base salary improve employee perceptions of the pay-performance relationship. Moreover, the findings here support Williams' (2010) claim that long-term effects on actual pay-performance correlations are larger than short-term effects (see Chapter 2, moderator effects).

In summary, other incentives can and should be considered in addition to, or instead of, merit pay. These plans need to be selected based on their intended objectives and the facilitating conditions discussed in detail by other authors. If multiple plans are used, considerable care must be taken to integrate and coordinate these plans. Integration and coordination can be achieved by using these plans as a routine part of the managerial process and by tying each plan to the mission of the organization.

Nonmonetary Rewards

A variety of nonmonetary rewards are available to organizations in addition to the monetary rewards just reviewed. Examples of nonmonetary rewards are shown in Table 3.5. Some of these rewards may be more feasible for organizations as they are virtually cost free. Also, nonmonetary rewards may actually be more attractive to some employees than monetary rewards. For example, with busy work and family schedules, some employees may prefer time off over an increase in pay. As shown in the discussion of expectancy theory (Chapter 2), outcomes with more positive valence to an employee are likely to be more motivational.

In using nonmonetary rewards, two points should be considered. First, if these rewards are to be used to maintain and improve performance, they must be made contingent on performance (Hinkin, Podsakoff, & Schriesheim, 1987). Only by making these rewards contingent on performance will they take on the motivational properties needed to improve performance. Second, it is sometimes possible to couple these nonmonetary rewards with monetary rewards. For example, an organization might not only reward a good performer with additional time off from work, but also provide pay during this time off. One reason to use monetary and non-monetary rewards as complementary incentives is that there is some evidence that monetary rewards are associated with higher levels of productivity than are nonmonetary rewards (Locke et al., 1980).

Organizations may use nonmonetary rewards as substitutes for monetary rewards from time to time. A good example is the situation described in Chapter 5, in which it may not be possible to provide good performers with merit increases because there are maximum amounts employees can earn (ceilings) that allow the employer to control labor costs and earn a profit. Over a number of years of good performance, an employee may reach the maximum that can be paid to a person holding that job. As any manager who has faced this situation will tell you, it is very difficult to maintain the employee's high level of performance when it is no longer possible to grant a merit increase.

Table 3.5

Examples of Nonmonetary Rewards

Formal commendation
Formal recognition
Informal recognition (e.g., a "pat on the back")
Unofficial time off (e.g., allowing late arrival or early departure)
Vacation scheduling (giving favorable vacation times)
Favorable job assignments (e.g., easy, comfortable, involves challenge)
Informal performance feedback
Mentoring, coaching, and development
Participation in unit decision making
Off-job socializing and friendship
Considerate, personally supportive behavior (e.g., giving personal advice or help)
"In-group" membership (giving inside information, special consideration, etc).
Career advice, counseling, and help

Source: Hinkin, Podsakoff, & Schriescheim (1987). Reprinted with permission.

What sometimes does work in this situation is to grant nonmonetary rewards instead of merit pay to continue to motivate good performance. For example, the manager may give the employee a greater voice in decisions that have a bearing on how work is performed in the unit. Along with greater participation in decision making, the manager might also involve the employee in training less senior employees. Even when monetary rewards are not possible, as in this example, there are still additional ways to motivate good performance, as shown in Table 3.5.

Summary of Major Points

1. *Feasibility of merit pay.* Merit pay is not appropriate in all situations. Even if merit pay appears to be desirable, an assessment needs to be made of conditions that may facilitate or hinder the use of merit pay.
2. *Conditions that need to be diagnosed.* At a general level, attention must be given to characteristics of the environment and organization in which merit pay decisions are made. Attention also needs to be directed toward the allocators and recipients involved in and affected by merit pay decisions.

3. *Economic conditions that favor using merit pay.* One aspect of the environment and organization that has a direct impact on the use of merit pay is present and anticipated economic conditions. Economic conditions favorable to the use of merit pay include the following:
   - Price stability
   - No wage and price guidelines or controls
   - Low marginal tax rates
   - Government subsidies
   - Adequate budget
4. *Institutional arrangements that favor merit pay.* The interaction of the organization and environment result in various institutional arrangements that influence the use of merit pay. Institutional arrangements that seem to favor merit pay are as follows:
   - Service-sector organizations
   - Private-sector organizations
   - Middle stages of an organization's life cycle
   - Flexible specialization technologies
   - Competitive culture
   - Nonunionized
   - Low politics
   - Well-defined job characteristics
   - High level of discretion in performing work
5. *Preferences for merit pay.* Not all employees favor pay increases allocated on the basis of performance. Some employees prefer alternative allocation procedures such as pay increases based on seniority. Groups that tend to favor merit pay are as follows:
   - White-collar employees
   - High performers
   - Achievement-oriented employees
   - Those who already work under a merit plan where performance differences are emphasized and teamwork is not diminished
6. *Alternatives or additions to merit pay.* If the reader concludes that merit pay is not feasible, or that merit pay needs to be supplemented, a variety of other reward systems are available. These reward systems include promotions, other incentive plans, and nonmonetary rewards.

Conclusions

In Chapter 2, we argued that merit pay ha some desirable features, and that those who reject merit pay under all circumstances have gone too far.

Based on the material presented in Chapter 3 on the feasibility of merit pay, it can be concluded that those who endorse merit pay in all circumstances have also gone too far. Simply put, there are times when merit pay should not be used. There are some organizations currently using or contemplating using merit pay that should not use merit pay.

Merit pay should clearly *not* be used under the following three sets of circumstances:

- The budget is too small or economic conditions are too tight to allow the granting of large increases to good performers.
- Employees value leisure, recognition, or some reward other than pay increases, or they prefer the allocation of rewards on the basis of equity, seniority, or some basis other than merit.
- Institutional arrangements are such that ratings of employee performance do not capture performance valued by the organization.

When faced with these circumstances, an organization needs to find alternatives to merit pay. One obvious approach is to use an across-the-board increase for all employees. As discussed in Chapter 1, this approach could be less offensive to employees than a merit pay plan under any of the circumstances listed above. It may be more effective to tell employees, "Pay increases will be the same for each employee because of the current economic crunch, your preferences for equality, and the limited capabilities we have to measure performance," than to simply tell employees, "You should be motivated by a merit increase," which employees know is less than inflation, is the same for each employee, and is based on a poorly defined standard of performance.

It should be noted that alternatives other than across-the-board increases can be used as well. These alternatives include other incentive plans, promotions, and nonmonetary rewards. There is no reason to be stuck with a merit pay plan when it will not work.

Three issues need to be considered when deciding if merit pay is feasible. These three issues are shown in Figure 3.4.

First, organizations need to assess whether current conditions favor the use of a merit pay plan. The summary of major points in this chapter can be used as a checklist. If conditions do favor merit pay, then it can be used and, as described in Chapter 2, there are many potential benefits to the organization in using it.

Second, if conditions faced by the organization do not favor merit pay, then the question is whether the current conditions can be altered or managed to create a more feasible environment for merit pay. Some of the conditions described in this chapter are more easily altered than are others. For example, an organization has greater influence over the way jobs are

Figure 3.4

Deciding whether Merit Pay Should Be Used.

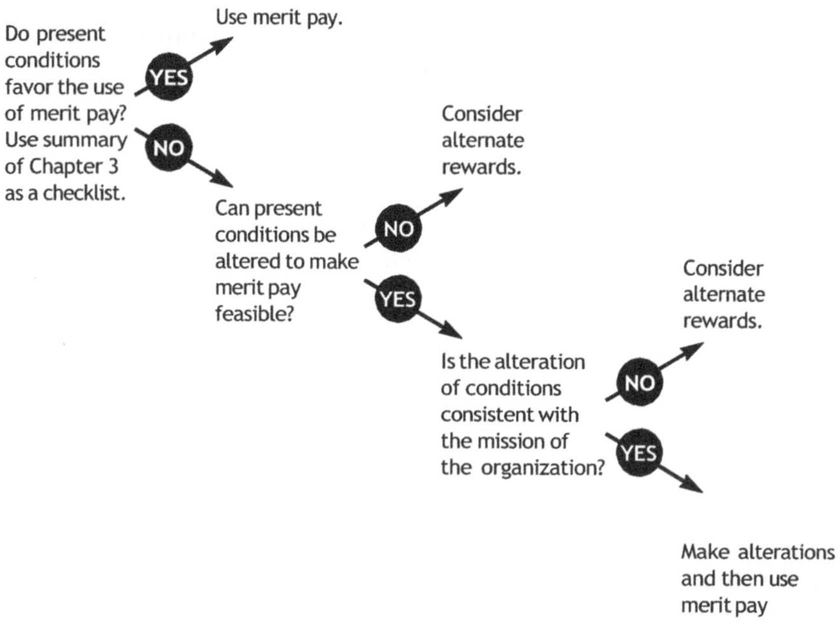

designed than they have over price inflation in the national economy. If conditions are not favorable to merit pay and cannot be altered, merit pay should not be used.

Third, if conditions can be altered to make merit pay more favorable, the desirability of these alterations and their impact on other aspects of business needs to be considered *before* going ahead with them. The alterations should be consistent with the mission, strategic plan, and culture of the organization. If the conditions are alterable and the alterations make business sense, then the alterations can be made, and merit pay becomes a feasible pay plan.

Study Questions and Case Study

1. Briefly discuss the contextual characteristics and conditions that influence the merit pay process. Are they equally important, or are some more important than others? Explain.
2. Explain why merit pay tends to be more successful in private sector organizations than in public sector employers. How could merit pay be more successful in the public sector?

3. Successful merit pay plan rely on favorable conditions. Assume you are the director of compensation contemplating such a plan in your company. What conditions should be present for an effective merit pay plan? (Hint: refer to Figure 3.4 to help you)
4. If merit pay is not suited for an organization, what other options do HR directors have to improve motivation?

Case Study: California Utility Company (CUC)

Assume you are a consultant hired by CUC's vice president of human resources. She wants you to decide which position below is better suited for a merit pay plan. Then, what type of financial incentive would you suggest for the other position. Give a rationale for each decision (Hint: Refer to Chapters 1 & 2 for additional information).

Organization

The California Utility Company (CUC) provides gas and electricity to 400,000 residents in central California. The company enjoys a favorable reputation from employees and customers alike. It is not uncommon to hear employees boast about their salaries, benefits, long tenure, and working conditions. Customers feel they receive excellent service at rates that are among the lowest in the state and frequently attend stockholder meeting to express their satisfaction with both. The CEO strongly believes in rewarding employees who "go the extra mile." The organization prides itself on using cutting edge technology and providing employees with comprehensive training.

Computer Technician Position

Computer technicians install, maintain, and repair all company PC's and networks. They typically work alone, assigned to specific departments in the organization. Because of the company's position on technology, replacement parts and peripherals are adequately supplied in the event problems arise. All technicians are paid at or just below the market average. Their supervisors continually complain to Human Resources about good and poor performers receiving the same pay, even though clearly performance differences exist between them. Also accepted is the appraisal system used to measure the performance of computer technicians. For eight months, several departmental managers have complained about the length of time it takes for computer installations and repairs.

Meter Reader Position

Meter Readers visit customer homes within a prescribed territory to assess their gas and electric usage. They almost always work in teams. Performance is measured on two outcome metrics - number of meters read and accuracy of recording data from meters; a typical appraisal system is not used to assess reader performance due to the existence of objective measures. In recent months, productivity has dropped considerably, while absenteeism and tardiness have increased at an equal rate. A study aimed at uncovering reasons for this revealed that 91% of all meter readers is married with at least one child, 89% felt very satisfied with the pay, and 84% felt management treated employees fairly and communicated clearly.

PART II

DEVELOPMENT AND ADMINISTRATION OF A MERIT PAY PLAN

CHAPTER 4

MEASURING PERFORMANCE

It is essential that adequate performance measures be developed if pay increases are to be linked to performance under a merit pay plan. In this chapter, we argue that the measurement of performance is best viewed as a *set of judgments*, rather than an end state, product, or form. This set of judgments is called *validation* and refers to the extent to which performance standards measure what they purport to measure. We will show that: (1) there are several different types of performance standards, ranging from traits to behaviors to results to relative comparisons; (2) there are multiple indicators of the extent to which we can infer that these standards of performance possess validity; and (3) there are several steps that can be taken in developing and using performance standards to maximize our chances of meeting these indicators, which allow us to infer validity.

The Importance of Adequate Performance Measures

Performance management in general, and performance appraisal in particular, have been increasingly criticized as ineffective, inefficient, and counterproductive (Adler et al., 2016; DeNisi et al., 2021; Pulakos & O'Leary, 2011; Schellhardt, 1996). Particular appraisal practices, such as forced ranking or forced distribution approaches that some large organizations have been using, are especially controversial (Bates, 2003b; Meisler, 2003; Schrøder-Hansen & Hansen, 2023). Nevertheless, as many observers of incentive pay plans have pointed out, a critical component of the success of these plans, including merit pay, is the adequacy of performance measures (Campbell et al., 1998; Hamner, 1975; Heneman & von Hippel, 1996;

Merit Pay, pages 123–173

doi:10.1108/978-1-80686-701-120263004

Lawler, 1971; Pearce & Perry, 1983; Wiscombe, 2001). There seems to be much stronger support for this view than for other contentions regarding various aspects of merit pay (see Adler et al., 2016). This support can be found in theory, research, and practice. While we do not wish to minimize the very real difficulties that individuals and organizations experience in measuring performance, our intent in this chapter is to provide a theoretically sound, yet workable approach to this essential topic.

The psychological and economic theories reviewed in Chapter 2 support the importance of adequate measures of performance. From a psychological perspective, an adequate measure of performance is needed so that employees can see that improved performance is instrumental in the attainment of a salary increase. An employee can only make the association between a desirable outcome, such as pay, and performance if performance is adequately measured. From an economic perspective, adequate measures of performance are needed for both the employer and employee to minimize costs. If performance is not adequately measured, an employer may end up overpaying employees whose performance was rated higher than it should have been, and underpaying employees whose performance was rated lower than it should have been. In either case, unnecessary costs may be incurred by the employer and employee because of inadequate performance measures.

Empirical research also points to the importance of adequate performance measures. While the adequacy of performance measures appears to have only a moderate impact on actual merit pay decisions (Huber et al., 1987; Schwab & Olson, 1990), adequacy of measures does have a larger impact on employee *perceptions* of the extent to which pay is tied to performance. As noted throughout the book, these perceptions are just as important as the actual link between pay and performance when it comes to employee motivation (Laguerre, 2022). Miceli and Near (1988) found that pay-for-performance perceptions and satisfaction with pay were stronger when allocators adhered to formal performance appraisal standards than when they did not adhere to such standards. Vest and colleagues (1989) found that low-performing employees in a transit agency were more likely to perceive a relationship between pay and performance when they believed that performance was accurately measured than when they believed that performance was not accurately measured. Although far from conclusive, the Miceli and Near and Vest and colleagues studies provide support for the importance of adequate performance measures as they relate to pay-for-performance perceptions. A study by Montemayor (2003) built on these studies. Based on research on organizational fairness, Montemayor developed and tested four factors that should increase employee satisfaction with merit pay. One of the factors was the "performance to rating link." This scale included items such as having clear performance standards, and consistently applying performance standards. Montemayor (2003) found suitable support for his four factors model of merit pay satisfaction via confirmatory factor analysis in both an American and a Venezuelan sample. This would suggest that one critical aspect of merit pay satisfaction is that employees perceive clear performance standards.

Recent research supports the importance of perception in the link between pay and performance. Chen et al. (2023) completed a meta-analytic study, supplemented with path analysis showing how perception affects merit-based pay. The results indicated that the actual relationship between pay and performance was partially mediated by employee perceptions of distributive justice and procedural justice. Like previous studies, the saliency of perceptions must be considered in a successful merit pay plan.

Finally, employer practices and experiences also demonstrate the importance of adequate performance measures. Surveys of employer practices (Bureau of National Affairs, 1983; Cleveland et al., 1989) show that a major reason for using performance appraisals is for making compensation decisions, merit pay decisions in particular (Peck, 1984). In a survey of large companies by Bretz and Milkovich, the top reason for using performance appraisal was "improving work performance," followed by "administering merit pay" (cited in Thomas & Bretz, 1994).

While deemed important in these surveys, performance measurement has also been reported as being problematic (Coens & Jenkins, 2000). Downs and Moscinski (1979), for example, reported that one of the most frequently mentioned weaknesses of large companies' performance appraisal systems is the subjectivity of ratings. A large-scale case study of the federal government's experience with merit pay also points to the importance of adequate performance measures. Pearce and Perry (1983) attributed the lack of success with merit pay in the public sector to a number of causes, including a performance appraisal system that was not adequately pretested. This resulted in inaccurate measures of performance being used to make merit decisions.

A survey of public-sector employees found considerable dissatisfaction with the extent to which their agency's appraisal system linked merit pay to performance. Thirty-nine percent of the employees surveyed agreed that better clarification of performance standards was needed, and 21% of managers agreed that there needed to be greater consistency between managers in rating performance (Longenecker & Nykodym, 1996). Additionally, in a survey of employees at a public university, only 39.1% expressed satisfaction with the university's appraisal system (Mani, 2002). Thus, both survey data and individual case studies point to the importance of adequate measures of performance, as well as the difficulties of adequately carrying this out.

Types of Performance Measures

Pay increase decisions are made on the basis of performance ratings under a merit pay plan. Performance ratings are appraisals or evaluations of employees' individual contributions to an organization. To assess the contribution of the employee to the organization, the employee is compared to a standard. Both absolute standards and relative comparisons can be used. They are considered in turn in this chapter.

Absolute Standards

Employee performance can be rated by comparing characteristics of the employee to definitional statements about the contribution or value of certain characteristics to the organization. Standards that are used in making these absolute comparisons include traits, behaviors, and results.

Many surveys have assessed the extent to which each of these sets of standards is actually used by organizations (Bernardin & Matt, 1985; Bretz & Milkovich, 1989; Bureau of National Affairs, 1983; Downs & Moscinski, 1979; Peck, 1984; Sibson & Company, 1989). Their findings indicate that results are the most frequently used performance standard, followed by traits and then behaviors. In the 1980s, there was a move toward a greater use of behaviors than traits (Sibson & Company, 1989), and a greater use of behaviors and results as a combined standard (Bernardin & Matt, 1985; Gosselin et al., 1997). Each of these three sets of standards—traits, behaviors, and results—will be described in turn, along with a discussion of their advantages and disadvantages for the purposes of merit pay.

Traits

Employee traits refer to personality characteristics of the employee. An example of a trait rating scale is shown in Table 4.1. As can be seen in this table, traits have an obvious appeal. Although the traits listed in the table were for the job of production supervisor, they would seem to be applicable

Table 4.1

Sample Items From a Trait-Rating Scale for Production Supervisors

	Strongly Disagree	Disagree	Neutral	Agree	Strongly Agree
Is active and energetic	1	2	3	4	5
Seldom sticks to business	1	2	3	4	5
Is self-controlled	1	2	3	4	5
Has common sense	1	2	3	4	5
Is proud of work	1	2	3	4	5

Source: R. Heneman (1984a).

to virtually all jobs. One advantage of using traits as a standard is that they appear to be applicable to a wide range of jobs. A second advantage to traits is that they can be generated fairly quickly. It takes little prompting to get organizational members to develop lists of desired personality characteristics. Perhaps this is because we think about performance using trait-like categories (Borman, 1987; Feldman, 1981; Werner, 1994).

Although traits are frequently used as a standard, they are very troublesome in measuring performance for merit pay. One disadvantage of traits is that they are vague and subject to varying interpretations by different raters (Borman & Dunnette, 1975). To illustrate this, ask a group of people, one at a time, to give their definition of traits like "aggressive," "dominant," or "self-starter." Then see how many different definitions of the same trait people come up with. Because of the likelihood of differing interpretations, merit pay decisions that rely too heavily on the evaluation of traits are very likely to be inconsistent (i.e., unreliable).

An implication of goal-setting theory (see Chapter 2) is that performance must be clearly specified for merit pay to help maintain or improve current performance. A disadvantage of traits is that they cannot be specified clearly enough. It is difficult, if not impossible, to improve employee performance when it is related to a personal characteristic that is difficult to define and potentially unalterable.

Behaviors

Employee behavior refers to the manner in which employees carry out their activities or duties. An example of a frequency-of-behavior scale, similar to behavioral observation scales (Latham & Wexley, 1994), is shown in Table 4.2. With a frequency-of-behavior scale, employees' behavior is compared to desired behaviors. The more frequently employees exhibit these desired behaviors, the better their performance.

Measuring behavior offers two advantages over measuring traits. First, behavior appears to be less vague, more clearly defined. You would expect to get more consistent merit pay decisions when using behavior as a standard. Also, you would expect improved motivation by using a more specific definition of expected performance. For example, you often hear about the need to be "professional" at work. While we all may agree this is a desirable trait, what does it mean? What is required? Clearly, the trait "professional" needs to be spelled out in behavioral terms for employees to understand what is expected of them. An example for the position of salesperson is as follows: Be courteous to customers; submit sales reports in a timely and accurate manner; keep shelves stocked with goods; and so forth. These behavioral standards give employees concrete performance objectives to work toward.

Table 4.2

Sample Items From a Frequency-of-Behavior Scale for Receptionists

	Almost Never	Seldom	Sometimes	Frequently	Almost Always
Desired Behaviors	**0**	**1**	**2**	**3**	**4**
1. Answers the phone by the second ring	0	1	2	3	4
2. Takes correct names and numbers on messages	0	1	2	3	4
3. Does not keep a person on hold any longer than 2 minutes without getting back and explaining why	0	1	2	3	4
4. Answers the phone in a pleasant manner and is always willing to help people	0	1	2	3	4
5. Offers guests coffee	0	1	2	3	4
6. Offers to take the guest's coat	0	1	2	3	4
7. Sorts mail no longer than 30 minutes after it arrives	0	1	2	3	4
8. Distributes mail to the correct personnel	0	1	2	3	4

Source: Reprinted with permission from the National Church Residences, Columbus, Ohio.

The second advantage that measuring behavior offers is that behavior is under the control of individual employees. Employees can more directly influence their behaviors than their traits or their results (described in the next section). Traits are a combination of innate characteristics and early learning. Results may be influenced by factors outside the employee, such as coworkers and budget constraints. Hence, it is more possible for the employee to alter behavior than traits or results to work toward the desired merit increase. The use of behaviors as measurement criteria, however, comes with a cost. Creating behavioral measures of performance is a more cumbersome, difficult, and time-consuming process than creating trait measures. However, these costs can be offset by avoiding the potential legal liability associated with performance measures that rely solely upon traits (Wiersma & Latham, 1986; see Chapter 6). Furthermore, in a series of studies in both Israel and Canada et al. (2002) found that employees responded more favorably to behaviorally-based, rather than trait-based, appraisals.

Results

Results-oriented measures of employee performance evaluate employee contributions in terms of actual products or services provided by an employee. Results measures are often used to evaluate individuals working in sales positions (Pettijohn et al., 2001). For professional positions, a common approach is to use management by objectives (MBO). An example of items from an MBO plan for lawyers in a large law firm is shown in Table 4.3.

As shown in this example, the major advantage of results-oriented measures is that they are highly specific and well defined. As a result, when these standards are set at challenging levels and accepted by employees, they have desirable motivational properties, as discussed concerning goal-setting theory in Chapter 2. In addition to their motivational potential, another advantage of results-oriented measures is that results can be directly coupled with merit increases of a specific size.

There are also, however, some distinct disadvantages to results-oriented measures of performance like MBO (Bowman, 1999). Results may be outside the control of individual employees. For example, billable hours for associates in a large law firm may be determined as much by the assignments they receive from senior partners as by their own efforts. Results may also fail to capture important aspects of employee performance. Using the same example, while billable hours might be an indicator of the *quantity* of service provided, those hours may indicate very little about the *quality* of service.

Relative Comparisons

Another standard is comparing employees to other employees. This is known as the process of relative comparisons, rather than the absolute

Table 4.3

Sample Items From an MBO Plan for Attorneys

Statistic	Desired Results	Actual Results	Improvement Plans
(1) Fee credits billed	$520,000.00		
(2) Cash receipts	$520,000.00		
(3) Realization (2-:-1)	100%		
(4) Billable hours	1,700 hrs.		
(5) Nonbillable hours	400 hrs.		
(6) Total hours	2,100 hrs.		

Source: Adapted with permission from the law firm of Porter, Wright, Morris, & Arthur, Columbus, Ohio.

comparisons that we just reviewed. The simplest method of relative comparisons is known as ranking: Employees in a work group are rank-ordered from the employee contributing the most to the organization, down to the employee contributing the least. Another way to make relative comparisons is to use the method of paired comparisons. An example of paired comparisons is shown in Table 4.4.

With this procedure, each employee is compared to every other employee. If the employee is a better performer than another employee, then the better employee earns a checkmark. A relative order is established based on the number of checkmarks a particular employee receives. The more checkmarks, the higher the rank.

Results of a national survey showed that relative comparisons are not used nearly as frequently as absolute comparisons for performance appraisal (Bureau of National Affairs, 1983). However, relative comparisons may actually be used more frequently than indicated in this survey. In two articles, it was estimated that as many as 20% of *Fortune* 500 companies use some form of forced ranking approach (Bates, 2003b; Meisler, 2003). Furthermore, you would expect ranking to be a common practice in small organizations (e.g., a corner convenience store), where resources are not available to develop absolute standards. Had these types of organizations been included in the survey, the results may have shown greater usage for relative comparisons.

An obvious advantage of relative comparisons is that, like traits, they can be quickly and easily constructed for at least a small number of jobs. Also, the rating task may be easier with relative comparisons because the rater is only expected to indicate who is better, not how much is one person better than another.

However, simplicity may also bring problems as well. A disadvantage of relative comparisons is that rank orderings made by different raters may not be comparable. For example, the difference in the performance levels of the first and second-ranked employees by rater A may be different than the difference in performance levels of the first- and second-ranked employees

Table 4.4

Paired Comparisons Method of Rating

	(1)	(2)	(3)	(4)	(5)	Total
(1) Goldie G.		X	X	X	X	4
(2) Pablo E.			X	X	X	3
(3) Denise W.				X	X	2
(4) Dave B.					X	1
(5) Phil Y.						0

for rater B. This is problematic when a common performance metric is needed to allocate merit increases across work groups.

A second disadvantage is that it is difficult to establish a relationship between pay and performance for purposes of employee motivation. Relative comparisons do not make it clear why one person is rated above another. Hence, it is difficult for employees to know what aspects of their performance they need to improve. A third disadvantage arises when there are severe, overall performance problems in an organization. In such cases, relative ranking may actually conceal poorly performing individuals. The employer may be ranking employees along the lines of "the best of the worst," which may overlook the fact that the performance of the entire work group is unacceptable. A relative ranking, in and of itself, tells us little about the contribution of a particular employee to the organization.

Current Trends in Merit Pay

Ratingless Feedback Reviews: A New Form of Performance Appraisal?

For decades, managers and employees alike have voiced their discontent with performance ratings. Some organizations have even abandoned them. Yet, performance appraisal remains necessary for administrative, legal, and developmental reasons. Instead of eliminating rated feedback, the use of ratingless reviews has recently garnered much attention (Gerhart, 2023).

Unrated reviews contain only narrative feedback. No labels or numbers showing gradations of individual performance exist. In addition, two other practices—ongoing feedback (feedback four or more times per year) and crowd-sourced feedback (the use of social media to collect feedback from peers and others)—are jointly used as a bundle of cutting-edge practices. These practices have become popular in the media and business press. Large companies, such as, Gap, IBM, and Microsoft have abandoned traditional performance appraisals and have adopted these cutting-edge practices (Gerhart, 2023).

Survey research, in general, shows organizations that adopted these cutting-edge practices had three objectives in mind (Ledford & Benson, 2019; Ledford et al., 2016a; Ledford et al., 2016b):

1. To improve the effectiveness of the performance management process (e.g., improved feedback, greater satisfaction in the process)
2. To improve strategic alignment (e.g., better support for the business strategy, increased organizational performance).
3. To help meet traditional reward objectives (rewarding, motivating, attracting, and retaining employees).

Results from this research indicated that the combined effects of the three practices had a slight positive impact on process effectiveness and strategic alignment, but little effect on reward objectives. Moreover, ratingless reviews could not be disentangled from the other two practices to determine its own effectiveness.

Evidence showing the effectiveness of ratingless reviews also comes from internal (case) studies conducted by managers in organizations, such as, Adobe Systems

(Morris, 2016); Cardinal Health (George & Holbein, 2016); Sears Holdings Corp (Engler & Mason, 2016). The studies often included pre- and post-measures, plus quasi-experimental designs testing ratingless reviews against the traditional system. All case studies reported positive effects and no negative effects from ratingless reviews (plus the use of ongoing feedback).

The major drawback from the surveys and case studies above is disentangling the effects of ratingless reviews from other performance management activities (e.g., on-going feedback). Empirical research looking to address this is scarce. As far as we know, only one empirical study attempted this. Ledford and Benson (2019) conducted a large-scale, pre- and post-test, comparative quasi-experiment in a large organization. They collected data from a treatment group of 1,061 employees (ratingless feedback) and a comparison group of 601 employees (rated feedback) before and after the change to ratingless reviews. Data were collected on three outcome measures: Satisfaction with performance feedback (e.g., fairness in compensation), employee outcomes (e.g., development), and organizational outcome (e.g., intent to quit). In all three outcome measures, the results show that some positive changes and no clear negative changes for the treatment group compared to the comparison group. Moreover, no definitive word on the effects of ratingless reviews could be made.

In conclusion, we want to emphasize that unrated reviews have been implemented with ongoing feedback, another cutting-edge practice. Thus, the effects of ratingless reviews must be uncoupled and assessed from other practices effects, which will take research and time. Until then, rated performance reviews will remain the de facto performance measure for individuals.

Choosing a Performance Standard

Choosing which measure(s) of performance to use in evaluating employees for purposes of merit pay is difficult. In making this choice, several factors must be considered. One obvious factor is the strengths and weaknesses of each standard just described (Bowman, 1999; Posthuma et al., 2018). Depending on circumstances (e.g., limited resources), some arguments may be more compelling than others (Keely, 1978).

A second factor to consider is whether standards can be substituted for one another. Sometimes you hear the argument that standards, whether traits, behaviors, results, or rankings, all basically measure the same thing. Hence, in choosing a standard for merit pay decisions, one need only look for the most convenient standard or one that is easiest to come by in an organization. However, at least two studies cast serious doubt on this assertion. R. Heneman (1986) found that, across 23 studies of performance, there was only a low-to-moderate correlation between behaviors and results. This result was confirmed in a meta-analysis that replicated and extended the Heneman meta-analysis (Bommer et al., 1995). While you would logically expect standards to be related to one another, in fact, the magnitude of the relationship does not appear to be strong enough to substitute them for one another.

A third factor to consider is that, given that measures are not interchangeable, a "mix" of standards may be better than just one. It is unlikely that any organization values only one type of employee contribution to the organization. Following this logic, it does not make sense to think about one "best" standard for performance measurement. Instead, multiple types of performance standards probably should be used, with the mix dependent on the strategic mission of the organization. In a survey of employee preferences concerning appraisal criteria, 42.3% most preferred to be evaluated based on their results, 30.4% based upon their behaviors, and 27.3% based on traits (Gosselin et al., 1997). The diversity of preferences across the three categories is somewhat surprising. Using a mix of appraisal standards is one way that organizations can address this diversity of employee preferences concerning this topic.

An example of this mix can be seen at General Electric and Westinghouse (Stonich, 1984). In mature business units within these companies, where the emphasis was on maintaining the current position in the industry, results-oriented performance measures such as profit, cash flow, and market share were used. On the other hand, in high-growth business units within these companies, behavior-oriented measures of performance were needed to measure the effectiveness of long-term goals such as effective research and development and the creation of new marketing opportunities. Another example comes from Praxair. Praxair had a results-oriented, MBO performance management program that had been emulated by other firms. However, in the late 1990s, Praxair changed their MBO program to one where there was equivalent weight given to how goals were achieved (i.e., the behaviors and skills involved) as to the actual goals and results obtained (Harris et al., 1999).

In conclusion, it does not appear that there is one best measure of performance to use for merit pay decisions. Thus, a "multiple" measurement strategy will probably produce the best outcomes. As discussed, there are a number of factors that can be considered in deciding which measure(s) to use. From a measurement standpoint, the greatest caution needs to be used with relative and trait-based measures of performance, with less concern if well-developed measures of employee behaviors and/or results are used. As we discuss later in this chapter, there are also indicators that can be used to assess the adequacy of the performance standards that have been selected. A preferred strategy for selecting performance standards might therefore be one of reasoned selection, followed by an empirical evaluation of the standards selected.

Alternative Measures of Performance for Merit Pay

Along with the general issues just reviewed, some specific issues need to be addressed as well. These issues center around the question of what actually constitutes performance under a merit pay plan. Heated conversations in many organizations point to the controversies that can arise concerning how organizations define individual contributions. Unfortunately, only limited research has been conducted to guide decision-makers. Nevertheless, these issues need to be considered and dealt with if a merit pay plan is to be effective. John Campbell and colleagues (Campbell, 1990; Campbell et al., 1993) clearly articulate the need for a model defining employee performance that is relevant to organizational effectiveness. In this section, we look at these alternative, and potentially controversial, issues in performance measurement for purposes of merit pay.

Promotions

It is no surprise that people in organizations usually receive a pay increase in conjunction with an upward promotion. What is less clear, however, is *why* people receive a pay increase for a promotion. Is the pay increase due to the acquisition of new skills, an increase in job responsibilities, good performance in the previous position, or some combination of these factors? If a pay increase for a promotion is granted at the same time as a merit increase, the employee will not be able to figure out which of these factors is being reinforced, and which are most likely to contribute to subsequent raises.

In a study of a large manufacturer, performance, promotions, and salary increases were shown to be related to one another (Medoff & Abraham, 1981). This suggests that performance may be used to make both promotional and merit pay decisions. Certainly, it may be desirable to reward employees for both promotions and merit. It may not be seen that way to employees, however, if only *one* merit pay increase is given to reward *both* promotion and merit. If only one rather than two pay increases are granted, then promotions may be a controversial measure of performance, because a promotional increase is viewed by employees as a substitute for, rather than an addition to, merit pay.

Seniority

Organizations seem to differ in how they treat seniority, or length of service with an organization, in merit pay decisions. In some studies, there is no observed relationship between merit pay and seniority, in other studies there is a positive relationship, and in others a negative relationship (R. Heneman, 1990). Regardless of whether or how seniority is used in merit pay, it invites controversy.

If seniority *is* used, at least in part, to determine merit increases, it is controversial. The use of seniority runs contrary to the evidence presented by some empirical research on the relationship between traditional measures of performance and seniority. In a study of two large manufacturing organizations, Medoff and Abraham (1980) found little evidence of a positive or negative relationship between performance and seniority. Three metanalytic studies (where results from previous studies are combined) produced conflicting findings. First, Gordon and Johnson (1982) found no evidence to support either a positive or a negative relationship between seniority and performance. Second, Quiñones et al. (1995) found a sizeable (mean $r = 0.43$) correlation between amount of work experience and employee performance. Third, Sturman (2003) found contrasting results for jobs with high versus low levels of complexity. For jobs with high complexity, amount of job experience became a stronger predictor of job performance over time. That is, individual performance increased over time for experienced individuals working in complex jobs. For jobs low in complexity, seniority was only a valid predictor of performance for individuals with low levels of organizational tenure. In short, the data do not support old arguments that senior employees are either more or less productive. Interested readers are encouraged to consult the following references for a more detailed discussion of these issues: Quiñones et al. (1995), Sturman (2003), and Tesluk and Jacobs (1998).

If merit pay is given based on seniority, the organization may fail to contain compensation costs. More senior employees tend to be at higher levels in the pay grade. If they all get higher increases, overall merit increases may exceed the maximum level permissible under company policy for that pay range (discussed in Chapter 5).

On the other hand, it may not be prudent to totally avoid using seniority in merit pay decisions. As pointed out by Mitchell (1989), implicit contract theory (covered in Chapter 2) suggests one reason why employers may want to consider seniority. Employers providing smaller pay increases to less senior employees could motivate these employees to remain with the firm by holding out the "carrot" of more substantial pay increases later.

Merit increases can be considered "prizes," and relative comparisons help employees gauge how successful they need to be to secure a valued merit increase. Tournament models of competitive pay situations (Lazear & Rosen, 1981) suggest that relative comparisons are considered by employees in determining the level of effort to expend at work. Employees assess the performance of others in order to determine their chances of capturing a tournament prize. Research by Schmidt et al. (1988) addressed whether seniority should or should not be used. Using a large military data set and a sensitive measure of seniority based on months rather than years, they found that several different measures of job performance were positively related to seniority for the first 12 months or so on the job. From that point on, however, up to the 5-year mark, there was little change in performance due to seniority. These data suggest that seniority could be considered as a measure of performance for relatively new employees. This concept is also consistent with the common practice of paying new employees according to seniority, until they reach the average salary in the market. From then on, they are paid according to traditional performance ratings, without regard to seniority.

Market Worth

Sometimes merit increases do not simply reflect an individual's contribution to the organization, but indicate the individual's worth on the outside market as well. Examples of this practice come from both research and the field. Landau and Leventhal (1976) found in a laboratory study that larger merit increases were granted to employees with more attractive job offers in the external labor market. In 1981, both Ford Motor Company and General Motors Corporation gave merit pay raises to salaried employees to try to retain the services of good performers who were leaving for better-paying jobs in other industries ("Two automakers," 1981). Bates (2003c) discusses creative ways that organizations can reward (and hopefully retain) their top performers.

For some jobs, there is a certain logic to basing pay increases on the employee's worth in the external market, because it is difficult to separate an individual's contribution inside the organization from his or her contribution outside the organization. An example here might be scientists or professors whose research has generally equal value across the labor market. Along these lines, Hansen (1988) distinguished between internally determined and externally determined merit for professors. The stature of a university is enhanced by having professors provide good service to the university (typically in the form of teaching and service within the university), and by having professors whose contributions (typically in the form of research) are valued by other institutions as well. Internal merit pay could be provided in the former case, while external merit pay could be provided in the latter case. This strategy could be accomplished by soliciting information on a professor's performance from both internal and external sources. This is a common practice in promotion and tenure decisions at universities and could be extended to merit increase decisions as well in other organizational environments.

However, basing merit increases on the market, or market adjustments as they are sometimes called, also has its problems. One problem is that market value may be determined by forces outside the control of employees. For example, a professor of engineering may have great market value because of a shortfall in the engineering labor supply rather than because of their performance. In fact, there are few people being graduated with PhDs in engineering. Given the scarcity of engineers with doctorates; their worth on the market is high. Some may argue that market adjustments are unfair because they do not reflect actual performance, but are forces that cannot be controlled in the outside labor market.

Organizational Citizenship Behavior

Dennis Organ (1988, 1997) argued that an important contribution that employees can (and do) make to their organizations is organizational citizenship behavior. This type of behavior includes activities above and beyond those normally required by the organization. Examples include altruism (e.g., covering for a sick coworker), conscientiousness (e.g., keeping a clean work station), and courtesy (e.g., providing people with information in advance). Such behaviors are less likely to be expected behaviors, and are less likely to be included in a written job description (Werner, 1994).

An interesting and debatable question is whether organizational citizenship behavior should be rewarded by organizations (Werner, 2000; Thomas et al., 2019), and therefore included in merit pay systems. Although not calling these contributions organizational citizenship behavior, Patten (1977) argued that these behaviors should be rewarded with merit pay, as they contribute greatly to the success of organizations. Research has demonstrated that supervisors consider both "task" and "citizenship" behaviors when making overall ratings of employee performance (Barksdale & Werner, 2001; Werner, 1994). Other research has extended these findings to the process of making pay increase decisions (Allen & Rush, 1998; Kiker & Motowidlo, 1999). That is, the highest raises were recommended for employees who were strong on task performance, and also engaged in high levels of organizational citizenship behaviors. In another study, the highest raises were recommended for individuals with a good reputation who were also observed engaging in helpful behaviors (Johnson et al., 2002). On the other hand, it might be argued that since these behaviors are not, by definition, required by the organization, it would be unfair to monetarily reward those who voluntarily engage in these activities.

Our view is that citizenships *are* properly viewed as a part of overall employee performance (Arvey & Murphy, 1998; Barksdale & Werner, 2001; Campbell et al., 1993; N. Podsakoff et al., 2009). However, as Organ (1997, p. 91) noted, citizenship behaviors are "less likely to be considered an enforceable job requirement," and are "less likely than task performance to be regarded by the performer as leading confidently to systemic rewards." Organizations that choose to include citizenship behaviors within their definitions of employee performance need to be clear in defining the performance dimensions that they wish for employees to be evaluated against (i.e., both task and citizenship dimensions), as well as in how these dimensions will be utilized or combined for merit pay purposes. This will by no means be an easy process, and therefore invites some controversy, as mentioned above (Elsner Twesme et al., 2021; Johnson et al., 2002; Werner, 2000).

Typical versus Maximum Performance

Performance levels of employees are usually not constant over time (e.g., Rothe, 1946). Instead, performance varies over time. One way to think of this variance in performance is in terms of typical and maximum performance (Kirk & Brown, 2003; Ployhart et al., 2001; Sackett et al., 1988). Typical performance takes place when individuals are not being evaluated, not attempting to work as hard as they can, for extended periods of time. Maximum performance takes place when individuals are being evaluated, working as hard as they can, for short periods of time. The research on this distinction indicates that supervisors attend more to maximum than typical performance (DiNisi et al., 1984), and that supervisory ratings are more closely related to maximum than typical performance (Sackett et al., 1988).

This line of research raises the policy issue of which level(s) of performance *should* be rewarded with merit pay. It would appear, based on this research, that maximum performance is being rewarded more than typical performance. In some jobs, this may be appropriate. For example, a sponsor of a professional bowler may be most concerned with maximum performance during a nationally televised event. In other jobs, however, typical performance may be of greater importance. An example here might be a nurse in a long-term health care facility, where the issues are more about patient care over extended periods of time, without much direct supervision.

The point is that maximum performance receives more rating attention than average, consistent, and regular performance. This imbalance is also most likely reflected in merit pay decisions, as pay increases are based on ratings. This practice may or may not coincide with the intended policy of merit pay in a particular organization. Therefore, the issue needs to be carefully considered. If the intent of merit pay is to reward typical performance, performance reviews should be conducted more than once a year, so that a representative sample of total performance can be obtained for merit decisions. Other administrative practices such as diary keeping, described later in this chapter, should also be followed to ensure that typical performance is being evaluated.

Job Level

In a literature review, R. Heneman (1990) reported a positive relationship between job level and size of merit pay increase. For example, Gerhart and Milkovich (1989) found that larger merit increases were granted to employees in higher-rather than lower-level positions for a large manufacturing company. Certainly, this relationship is reasonable if job level is related to merit increase dollars. You would also expect larger absolute increases in merit pay for high-level jobs because the base salary is larger in these high-level jobs. Even if a high- and low-level job receive the same percentage merit increase, the total amount for each differs because the absolute amount is a percentage of base salary. The relationship between job level and the amount of merit increase is shown in Table 4.5. While both the production manager and production associate receive a 4% merit increase, the absolute amount of the increase is larger for the manager ($4,800) than for the associate ($1,840), because of the higher base pay level of the manager's job ($120,000) versus the associate's job ($46,000). In other words, the same percentage increase applied to two job levels will always result in a larger absolute increase for the job with the higher pay level.

The relationship between job level and merit may be troublesome when merit pay decisions are made in the form of a percentage increase, rather than in the form of absolute merit dollars. This would be depicted in Table 4.5 if the percentage increase was, say, 6%, rather than the 4% shown for the production manager. A relationship between job level and percentage increase suggests that job level is being used as a measure of performance, with higher-level jobs receiving larger percentage merit increases. Whether this practice is desirable depends on other human resource practices. A positive relationship between job level and merit may be desirable if the better performers are promoted. Since most promotion systems are less than perfect, however, this assumption is a controversial one. A positive relationship may not be desirable if people already receive adequate pay for the level of job they hold. The level of job is sometimes used to determine the base wage or salary, using a procedure known as job evaluation, which is described in Chapter 5. A positive relationship between job level and merit pay may not be desirable in this situation because people would be paid for job level twice—once for merit pay and once based on job evaluation.

Table 4.5

Comparison of Percentage and Absolute Merit Increases by Job Level

				Merit Pay		
Title	Job Level	Performance	Current Salary ($)	Increase (%)	Amount of Increase ($)	New Salary ($)
Production Manager	6	5	120,000	4	4,800	124,800
Production Associate	3	5	46,000	4	1,840	47,840

Immediate versus Distant Past Performance

A question that arises in the administration of a merit pay plan is how far back in time should the employer go to reward performance. Based on limited empirical research, it seems that allocators should look at performance over multiple merit pay periods. Birnbaum (1983) reported that, for samples of professors and students, allocators tended to look at the amount recipients were underpaid in the past in determining current merit increases. This may have been done by allocators to restore perceptions of equity for the recipient (see Chapter 2 for a review of equity theory).

By considering performance prior to the current merit pay period, the allocator can resolve previous inequities in merit increase decisions. But, when distant rather than immediate performance is considered, it may just as likely create equity problems as solve them. In effect, performance may be double counted. An employee may receive an increase for the same episode of good performance in two pay periods. An inequity may be created if other employees only receive one merit increase for the same level of performance. One way this situation could be handled would be to offer "equity" adjustments on a limited basis, under a policy that takes into account exceptional circumstances. Exceptional circumstances could include, for example, a monumental feat performed by an employee two merit pay periods ago that was inadequately compensated at the time because of a limited merit pay budget. Such an approach, however, could invite bargaining behaviors by the allocators and recipients. Hence, an equity adjustment should only be made under exceptional circumstances that have been documented and approved.

Policy Guidelines for Alternative Performance Measures

As shown in the preceding section, it is not always clear which measures of performance are appropriate for merit pay decisions. Additional research is needed to guide decision-makers as to which criteria to use. Given the potentially controversial nature of some criteria, it appears that not only is further discussion of the issues critical, but it is incumbent on policymakers to communicate the resulting decisions. If an organization has not clearly communicated its position on these issues, the organization may encounter unanticipated (and likely undesirable) outcomes with their merit system. As shown by reinforcement theory (reviewed in Chapter 2), organizations are likely to encounter different outcomes depending on which measures of performance lead to rewards. Also, feelings of inequity may result if employees consider these measures as inputs, while the organization does not.

Adequacy of Performance Measures

Fortunately for decision-makers in organizations, the process of performance measurement has established criteria that can be used to evaluate the adequacy of the measures that are developed. While judgments are, of course, required in deciding which measures to use, these judgments can be guided by a number of indicators of adequacy, discussed in this section. These indicators concern the validity or extent to which performance standards measure what they purport to measure. Indicators of or approaches to assessing validity at various levels of performance measurement are shown in Figure 4.1.

Figure 4.1 is a guide for the discussion of the adequacy of performance measures. Each indicator provides an important and unique piece of information for deciding which performance standards to use. In line with the writings of others on criterion and validity issues (Binning & Barrett, 1989; James, 1973; Landy, 1986), we argue that multiple indicators need to be used to make inferences about the validity or adequacy of performance measures.

Figure 4.1

Indicators of Validity at Various Levels of Performance Measurement.

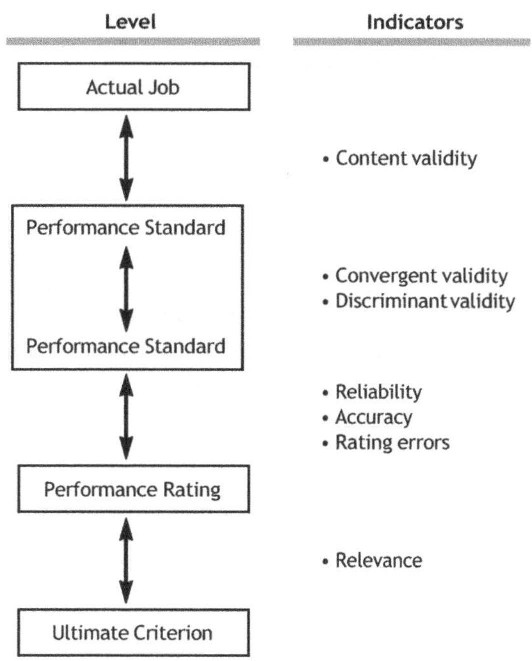

Content Validity

One indicator of the adequacy of performance measures is known as content validity. As shown in Figure 4.1, content validity refers to the job relatedness of performance standards, or the extent to which performance standards are related to the actual job. A numerical estimate of content validity can be generated using formulas by Aiken (1980) and Lawshe (1975), which rely on judgments of the job relatedness of performance standards by subject-matter experts. An example of both Aiken's and Lawshe's procedures is found in Distefano et al. (1983). These authors developed a behavioral rating scale for aides in psychiatric hospitals. Job experts generated behavior-based performance standards. In turn, another group of job experts rated aides using these standards. These ratings were then used to calculate the degree to which these standards were job-related using the Lawshe and Aiken formulas.

To illustrate the importance of content validity, you need only envision a situation where performance standards are not job related. Under such a system, employees are likely to feel that their duties on the job are inconsequential, and perform accordingly. Merit pay may, in turn, reinforce non-job-related behaviors, such as political behaviors intended only to garnish a larger pay raise.

Convergent and Discriminant Validity

Two other indicators, convergent and discriminant validity, have to do with the relationship among performance standards as shown in Figure 4.1. These indicators are used to show the degree to which performance standards are measuring the same construct. A construct is a summary label attached to a category of employee performance. For example, "attention to detail" is a construct or category of employee performance that might be valued for many jobs. Convergent validity refers to the degree to which performance standards, thought to be similar to one another, is indeed correlated with one another. A correlation shows the strength of the relationship between performance standards. If performance standards are measuring the same construct, they should be highly correlated with one another. Discriminant validity refers to the degree to which performance standards, thought to be dissimilar to one another, are indeed uncorrelated with one another. If performance standards are measuring the same construct, then they should not correlate with dissimilar standards. In short, similar measures of performance should be more strongly correlated to one another than dissimilar measures of performance.

An empirical procedure to test for convergent and discriminant validity is the multitrait–multimethod matrix developed by Campbell and Fiske

(1959). Refinements to the original procedure can be found in Schmitt and Stults (1986). An example of the statistics involved with this procedure as it relates to performance standards is found in Kavanaugh et al. (1971).

A descriptive rather than statistical example may help to clarify the concepts of convergent and discriminant validity. For example, service supervisors in a state government are responsible for managing vocational rehabilitation counselors and their own caseload of clients (Moore & Heneman, 1983). Two standards by which supervisors are held accountable for the management aspects of their job are performance planning and performance problem solving. If these two standards, and others like them, do indeed measure management, they should be correlated with one another. If they are correlated, then this is evidence for the convergent validity of the management aspect of the work. It would also be expected that these two standards would not be as strongly related to how well the service supervisors provide services to their own individual clients. After all, the handling of clients involves a different set of skills and activities than the management of subordinates. The extent to which performance planning and performance problem solving are more strongly correlated with one another than they are with how well the supervisors provide services to their clients is evidence for the discriminant validity of the management aspect of work.

The importance of establishing the convergent and discriminant validity of ratings was highlighted by Kavanaugh and colleagues (1971). Convergent and discriminate validity enables organizations to be efficient in the development of performance standards. In terms of time and money, it is more efficient for an organization to use fewer than more standards to measure performance. That is, of course, assuming the same performance constructs can be measured using fewer standards. Tests for convergent and discriminant validity help assess to what degree this assumption is a reasonable one.

Reliability

At a general level, reliability refers to the consistency of ratings. As shown in Figure 4.1, ratings are the actual values assigned to performance standards by evaluators reviewing employee performance. Consistency can be thought of in terms of consistency across time, raters, and/or performance standards. Depending on which perspective you take regarding consistency, that perspective will define the form of reliability that should be calculated.

There are three primary forms of reliability. *Test–retest reliability* looks at the stability of ratings over time. To examine stability, ratings in one time period are correlated with ratings in another time period, given by the same set of raters. *Interrater reliability* refers to the consistency of ratings across different raters. It is assessed by calculating the correlation between the ratings made by different raters who are evaluating the same employee and using the same performance standards. *Internal consistency reliability* captures the degree to which measures of the same performance standard (e.g., different items or questions) are correlated with one another. The formulas needed to calculate these forms of reliability can be found in any test construction text (e.g., Ghiselli et al., 1981; Nunnally & Bernstein, 1994).

The importance of reliability to the merit pay process can be examined in at least two ways. First, the reliability of the performance measure used for merit pay can be viewed as the upper boundary or limit to the strength of the relationship between performance ratings and merit increases (Rothstein, 1990). Second, the less consistent you are in measuring performance, the less likelihood you have of linking pay increases to actual employee performance. If employees are unsure as to how you measured their performance, how can you expect them to see any relationship between their pay and performance? This question is at the heart of the notion of reliability as an "upper bound." It should be noted, however, that the magnitude of the impact of reliability on the actual relationship between pay and performance may not be very substantial when the reliability of performance measures varies by a small amount (Schwab & Olson, 1990).

Even though the impact of reliability on the actual pay-for-performance relationship may not be that strong, there is a second and perhaps more compelling reason for ensuring reliability. If ratings are not reliable in a merit pay plan, or not perceived as reliable, it is unlikely that employees are going to accept the decisions being made. Employees are likely to reject a merit pay plan when merit increases depend more on the timing of ratings, the rater being used, or the standard being used, than upon the actual performance level of the employee. As shown by Folger and Konovsky (1989) and discussed in Chapter 6, procedures as well as outcomes are important to employee acceptance of a merit pay plan. Reliability is one important component of the procedures used in determining merit pay.

Accuracy

As shown in Figure 4.1, another indicator of the adequacy of performance measures is the accuracy with which ratings are made of performance. Accuracy refers to the relationship between *ratings* of employee performance and actual, correct, or "true" employee performance (R. Heneman et al., 1987; Murphy & Balzer, 1989). The stronger the relationship between ratings and true performance, the greater the accuracy. Because accuracy implies some true or correct measure of performance, there is considerable controversy as to how to best assess accuracy (Kruglanski, 1989; Padgett & Ilgen, 1989; Sulsky & Balzer, 1988). A common method of assessing accuracy is to use using ratings by "experts" who view the (often videotaped) performance of a sample of employees in simulated or actual work settings. These ratings from experts become true scores, which are then used to gauge the accuracy of others' ratings of the same performance (cf. Werner, 1994).

Although problematic to assess, the concept of accuracy is certainly an important one when it comes to the adequacy of performance measures. If performance ratings are not accurate in a merit pay plan, pay increases may be allocated to the wrong employees (Ball & Heneman, 1988). That is, employees incorrectly rated as good performers may receive large pay increases, while employees incorrectly rated as poor performers may receive small increases. The accuracy of raters' decisions may need to be assessed from time to time using expert ratings to prevent incorrect decisions.

Rating Errors

Like reliability and accuracy, rating errors also have to do with ratings of performance standards as shown in Figure 4.1. In the discussion of reliability, consistency in ratings was portrayed as a desirable property of performance measures. This is true, however, only up to a point. If consistent ratings are granted in the face of true performance that is inconsistent, this may be a rating error. For example, a manager may rate an employee as excellent for three consecutive years. But actual employee performance may have been excellent for two of the three years, and average for one year. In this case, there was an error committed because while the ratings were consistent, actual employee performance was inconsistent. Major rating errors include halo, leniency, and central tendency. The absence of these rating errors is sometimes used to assess the adequacy of performance measures. Each of these rating errors will be described below.

Halo error takes place when a rater generalizes from one aspect of an employee's performance to other aspects of an employee's performance without regard for the true or actual level of employee performance. Examples could include rating professors good in teaching because they are good in research, or rating supervisors good in management duties because they are good in the technical duties of their job. Sometimes this pattern of ratings does not turn out to be an error (Nathan & Tippins, 1990). Some people do indeed perform at the same level in other aspects of their work. However, this pattern of rating can also be an error. People good at research are not necessarily good at teaching, and people good at technical work are not necessarily good at management.

Another rating error, known as *leniency error*, is a specific type of halo error. Positive leniency takes place when employees are rated high on one or more aspects of their performance, while negative leniency (also called strictness) takes place when employees are rated low on one or more aspects of their performance. In both cases, these patterns of ratings are errors if they run contrary to the pattern of ratings of true performance. One possible reason for these errors is that they may allow raters to justify a large merit increase for themselves. If a rater commits positive leniency error, the rater can tell the boss what a good job they have done at managing their subordinates. If a rater commits negative leniency, the rater can use poor-performing subordinates as an excuse for his or her poor performance.

Along with leniency, *central tendency* is another specific type of halo error. When central tendency error takes place, employees are rated average on one or more aspects of their performance. In a sense, this is a "play-it-safe" approach for raters. It is difficult to be accused of favoritism under this scenario. It is an error, however, if true employee performance is not average.

While it may be easy to see why these errors occur, the explanations do not minimize the problems that rating errors cause with merit pay. Examples of these problems abound in organizations. Accusations of favoritism and discrimination take place when leniency error is present. Good performers feel cheated when the supervisor commits central tendency error. Managers are upset with other managers who commit positive leniency errors and, as a result, get a larger share of the merit budget than those who did not commit the error. These examples point to the importance of diagnosis and correction of rating errors.

To have a high degree of certainty that the rating patterns just described are rating errors rather than ratings of actual employee performance, it is essential to calculate these errors relative to true scores (Pulakos et al., 1986). However, true scores are often difficult to develop (R. Heneman et al., 1987). Consequently, inferences need to be made, in the absence of true scores, as to the degree of rating errors actually present. For example, you might infer that positive leniency is at work when the rater gives high ratings to all aspects of an employee's performance. This inference might be further strengthened if there is evidence that the rater not only rates all aspects of one employee's performance high, but also rates all aspects of all employees' performance high. While you may encounter a work group where all members perform well at all aspects of their jobs, a more likely scenario is that some people perform better than others and that each person performs some aspects of their job better than other aspects. When inferences such as these can be safely made, it is possible to calculate rating errors without true scores. Formulas to calculate rating errors without true scores can be found in Saal et al. (1980).

An important task of the human resource function is to call such erroneous rating patterns to the attention of line managers. Performance appraisals should be collected and reviewed by Human Resource professionals. If troublesome or questionable patterns are detected, documentation and/or an explanation may be solicited to show that the pattern of ratings is not an error. If rating errors are revealed, the problem can be referred to the raters' supervisors for corrective action.

Relevance

The concept of relevance, as shown in Figure 4.1, refers to the relationship between performance ratings and some measure of an ultimate criterion (Thorndike, 1949). The ultimate criterion is the final or ultimate goal of the organization in terms of individual job performance. It is a more distant and abstract standard than traits, behaviors, and results, which are more immediate and measurable. It may be, for example, the overall contribution of the organization to the product or service market in which the organization competes. Relevance is similar to the notion of accuracy, as previously described, but with the major distinction that the measure of individual performance has been moved up to (i.e., linked with) an organizational-level measure of effectiveness.

Relevance is usually less than perfect because of two factors known as deficiency and contamination (Brogden & Taylor, 1950). *Deficiency* refers to variance in the ultimate criterion that is not captured in the performance ratings. Ratings may not capture all of the ultimate criterion because raters may, for example, have limited opportunity to observe employee performance. As an illustration, supervisors often have a large number of employees reporting to them and, as a result, have limited opportunity to observe the performance of any one employee.

Contamination refers to variance in performance ratings that is unrelated to the ultimate criterion. Ratings may be contaminated, for example, when they capture aspects of the performance outside the control of the individual employee. In an outside sales position, the number of sales made may be more closely linked to the state of the economy than to the effort of the salesperson. As would be predicted from expectancy theory (reviewed in Chapter 2), pay is unlikely to motivate performance when performance is not under the control of the employee.

The relationship between the concepts of relevance, contamination, and deficiency is shown in Figure 4.2. As illustrated in this figure, the level of relevance for performance ratings depends on the amount of contamination and deficiency in ratings. There is a greater level of relevance possible when there is less deficiency and less contamination.

An example may help to clarify the concepts of contamination and deficiency. The National Football League (NFL) uses a passer rating system to evaluate the passing performance of quarterbacks in the NFL (Ordine, 1990; Pasteur & David, 2017; Stimel, 2009). Passing performance is assessed using four categories: completion percentage, touchdown percentage, interception percentage, and average gain per attempt. A rating for each category and an overall rating is determined by comparing a quarterback's performance to statistics of quarterback performance in the NFL and the old American Football League (from 1960 to 1971).

Figure 4.2.

The Relevance of Performance Ratings.

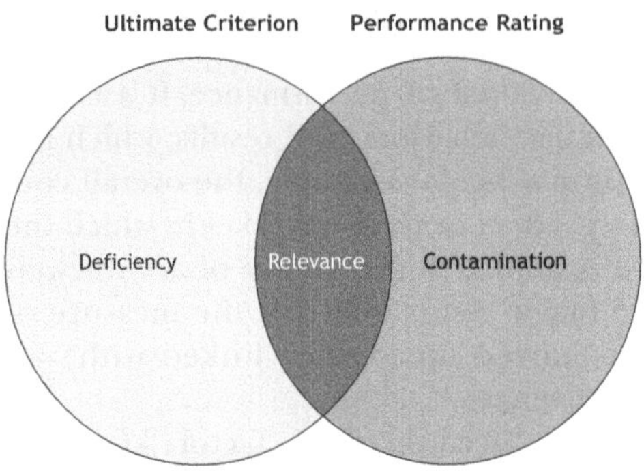

This rating system for quarterbacks has been controversial and disliked by some quarterbacks, since incentive bonuses are frequently based on these ratings (Ordine, 1990). Complaints about the system center around the concepts of contamination and deficiency. Some think that the ratings are unfair because the ratings are contaminated by the play of other players on the team. You would expect that the ratings would be higher for a quarterback with a high-performing offensive line than a quarterback with a low-performing offensive line. Others think that the ratings are unfair because they are a deficient measure of the total contribution of the quarterback to the performance of the team. Missing from the calculations are contributions other than passing, such as rushing yardage and play-calling ability.

In actual practice, relevance is a difficult, if not impossible, concept to measure, due to the abstract and distant nature of the ultimate criterion. Hence, unlike the other indicators reviewed, formulas are not available to assess relevance. Instead, relevance is inferred based on the conditions surrounding performance measurement. One way to do this is to look at the relationship between performance ratings and some intermediate representation of the ultimate criterion, such as the strategic mission of the organization. Another way to infer relevance is to look for an *absence of* conditions that are likely to lead to contamination and deficiency in ratings. The less present are contamination and deficiency, the higher the level of relevance. For example, we might expect relevance to be greater when supervisors have a small rather than large number of employees reporting to them. With a small number of employees, deficiency may be less because there may be a greater opportunity to observe each employee. In turn, the less likely that there is deficiency, the greater is the likelihood of relevant ratings.

While relevance is difficult to assess, it is essential to the merit pay process. If performance is viewed as being outside the control of the individual or not adequately reflecting actual contribution to the organization, then, as discussed in Chapter 2, it is doubtful that employees will be able to make the desired link between pay and performance.

Selecting an Indicator to Evaluate Performance Standards

Multiple indicators are needed to evaluate the validity or the adequacy of performance standards. Each of the indicators provides a unique bit of information about the adequacy of performance measures. To put it another way, there is no one best way to assess the adequacy of performance measures. Furthermore, the research evidence indicates that indicators are not substitutes for one another. For example, it has been shown across many studies that the magnitude of the relationship between halo error and rating accuracy is modest (Murphy & Balzer, 1989; Werner, 1994; Goffin et al., 2003). Even if halo error is reduced, accuracy is not always improved. Even the relationship among alternative measures of the same indicator may be modest. Pulakos and colleagues (1986) found this to be the case for alternative measures of halo error, while Murphy et al. (1982) found it also to be the case for alternative measures of rating accuracy. So, different ways to measure the same indicator of validity may lead to different results.

If you found our discussion of accuracy and relevance to be abstract, we wouldn't blame you, as these are difficult issues to describe and measure. Obviously, we would like to see organizational measures of performance be accurate and relevant, though documenting this can be challenging. Ideally, organizations would like to see their performance measures possess high levels of *each* of the indicators described above (and depicted in Figure 4.1). Realistically, we recognize that there is often not the time and resources available to collect data for all of these indicators for every performance measure. At a minimum, we would argue that organizations need to be confident about the *content validity* and *reliability* of all performance measures they use. It is crucial that there is confidence that the performance measures used are measuring the most important aspects of employee work (i.e., are content valid), and are doing so in a consistent or reliable fashion (Bowman, 1999).

The Upper Boundary of Performance Rating Validity

To interpret the results of studies designed to assess the adequacy of performance standards, it is useful to know what the upper bound, or maximum possible level, of validity is for performance ratings. Several attempts have been made to estimate the upper bound of performance rating validity using some of the alternative indicators of validity just reviewed. Even though different methodologies were used, the results were similar and suggest that the upper bound of validity for performance ratings is about 0.60, with a value of 0 representing no validity and a value of 1.00 representing perfect validity. What this value of 0.60 indicates is that about 36% (0.6 × 0.6) of the variability in the indicators being used to assess validity is due to performance ratings. Although it is a judgment call, a value of 0.60 can be viewed as a respectable level in human resource management research. Furthermore, this value of 0.60 is comparable to the validity of more objective performance indicators such as output (R. Heneman, 1986). However, although this value is "respectable," it must be acknowledged that this is the highest value that can be expected. It can be lower and, even at its highest value, it suggests that about 64% of the variability in standards being used to assess validity are due to factors *other than* performance ratings. What this means is that most measures of performance are less than perfect representations of the employee's ultimate performance contribution to the organization.

In one study, interrater reliability, convergent validity, and rating errors were assessed in near-perfect laboratory conditions (Borman, 1978). These conditions consisted of raters who were very knowledgeable about the jobs rated, had ample opportunity to observe performance, and used a well-developed rating scale. In another study, there were near-perfect field conditions (Weekly & Gier, 1989) to assess reliability, convergent validity, and discriminant validity. These conditions were found in a world-class figure-skating event where the judges were very experienced, well trained, and had excellent observational opportunities. A large-scale investigation by Rothstein (1990) for 9,975 ratees in 79 organizations examined the interrater reliability of a well-developed rating scale. King et al. (1980) conducted a review of several studies concerned with the reliability of single raters. As can be seen from these brief descriptions, a variety of different methodologies were used and, as previously noted, similar results were obtained. When a variety of different methods yield the same results, considerable confidence can be placed in the results (Jick, 1979). To reiterate, the upper limit for the validity of performance ratings appears to be around 0.60. This is a sobering statistic, with important implications for the effectiveness of merit pay plans.

Methods to Improve the Validity of Performance Standards

Although it may not be possible to develop performance standards with perfect validity for merit increase decisions, it is possible to take some steps that have been shown to be related to increases in the indicators of validity.

Such practices should also increase the perceived fairness and legal defensibility of an organization's performance measurement practices (Laguerre, 2022; Martin et al., 2000; Werner & Bolino, 1997). We now review these steps. They have to do with how the performance standards are used, as well as how they are developed. The way in which standards are used is as important, if not more important, than the standards themselves (Landy & Farr, 1980).

The steps shown here should also make it clear that the performance appraisal process is not without costs (cf. Coens & Jenkins, 2000). Efficiency wage theory (described in Chapter 2) suggests that there are administrative expenses when an organization attempts to monitor employee performance. These costs include the time and money needed to ensure that adequate performance measurement is taking place. In considering whether to use merit pay, an eye must be kept on anticipated costs, as well as anticipated productivity returns.

Linked to the Strategic Mission

One way to increase the relevance of ratings is to link performance standards and ratings to the strategic mission of the organization (Mueller-Hansen, 2020). The mission of the organization refers to a philosophical statement by upper-level decision-makers concerning the strategic direction of the organization. Schneier (1989b) provides an example from National Car Rental of how a mission statement can be translated into results- and behavior-oriented measures of performance. This example is shown in Figure 4.3.

In many organizations, a formal document known as a mission statement states what the mission of the organization is. It can be used to ground performance standards in the business of the organization and can also be used to make raters aware of desired end results. Henderson (1980) provides step-by-step instructions on how to do this, and these instructions are summarized in Figure 4.4. Examples of where procedures such as these have been followed are available (Harris et al., 1999; Hurwich, 1986; Schneier, 1989a, 1989b, Wilkinson, 1993; see also Chapter 2 in R. Heneman, 2001a).

Performance Management—Broader Than Performance Appraisal

The previous section introduced the idea of linking performance standards and rating to the strategic mission of the organization and, therefore, increasing the relevance of performance ratings. In this section, we expand on this idea under the broad label of performance management. The notion of performance management has grown popular (Bauwens et al., 2024;

Figure 4.3.

Strategic Performance Management: Linking Strategy to Performance Management and Recognition/Rewards (PMRR) Systems.

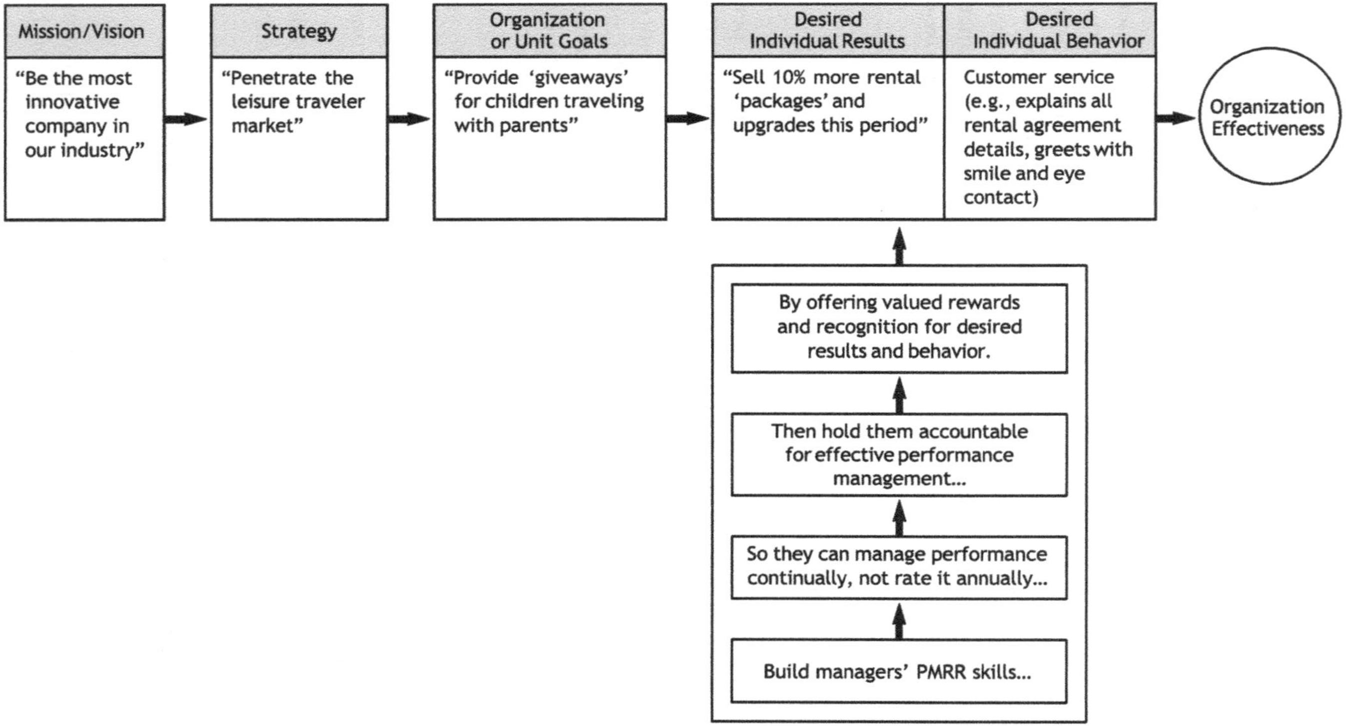

Source: Schneier (1989b). Reprinted with permission.

Figure 4.4.

Tying Organizational Mission to Workforce Productivity.

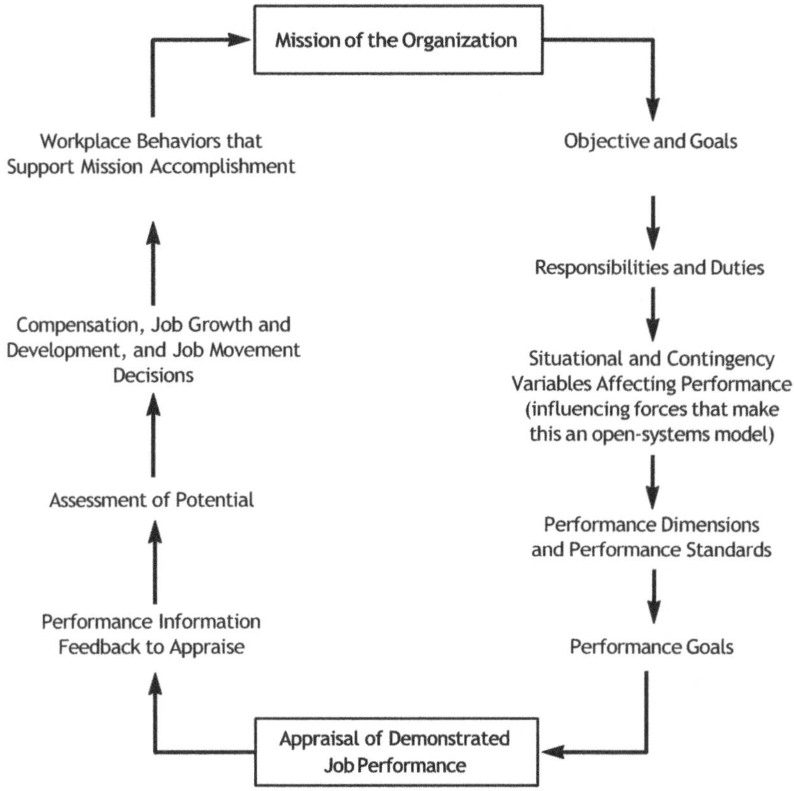

Source: Henderson, R. (1980). *Performance appraisal: Theory to practice* (p. 26). Reprinted by permission of Prentice Hall, Englewood Cliffs, NJ.

Brown et al., 2019; Maley et al., 2021; Pulakos & Battista, 2020; Pulakos et al., 2019; Werner, 2022). According to Murphy et al. (2019), a performance management system links "the goals and strategies of the organization with the goals and activities of every division, department, work team, and employee" (p. 24). It also exemplifies how performance appraisal (ratings) links with the goals and strategies of an organization. Figure 4.5. is a conceptual model of a *complete* performance management system that aligns with the above definition. There are several observations to note.

First, the model suggests that performance management consists of inverted, cascading triangles that represent the link between the goals and strategies of the organization and the goals and strategies of organizational units. Its cascading effect implies organizational goals drive successive unit objectives, ending with individual performance goals and behaviors. The bottom unit is traditionally known as performance appraisal (shown in the broken-lined rectangle). The arrow at the bottom extends upward to organizational units and the entire organization. It represents the flow of output data from company units to the top of the enterprise. Each unit contains indicators with performance data. Once the data are gathered, integrated, and analyzed, an overall index of company performance is calculated, providing decision-makers with the best course of action for the firm. Hence,

Figure 4.5.

A Conceptual Model of a Performance Management System for an Entire Organization. The Area in the Broken-Lined Rectangle Represents a Performance Appraisal System.

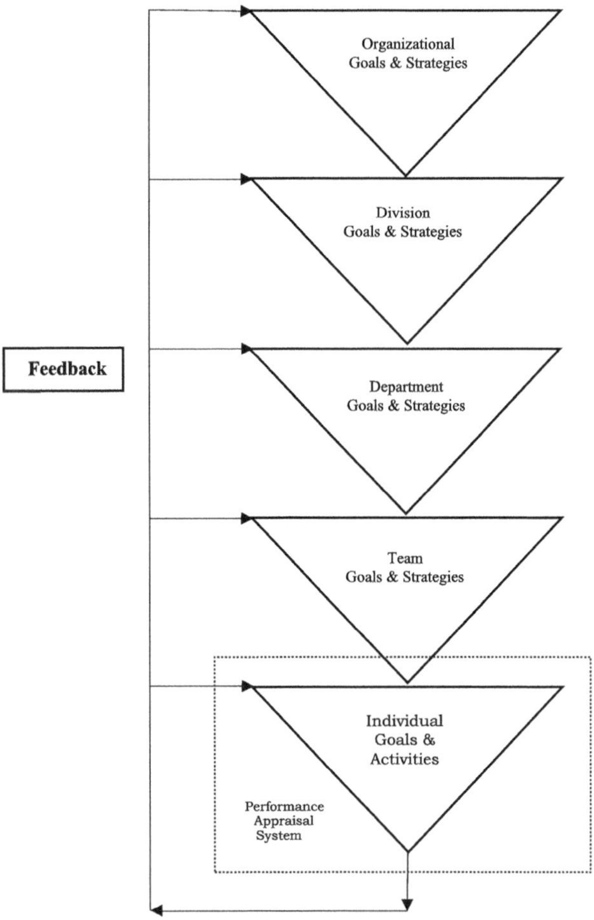

the model reflects how a performance appraisal/merit pay system can be directly linked to the entire organization.

Second, performance management and performance appraisal are not synonymous. The definition of performance management was introduced above. In contrast, performance appraisal focuses on two aspects of individual work. The first is time orientation, where evaluating employee achievements takes place over a period of time in the past, usually six months or one year (Murphy et al., 2019). The other, an orientation toward power, authority, and influence, is advisory, with employee input considered in previous activities and goals (Murphy et al., 2019). The bottom unit in Figure 4.5 constitutes a performance appraisal system (and by extension, merit pay). Conceptually, this is how performance ratings link with the organization's objectives and strategies. Below, we show how this connection is practically accomplished.

Third, a performance management system synthesizes concepts presented in Chapter 3 regarding business strategies and the notions above in linking performance ratings (appraisal) to the organization's strategic mission. The model also suggests that consequences of performance ratings (and by implication, merit pay) play a larger role in performance management. This was discussed in Chapter 2 when we introduced the transition of merit pay from a motivational tool in the past to a strategic perspective today.

So, how can performance ratings and organizational goals be systematically connected in practice? As mentioned above, while the previous section offers a good starting point, it omits additional depth and breadth based on the most recent scholarly writing and research. This section provides that additional depth and breadth. The process consists of two broad steps. It begins with understanding a conceptual model of a performance management system covering the entire organization, as the one in Figure 4.5. Then, it proceeds with the incorporation of a comprehensive measurement system located in the management and/or industrial-organizational literature. Although an exhaustive list and descriptions of these systems are beyond the scope of this book, we will mention a few popular ones. For a comprehensive view of assessing organizational performance (and the integration of organizational units), we refer the interested reader to Tatum (2018), from which much of the following is adopted.

Brinkerhoff and Dressler Seven-Step Process

Brinkerhoff (2015) and Brinkerhoff and Dressler (1990) provide a comprehensive measurement system based organizational productivity, consisting of detailed measures of outputs and inputs. It also includes measures for white collar and professional work. The authors' approach integrates measures from organizational units—individual, team, department, division—to form an overall performance metric. Note that the individual unit denotes performance ratings and goals (performance appraisal system). The measurement system consists of seven steps:

1. Start with a mission statement to develop measurement system.
2. Understand customer expectations.
3. Identify key outputs that express customer needs.
4. Understand how inputs transform into outputs.
5. Select output measures.
6. Select input measures.
7. Construct a productivity index of outputs to inputs.

Performance Indexing

Performance indexing (Tatum, 2018; Tatum & Nebeker, 2002; Tatum et al., 1996) derives from Felix and Rigg's (1983) objectives matrix (OMX), a productivity measurement system. Similar to the Brinkerhoff and Dressler approach above, performance indexing can identify and measure outputs of white collar positions and integrate the performance of organizational units (including individual units) to derive an overall index of organizational effectiveness. A useful aspect of this system is the ability to jointly assess the performance of work teams and their members. These assessments, in turn, may be used for team incentives and merit pay awards.

Productivity Measurement and Enhancement System (ProMES)

ProMES (Arapovic-Johansson et al., 2020; Pritchard, 1990; Pritchard et al., 1989; Schermling & Scaduto, 2016) follows the two measurement systems above in that ProMES identifies and measures indicators of organizational units (Including individual measures). It also accommodates metrics of goals for professional positions. An interesting aspect of the system is the use of contingencies, graphs showing the relationship between the amount of an indicator (an output measure similar to those in the measurement systems above) and effectiveness of that indicator. Contingencies form quantitative feedback for identifying unit effectiveness. The aggregation of effectiveness data from contingencies are compiled to form an overall index of organizational success.

In conclusion, this section emphasizes several important points:

1. The use and effectiveness of merit pay should consider the entire organization. Advanced technology, recent scholarly writing and research, and more sophisticated research tools make it possible to

look beyond a simple relationship between merit pay and individual performance. Performance appraisal (and by implication, merit pay) should be linked to an organization's strategic mission, therefore, improving content validity in performance standards and ratings.

2. Performance appraisal and performance management are not equivalent. Performance management systems identify, measure, and integrate all organizational units. Performance appraisals focus on individual behavior and goals. Merit pay, by definition, must relate to performance appraisal before it *can* link to other organizational indicators. Reciprocally, a performance management system without individual ratings cannot accommodate a merit pay plan.
3. As a matter of practice, organizations considering a performance management system ought to rely on conceptual models and measurement system systems found in the scholarly literature.
4. The measurement systems mentioned above consist of common elements that should be considered for a sound performance management system. First, all organizational units ought to have reliable and valid indicators. Second, the system must be systematically linked from the top of the company to the bottom (to include a performance ratings) with a feedback loop. Third, the system must accommodate the output and performance of white collar positions and other non-professional jobs (e.g., administrative support).

Job Analysis

A review of textbooks, court cases, and research in performance appraisal indicates that it is essential for performance standards to be based on job analysis for validity to be improved (Bernardin & Matt, 1985; Posthuma et al., 2018; Werner & Bolino, 1997; Williams & Werner, 2022). Unfortunately, this prescription does not appear to be widely followed (Bernardin & Matt, 1985; Posthuma et al., 2018; Werner, 2024).

Job analysis refers to procedures used to come up with a systematic description of the duties and requirements of a job. One method of job analysis that job analysts believe to be effective in establishing performance standards (Levine et al., 1983) is the critical-incident technique (Flanagan, 1954). With this approach, job experts are asked to generate lists of highly effective and ineffective behaviors observed in the past. In turn, these behaviors, or incidents, are used to develop behavior-based measures of performance, such as the frequency-of-behavior scale shown in this chapter, behavioral observation scales (Latham & Wexley, 1994), and behaviorally anchored rating scales (Smith & Kendall, 1963). Hence, performance standards based on the critical-incident technique are very job related and should be more likely to lead to more accurate (Osburn, Timmreck, & Bigby, 1981) and reliable (Borman & Dunnette, 1975) ratings than non-job-related performance standards.

Cognitive task analysis (CTA), a form of job analysis, has gained attention in research and practice, especially since many jobs today are knowledge based. These jobs usually are cognitively demanding and require formal training and education. CTA employs various interviews and observations to capture strategy differences between experts and novices, based on explicit and implicit knowledge, in completing complex tasks (Clark et al., 2008; Morgeson et al., 2020). The captured knowledge is most often transferred to training or the development of expert systems. However, gathered knowledge may also be used to develop more precise performance standards that can guide raters on rating employee performance on complex jobs, such as, *healthcare providers* (Swaby et al., 2022), *pilots* (Seamster et al., 2017), and *software engineers* (Karambir et al., 2024). Hence, greater precision in performance measures should yield higher validity.

Multiple Raters

A common prescription in performance appraisal/management is to use multiple raters, and this prescription appears to be used by organizations to a moderate degree (Bernardin & Matt, 1985; Werner & Bolino, 1997; Bayo-Moriones et al., 2020). Typically, the immediate supervisor is the only rater. Others can, however, be used to generate ratings including peers, incumbents, subordinates, customers, and clients.

Current Trends in Merit Pay

Competency Modeling: The Death of Job Analysis?

A recent understanding of jobs has surfaced under the broad label of competency modeling. Moreover, much debate has since ensued (Arribas-Aguila et al., 2024; Morgeson et al., 2020; Shippmann et al., 2000).

A competency model (CM) is a framework that defines the knowledges, skills, abilities, and behaviors required for successful employee performance (Shippmann et al., 2000). A traditional job analysis (JA) also yields comparable information. So, what are key similarities and differences between CM and JA? Is one method superior to the other? The results of two seminal studies address these questions. Sanchez and Levine (2009) compared job analysis and competency modeling and noted six key differences based on the following dimensions:

1. Purpose: JA focuses on better understanding and measuring work assignments. CM concentrates on how work assignments are performed to match the organization's business strategies.
2. View of the job: JA views the job as a fixed object to be described. CM views the job as a dynamic role to be enacted by each employee.
3. Focus: The focus of JA is solely the job. CM focuses on the performance of jobs in the organization based on certain behavioral themes that connect jobs to the firm's business strategies.
4. Time orientation: JA looks at the past, while CM concentrates on the future.
5. Performance level: JA highlights typical performance. CM focuses on maximum performance.
6. Measurement approach: JA relies on content validity (judgment) for measuring job characteristics. CM concentrates on construct validity, a view of developing behavioral themes of jobs that ostensibly depend on statistical procedures.

Overall, CM can be more dynamic, future-oriented, and organizationally-focused than JA. Rather than merely describing jobs, CM guides employees toward values and high-level performance that align with company objectives and strategies.

In another study, Shippmann et al. (2000) asked several subject matter experts to judge the similarities and differences between CM and JA on the following characteristics: method of investigation, type of descriptor, procedures for developing descriptor content, level of detail of descriptors, link to business goals and strategies, content review, ranking of descriptor importance, assessment of reliability, process of content revision, and documentation of the procedures. The findings suggest that JA is superior to CM except for linking jobs to business goals and strategies. While JA covers job specific information well, CM goes above and beyond by revealing the value of job information as it relates to the organization's context, goals, and strategies (Morgeson et al., 2020).

In summary, competency modeling is a fairly novel approach to understanding work. The results of both studies above reveal similarities and differences of CM and JA. A distinct advantage for competency modeling resides in linking business values, goals, and strategies to the workforce. Organizational outcomes yielding a competitive advantage can be translated to all firm levels. Major drawbacks of CM are its abstract nature, unstandardized methods, and a barely tested track record (insufficient empirical research). These idiosyncrasies can leave companies more vulnerable to legal action than JA, which has stood the test of time.

Is job analysis dead? We think not. Instead, we agree with authors (Arribas-Aguila et al., 2024; Morgeson et al., 2020) who suggest integrating the best of both approaches. Moreover, from the perspective of increasing the relevance of performance measures, this idea makes sense since doing so is indeed one method of increasing the validity of performance standards and ratings.

The reason that multiple raters are recommended is that multiple rating may yield a more complete picture of actual employee performance. Each rater should have a unique perspective on the performance of the rated employee. By using multiple raters, any deficiency in ratings by one rater may be compensated for by the perspective of another rater. Overall, multiple raters should lead to more relevant ratings.

While multiple raters may be desirable to remove deficiencies, they may also create problems when used for merit pay purposes. In particular, multiple raters may lead to contamination in ratings. For example, incumbents may inflate their ratings to receive a larger merit increase. Peers may deflate their ratings of incumbent performance to prevent the incumbent from getting a larger increase than they would. These distortions would seem to be more likely in a competitive reward situation (e.g., fixed merit budget), in which one person's gain is another person's loss.

Given the potential problems, organizations must be cautious when using multiple raters for merit pay purposes. That is, if multiple raters are used, the process must be managed carefully. The immediate supervisor could use performance incidents that come to his or her attention from other parties. To use these pieces of information, the following conditions are necessary. First, performance-related observations, rather than judgments by other parties, should be used. The supervisor, rather than other parties, should make the overall judgment of performance and corresponding merit. Second, information collected by the supervisor from other parties should be kept confidential. Third, information should be used only from those parties who are knowledgeable about the incumbent's job and have the opportunity to observe the incumbent perform the job.

In short, an uncritical use of multiple raters does not appear to be appropriate for merit pay decisions. On the other hand, it would be naive to think that merit allocators do not draw upon the opinions or feedback of others. A compromise position would be to use other parties as sources of observation, rather than judgments.

Barclay and York (2003) examined the influences on actual merit pay decisions at a business school at a state university. Merit pay decisions were made by a Merit Committee consisting of four department chairs, with the college dean as an ex officio member. As a committee, the greatest weight was assigned to research, then to teaching, with the least weight given to service. Committee members were in substantial agreement in their initial ratings of faculty members, though some influence on the consensus ratings could be seen from particular committee members. Barclay and York point out that the amount of weight given to research by the Merit Committee (80%) was considerably higher than the weight that faculty members thought was assigned to this aspect of their performance (50%).

In a recent study, Ockenfels et al. (2024) compared evaluations of employee performance by individuals and groups of raters. The authors applied a hybrid research design in which they (a) developed and tested a predictive model and (b) conducted a controlled laboratory experiment, where participants completed a simple task. The model predicted that multiple-rater evaluations were more precise than single-rater evaluations when groups of raters rationally aggregate their judgments about employee performance. The results of the controlled laboratory experiment confirmed model predictions and showed that group-rated performance positively related to incentive pay.

Overall, there remains limited empirical research regarding multiple raters and merit pay. Thus, it is premature to make anything other than tentative recommendations concerning the use of multiple raters when making merit pay decisions.

Participation in Scale Development

The importance of getting those parties who are affected by performance ratings involved in the development of performance standards has been shown in four studies. Friedman and Cornelius (1976) found that when raters participated in the development of performance standards, the resulting ratings had less halo error and more convergent validity than did the ratings of raters who did not participate in scale development. Silverman and Wexley (1984) reported that ratees involved in the development of performance standards were more satisfied with the appraisal and more willing to improve than were ratees not involved in the development of performance standards. Balkin and Gomez-Mejia (1990) found that participation in scale development by ratees was correlated with perceptions of the overall effectiveness of the pay system. Finally, in a survey of HR and senior executives, a major recommendation for improving performance management and reward systems was to promote greater employee involvement in the process. These executives also agreed that senior management needs to be involved in the design and implementation of such systems (Mcdonald & Smith, 1995, cited in Rheem, 1995).

Taken together, these studies indicate that both raters and employees should participate in the development of performance standards for merit pay. A survey by Bretz and Milkovich (1989) suggested that while this was being done for upper-level jobs, in lower-level jobs, employees are infrequently used in developing performance standards. Based on the research, however, it would seem that organizations should consider inviting greater employee participation in scale development for lower-level as well as for upper-level jobs.

It should be noted that participation is not for everyone. Those involved must have the skills and motivation to develop meaningful performance standards (Lawler, 1981). The organization may need to train both managers and subordinates on how to develop performance standards. Also, turnover has to be low for participation to make sense. If employees are frequently leaving the organization, the participation process may need to be repeated with new employees. This would be a costly procedure for organizations to follow on a repeated basis.

The steps that can be taken in a participative approach to scale development are illustrated in Box 4.1 and contrasted with a nonparticipative approach. In large organizations, it may not be feasible to have all employees involved in the development of performance standards. However, participation may still be possible by using task forces composed of representatives of both raters and employees. Examples of the use of task forces in developing performance standards in large organizations can be found in Schneier (1989a), Cowan (1978), and Goodale and Mouser (1981). It may also make sense to get customers involved in developing performance standards. One of us (Robert Heneman) once made this recommendation to a small manufacturing firm. The mission statement of this firm clearly stated that the firm was to place a premium on responsiveness to customers' needs. To support this vision, it was recommended that customers be involved in establishing standards of performance for such things as quality and delivery time. This approach is consistent with the increased emphasis on quality service found in many organizations.

Rating Format

Over the years, there has been considerable controversy about the superiority of various rating formats or scales relative to the indicators of adequate performance standards. A prime example is the lively debate on the virtues of behavioral observation scales versus behavioral expectation scales. Dossett (1989) provides a review of this debate, and the data having a bearing on these arguments. Tziner and Kopelman (2002) provide evidence from four samples that employees react more favorably to behavioral observation scales than to scales emphasizing employee traits.

Unfortunately, there are no data on the adequacy of various formats when it comes to merit pay appraisal. Given the somewhat mixed results on the adequacy of various formats used for purposes other than merit pay (Landy & Farr, 1980), you would expect differences between different formats used for merit pay. Organizations may wish to conduct empirical studies to explore the adequacy of alternative formats in developing merit pay plans. Banks and Roberson (1985) provide a good set of guidelines on how performance appraisal formats should be developed.

Rater Training

A well-documented method of improving the validity of ratings is to train raters. Smith (1986) reviewed 24 studies that looked at the effectiveness of alternative rater training programs. His review suggests that the effectiveness of rater training programs varies by method of presentation and content

Box 4.1 Nonparticipative and Participative Approaches to Developing Performance Standards.

Nonparticipative Approach

1. Supervisor gathers data on the performance measures.
2. Supervisor completes the performance appraisal forms.
3. Supervisor shows completed appraisal to immediate boss and gains concurrence that it has been completed in acceptable form.
4. Supervisor presents completed performance appraisal to subordinate and asks subordinate to react and sign.
5. Appraisal is entered into information system and predetermined consequences result.

Participative Approach

1. Supervisor and subordinate separately gather data on the appraisal measures.
2. Superior and subordinate meet to compare the data they have collected.
3. Superior and subordinate jointly agree on a tentative set of results for the subordinate's appraisal.
4. The tentative appraisal is shown to supervisor's boss, who reacts to it.
5. Appraisal result is communicated to the subordinate.
6. Appraisal results are put in the information system and appropriate action is taken.

Source: Adapted from Mohrman et al. (1989). Reprinted with permission.

being presented. In terms of method of presentation, the more active raters are in training, the better the outcomes. Hence, giving raters the opportunity to discuss issues and to participate in practice and feedback sessions during training resulted in fewer rating errors and more accuracy than did training presented in a lecture format.

In terms of the content presented, it appears that emphasis must be placed on both the observation and judgment of performance (R. Heneman, 1988). As shown in the Smith (1986) review, training that emphasizes the observation of performance, by having raters become familiar with the actual performance standards used, results in more accurate ratings. Training that emphasizes performance-related judgments by training raters to minimize ratings errors is related to a reduction in rating errors. Because both rating errors and accuracy are important indicators of validity, the content of training programs should emphasize both observation and judgment. Several surveys of employer practices have been conducted, which shed some light on the degree to which these research findings are being followed by organizations. On a positive note, there was an increase in the 1980s in the number of organizations providing rater training (comparing Bernardin & Matt, 1985; Bureau of National Affairs, 1983, to Bretz & Milkovich, 1989; Hall, Posner, & Harder, 1989). On a negative note, the content of these programs during this same period did not appear to have changed much. Emphasis continued to be more on how to fill out forms than on how to observe and judge employee performance (Bureau of National Affairs, 1983; Bretz & Milkovich, 1989; Downs & Moscinsky, 1979; Hall et al., 1989).

Research has focused more on the *processes* used to present rater training programs (see Hauenstein, 1998; Woehr & Huffcutt, 1994). Training focused on reducing rater errors, increasing understanding of the performance dimensions used, providing a common frame of reference to raters, and in increasing the accuracy of behavioral observations have all been found to be moderately to strongly successful using various outcome measures (Schleicher & Day, 1998; Woehr & Huffcutt, 1994). For example, a series of studies by Lorne Sulsky and colleagues have pursued and identified factors influencing the effectiveness of frame of reference (FOR) training (Day & Sulsky, 1995; Keown-Gerrard & Sulsky, 2001; Noonan & Sulsky, 2001; Sulsky et al., 2002). In general, rater training seems to be very important in increasing employee acceptance of appraisal/merit practices (Roberts, 1996), as well as in promoting the legal defensibility of such practices (Martin et al., 2000; Werner & Bolino, 1997). In particular, frame of reference training seems especially beneficial (Gorman et al., 2024). Thus, it would appear critical for the success of merit pay plans that all raters involved in the appraisal process receive thorough training in the content and procedures of their organization's appraisal system.

Understanding Generational Differences in Performance Feedback

In the introduction of this edition, we noted that the current workforce contains five generations, something unprecedented in the United States, i.e., many Americans who had retired (or who were thinking about retirement) decided to reenter the workforce (or remain employed) for various reasons, such as, a need to supplement their incomes, a desire to stay active and engaged, or a combination of both (Interestingly, young managers today may supervise employees the age of their parents). No matter the reason however, understanding (through rater training) generational differences in performance feedback preferences can improve the reliability and relevance (validity) of performance measures. Let's take a closer look at what this means.

Feedback-seeking behavior. In varying degree, workers seek feedback on how well they are performing their jobs. Ashford et al. (2016) contend that performance assessment can be improved by managers taking the time to understand which employees seek more attention on their performance. This knowledge can help both raters and ratees stay focused on performance standards. Research supports this claim, as younger cohorts (Millennials and Gen Z) expect, and respond well to, more frequent and detailed feedback than their older cohorts (Ashford et al., 2016; Locker & Teague, 2024).

Socioemotional selectivity theory (SST). Generational differences in performance feedback preferences and reactions have implications for optimizing such feedback. SST (Cubrich & Petruzzelli, 2020; Wang et al., 2015) suggests that younger workers (Millennials and Post-Millennials) tend to see "time" in a future orientation, as limitless, where feedback is useful for developing competencies for future careers and goals. Older workers (Baby Boomers and Generation X) tend to perceive "time" in the workforce as present oriented and limited in scope. They are more open to receiving feedback on social awareness and less open to improving skills for future performance. Research on SST supports these propositions (Carstensen & Hershfield, 2021; Wang et al., 2015). The implications here are similar to feedback-seeking behavior. Managers who provide generation-specific performance feedback stand a better chance of leading and reinforcing what is important for successful job performance (increased relevance) than managers who do not provide such information.

Administrative Practices

Administrative practices, such as how and when ratings are conducted, influence the adequacy of performance measures. It seems that often what is required by the organization is in conflict with the capabilities of the rater to "mentally process" performance information. As a result, the accuracy of ratings is diminished. Therefore, to increase the accuracy of ratings, required administrative practices should be made consistent with the mental processes of the raters.

Time Delay in Ratings. One specific application of this general statement has to do with the timing of ratings. According to a national survey in 1983, 85% of U.S. organizations only conducted ratings once a year (Bureau of National Affairs, 1983). A 1988 survey estimated this figure to be almost 70% (Locher & Teel, 1988). Eskew and Heneman (1996) found that many organizations now assess performance for merit pay decisions twice a year. One implication of these findings is that a considerable period of time typically passes between the observation and rating of employee performance. Raters are, in effect, being asked to evaluate performance that took place up to 6 or 12 months earlier. Given the time delay in ratings, considerable demands are made upon the memory capabilities of raters. Given less-than-perfect memories, less-than-perfect ratings should be expected as well. A study by R. Heneman and Wexley (1983) suggested that this speculation is indeed the case. They reported that the longer the delay between the observation and rating of performance, the less accurate were the ratings. This decrease in accuracy took place after a mere 3-week delay in ratings. Imagine the potential decline in accuracy after 6 or 12 months! These data suggest that ratings need to be made more frequently than once a year.

Ratings should be made at least twice a year and, if feasible, every quarter. This also matches the most common employee preferences in this matter, that is, in a survey of Canadian employees, 45.3% indicated that they wished to be appraised twice a year, with 16.4% wishing to be appraised more than twice a year, and 38.3% indicating a preference for annual appraisals (Gosselin et al., 1997). Recent research strengthens this recommendation. Gerhart (2023) and Ledford and Benson (2019) present survey data from organizations adopting a performance management system with ratingless reviews and continuous feedback with quarterly intervals. Both show an increased employee and manager satisfaction in performance feedback meetings.

Amount of Information Observed. Many, if not most, supervisors have limited opportunity to observe employee performance. This limited opportunity is a result of large spans of control, physical distance from the ratee, and responsibilities not requiring interaction with the ratee. In any event, what this means is that the rater is making a summary judgment of employee performance on the basis of a limited sample of the employee's total performance. You would expect, and it has been empirically verified, that ratings would be more accurate the greater the amount of observation time (R. Heneman & Wexley, 1983). Also, greater opportunity to observe is associated with higher levels of interrater reliability (Rothstein, 1990). Hence, arranging work conditions to facilitate the observation of employee performance is recommended. For example, the observations of peers could be used if a supervisor has a large number of people reporting to him or her, thereby limiting the opportunity to observe. In large consulting firms, partners are sometimes asked to evaluate the performance of associates who spend large amounts of time working at client organizations. However, the partners have limited opportunity to observe the actual performance of associates. In these cases, it would be better to ask the client organization to evaluate the associates, as the client has had more opportunity to observe them.

Diary Keeping. Time and other resource constraints may make it difficult, if not impossible, for organizations to require anything but limited observation of employees and once-a-year ratings. But even under these less-than-favorable conditions, organizations can still attempt to make administrative practices consistent with the rater's mental abilities by requiring diary keeping. By carefully recording employee performance, the rater is relying more on documentation and less on memory when rating performance. Moreover, a diary or log can be used to impose some structure on a large amount of performance information that may seem scattered. With structure, the information may be easier to recall.

DeNisi et al. (1989) conducted a study to look at the effects of diary keeping. They found that raters who kept a diary were more accurate in their ratings than were raters who did not keep a diary. Also, they found that raters who organized their diary by the ratee, rather than by the task being performed by ratees, were more accurate. Finally, they found that raters preferred to organize their diaries by ratees rather than by tasks. In a field study, DeNisi and Peters (1996) found that, after structured recall and diary keeping were introduced, raters recalled more performance information, were more discriminating in their ratings, and were more satisfied with the appraisal process. The findings of these two studies clearly point to the utility of diary keeping in performance measurement (see also Varma et al., 1996). While it may be naive to expect raters to keep extremely detailed diaries given their busy schedules, it should be a required practice that raters document the critical episodes of employee performance. Advances in technology, including stand-alone appraisal software, or incorporating appraisal within enterprise resource planning (ERP) software systems, makes note taking/diary keeping much more feasible than when it had to be entirely a paper-based system (Miller, 2003).

Social Comparisons

Two studies showed that indicators of the convergent validities of ratings were increased by providing raters with comparative performance information on other subordinates. R. Heneman (1986) reported stronger correlations between ratings and objective measures of performance, while Farh and Dobbins (1989) reported stronger correlations between self and supervisory ratings, when relative comparisons rather than absolute comparisons were made. In another study, the criterion-related validity of relative comparisons was greater than the criterion-validity of absolute comparisons in a sample of Canadian managers (Goffin et al., 1996). The results of these three studies suggest that the convergent validity of ratings is increased when relative rather than absolute comparisons are made in performance ratings.

There are several reasons why ratings may be more valid with relative rather than absolute comparisons. First, individuals typically seek out comparative information about the performance of others when making performance judgments. The sought-after information provides a context or point of reference for the ratings to be made (Farh & Dobbins, 1989). Second, relative comparisons may be a less complex rating task for the rater. It may be easier to compare ratees to one another than it is to compare ratees to a poorly defined anchor on a rating scale (R. Heneman, 1986).

As discussed previously, relative comparisons are not used extensively. Our current discussion would suggest that greater use of relative comparisons might improve the convergent and criterion-related validity of ratings. Given the limited research, we are not suggesting that relative comparisons be used to replace absolute comparisons. However, the data seem strong enough to warrant that relative comparisons may be used as a *supplement* to absolute comparisons. Along those lines, more organizations are making use of forced rankings to evaluate managers and other professionals. However, as noted in Chapter 1, great care needs to be taken to ensure that relative appraisal practices are done in a manner that is perceived as fair, and that is legally defensible (Bates, 2003b; Meisler, 2003).

Rater Motivation

The discussion of ways to increase the validity of ratings thus far has focused on ways to improve the rater's skills, or on ways to arrange working conditions to promote the rater's ability to mentally process performance information. Another way to improve the validity of ratings, which may be as good as or better than focusing on the rater's skills and abilities, is to increase the rater's *motivation* to make valid ratings (Murphy & Cleveland, 1991). Unfortunately, limited research has been conducted along these lines (Harris, 1994; Salvemini et al., 1993). The importance of rater motivation in the validity of ratings is illustrated in a study by Napier and Latham (1986). They found that raters did not see any personal consequences for the ratings they assigned, such as appreciation from the boss, a pay raise, or a promotion. Although conducted with small samples of employees, their results were consistent for two different industries (newsprint and banking) and methods of research (interviews and questionnaires). Based on these results, the authors suggest that it may be naive to expect valid ratings in the absence of any motivating outcomes for those conducting the ratings. One way to motivate raters is to hold them accountable for their ratings. Methods to hold raters accountable for performance ratings and merit increase decisions are discussed in Chapter 6.

In a study of public-sector managers in Quebec, Morin et al. (1999) found that there was some rating inflation when "public" ratings were compared to "private" ratings made by managers. These authors suggest that inflated ratings are more likely to occur when there are political influences within the appraisal process.

Statistical Control of Halo

One approach to improving the validity of ratings is to statistically control halo error. Under this approach, time and other resources are not devoted to minimizing rating errors. Instead, rating errors are allowed to occur and be statistically partialed out from the ratings. You might expect that this procedure would yield ratings free from error at a reduced cost to the organization, as a statistical manipulation is used rather than more costly interventions such as rater training programs. A good example is a study by

Landy et al. (1980) in which they reported greater discriminant validity after statistically partialing out halo error.

The major problem with this approach is that it assumes halo is an error rather than true employee performance (e.g., Barksdale & Werner, 2001; Hulin, 1982). There may, in fact, be work situations where uniform ratings of employee performance does and should take place, because it reflects true performance. In some settings, the same abilities are required to perform different aspects or dimensions of the job (Cooper, 1981). Given the difficulty of separating out valid from invalid halo in ratings, this procedure has not received widespread acceptance and use.

Bartlett (1983) presented an approach to the statistical control of halo. Under his procedure, Bartlett is explicit as to what constitutes valid and invalid halo. He then uses a rating technique, known as forced choice, to remove invalid halo from overall ratings. Just as important as the procedure that he offers is the explicitness with which he treats halo. If you use the statistical control of halo, you must be explicit as to what constitutes halo error to provide logical justification for its removal.

Current Trends in Merit Pay

Use of Artificial Intelligence (AI): Computers Replacing Humans?

Technology has ushered in an era of machine learning replacing human judgment in many aspects of human resource management. Both popular media and early research have touted the idea that machine learning (or AI as it is commonly known) will transform many HR functions—including performance measurement. Recent research shows the potential for AI to enhance accuracy in supervisory ratings. This results from reducing rater bias because of increased objectivity in observing employee behavior (Eubanks, 2018; Orben, 2020; Tambe et al., 2019). Ironically, many subject matter experts (SMEs) found a reduction in rater bias rather than an elimination of it to be a disappointment. Early expectations held that AI would eliminate rating biases. However, research has shown that programmers coding AI algorithms carry their own prejudices and unintentionally include them in their code (Orben, 2020). Algorithms may inadvertently carry sources of bias that lead to adverse impact as well as other illegal and unethical consequences.

In a different vein, Walker and Larson (2025), examined the degree to which AI can help human resources students collect job data (through interviews) with 10 real job holders and write job descriptions. The results reveal that AI indeed complements student learning on job analysis tasks and job description writing. Students gasp an understanding of the benefits and limitations of the new technology.

It is important to note that AI is in its infancy and seems to hold promise for supplementing decision makers in human resources. However, it will never, or should never, be considered a substitute for human judgment. Many ethical questions will need answering as well as much research to determine AI capabilities and limitations. One advantage of AI may be predicting performance of employees in remote jobs, where rater exposure of ratees is limited. Thus, AI holds promise for increasing the validity of performance measures and job descriptions by increasing rating accuracy. However, time will tell how much.

Summary of Major Points

1. *The importance of performance measurement.* The first and foremost step in the development of a merit pay plan is the adequate measurement of performance. Based on theory, research, and practice, it is not possible to have an effective merit pay plan if performance is not adequately measured. This is true regardless of the desirability and feasibility of merit pay.
2. *A variety of performance measures can be used.* These measures include traits, behaviors, results, rankings, and paired comparisons. Each approach has distinct advantages and disadvantages. These sets of performance standards should not be treated as substitutes for one another. No one approach is clearly superior to another for all considerations (Jelley & Goffin, 2001). As a general matter, though, it can be stated that behavioral and results measures should be emphasized most heavily (Gosselin et al., 1997; Latham & Seijts, 1997; Posthuma et al., 2018; Werner & Bolino, 1997). A preferred strategy for selecting which standards to use includes reasoned selection, followed by an empirical evaluation of the standards selected.
3. *Alternative measures of performance.* Some specific measures of employee performance can be controversial and need to be carefully considered before being used for merit pay. These measures include promotions, seniority, organizational citizenship behavior, maximum versus typical performance, and job level.
4. *Adequacy of performance measures.* The adequacy of performance measures refers to the concept of validity, or the extent to which performance standards measure what they purport to measure. Overall validity is assessed with a number of indicators including content validity, convergent validity, discriminant validity, reliability, accuracy, rating errors, and relevance. These indicators are not substitutes for one another, and each indicator provides a unique source of information from which to make inferences about validity.
5. *Methods to improve the validity of ratings.* The validity of ratings can be improved by how performance standards are developed and how the standards are used. Validity appears to be greater when the following conditions are present: (a) ratings are tied to the strategic mission of the organization, (b) performance standards and ratings are based on job analysis, (c) multiple sources of performance information are used, (d) raters and employees participate in the development of performance standards, (e) rater training is provided, (f) rating formats are based on sound test

construction principles (Nunnally & Bernstein, 1994), (g) the delay between observation and ratings is minimized, (h) the opportunity for the rater to observe the employee is maximized, (i) the rater keeps a diary organized by employee, (j) social comparison information is provided to the rater, (k) raters are held accountable for their ratings, (l) the statistical control of halo is only used under well-defined conditions, (m) relative comparisons supplement absolute comparisons, and (n) AI is applied mindfully in rating performance.

Conclusions

The most difficult aspect of developing a merit pay plan is creating a valid way to measure performance. If a valid method of measuring performance is not developed, it is unlikely that employees will see the link between their pay and performance. And, in turn, if employees do not see the link between their pay and performance, merit pay will not lead to improved performance (as presented in Chapter 2).

A central theme in this chapter is that there is no one best way to measure performance, to assess validity, or to improve upon the validity of performance measures. A variety of guidelines have been offered as to the development of performance standards, the assessment of validity, and ways to improve validity. While there is no one best way, some guidelines to measuring performance appear to be more promising than others when it comes to using performance measurement for purposes of merit pay. In particular, three main points stand out. At an absolute minimum, the following three guidelines need to be followed.

First, alternative measures of performance need to be clearly defined and communicated to employees. It must be clear to employees what the organizational policy is regarding how merit pay will be linked to promotions, seniority, organizational citizenship behavior, maximum versus typical performance, and job level. If these factors are not explicitly treated by the organization, even the most sophisticated rating scales may be ineffective for merit pay decisions. If the employee hears that pay is based strictly on performance, but sees that merit increases are based on other factors that may or may not be related to performance (as defined in the rating scale), then the scales and merit pay plan will fail.

Second, no matter which performance standards are selected, an empirical study should be conducted on the validity of these standards. As shown in this chapter, with the exception of accuracy, which requires a true score, and relevance, which requires an ultimate criterion, there are a number of straightforward indicators that can be used to assess the validity of performance standards. We discuss measurement issues in more detail in Chapter 7.

Third, the validity of ratings appears to be heavily contingent on the acceptability of the standards to the affected parties. To enhance the acceptability of standards, both raters and employees should be involved in developing standards, the rating task should be made consistent with the ways in which raters mentally process performance information, raters should be trained and held accountable for their ratings, and the system of performance measurement should be related to the job. If the standards used to assess performance are well defined, show evidence of validity, and are acceptable to the affected parties, then there should be a strong relationship (both actual and perceived) between merit increases and performance ratings. If these three guidelines are not followed, then judgments regarding performance may be inconsistent with judgments about merit increases. Obviously, this inconsistency will create dysfunctional consequences if pay is to be linked to performance under a stated merit pay plan.

In short, a great deal of effort has been spent trying to find the "one best way" to measure performance (Werner, 2000). Considerable academic journal space has been devoted to comparing alternative rating formats, and organizations frequently change their methods used to assess performance. Unfortunately, these lines of inquiry have failed to produce the one best way to measure performance (Kozlowski et al., 1998). A better use of resources is to develop measures of performance with clearly defined standards, with known validity properties, and that are acceptable to the affected parties.

Some may argue that the development of standards with known validity properties is not "practical" for organizations. In our opinion, nothing could be further from the truth! As shown in this chapter, the procedures used to develop standards with reasonable levels of validity make good "business sense." Many organizations, for example, are looking for a way to achieve greater adherence to their strategic plans. One way to do so is to use the mission statement and strategic organizational objectives to develop performance standards, so that behaviors consistent with the strategic plans will be rewarded.

The standards, in and of themselves, are also important for business purposes. The obvious argument is that standards must be measuring what they purport to measure for actual performance to be linked to merit pay. A less obvious, but perhaps more important, argument is that for performance standards to be accepted and acted upon, the standards must be seen as reasonable by the affected parties. Greater attention needs to be given to discussing the desired status of controversial performance measures for particular organizations and to the acceptability of performance standards to the affected parties than has been done in the past (Gilliland & Langdon, 1998). Standards are much more likely to be acceptable to managers and employees when the standards themselves have adequate validity properties. Again, sound measurement is a very "practical" consideration.

To say it as strongly as possible, it would be reckless, even dangerous, for an organization to implement a merit pay plan without a sound (i.e., valid) means of measuring employee performance. We hope this chapter has provided practical guidance to assist organizational leaders in their efforts to validly measure employee performance. As we said at the start of this chapter, adequate performance measures are *essential* in order for merit pay plans to be effective. Many other things are necessary as well, but without solid performance measurement, merit pay plans cannot work as they are intended. We now turn our attention to some of these "other" issues involved in administering a merit pay plan.

Study Questions

1. Explain how both theory and research reveal the importance of adequate performance measures. Give examples.
2. Compare and contrast various performance standards. What things should a manager consider in selecting a performance measure? Is there a "best way" to choose performance measures? Explain.
3. In your view, what characteristics make up a good performance measure? Include the concepts of reliability, validity, and relevance in your explanation. Be as specific as possible.
4. Why should merit pay be linked to the organization's strategic mission? What roles do performance management and performance appraisal play in this connection?
5. What is the role of job analysis in performance measurement. Compare and contrast job analysis with competency modeling.
6. You are an HR director in a manufacturing company. What should you consider in training new supervisors in rating employee performance? How many raters should you include in this task? Why?
7. What is statistical control of halo? How does it affect performance measures?
8. How can AI benefit human resources in performance appraisal? In your opinion, will it ever replace human judgment? Why or why not? What ethical issues about AI should be addressed?

CHAPTER 5

ESTABLISHING PAY INCREASES

This chapter discusses how pay increases can be tied to performance—once adequate measures of performance have been developed. Establishing pay increases is the second step in the development and administration of a merit pay plan. To establish pay increases based on performance, two major activities must take place. First, a policy, or set of guidelines, must be developed regarding pay increases and their relationship to performance. Second, this policy needs to be introduced and implemented in the organization. Both topics are covered in this chapter.

Creating a Merit Pay Policy

In creating a merit pay policy, attention must be given to the size, form, and timing of pay increases that will be linked to various levels of performance. The size, form, and timing of pay allocated to merit increases depends on many factors, including the budget and pay structure. Before considering these issues, the concept of "just-noticeable differences" (JNDs) is discussed, as this is the frame of reference for a sound merit pay policy.

Just-Noticeable Differences

A just-noticeable difference (JND) refers to the minimum pay increase that employees would perceive as "making a difference" with regard to their

Merit Pay, pages 175–208

doi:10.1108/978-1-80686-701-120263005

Figure 5.1.

The Role of Just-Noticeable Differences in the Merit Pay Process.

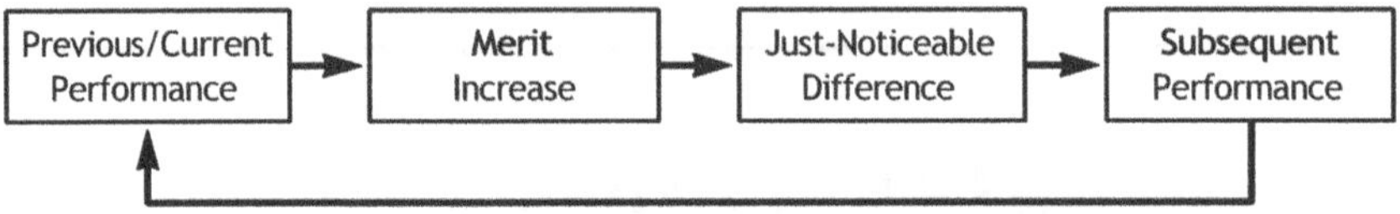

attitudes and behaviors (Conroy, Roumpi, Delery & Gupta, 2022; H. Heneman & Ellis, 1982; Kim, 2025). This concept has also been referred to as a "just meaningful difference" (Ze deck & Smith, 1968) and a "smallest meaningful pay increase" (Krefting & Mahoney, 1977; Mitra et al., 1997). Regardless of how it is labeled, the concept of a JND is important for merit pay, as it is thought to mediate the relationship between merit pay and subsequent performance, as shown in Fig. 5.1. What this means is that a just noticeable difference or JND is the psychological state that translates merit increases into subsequent employee performance. If merit increases are not large enough to have a JND, they may not produce increases in future performance. Hence, one critical goal in establishing pay increases is to create a JND. Another competing goal, of course, is to minimize cost, as described throughout the book.

A common question is how large a merit increase is required for the increase to have a JND? Two studies shed some light on this question. First, Mitra et al. (1997) studied the reactions of 192 student employees, and found that increases below approximately 7% were unlikely to evoke positive reactions. Second, Katkowski et al., (2002) conducted a meta-analysis of 11 studies on this subject (including Mitra et al., 1997). The majority of the studies produced JND estimates between 6–8 percent. After some methodological adjustments, they conclude that "it appears that an estimate of around 7.5% is a rough indicator of how large a pay raise needs to be before it becomes just noticeable to employees" (p. 9).

As Katkowski et al. (2002) state, this figure is an estimate, as the amount of increase likely to cause a JND will depend on both personal and situational factors. Other research has shown that a smaller pay increase is likely to produce a JND when employees are in lower- rather than higher-level jobs (Zedeck & Smith, 1968); have lower rather than higher earnings (Hinrichs, 1969); anticipate a low rather than high cost of living (Krefting & Mahoney, 1977); anticipate great difficulty in attaining a new job; have a small rather than large current wage; anticipate a small rather than large pay increase; work a long rather than a short work week (H. Heneman & Ellis, 1982); and a field study rather than a controlled study is conducted (Mitra et al., 2015). Furthermore, when determining what size increase is needed to create a JND, three other factors need to be considered. First, simply increasing the amount of money allocated to merit increases does not necessarily produce a JND. Rambo and Pinto (1989) showed that there is not a one-for-one return in the form of a JND for each dollar spent on increases. Instead, they found diminishing marginal returns on each additional dollar allocated. That is, each additional merit increase dollar resulted in smaller increases in JND.

Second, the amount of influence that characteristics of the employee and situation have on JNDs may depend on the attitudes of employees. In two studies, it was shown that the ability of person (i.e., employee) and situational variables to predict JNDs depended on attitudes toward rewards (Krefting & Mahoney, 1977; Varadarajan & Futrell, 1984). For those who value pay for its purchasing power, or the amount of goods and services that can be bought, JNDs seem to be best predicted by the cost of living. For those who value pay as a form of organizational recognition, JNDs seem to be best predicted by the size of the anticipated pay increase (Krefting, Newman, & Krzystofiak, 1987).

Third, equity considerations need to be kept in mind as well (see Chapter 2 for a review of equity theory). For pay to have a just-noticeable difference, the employee must see the size of the increase as meaningful in a relative sense, as well as in an absolute sense. Equity theory (Adams, 1965) suggests that the employee must regard his or her own ratio of merit pay to performance as roughly equivalent to the ratio for other comparably performing people in the organization. This leads to the question of whether actual merit increases are large enough to change employee attitudes and behaviors, or whether they are viewed as a "drop in the bucket" (Mitra et al., 1997). For various reasons, the size of merit increases has been trending downward for the past two decades (Hewitt Associates, 2003; HR Focus, 2003; Peck, 1984; Teel, 1986).

Actual Size of Merit Increases

Fig. 5.2 shows the trend of average merit increases from 2005 to 2024 (WorldatWork, 2005–2024). From 2005 to 2009, average increases had some yearly variance, but nothing extreme. Then, in 2010, the average merit pay increase dipped substantially from 3.6 to 2.3. The overarching reason for this was the lagging effect of the U.S. economic recession of 2008, which was described in Chapter 3. From 2011 to 2019, merit increases rose initially then hovered around 3.0% for the rest of the duration. In 2020, the global pandemic occurred, seriously affecting compensation decisions around the world. Merit pay increases dropped to 2.4 that year. In the next four years, average increases bounced back to 3.8.

Since the pandemic, several observations are notable (WorldatWork, 2024). First, compensation budget surveys show that average merit increase

Figure 5.2.

Average Merit Pay Increases From 2005 to 2024.

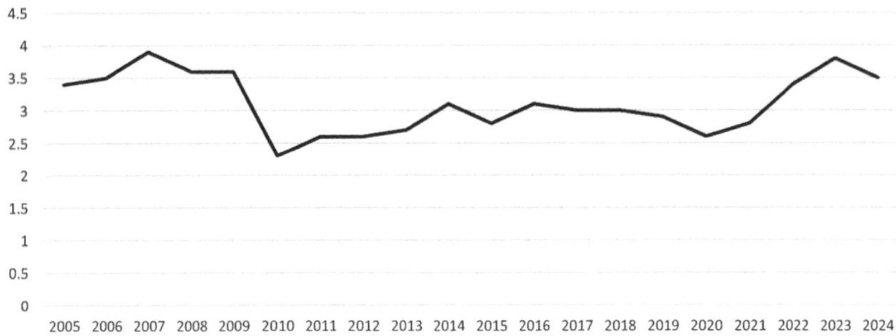

budgets have risen, with employers allocating a larger portion of their compensation budget towards merit pay to attract and retain employees in a competitive market. The scarcity of employees for hire and retention was and still remains a huge problem for both national and international organizations (The reader ought to note the strategic effect of merit pay plans here.) Second, while merit pay increases have gone up, they often haven't kept pace with inflation. This indicates many employees are seeing a decrease in real purchasing power despite receiving a raise. Third, different industries have experienced varying levels of merit pay increases, with sectors like technology and healthcare often seeing larger increases due to high demand for skilled workers. Fourth, many companies are increasingly tying merit pay increases directly to individual performance metrics, emphasizing a more meritocratic system to reward top performers.

Form of Merit Increases

In addition to determining the size of merit increases, consideration must also be given to the form that merit increases will take. Two notable features taken from current practice need to be discussed here: the type of increase and the permanence of the increase.

Type of Merit Increase

In virtually all organizations, merit pay comes in the form of direct pay. That is, merit pay represents an increase in wages or salary, which shows up in the employee's paycheck. However, there has been some discussion of allocating indirect pay or employee benefits on the basis of performance as well. Brunker (1982) appears to have first advocated the use of benefits as a type of merit pay.

In the 1980s, a Houston-based organization, CRS Sirrine, Inc., put a performance-based benefits plan into place for its 3,000 employees in architecture, engineering, and construction ("How one company," 1989). Under the plan, the organization contributed to employees' health plan costs only if employees' performance ratings were adequate. Employees with less than adequate ratings had to pay the full cost of their health care until their performance reached an adequate level. Reasons for undertaking this plan included a desire to strengthen the pay-for-performance philosophy by linking all types of pay to performance, and to get employees to view benefits as a reward for performance, rather than an entitlement based on membership in the organization. It should be noted that it does not appear that this company ever realized any cost savings with the plan. CRS Sirrine was acquired and then dismantled in 1994 (King & Langdon, 2002).

Speaking more generally, however, an obvious advantage of benefits over pay increases for purposes of merit pay is the tax savings available for the employee. Under present tax laws, direct pay increases are treated as taxable income, but most benefits are not. Hence, if benefits are used in lieu of merit increases, the reward may not be taxed. A potential, yet solvable, problem with performance-based benefits is that some benefits (e.g., Social Security) are legally mandated for employees, regardless of performance. Hence, legally mandated benefits would have to be excluded from the plan. Another problem may be that if the amount of benefits granted is based on performance, some employees could be left defenseless in the face of a catastrophic illness. This may create pressure on the supervisor to evaluate employees as average or better, even if actual performance does not warrant such ratings. A way around this problem may be to make *employer contributions* beyond a minimum (survival) level contingent on performance, rather than the total amount of benefits.

In short, performance-based benefits represent a controversial approach to performance-based pay, including merit pay (Balkin & S. Werner, 2023). Organizations considering such a plan need to pay careful attention to current tax laws (Brunker, 1982). We point out that many efforts to promote employee wellness move in this direction, for example, providing health insurance discounts for nonsmokers or for employees participating in wellness activities (Blassingame, 2003). Given the rising costs for many employee benefits such as health care (Bates, 2003a; Sweeney, 2003), there may be organizations that will consider linking the provision of certain (nonlegally mandated) benefits to measures of individual employee performance. There would be clear and substantial risks as well as administrative difficulties involved in such an effort, and so we would recommend that organizations proceed with great caution. However, the pressures to manage total compensation costs may make this an attractive option for some organizations to consider.

Permanence of the Increase

A merit increase can become a permanent addition to base pay. For example, an employee who receives a 4% increase in pay would continue to receive that 4% increase as long as they remain with the organization under a *traditional merit pay plan*. Merit pay is typically granted on a permanent basis. A permanent increase, if costed out over time, represents a very large reward for future increased and sustained performance. If employees perceive the total value of the merit increase over time, they may see the increase as very large and be very motivated. In the 1980s, it was estimated that about 78% of U.S. organizations had traditional merit pay plans (Wyatt Company, 1987). Hewitt Associates (2003) estimated that 77% of U.S. organizations use at least one form of variable pay plan. Variable pay includes business incentives (59%), special recognition (55%), individual performance/merit pay (47%), and stock ownership (32%). Thus, while merit pay is no longer the primary means that organizations use to provide individual incentives, it continues to be widely used, in conjunction with other forms of variable pay (IOMA, 2003). The traditional merit plan has been criticized for a number of reasons.

First, the costs associated with permanent increases can be huge. Minken (1988) offered an example of the mathematics involved. Under a traditional plan, an employee earning $30,000 a year who gets a 5% merit increase would receive a $1,500 (0.05 × $30,000) raise in year 1, and a $1,575 (0.05 × $31,500) raise in year 2—for a total merit increase over 2 years of $3,075. Had this same employee not received a permanent increase, they would have received $1,500 in year 1, another $1,500 in year 2, with a total of $3,000 for the 2 years. While a total payout difference of $75 ($3,075 minus $3,000) between a permanent and nonpermanent increase may not seem large, consider that an employer may have thousands of employees working for an extended number of years. These cumulative costs can be substantial.

A second problem with traditional merit pay plans is that they may lessen the strength of the perceived pay-for-performance relationship. As noted by Belcher (1980), traditional merit pay plans pay not only for performance, but for membership in the organization as well. The longer an employee is with the organization, the larger the merit increase becomes in any one year. Over time, the size of the increase is compounded by the increase built into the base salary. Whether this correlation between seniority and pay is desirable or not depends on your view of seniority as a measure of performance (see the discussion in Chapter 4).

A third problem with traditional merit plans is that the statistical effects of a permanent increase may result in the relative pay status of employees being unalterable. In an interesting study, Haire, Ghiselli, and Gordon (1967) found that if there is a strong correlation between pay level and increase, as one would expect with a permanent increase, the rank ordering of the lowest to highest paid employees would continue to remain the same, regardless of changes in employee performance. To the extent that merit pay possesses status properties as well as consumption properties (Frank, 1984), merit increases may produce an unalterable status hierarchy that may be unacceptable to many employees.

A fourth problem with a permanent increase is the potential for a decrease in the actual relationship between pay and performance. The magnitude of the relationship may decrease because, as time goes on, pay increases will become compounded more by the passage of time than actual performance. Schwab and Olson (1990) found that the permanence of merit increases had little impact on the actual relationship between pay and performance. However, as noted by the authors, these results occurred in a situation where the "maximums" (reviewed at the end of this chapter) paid by the organization were increased to keep up with pay increases in the market. Had these adjustments not been made or been done less frequently, the impact of the permanence of the increase may have been more pronounced. The actual pay-for-performance relationship would have been weakened because long-tenured employees would no longer be eligible for pay increases, having reached the maximum allowable rate of pay.

An alternative to the traditional merit pay plan exists and is known as *lump-sum bonuses* (Bergmann & Scarpello, 2001; Minken, 1988; Overstreet, 1985). Under this form of merit increase, the increase received is not permanent, but instead is a one-time increase that is not rolled over into base pay. As shown in Box 5.1, there are a variety of lump-sum merit pay plans. Many organizations have used lump-sum merit plans (Kanter, 1987; Terry, 2003; UAW DaimlerChrysler, 2003).

Lump-sum plans appear to have developed in response to the criticisms of traditional merit plans. By not making merit pay a permanent addition to base pay, costs can be minimized and the pay-for-performance relationship may be strengthened. Also, benefit costs may be reduced as benefit amounts are sometimes linked to the base pay amounts (Minken, 1988). Under a lump-sum plan, base pay is not increased as with a merit increase and, hence, the amount of benefits may remain the same. Another potential advantage with lump-sum plans has to do with tax savings ("Lump-sum salary increases," 1983). Under the salary advance plan shown in Box 5.1, any employee could choose to distribute increases over two years rather than receive the increase in one year. Tax savings would be greater if pay were deferred to a second year in which the marginal tax rate is lower.

Box 5.1 Lump-Sum Merit Plans.

No-Strings Approach

Employees are given the option to receive the increase in the traditional manner or to take the total amount in a lump sum. Employees who take the lump-sum option are under no obligation to repay an unearned portion should they leave the company for any reason.

Salary-Advance Approach

Employees who elect to receive a lump-sum increase must sign a contract obligating them to return the unearned portion should they leave the company. Installments are possible under this approach as well.

Earned-Out Approach

Lump-sum increase is paid in advance, but is excluded from pension plans, profit sharing, and other benefit programs until the increase has been earned out over the future period by the lump-sum amount.

Source: Small Business Reports, June 1983. Published by the American Management Association, Monterey, CA. Reprinted with permission.

Although lump-sum merit pay plans seem to offer some advantages over traditional pay plans, only limited research has been conducted on this subject. For instance, Bell and Neumark (1993) studied the use of lump-sum payments in unionized U.S. firms in the 1980s, and concluded that, from an economic standpoint, such payments were *not* provided as a form of performance-related pay. Sturman and Short (2000) developed and tested a four-item measure of lump-sum bonus satisfaction that is meant to supplement the scales in the Pay Satisfaction Questionnaire (H. Heneman & Schwab, 1985). Lowery et al. (2002) studied the impact of a merit bonus plan that was used in a large service organization. Two variables had the strongest relationship to employee satisfaction and job performance, that is, reward contingency (the extent to which employees perceived that their bonus was based on their performance) and goal quality (the completeness of goals, as well as control over their accomplishment). Thus, despite some enthusiasm for lump-sum bonuses as a means of controlling compensation costs (Martinez, 1994), research has yet to verify the purported advantages of this approach. In 1987, it was estimated that about 14% of U.S. organizations used lump-sum merit plans (Wyatt Company, 1987). In 2000, 28% of the organizations surveyed by IOMA reported having lump-sum merit pay (HR Focus, 2001). There is an obvious need for more evaluative research on lump-sum merit plans. It could be argued, for example, that cost savings associated with a lump-sum plan are offset by decreased motivation due to a reduction in the total value of a merit increase to the employee. In fact, although they are fairly widely used, respondents in the IOMA survey just cited also rated lump-sum plans as the *least* effective of the 17 incentives studied (HR Focus, 2001).

Timing Considerations

There have been recommendations in the literature that merit payouts be made more frequently than once a year (Wiscombe, 2001). However, in most organizations, merit and other increases (such as cost-of-living) continue to be allocated once a year (IOMA, 2003; Wyatt Company, 1987) or, at best, twice a year (Eskew & Heneman, 1996). This seems to be largely an administrative or a convenience issue. A question that arises, then, is when during the year should the annual merit review take place? Two different approaches seem to exist in practice, each of which has its advantages and disadvantages.

One approach is to have a *common review date* for all merit increase decisions. One advantage to this approach is that the amount of paperwork may be decreased over having different review dates for different employees. A second advantage may be that relative performance information is more readily available to allocators and covers the same time period for each employee (R. Heneman & von Hippel, 1996). This may be desirable for enhancing the accuracy of performance ratings (as discussed in Chapter 4). A disadvantage to this approach is that allocators may have a large number of decisions to reach during a short period of time. Also, depending on the size of the merit budget, this approach may put a large monetary burden on the organization once a year rather than spreading it out over the entire year.

A second approach is to use each employee's *anniversary date.* With this approach, employees are reviewed on the day they began work with the organization. By having, in effect, staggered review dates over the course of the year, the review burden placed on the allocators and the monetary burden placed on the organization is spread out over the year. This may be why some organizations use anniversary dates instead of a common review date (R. Heneman, 2001b). However, additional paperwork may be required in the form of reminders to allocators, and relative performance information may not be current or readily available.

The decision as to which approach to use may be dictated by current circumstances. If relative comparisons are used as a method of performance appraisal, and departments "compete" for budget money, then a common review date is needed. By having a common review date, employees and departments are compared to one another over the same time period. If absolute comparisons are used for performance appraisal, and there are fixed raise amounts to which all departments must adhere, then using service/anniversary dates of employees could be a better approach—provided that the performance standards and merit raise guidelines remain constant over time.

In practice, a common review date is used more frequently than an anniversary review date. In a survey by Bretz and Milkovich (1989), merit increases were granted on common review dates in 58% of organizations, on the employee's anniversary date in 27% of organizations, and on a rolling date based on some factor other than the employee's anniversary date in 15% of the organizations. Another timing issue that arises in merit pay policy is whether the period between merit increases should be constant or variable. In some organizations, the time that elapses between merit reviews is not uniform for all employees. Instead, the time between reviews depends on performance. The better an employee's performance under this arrangement, the more frequently they are reviewed for another pay raise (for an example, see the discussion of guide charts later in this chapter).

From a motivational perspective, it has been argued that this approach is problematic (Mohrman et al., 1989). If the review dates for poor performers are stretched out, there is little incentive for them to improve. From a budgeting perspective, however, it has been argued that variable review periods based on performance are advantageous (Farmer, 1978). By paying below-average performers less frequently, more money is available for better performers.

Budgeting Issues

The budgeting process behind merit pay increases is not well described or researched (R. Heneman, 1990). Nevertheless, it is a topic of crucial importance for establishing merit increases. The importance of financial considerations is clearly spelled out in economic theory (as reviewed in Chapter 2) and is a continuing theme of this book. The limited information available on budgets is reviewed here. Readers interested in case study examples of the merit pay budgeting process can look at descriptions of Armstrong Cork (Farmer, 1978), a private-sector organization; a review of practices by various public-sector organizations (Van Adelsberg, 1978); or view the practices in use at the University of New Mexico (University of New Mexico Human Resources Department, 2003). Consideration will be given in this section to budgeting models that can be used and issues that arise in the use of these models.

Before describing some of these more formal budgeting procedures and issues, it should also be noted that many informal, yet important, practices also accompany merit pay budgeting. For example, a great deal of "horse-trading" can go on concerning merit pay budgets. A new manager may see, for example, that when they request and argue for a $20,000 budget for merit increases in the next year, they receive a $10,000 budget. It doesn't take a new manager very many budgeting periods to realize that to be assured of the $20,000 budget they need, the manager will need to submit a proposed merit increase budget of $40,000. The point here is that many rituals and other informal behaviors accompany merit budgeting and may be just as influential in determining the ultimate size of the budget as formal dollar-and-cents considerations.

Uniform versus Flexible Budgets

The majority of U.S. organizations appear to allocate their merit pay budgets as a uniform percentage of pay-roll (Peck, 1984). What this means is that a uniform percent of the total payroll is allocated to each business unit in the organization for merit increases. No allowance is made for differences in costs or revenues associated with employees in each business unit. Alternatively, flexible budgets make allowances for differences in costs and revenues for each unit.

The frequent practice of uniform budgets is potentially problematic (Brennan, 1985; R. Heneman, 1990). If one business unit is very profitable because of employee efforts and another unit is not, when pay increase monies are allocated on a uniform basis, pay-for-performance perceptions may be low for the more profitable unit. As a result of the budgeting process, money is, in a sense, being taken away from the more profitable unit to pay for the less profitable unit. Given this potential problem with uniform budgets, some organizations use more flexible budgets, which take into account differences between business units. The risk of using flexible budget models is, of course, the chance of creating perceived inequities across business units. The hope, however, is that linking merit budgets to individual unit performance will strengthen the linkage between merit pay and performance, aligning merit pay more closely with organizational strategy (R. Heneman, 2001b).

Top-Down versus Bottom-Up Models

If flexible budgets are used, distinctions between business units can be made using a "top-down" approach, a "bottom-up" approach, or some combination of the two (Rock, 1988). A top-down approach is based on a valuation of cash generation received by capital markets. Business units that generate greater revenues receive a larger merit budget. In the public sector, cash generation may be supplemented with funds not only generated by capital markets, but by the legislature as well. Lawther et al. (1989) reported that many states receive merit budgets solely on the basis of legislative funds.

A bottom-up approach is based on management projections of cash uses and sources. An example is the setting of merit budgets on the basis of anticipated comparative salary ratios. According to Peck (1984), about 13% of U.S. organizations grant merit budgets on the basis of comparative salary ratios, with business units with larger comparative salary ratios receiving larger budgets. Another example comes from the public sector. Merit increases for state employees in Alabama, Idaho, Minnesota, Montana, Nebraska, and Texas have been funded by turnover, retirement, and open positions in the state (Lawther et al., 1989). Savings from these sources were used to fund merit increases.

Fay (1972) described top-down and bottom-up budgeting procedures. He concluded that a bottom-up procedure is superior to a top-down approach for a variety of reasons. Among them is the consideration given in the bottom-up procedure to changes in cash flow and human resource requirements over the budgeted time period. Under a top-down approach, changes in these variables are not taken into consideration. Also, a bottom-up approach facilitates the strategic planning process by involving business unit managers in the budgeting process. Under a top-down approach, budgets are established by the finance department, in conjunction with compensation professionals. Such an approach may not take into consideration the strategic direction of individual business units.

While a bottom-up procedure appears to be desirable from both time and managerial perspectives, Fay (1972) noted that this procedure is not without costs. In particular, if an organization is to be successful with a bottom-up model, it is essential that it has the information-processing capabilities required to make changes in resource requirements over time. By having an effective human-resource information system (HRIS), the line manager can see the impact of salary decisions under various sets of circumstances. Along with a HRIS, it is also essential that line managers be trained in the salary and budgeting process as it relates to strategic planning. The Human Resource department can be helpful in this training, as well as in auditing the results of the budgeting process.

Overall Size of Budget

Regardless of the procedure used to allocate budgets among business units, consideration also needs to be given to the overall size of the budget. The Peck (1984) survey suggested that while the financial performance of the organization is important, the competitiveness of the organization in terms of pay is even more important in setting merit pay budgets. This can be seen in Table 5.1. These figures are quite consistent with economic theory (reviewed in Chapter 2). As would be expected under the theory of marginal revenue product, employers seem to base merit budgets on

Table 5.1

Considerations in Establishing Merit Increase Budgets

Factors	Number of Mentions	Average Rank*
External pay relationships	503	1.9
Company financial results	471	2.6
Company financial prospects	452	2.9
Internal pay relationships	419	3.7
Cost-of-living changes	420	4.3
Ability to hire	386	4.7

Source: Peck (1984). Reprinted with permission. *Note:* * 1 = most important.

financial considerations concerning the price of the product. Also, as would be expected from efficiency wage theory, employers also base merit budgets on labor market considerations.

Gross versus Net Costs

There is confusion as to the actual costs involved in developing, using, and reporting merit pay budgets. According to Mitchell (1989), this confusion comes from a failure to distinguish between gross and net costs. He provides an example to show how easily actual costs can be overstated by failing to subtract turnover savings from gross merit costs in getting to net or actual merit increase costs. In his example, four employees are granted a $1.00 merit increase. Another employee retires and saves the firm $14.00, while a new employee replaces the retired employee at a cost of $10.00. The gross cost of merit pay in this situation is $4.00, as four employees each receive a $1.00 merit increase. The net cost, however, is zero because of the turnover savings of $14–$10 = $4. When the turnover savings of $4 is subtracted from the gross cost of $4, the net cost is zero. As can be seen from this oversimplified example, care must be taken in specifying gross versus net costs in budgeting procedures. It should also be noted that an argument can be made against subtracting out turnover savings that are not directly attributable to the merit pay plan.

Pay Structure Issues

A pay structure is an organizational policy that specifies the rates that can be paid to employees holding jobs of varying worth to the organization. An example of a pay structure is shown in Box 5.1. Each box in this figure depicts the rates of pay that can be allocated to individuals who hold a particular job. To simplify the discussion, each box represents one job. However, each box could be viewed as representing a collection of jobs of similar worth to the organization. Such a collection is known as a pay grade. For example, an individual in entry-level job A can be paid anywhere from $30,000 to $35,000 per year. Rates of pay are similarly shown for individuals in jobs B, C, and D. The rates of pay specified for each job in a pay structure are determined by two procedures known as job evaluation and salary surveys. Both of these procedures are described in detail by Gerhart (2023), Martocchio (2023), and Williams & Werner (2022).

Job Evaluation

Job evaluation is a procedure undertaken in many organizations to determine the worth of jobs to the organization. Some jobs are graded or evaluated higher than other jobs because they have more of certain characteristics believed to be of value to the organization. For example, in Fig. 5.3, Job B may be evaluated higher than Job A because more independent judgment is required by the jobholder and because the duties of the job are more complex. Jobs evaluated as having greater worth or value have corresponding rates of pay that are, on average, greater. So, for example, in Fig. 5.3, the rates of pay for Job B tend to be greater than the rates of pay for Job A. By paying people on the basis of the relative worth of the job, the

Figure 5.3.

Example of a Pay Structure.

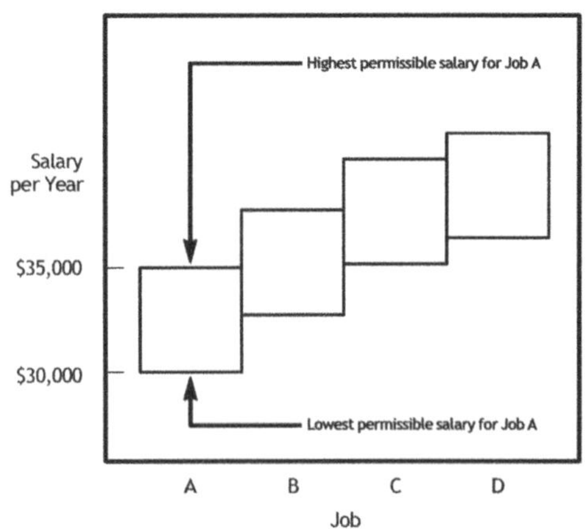

organization is attempting to create a pay system that is equitable (see Chapter 2 for a discussion of equity theory).

Salary Surveys

A salary survey is a procedure used to evaluate the worth of jobs in the marketplace. This procedure helps the organization to establish the pay levels that are assigned to evaluated jobs. In Fig. 5.3, for example, the starting salary for a person in Job A is $30,000 because this is the amount that is being paid as a starting salary in the marketplace for entry-level workers in Job A. Pay rates are made competitive with the market to attract, retain, and maintain a quality workforce. To conduct a salary survey, organizations solicit pay data for jobs similar to theirs from other organizations providing similar products or services in similar geographic areas. It may surprise some readers that there is an incentive for organizations to release their pay data to other organizations, as the participating organizations are usually promised a copy of the results of the survey by the organization conducting the survey. In turn, they can use these results to make the rates of pay for their own jobs competitive with the market.

In summary, pay structures establish the rates of pay for employees based on the value of the jobs they hold. The value of a job is typically established by looking at the results of *both* the job evaluation and the salary survey. Pay structures, like budgets, set boundaries, or limits, on merit increases. Merit increases for an individual employee must not exceed the salary parameters for his or her job, as defined by the pay structure. Pay structures can be further explained by looking at certain characteristics of these structures. Characteristics that are likely to have an influence on merit pay increases are described in detail below.

Pay Ranges

It is possible for a pay structure to be even simpler than the one in Fig. 5.3. In a single-rate structure, for example, there is one rate of pay for each job rather than a range of rates, as shown in Fig. 5.3. So, under a single-rate plan, a person in Job A could only receive a particular rate, say $32,500, rather than being assigned a rate somewhere between

$30,000 and $35,000. The advantage of paying a single rate is that such a structure is straightforward to communicate and easy to administer. The problem with single rates, however, is that they fail to account for differences among employees in their contribution to the organization. For example, under a single-rate structure, both a well-performing and poor-performing employee in Job A would receive a base salary of $32,500 per year. Applying any of the motivational theories discussed in Chapter 2, this arrangement is likely to put a damper on employee motivation.

Because single-rate structures can be problematic, many organizations provide a range of pay levels for people working at a particular job. As in Fig. 5.3, a range of pay levels are granted, depending on the individual contribution of the jobholder. For example, as in Fig. 5.3, an average-performing employee in Job A may receive a salary of $32,500 a year, while an excellent-performing employee may receive $35,000. When a range of rates is used, pay should hopefully be more clearly linked to performance, which, in turn, should motivate employees.

A more detailed treatment of a specific pay range is shown in Fig. 5.4. This figure shows the range of pay for people holding a specific job. For the sake of illustration, the salaries correspond to the range of salaries for Job A in Fig. 5.3. Of course, there are also ranges of salaries for Jobs B, C, and D.

A pay range is defined by three values: the minimum, midpoint, and maximum. The *minimum* is the lowest rate paid to a jobholder, and may correspond to a starting salary for a person with no previous experience.

The *maximum* is the largest amount that can be paid to an individual in this job. The maximum represents the most the job is worth to the organization, regardless of the job incumbent. The *midpoint* represents the desired average that the organization wishes to pay for a particular job. The midpoint can, but does not have to be, set at the market average, as identified in a salary survey. An organization may choose to set the midpoint above or below the market average, in order to either lead or lag the competition. The supervisor uses this range of values in deciding how much his or her subordinates are to receive. Allowances can be made for differences in performance levels of

Figure 5.4.

Example of a Pay Range.

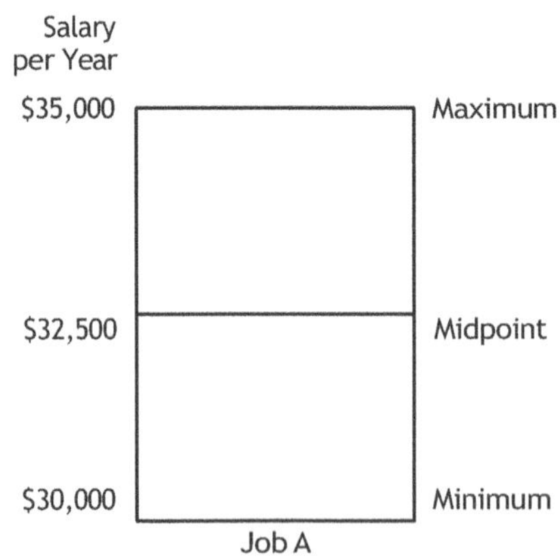

employees holding the same job. Typically, more senior and better-performing employees are between the midpoint and maximum salaries, and less senior and poorer-performing employees are between the midpoint and minimum.

Adjustments are periodically made to pay ranges by organizations (IOMA, 2003). These adjustments are usually in the form of increases to the minimums, midpoints, and maximums. Increases are usually made in response to many factors, including rising costs of goods and services, rising pay levels in the market, increases in the minimum wage required by law, and large numbers of employees reaching the maximum of their pay ranges. Employers must be careful when making these adjustments, so that employees do not become confused as to why their pay is increasing. If employees do not know whether they received a pay increase for performance or for cost-of-living, for example, they will be unable to make the link between pay and performance. As shown in Chapter 2, merit pay is unlikely to be motivational when pay is not linked to performance. This means that organizations need to carefully communicate to employees on what basis they are receiving additions to their pay. Once again, the perceived relationship between pay and performance is as important as the actual relationship between pay and performance. In short, adjustments in pay level for reasons other than performance should be kept separate from merit increases to manage the perception that pay is linked to performance.

Both the maximum and the spread between the minimum and maximum have implications for merit pay. The maximum obviously sets an upper boundary to the size of the merit increase. An increase cannot be so large as to put an employee's pay over the maximum allowed by policy. The size of the spread between the minimum and maximum may also have an influence on performance levels. Obviously, the greater the spread between the minimum and maximum, the larger the potential spread of salary increases. Kopelman and Reinharth (1982) found in a study of white-collar employees in a large financial institution that the greater the range of salary increases awarded, the better the business unit performance. A survey by the Bureau of Labor Statistics indicates that for white-collar occupations, the most likely occupations to have merit pay plans, the average spread between the minimum and maximum is about 50% (Personiak, 1984). Similarly, Zingheim and Schuster (2000) estimate the average spread at 50% for exempt jobs, and at 35% for nonexempt jobs.

Comparative Salary Ratios

Along with the boundaries of the pay structure, another variable that may influence employees' merit increases is position within the pay range. The position of an employee within the pay range can be defined with a comparative salary ratio, or compa-ratio as it is sometimes called. A compa-ratio is simply the pay level for an employee divided by the midpoint or average pay level desired by the organization for employees in the pay range. An example of the calculation of a compa-ratio is as follows:

Employee ID	1,439
Current salary	$51,000
Salary range midpoint	$60,000
Compa-ratio	0.85

It is a common policy in organizations to grant larger merit increases to those with lower compa-ratios. The reason for this policy is to ensure adherence to the desired policy of paying at the budgeted midpoint. Individuals with a compa-ratio greater than one are granted smaller increases to slow down their ascent from the midpoint and to prevent them from exceeding the maximum. Individuals with a compa-ratio less than one are granted larger increases to hasten their progression to the pay midpoint and to prevent them from falling below the minimum. What this means is that individuals with identical performance ratings may receive different merit increases depending on their position in the pay range. While this type of policy may be desirable from the standpoint of minimizing costs, it may conflict with the goal of motivating subsequent performance. In recognition of this tradeoff, some organizations have implemented lump-sum merit increases, where the merit increase is not permanent, to control costs. The increase is not made contingent upon the compa-ratio so as to motivate performance (Sullivan, 1988).

Locked or Fixed-Step Systems

In some organizations, primarily in the public sector, a fixed or locked-step approach to pay ranges is taken (Van Adelsberg, 1978). What this means is that the progression of employees' pay increases within a pay range is based on a series of steps or defined increments. Under such a plan, each level (or step) of performance corresponds to a particular merit increase amount. Hence, the size of a merit increase is locked or fixed for each level or performance rating. For example, a rating of three might correspond to an increase of 3%. This approach is in contrast to other merit pay plans where a range of pay increases is possible for a particular level of performance rating. For example, a rating of three might correspond to an increase anywhere from 2 to 4%.

An obvious advantage to a fixed or lock-step system is that it is a simple plan to follow and administer. Allocators are only required to evaluate the level of performance. The increase associated with the level of performance is automatically determined. On the other hand, this approach may be problematic from a motivational standpoint. It may be possible to more accurately match pay and performance when there is a range of values that can be allocated. Also, allocators may be more motivated to use merit pay, the more discretion they have in allocating pay increases. Merit pay is an important source of authority for supervisors in managing employee performance. The potential downside to this greater amount of discretion, however, is the possibility of creating inequities in pay increases.

Forced Distributions

To control the amount of money allocated to merit increases, forced distributions are sometimes used for performance ratings. A forced distribution (also called a forced ranking) requires that a predetermined percentage of employees be rated at various levels of performance (Smith et al., 1987). This forced distribution of performance ratings in turn leads to a forced distribution of merit increases within pay ranges. Given the amount of discussion and controversy generated by this topic, it is important to estimate the actual frequency with which forced distribution systems are used. Peck (1984) reported that 10% of the organizations he surveyed formally use forced distributions, but that an additional 37% used forced distribution informally. Bretz and Milkovich (1989) reported that 27% of the *Fortune* 100 used forced distributions for professionals. Some estimates are that between 20–25% of organizations use forced distribution systems to make individual performance assessments (Fuller & Tinkham, 2002; Gary, 2001).

Forced distributions seem to be used in response to the positive leniency effect (discussed in Chapter 4) found in some organizations. Ratings are sometimes skewed to the positive extreme, which, in turn, creates cost pressures due to the corresponding large number of large merit increases granted (Smith, 1986). A further rationale for forced distribution is the argument that true performance is normally distributed along a bell-shaped curve. Hence, actual ratings should be normally distributed to capture true performance.

These arguments for the practice of forced distributions have met some conceptual and empirical counterarguments that question even the informal use of forced distributions (Meisler, 2003). Mohrman et al. (1989) pointed out that the assumption that employee performance is normally distributed only holds for a large population of employees. In most merit pay situations, allocators are dealing with a small number of employees. Moreover, these employees have been influenced by other human resource interventions (e.g., selection and training), which may skew true as well as actual performance in a positive (or negative) direction.

McBriarty (1988) presented an interesting case study on the use of forced distributions in the U.S. Air Force. Based on the results of some 200 interviews with participants in this system, McBriarty concluded that the system led to decreased motivation as well as increased turnover, competition among subordinates, and conflict between subordinates and supervisors.

Overall, we recommend that forced distributions should generally be avoided. However, although they are problematic, the goal of cost minimization may sometimes drive employers to use forced distributions. If a forced distribution is necessary, the guidelines set forth by Mohrman et al. (1989) are reasonable. A forced distribution should only be used when absolute rather than relative ratings are used, when work groups are at least 50 members in size, and when only a few categories are "forced" on the allocator, with the bulk of employees being rated in the middle category. Finally, any appraisal system needs to align individual and team efforts with the goals of the unit and organization, and this holds for forced distribution systems as well.

Range Penetration

In addition to *current* position within the pay range, the desired *future* position within the pay range can also be considered. It is possible to provide allocators with spreadsheets and mathematical formulas showing the recipient's position in the pay range over time (Basnight, 1980; Davis, 2002; Moran, 1986; Seithal & Emans, 1983; Stokes, 1981). Position in range is predicted on the basis of various assumptions regarding expected performance levels, range widths, and changes in the pay structure, among other things. These formulas can be used to ensure that an actual merit increase in one year will *not* lead to an employee exceeding the maximum in future years. Also, the formulas can be used to develop merit pay guidelines, so that certain combinations of merit increases over time do not exceed the maximum.

This process of basing merit increases on anticipated range penetration as well as actual performance makes some sense from a cost containment perspective. It is most likely to be used when organizations have limited opportunities for promotions and want to ensure that adequate performers receive a pay increase each year. From a motivational perspective, however, it seems to be a less effective procedure. As discussed in Chapter 2, when pay is *not* contingent on performance, it is unlikely to motivate future performance.

Guide Charts

A summary statement of organizational policy regarding merit pay is sometimes known as a merit pay guide chart (or guideline). A guide chart details the amount and timing of merit increases for various levels of performance at various locations in the pay grade. In a sense, a merit pay guide chart is an operational statement of an organization's pay-for-performance theory or policy. It spells out the contingency between pay and performance in specific terms.

Merit pay guide charts range from the simple to the complex, depending on the number of variables on which pay is made contingent. A simple merit pay guide chart is shown in Table 5.2, in which pay is made contingent solely on performance; the better the performance, the larger the increase. According to reinforcement theory (see Chapter 2), such a policy is likely to motivate improved performance. Also, this policy is consistent with the theme of doing more with less. It is less expensive to give larger increases to good performers and no increases to poor performers than it is to give large increases to both good and poor performers. Merit is usually in the form of a percentage increase in base salary, rather than in the form of an absolute increase for purposes of equity. If an absolute increase amount had been used in Table 5.2, then the percentage increase for high salary employees would have been less than the percentage increase for low salary employees, even though the performance levels of high and low salary employees were the same. Under this absolute increase scenario, employees probably would perceive inequity (see Chapter 2).

As in Table 5.2, it should also be noted that, in order to emphasize the importance of good performance, anything less than adequate performance is usually given a low, or even zero, percent increase. In some organizations, a modest increase may be granted instead of no increase, in order to retain employees. This practice of giving increases to poor performers is curious, though, as it appears that the organization wants to retain rather than lose poor performers! Although negative increases or reductions in salary have

Table 5.2

Simple Merit Guide Chart

Performance Rating				
Unsatisfactory	Needs Improvement	Fully Satisfactory	Above Expectations	Clearly Outstanding
(1)	(2)	(3)	(4)	(5)
0%	1%	4%	5%	6%

Table 5.3

Complex Merit Guide Chart

Position in Range	Unsatisfactory (1)	Needs Improvement (2)	Fully Satisfactory (3)	Above Expectations (4)	Clearly Outstanding (5)
4th quartile	0%	0%	2–4% 15–18 months	4–6% 12–15 months	6–8% 9–12 months
3rd quartile	0%	0–3% 15–18 months	4–6% 12–15 months	6–8% 9–12 months	8–10% 9–12 months
2nd quartile	0%	0–3% 12–15 months	6–8% 9–12 months	8–10% 9–12 months	10–12% 6–9 months
1st quartile	0%	0–5% 9–12 months	8–10% 9–12 months	10–12% 6–9 months	12–14% 6–9 months

been advocated (e.g., Silverman, 1981) for less than adequate performers, this seldom seems to be done in practice.

A more complex guide chart is shown in Table 5.3. It is more complex in three ways. First, a range of merit increases is offered, rather than a single value for each level of performance. This is done to more closely link pay to performance and to give allocators more discretion in the process. Note also that the salary increase ranges do not overlap, to prevent perceptions of inequity. Second, increases depend upon position in the pay range as well as performance. Employees in higher quartiles receive smaller increases than employees in lower quartiles to prevent those in higher quartiles from exceeding the maximum. Third, the timing of increases varies. Better performers are rewarded more frequently than are poorer performers.

A different task confronted by managers who are required to use complex guide charts is deciding the specific percentage increase to grant to subordinates when a range of values is possible. For example, using Table 5.3, if a manager has a fully satisfactory performing subordinate in the second quartile of the pay range, the manager can grant that subordinate a 6 to 8% merit increase. Which increase to give—6, 7, 8%, or some value in between—is a tough decision.

It seems likely that when managers need to make decisions at the margins, they look at some of the alternative measures of performance described in Chapter 4. That is, they look at factors like seniority, promotability, organizational citizenship behaviors, and market value. For example, a manager may be more likely to grant a 6% instead of a 4% increase when the fully satisfactory employee has been on the job a short period of time, is seen as being promotable, exhibits high levels of citizenship behaviors, and has talents that are in demand in the labor market. Factors such as these should be considered on the margins when they are related to the business mission of the organization, are clearly communicated to employees, and do not violate the laws and regulations discussed in Chapter 6.

There is almost no research on employees' reactions to merit guide charts. In a study of employees in a transit agency, merit pay satisfaction was highest for employees rated highest, as well as for those lower in their pay ranges (Scott, Markham, & Vest, 1996). Stated another way, employees were generally satisfied with their merit increases (paid on the basis of guide charts), except for those in the highest pay quintile with the lowest performance ratings. One might also expect to find that reactions to guide charts would depend on social comparisons made. In two studies, it has been shown that reactions to pay vary according to the selection of comparison others (H. Heneman, Schwab, Standal, & Peterson, 1978; Scholl, Cooper, & McKenna, 1987). It might, therefore, be expected that reactions to guide charts depend on the comparisons employees make between the guide chart they operate under and the guide charts that the comparison others they have selected are believed to work under. For example, a 4% increase for excellent performance may be upsetting in the absence of information about merit increases in other organizations. The same 4% increase may lead to being pleased rather than upset when it is known that in other similar organizations, a 2% increase is granted in a given year for excellent performance.

Allocator Selection

A final policy issue that arises is who should be making merit increase decisions? In the majority of cases, the individual allocating merit increases is the recipient's immediate supervisor, who makes the decision in conjunction with the business unit head and human resource manager (R. Heneman, 2001b; Wyatt Company, 1987). This most-often-followed policy makes sense, in that performance information is available through the immediate supervisor, as discussed in Chapter 4. Budget information is perhaps best known by the business unit head, and the human resource manager can ensure consistency across business units. This approach is consistent with the traditional model of management in which managers are responsible for the performance of their subordinates and are given discretion within limits to manage their subordinates.

As traditional models of management change, however, so too may those involved in merit allocation decisions. An example is work settings where individuals perform in a more autonomous fashion with less immediate supervision. In these situations, organizations may have to draw upon allocators other than immediate supervisors. These could include peer nominations for merit increases in public school systems, team leaders as allocators in matrix organizations, host-company supervisors as allocators for outside consultants, managing partners as allocators in law and accounting firms, and ratings of behaviors, rather than results for CEOs by their board of directors. Changes in the nature of work are having an impact on traditional merit pay systems (Gabor, 1989; R. Heneman, 2001a).

Implementing a Merit Pay Policy

It is unlikely that a well-designed merit pay policy will lead to desired outcomes, such as improved performance, in and of itself. In other words, a well-designed policy is a necessary but not sufficient condition for a merit pay plan to work (R. Heneman, 1984b). Attention must also be given to factors that facilitate the introduction and implementation of a merit pay plan. Although there is not a lot of research on factors that facilitate this process, several factors based on theory and case study reports are presented here. These factors that facilitate the implementation of a merit pay plan include the timing of plan introduction, upper-level support, participation in plan development, and employee trust.

Timing of Plan Introduction

A merit pay plan can be introduced in two ways: either as a lead or a lag system (Lawler, 1981). What this means is that a merit plan can be used either to bring about a change in the organization (a lead system), or to reinforce other changes being made in the organization (a lag system). There could, of course, be parallel change, where merit pay is introduced at the same time as another change in the organization. As pointed out by Lawler (1981), such an attempt is likely to produce chaos because of the drain on organizational resources and the difficulty of meshing the two changes. A good example of these difficulties is pointed out by two reports that examined the simultaneous implementation of both a new performance appraisal system and merit pay system in the federal government (R. Heneman, 1990; U.S. Congress, 1981).

Merit Pay as a Lag System

Under many circumstances, it would seem that merit pay should be introduced as a lag system. As described in Chapter 2, merit pay possesses strong motivational properties, which can be used to reinforce desired changes in the organization (Zingheim & Schuster, 2000). Reports by Patten (1977) and the Florida Power Corporation (1985) show how merit pay can be used to reinforce a desired change. Patten shows how merit pay was used to support the introduction of an MBO program for sales employees. This method of management was reinforced by merit increases that were made contingent on the successful completion of agreed-upon objectives established by the employee and his or her supervisor. At Florida Power Corporation, merit pay was used to reinforce behaviors back on the job that employees learned in a new management development program. Successfully completing learning objectives from the development seminar back on the job was coupled with a merit increase.

Given the motivational properties of merit pay, it might seem that merit pay should be used solely as a lag system. This does not, however, seem to be the case. If merit pay is introduced following the implementation of another program with perceived negative properties, merit pay may be viewed or used in a negative fashion as well. Pagano (1985) reported on employees' reactions to a merit pay plan introduced after a reduction in force in a U.S. government agency. Rather than using merit pay for its intended purpose (i.e., rewarding past performance to motivate future performance), merit pay was used instead to retain staff members from a reduction in force. In short, merit pay, as a lag system, can be a powerful intervention in organizations. Therefore, care must be exercised to ensure that it is used to reinforce desirable rather than undesirable behaviors.

Merit Pay as a Lead System

Merit pay can also be used as a lead system with the intent of bringing about a change in the organization, rather than simply reinforcing some other change that has been implemented. One advantage to introducing merit pay as a lead system is that it shows the organization is committed to meaningful change (Lawler, 1981). A merit pay system may show employees that the organization is serious about change because resources are being devoted to change. This situation can be contrasted with one where resources are not devoted to change, and employees therefore view any change as merely cosmetic.

An example of merit pay as a lead system comes from the Evanston, Illinois, school district (Cohen & Murname, 1980). Merit pay was introduced as a lead system to demonstrate the school district's commitment to improved performance in the classroom. Comments by Evanston school teachers indicated that merit pay as a lead system did result in more teacher commitment to quality education. However, it did not necessarily result in improved teaching performance. Many teachers viewed merit awards as a vote of confidence by the community for quality education, rather than viewing these awards as an incentive to improve teacher performance.

The Evanston example indicates that merit pay as a lead system may not always produce the intended results. To achieve the intended results, those managing the merit process must carefully monitor users' reactions. Also, as pointed out by Lawler (1981), for a merit pay plan to work as a lead system, there often needs to be dissatisfaction with current conditions in the organization. If dissatisfaction is not present, employees may not be receptive to a change in the pay system.

Upper-Level Support

Another factor that should contribute to the successful implementation of a merit pay plan is upper-level support in the organization. Upper-level support consists of at least three features. The first feature is the linking of the merit pay plan to the strategic mission of the organization. By tying these two systems together, the message is communicated that merit pay is an integral component of the mission of the organization, rather than a tangential system (R. Heneman, 2001b). An example of this feature can be observed at Pratt and Whitney, where the performance standards on which merit increases were based were linked explicitly to the business goals of the organization (Schneier, 1989b).

A second feature that demonstrates upper-level support is endorsement of the plan by the top decision-makers in the organization. This is one of several factors attributed to the success of merit pay for managers in New York City (Allan & Rosenberg, 1986). Perhaps the best way for upper-level decision-makers to demonstrate support is to participate in the process. That is, if merit pay is to be used, it should apply to all levels of the organization, not just to the lower levels. This participative approach is one of the reasons given for the successful implementation of the merit pay plan at Pratt and Whitney (Schneier, 1989b). The reason this support is vital to the successful implementation of a merit pay plan is that it communicates the importance of performance for employees at all levels of the organization. A third feature is the use of performance-contingent rewards as a method of leadership by upper levels of the organization (Hinkin et al., 1987). What this entails is making sure that not only are rewards based on merit for upper-level managers, but that upper-level managers apply this same philosophy to their subordinates. Pay as well as other nonmonetary rewards, such as recognition, need to be made contingent upon successful performance. A merit pay plan should be more acceptable to employees when all rewards are made contingent upon performance for all employees than when merit pay is the only reward that is contingent on performance, and when this contingency applies to only some employees.

Participation in Plan Development

Both theory and research suggest that the successful implementation of a merit pay plan involves participation in the development of the pay plan by the parties who will be affected. Drawing upon motivational theory, Lawler (1981) suggested that participating in the development of a merit pay plan leads to the strengthening of pay-for-performance perceptions. The reasons for this strengthening of the pay-for-performance relationship is that, by participating in the development of a merit pay plan, employees have more knowledge about the plan, are more committed to the plan, feel that they have some control over the plan, and trust the system (Lawler, 1981). A proposed model of participation is shown in Fig. 5.5.

Figure 5.5.

The Effects of Participation on Perceptions of Pay.

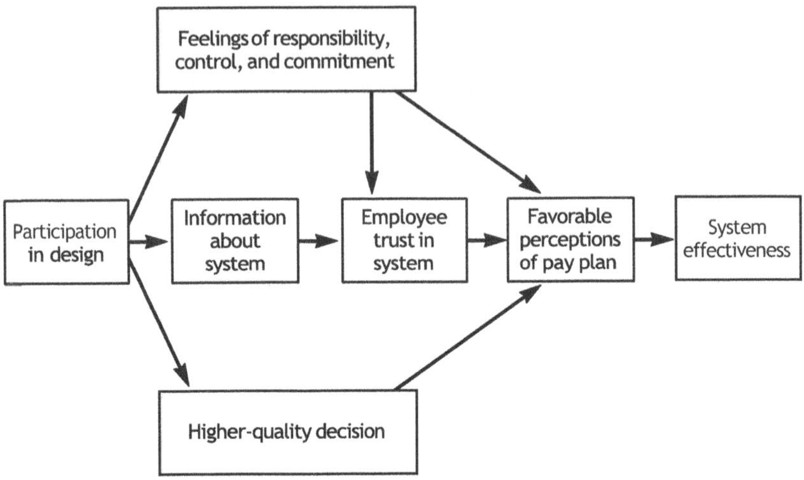

Source: From E.E. Lawler III (1981), Pay and organization development, © 1981 Addison-Wesley Publishing Co., Inc., Figure 4.1. Reprinted with permission.

Support for this model comes from two interesting studies conducted with custodial workers by Lawler and his colleagues (Lawler & Hackman, 1969; Scheflen et al., 1971). In the first study, comparisons were made among workers who developed their own bonus plan for good attendance, workers who received a bonus for good attendance based on a plan imposed by management, and workers who did not receive a bonus for good attendance. A significant improvement in attendance occurred—but only for the group that participated in developing the bonus plan. In the second study, it was shown that this improved attendance record was carried over into the next year even for custodians in the group that did not develop the original plan. These positive results were attributed by the authors to the increased commitment, knowledge, and trust of employees who participated in the development of the bonus plan.

These are the variables shown in Fig. 5.5 to explain the favorable effects of participation in pay plan development.

Three empirical studies also provide support for participation in the implementation of merit pay plans. One of the studies was conducted in a small manufacturing plant in Ohio (Jenkins & Lawler, 1981; Lawler, 1981). In this study, attitudes and behaviors were compared before and after implementation of the merit pay plan. After participative implementation of the plan, there were significant improvements in turnover, job satisfaction, and pay satisfaction. A second study was conducted in a public utility company

(Bullock, 1983). Again, reactions were measured before and after the plan was implemented. The results indicated that participation in the development of the plan led to strengthened pay-for-performance perceptions, increased commitment, and greater job satisfaction. Pay satisfaction was not, however, increased. A third study was conducted in the city government of Biloxi, Mississippi (Gabris & Mitchell, 1988; Gabris, Mitchell, & McLemore, 1985). Pay fairness was measured only after the implementation of the plan, and it was found that while the high performers believed the system was fair, low performers were less inclined to believe the plan was fair.

All three of these studies provide some support for participation in the implementation of merit pay plans. Some confidence can be placed in the generalizability of these findings, as the studies took place in very diverse settings. On the other hand, caution should be exercised in the interpretation of these findings, as there were no control groups (see Chapter 7 for a discussion of the importance of control groups). Without a control group, it is difficult to know if the observed changes were due to participation or some other factor.

The form that participation took in the three studies was very similar. A committee, council, or task force was established in each location. These task forces were composed of members from a representative sample of the workforce. Also, these task forces consisted of both employee and management representatives. In all three cases, the groups developed the actual merit pay plan that was used. From the reported characteristics of these groups, it seems that, for a merit pay plan to be successfully implemented, all of the parties who will be affected by the plan must have a voice in its development—at the least, through a chosen representative (or group of representatives).

While participation can have some very desirable results, it will not work in all situations. This was pointed out to one of us (R.L.H.) in a project with a Japanese parts manufacturer in the United States. The Japanese managers in this organization felt that participation was appropriate when it comes to technical matters, such as how parts are produced. They did not, however, feel that participation was appropriate in managerial decisions concerning how performance is measured, evaluated, and rewarded. Once again, as noted in Chapter 4, participation may or may not be acceptable to the affected parties. This issue clearly needs to be addressed in the administration of merit pay plans.

Employee Trust

A difficult-to-define, but important concept in the implementation of merit pay plans and other reward systems is employee trust (Avdul et al., 2023; Ferrin & Dirks, 2003; Lawler, 1971; Parco, Rapoport, & Stein, 2002).

Trust, as it relates to merit pay, seems to refer to a belief that management has developed and adheres to a fair set of performance standards used to grant merit increases. A study by Vest, Scott, Vest, and Markham (2000) demonstrated the importance of trust. A significant positive relationship between trust in top management and pay-for-performance perceptions was reported for a sample of employees in a transit authority. The more trust, the stronger the belief that pay was related to performance.

The importance of developing an agreed-upon and adhered to set of performance standards for merit increases also comes from a report about merit pay practices at the Dayton-Hudson Corporation (Schwadel, 1990). According to this news report, sales employees were disgruntled with the performance standards as well as other facets of the merit pay plan. For example, the longer the time on the job, the higher the sales quotas under the plan. If the quotas were not attained, employees were fired. You would expect employee trust to be low in a situation where the better you perform, the more likely you are to lose your job!

Trust also has to do with participation in pay plan development and the degree to which merit decisions are kept confidential (see the discussion of pay secrecy in Chapter 6). Some organizations encourage employee participation in the setting of performance standards, but limit employee access to salary information. Employees will question the motives of management when they are asked to develop standards that will influence the size of their pay increase, but are not allowed to know how their performance actually influenced the size of their pay increase. If participation is used, then there must be some openness concerning how merit increase decisions are reached.

Summary of Major Points

1. *Just-noticeable differences (JNDs).* Merit increases do not automatically influence subsequent employee performance. For a merit increase to influence subsequent performance, it must be large enough in magnitude to create a just-noticeable difference (JND) to the employee.
2. *Size of merit increases.* There is no ideal size for a merit increase. The size of the increase likely to create a JND depends on characteristics of the person and situation, including the job, performance, and earnings level. Research, however, suggests that the average increase needed to create a just-noticeable difference is likely to be considerably higher than the average merit increase actually received by most employees.
3. *Lump-sum merit increases.* Under a lump-sum merit pay plan, a merit increase is not rolled over into the base salary of the employee.

Instead, the merit increase is a one-time award. A lump-sum plan seems to be less costly to the organization and more likely to tie pay to performance over the long term. Concerns remain, though, over employee reactions to such plans.

4. *Common review date.* Many organizations have made a practice of reviewing merit increases for all employees on a common date. This practice seems to lessen the paperwork burden, but may impose time pressures on the allocator and cost pressures on the organization.
5. *Merit pay budgets.* Establishing merit increases depends, in part, on the budget for merit pay. The most common practice, allocating merit pay budgets as a uniform percentage of payroll, appears to be problematic as attention is not given to differences in business unit performance. Flexible budgeting procedures, such as top-down and bottom-up procedures that recognize differences in subunit performance, should be used more often.
6. *Pay structure considerations.* Establishing merit pay increases also depends on characteristics of the pay structure. To control costs and keep employees within the existing pay structures, organizations sometimes give consideration to rate ranges, maximums, comparative salary ratios (compa-ratios), forced distributions, and range penetration in determining merit increases. These other considerations may, however, detract from the purpose of merit pay, which is to motivate subsequent performance.
7. *Guide charts.* A guide chart is the formal policy statement issued by an organization regarding merit pay. A guide chart details the amount and timing of merit increases for various levels of performance at various locations in the pay range.
8. *Policy versus implementation.* A well-developed merit pay policy is important. Although necessary, it is not a sufficient condition for a merit pay plan to lead to desired outcomes, such as improved performance. For a merit pay plan to contribute to desired outcomes, management must also focus on the implementation of the plan.
9. *Implementation steps.* Considering the results of a number of case studies, it seems that merit pay plans are more successful when the plan is not implemented simultaneously with other large-scale organizational changes. There also needs to be upper-level support for the merit pay plan, employee participation in the development of the plan (at the least, by representatives of all those affected by the plan), and employee trust in management, as well as in the standards that are used to determine merit increases.

Conclusions

As noted in the first chapter, merit pay is an attempt by organizations to get more for less. The goal is to get more performance for less money. To do so, attention must be paid to both motivational and financial considerations. Motivational considerations help us guide reward systems toward greater performance. Financial considerations help us minimize the costs associated with reward systems. Attention must be given to *both* motivational and financial considerations, because the goals of improved performance may conflict with the goals of minimizing costs. Too often, it seems that attention is given to one, but not to the other. As a result, merit pay plans are developed that are likely to motivate improved performance, but are too costly to implement. Conversely, merit plans are developed that cost little to implement, but are unlikely to motivate improved performance. In either event, when motivation and finances are considered independent of one another, a merit pay plan is unlikely to produce the desired results.

In developing a merit pay plan, attention must be given to both the creation and implementation of a policy or intended statement about the relationship between performance ratings and pay increases. One development in merit pay policy is the creation of lump-sum merit plans. Compared to more traditional merit pay plans, lump-sum plans seem to strike a balance between the goals of performance maximization and cost minimization. Under a lump-sum plan, pay increases are not permanently rolled over into base salary as is done in traditional merit pay plans. Hence, pay is "earned as you go," rather than granted for the duration of your entire career on the basis of performance in one rating period.

This promising feature does not mean that organizations should rush into using a lump-sum plan. Organizations with preexisting, traditional merit pay plans need to exercise extreme caution in shifting to a lump-sum plan. The shift to a lump-sum plan may clash with the culture of the organization. For example, as a result of years of experience with a traditional merit plan, employees may believe they are entitled to an annual merit increase that rolls over into their base salary. A rapid shift to a lump-sum plan may shatter beliefs and lead to disruptive work behaviors.

Even organizations implementing a merit pay plan for the first time need to proceed slowly with lump-sum arrangements. When a lump-sum plan is implemented, the initial reactions of employees may be favorable. Who wouldn't be pleased with the possibility of a large cash bonus at the end of the year? However, these favorable reactions may not last very long when employees find that their monthly paychecks do not keep their incomes at acceptable levels, or when they find that their neighbors keep merit increases as a permanent addition to their salaries. A lump-sum plan simply will not work if it is used as a substitute for a well developed *total compensation system* that provides adequate levels of income in the form of salaries, incentives, and benefits (Zingheim & Schuster, 2000).

As with lump-sum plans, a note of caution should be added vis-à-vis employee participation in merit plan development. Two warnings are warranted. First, participation requires a certain level of expertise. For example, a merit pay plan must be integrated with other components of a total compensation system, such as salaries and benefits. This integration requires knowledge of pay systems. As a result, a leader knowledgeable in compensation matters should facilitate the participation process, and employees involved in the development of merit pay plans should receive training in compensation matters.

A major factor in the successful implementation of merit pay plans is employee participation. Participation in the implementation of merit pay plans is *in addition to* the participation that is recommended in the development of performance standards (see Chapter 4). Employee participation in the implementation of merit pay plans has both theoretical and empirical support. Research shows that participation works well when a task force of elected employees is used in an advisory capacity to help implement a merit pay plan. Such participation is likely to foster more favorable attitudes toward merit pay and commitment to the merit pay plan.

Second, participation requires a willingness to become involved in the development of a merit pay plan. Some employees may not see participation as desirable. While these employees may want to share in merit pay increases, they may not want to participate in determining the procedures to be used to link pay to performance. As a result, participation in merit pay plan development should be voluntary.

As you have seen, many factors need to be considered as an organization implements a merit pay plan and establishes individual pay increases. The actual administration of merit pay plans on a day-to-day basis requires that organizational decision-makers consider yet more issues. We turn our attention to these additional issues in Chapter 6.

Study Questions

1. What is a just-noticeable difference (JND)? How do JNDs relate to merit pay increases?
2. What has been the trend of average merit pay increases in the last few decades? What are some chief influences affecting major volatility in merit pay increases? Why would compensation practitioners find this information important?
3. What is the difference between traditional merit pay plans and lump-sum merit pay plans?
4. Briefly, describe budgeting issues as they relate to merit pay plans.

5. What is the purpose of a merit guide chart? Describe the difference between simple and complex merit guide charts.
6. Describe four aspects of implementing a merit pay policy. Is one aspect more important than the others, or are they equally important? Explain.

CHAPTER 6

MERIT PAY ADMINISTRATION

Numerous authors have called attention to the importance of the administration of merit pay plans (Allan & Rosenberg, 1986; Berger & Schwab, 1980; Fulmer et al., 2023; Hamner, 1975; R. Heneman, 1984b, 2001b; Kellough & Nigro, 2002; Velghe et al., 2024). Merit pay plans can be eloquently designed, yet ineffective, if they are poorly administered. In this chapter, attention is given to issues that must be considered to properly administer a merit pay plan. These issues center on what organizations can do to ensure that their merit pay policies are carried out as intended in actual practice. Perceptions of fairness are vital in this regard.

Organizational Justice

An important area of investigation for organizational researchers is known as organizational justice (Adamovic, 2023; Colquitt et al., 2001; Cropanzano et al., 2001). Organizational justice has to do with the perceived fairness of decisions made about employees in organizations. Major issues concerning organizational fairness have to do with distributive, procedural, and interactional forms of justice. Each form of justice has important implications for merit pay administration.

Theory

Greenberg (1986, 1987a, 1987b, 1990) made an important distinction between distributive and procedural justice that is relevant for the

Merit Pay, pages 209–250

doi:10.1108/978-1-80686-701-120263006

administration of merit pay. Distributive justice, as it relates to merit pay, refers to the perceived fairness of merit increases allocated. That is, distributive justice focuses on the perceived fairness of merit pay *outcomes* (i.e., the amount allocated for various performance inputs). Procedural justice, on the other hand, refers to the perceived fairness of the procedures or *process* used to determine merit increases. That is, procedural justice looks at the procedures organizations undertake to ensure a link between pay and performance. This has been described as a "due process" metaphor, akin to the focus in courts of law on the processes and procedures followed in a legal trial (Folger et al., 1993). A third form of organizational justice has also been proposed, namely *interactional* justice (Bies, 2001; Greenberg & McCarty, 1990). This form of justice appears to be related to procedural justice, yet emphasizes the manner in which individuals are treated (Cropanzano et al., 2001). Interactional justice can include the way that decisions concerning merit pay are communicated to employees by their supervisors (Ramaswami & Singh, 2003).

Much of what we have covered in this book so far relates primarily to distributive rather than procedural or interactional justice. For example, Chapter 5 discussed setting policy on the amount to be allocated in merit increase decisions. The research of Greenberg and others suggests that attention should also be given to issues related to procedural and interactional justice.

Importance of Procedural and Interactional Justice

A number of studies point out the importance of both procedural and interactional justice to merit pay. First, Hyde (1988) found that, for a large sample of federal managers, 90% were in favor of pay for performance, yet 74% felt that their present merit pay system was unfair. Second, Bretz and Milkovich (1989) reported that the most important issues large organizations faced regarding their performance appraisal systems concerned the fairness of how the systems were used. Third, St-Onge (2000) studied employees in a large manufacturing organization, and found that perceptions of procedural fairness (concerning both the appraisal and the merit pay systems) was the strongest predictor of perceptions that pay was based on performance. Interestingly, the perceptual fairness measure was a stronger predictor of pay-for-performance perceptions than was a measure of the actual pay-for-performance link. This result, however, may simply reflect the fact that both the measures of fairness and pay-for-performance perceptions were measured by questionnaire. Fourth, Jones (1998) found that perceptions of fairness concerning pay determination, pay communication, appraisals, and appeal processes (see Scarpello &

Jones, 1996) were predictive of voluntary turnover among county government workers. These effects were found after controlling for perceptions of distributive justice. A later study of retail employees found that distributive justice had a stronger effect on turnover when interactional justice was perceived as low (Jones & Skarlicki, 2003). Fifth, Ramaswami and Singh (2003) studied merit pay fairness perceptions among industrial salespeople. They found that interactional justice had a stronger relationship than procedural justice with the level of trust that salespeople had with their supervisors, as well as with their reported job satisfaction. They write that, "our findings suggest that when procedures and their enactment are separated, it is interactional fairness that affects work outcomes" (p. 60). Sixth, research has shown the moderating effect of procedural justice and other individual and organizational characteristics on various organization outcomes.

Collectively, these studies suggest that employees are likely to be very concerned about procedural and interactional justice issues, perhaps even more than over distributive justice issues (Jones, 1998).

Rules

Miceli and Lane (1991) provided a valuable summary of suggested rules that organizations can follow to attain perceptions of procedural justice. These rules (based on Leventhal et al., 1976) and their potential applications to merit pay are shown in Table 6.1.

Research

Empirical research gives further insight into the manner in which procedural justice relates to performance appraisal and compensation in general, and to merit pay in particular. The reader will note that the studies provide general support for the rules shown in Table 6.1. These studies also suggest additional rules that might enhance perceptions of procedural justice. While the focus of these studies has been on "procedural justice" issues, the variables studied in fact combine both the procedural and interactional forms of justice described above. Finally, the studies described below are divided in two broad categories for reading ease. The first collection concentrates on the relationship between procedural justice and *attitudes* such as pay satisfaction and organizational commitment. The second group looks at the effect of procedural justice on *behaviors* such as performance and engagement.

Table 6.1.

Procedural Justice Rules Applied to Merit Pay

Rule	Description	Potential Applications
Consistency	Procedures for allocation should be consistent across persons and over time	Reliable and valid measures of performance are used to make merit decisions
Bias suppression	Bias should be suppressed	Rater training is provided to eliminate rating errors
Accuracy	Decisions must be based on accurate information	Allocators are held accountable for their decisions
Correctability	Decisions should be correctable	Merit pay decisions can be appealed
Representation	The allocation process must represent the concerns of all recipients	Employee participation takes place in the development of a merit pay plan
Ethics	Participants should comply with ethical standards	Laws and regulations are followed; organizational codes of conduct are adhered to in all merit pay decision making

Source: Adapted from Leventhal et al. (1980); Miceli and Lane (1991). Reprinted with permission.

Procedural Justice and Attitudes

In a study of managers, Dyer and Theriault (1976) looked at the perceived adequacy of pay system administration. Their results indicated that the perceived adequacy of pay system administration provided an explanation of pay satisfaction above and beyond the explanation offered by characteristics of the job and person alone. The perceived adequacy of pay system administration appears to be very closely related to the concept of procedural justice. It is defined by employee understanding of the pay criteria, superiors' influence over pay decisions, superiors' accuracy in work assessments, and the congruence between the employee and superiors' preferences for pay criteria. Subsequent studies of the perceived adequacy of pay system administration also found this concept to be related to pay satisfaction (Miceli & Near, 1988; Weiner, 1980). One interesting aspect of this concept is that it requires the clear communication of rules and procedures of the merit pay system. To do so, training seems appropriate for both allocators and recipients of merit pay.

Greenberg (1986) looked at the determinants of perceived fairness of performance evaluations. He asked mid-level managers, by way of an open-ended questionnaire, to describe determinants of fair or unfair appraisals. He found that several of the determinants related to procedural/interactional justice. These determinants were: soliciting input prior to evaluation and using it, engaging in two-way communication during the appraisal interview, providing the opportunity to challenge or rebut the evaluation, the rater being familiar with the ratee's work, and consistently applying performance standards. These factors are consistent with the rules in Table 6.1.

In addition to providing some support for the perceived adequacy of pay system administration, Miceli and Near (1988) also formulated and tested another variable believed to be a part of the procedural justice concept. This variable was the perceived adequacy of merit funding. As expected, this variable was positively related to pay satisfaction for executives in the sample. Unexpectedly, this variable was negatively related to pay satisfaction for middle managers in the sample. Hence, there was some support for the perceived adequacy of merit funding. The reason why adequacy of merit funding may be related to pay satisfaction is because employees are more likely to be satisfied when they believe that the merit budget is large enough to reward all employees deserving of a merit increase (Miceli & Lane, 1991; Miceli & Near, 1988).

Folger and Konovsky (1989) examined distributive and procedural justice as they related to pay decisions for employees in a manufacturing plant. They found that procedural justice could be summarized in terms of how feedback was presented to the employee, the planning of the performance and salary increase review, recourse available to the employee in response to appraisal, and frequency of performance observation by the supervisor. These procedural factors were more strongly related to organizational commitment than were measures of distributive justice. Although they were related to pay satisfaction, procedural justice items were not as strongly related to pay satisfaction as were perceptions of distributive justice. An important implication of this study is that organizations and individuals can and should take a proactive stance toward procedural justice. This is reflected in the results of Folger and Konovsky for the planning aspect of procedural justice, and is consistent with Greenberg's (1987b) observation that procedural justice can vary from reactive to proactive.

Mulvey (1991) also studied procedural justice and merit pay. He examined the reactions of employees to pay outcomes and procedures in eight Midwestern service organizations with merit pay plans. In particular, he looked at the extent to which satisfaction with pay depends on procedural justice. His findings indicated that pay satisfaction is likely to be higher when employees believe they have the opportunity to appeal and modify pay decisions, and when pay decisions are clearly communicated and justified to employees. This is supported by subsequent research by Jones and colleagues (Jones, 1998; Jones & Skarlicki, 2003; Scarpello & Jones, 1996).

The relationship between procedural justice and merit-pay acceptance was also studied by van Dijke et al. (2009). They predicted that procedural and interpersonal justice would moderate the relationship between distributive justice and merit pay acceptance. Their analysis included two steps. First, the authors employed a factor analysis to ensure all fairness measures—procedural, interpersonal, distribution—were distinct factors. Second, the researchers used a multiple-regression procedure to examine the moderated effect of procedural and interpersonal justice on distributive justice and merit-pay acceptance. The results of the analyses supported the authors' hypotheses. The implementation of a new merit pay system based on favorable perceptions of procedural and interpersonal fairness promotes worker acceptance of such a system and the fairness in which merit increases are distributed. The findings of this study appear to align with the rules in Table 6.1. Employees participating in the development of a merit pay system are more likely to accept that program.

In a study of a public-sector organization, Choi (2011) explored how procedural and distributive justice affect employee perception of pay satisfaction, trust in management pay decisions, and turnover intentions. Using multiple regression, the results show that both forms of justice (distributive slighter greater than procedural) relate positively to pay satisfaction, and trust in pay decisions, while they correlate negatively with turnover intentions of employees. The findings shed light on two practical implications. First, procedural justice and distributive justice appear to be as important to governmental agencies as they are to private-sector employers. Second, failure to include both forms of justice in human resource (HR) processes may magnify the possibility of pay dissatisfaction, distrust in manager pay decisions, and turnover intentions.

Abd Razak et al. (2025) evaluated the effectiveness of performance-based pay and perceived procedural justice in companies linked to the Malaysian government. Specifically, the researchers examined the relationship between components of a performance-based pay system (i.e. communication, participation, and performance evaluation) and procedural justice. Using structural equation modeling (SEM), the results of the study showed (a) the relationship between communication and procedural justice was positive and significant, (b) the relationship between participation and procedural justice was non-significant, and (c) the relationship between performance appraisal and procedural justice was positive and significant. An important-performance map analysis revealed that performance evaluation is the most critical and well-executed component, followed by communication, and participation. The findings here reveal the importance of effective communication, participation, and systematic performance evaluation in implementing and managing performance-based pay to enhance employees' perception of procedural justice.

Procedural Justice and Behavior

Chien et al. (2010) investigated the effects of employee's perceptions of performance-based pay, procedural justice, on job performance among 258 R&D professionals in Taiwanese high-tech organizations. Data were analyzed with (a) factor analysis to validate the three construct measures and (b) multiple-regression to test the association of those constructs. The results showed that perceived performance-based pay positively related to procedural justice and job performance, and procedural justice moderated the pay-performance relationship. These findings emphasize the importance of procedural justice as an antecedent to the establishment of a pay for performance program.

Meng and Wu (2015) hypothesized that procedural and distributive justice in a merit pay plan positively relates to leader-member exchange (LMX), which in turn, positively affects job engagement. Using multiple regression, the authors analyzed data from 581 Chinese school teachers. The results supported the authors' hypotheses. Specifically, the relationships between (a) procedural justice of merit pay and LMX and (b) procedural justice of merit pay and job engagement were positive and significant. In addition, LMX partially mediated the relationship between procedural fairness perception and job engagement. The findings suggest that procedural justice plays a greater role in motivating teachers in a new merit pay system than distributive justice. Practically, an emphasis on procedural justice may prompt individual respect and dignity, promote teachers' acceptance of leadership styles, and thus, stimulate greater job engagement among employees.

In another study, Caza et al. (2015) examined the mediating effect of procedural justice on the relationship between reward (compensation) choice and employee performance. An experiment and a field study showed the same results: Reward choice increased employee performance, via the mediation of procedural justice. The findings suggest that perceived control over reward choice (a form of procedural fairness) leads to an increase job performance, according to self-assessed performance appraisals. In addition, these findings seem to align with rule six, concerning representation. Employee representation in reward choice provides workers with a sense of ownership in the distribution of rewards.

Khtabeth et al. (2020) investigated the mediating role of procedural justice on the relationship between job analysis and employee performance of 690 employees working in three Jordanian industrial organizations. Using SEM, the researchers found positive and significant relationships between (a) job analysis and employee performance, (b) job analysis and procedural justice, (c) and procedural justice and employee performance (self-assessed). In addition, they also found procedural justice mediates the relationship between job analysis and employee performance. The findings indicate that fair procedures in administering HR practices influence employees to increase job performance.

In addition, Gupta et al. (2024) examined the mediated effect of procedural justice on the relationship between performance-based pay and job performance, and the relationship between performance-based pay and organizational citizenship behavior (OCB). Participants were 226 workers in a technology company in India. Employees supplied perceptions of the performance-based pay system and procedural justice. Supervisors provided data on OCB, and researchers collected performance data from the organization's records. The results revealed that procedural justice mediated a positive relationship between performance-based pay and job performance, and a positive relationship between performance-pay and OCB.

Summary

Overall, the empirical evidence to date shows that procedural justice plays a critical role in designing and managing compensation systems in general, and for merit pay systems in particular. Empirical research shows that both sources of justice are different sides of the same coin. Generally speaking, procedural justice is the process (or antecedent) that can lead to a fair distribution of employee rewards. The notion of transparency, trust, and fairness produces a context in which an effective merit pay program can be optimized.

Appeals Procedure

The importance of setting up an appeals procedure for employees who have a concern about their merit increase can be seen in the correctability rule presented in Table 6.1. The correctability rule suggests that for there to be perceptions of fairness, merit decisions must be correctable if needed. An appeals procedure can be instituted to determine if corrections are needed and how to go about making them. From a legal standpoint, having a formal appeals mechanism is a recommended "best practice" for legally sound performance appraisal practices (see Malos, 1998, for a review). In addition, advances in technology have entered the arena of performance appraisal systems and should be also added to the conversation on best practices. Web-based, or e-performance appraisals have simplified employee performance ratings; however, the complexity of the new technology has generated questions about their accuracy and objectivity. Ullah and colleagues (2021) set out to study these concerns. Questionnaires from 352 employees in a non-profit organization were completed and analyzed with

SEM. The results indicate that rater competence and the possibility to challenge performance appraisals judged as unfair or inaccurate highly influence the employees' perception of accuracy of e-performance appraisals.

There are examples of appeals procedures for performance appraisal review, at least informally (Martin et al., 2000). Two national surveys (Bretz & Milkovich, 1989; Bureau of National Affairs, 1983) showed that about 55% of US organizations had informal procedures, about 30% had formal procedures, and only about 15% had no procedures. Another survey found that 32% of organizations reported having formal appeals mechanisms in place (cited in Nadler, 1998). A benchmarking project conducted at the University of Kentucky found that 14 of 22 public universities studied had an appeals process in place concerning performance appraisals, though there was considerable variability in how such appeals were conducted (). A meta-analytic study by Akhtar and Khattak (2013) found that appraisal systems containing appropriate appeal procedure, in conjunction with employee participation in its design, generally had high levels of employee acceptability and satisfaction with the system.

The extent to which *merit increase* decisions are appealed is not known. Anecdotally, it would seem that formal appeals mechanisms concerning merit pay decisions are more common in the public than the private sector (at least at the level of state government). Kellough and Selden (1997) surveyed HR managers at state agencies, and found that merit pay remains the most popular form of individual pay-for-performance plan utilized in state governmental agencies. This is in contrast to the federal government, which effectively ended their use of individual merit pay in 1993 (Kellough & Selden, 1997). Internet searches yield numerous examples of formal appeals mechanisms for state employees. For example, the appeals policy for college faculty at Northeastern University is provided in Box 6.1.

However, as noted by Perry and Pearce (1985), a formal appeals system does not guarantee the adequate resolution of concerns over merit increase decisions. Merit increases do not necessarily correspond to performance ratings, even when an appeals procedure is in place. Perry and Pearce reported that in some federal agencies, computerized payroll systems had to be reprogrammed to ensure that unsatisfactory performers did not receive merit increases.

This discussion of the federal government's troubled experiences with merit pay suggests that, among other things, an appeals procedure is needed for merit pay as well as for performance appraisal decisions (Bowman, 1999; Mulvey, 1991; Risher, 2002). Folger and Konovsky (1989) generated a list of characteristics, based on the procedural justice literature, which seem to be desirable features of an appeals procedure for merit pay decisions. Moreover, these features were found to be positively related to pay satisfaction, organizational commitment, and trust in supervision. These characteristics are listed in Box 6.2.

Box 6.1 Merit Appeals Procedure—Northeastern University Bouvé College of Health Sciences

A. Purpose

The purpose of merit review is to measure and to reward individual faculty members' contributions to the achievement of unit goals, and to provide a process to assess and to facilitate professional development.

. . . .

E. Appeals Procedure

Each faculty member shall have five working days after receiving the written evaluation to submit documentation for appeal. The faculty member will be provided the opportunity to meet with the persons responsible for the merit review, to discuss any concerns about the results of the review. This meeting shall take place within two weeks after the request is made. The committee shall respond to the faculty member within five working days after the meeting with the faculty member. In the event that the faculty member is not satisfied with the outcome of his/her appeal, he/she may pursue whatever rights are available in the Faculty Handbook.

Source: Bouvé College of Health Sciences Merit Policy, Northeastern University (June 14, 2001).

Box 6.2 Desirable Characteristics of an Appeals Procedure for Merit Pay Decisions

1. *find out why you got the size of raise you did.*
2. *make an appeal about the size of a raise.*
3. *express your feelings to your supervisor about your salary decision.*
4. *discuss with your supervisor how your performance was evaluated.*
5. *develop with your supervisor an action plan for future performance.*

Source: Folger and Konovsky (1989). Reprinted with permission.

Merit Pay Communications

Another issue of importance in the administration of merit pay is the communication of merit pay information. Marriott (1962) reported that one of the biggest complaints about merit pay by factory employees was the "lack of information and understanding" about merit pay. This lack of understanding may in turn diminish perceptions of procedural/interactional justice (Dyer & Theriault, 1976; Miceli & Lane, 1991; Miceli & Near, 1988; Ramaswami & Singh, 2003). It also may diminish employee motivation, as there may be misunderstandings concerning pay and performance links (Stiglitz, 1987). From the perspective of expectancy theory (see Chapter 2), instrumentality perceptions are likely to be strengthened when the link between pay and performance is clearly communicated.

Communicating merit pay decisions to employees can be difficult. As noted by Scheele (1991), employees frequently are not passive recipients of annual merit increases, but may instead ask or even demand a merit increase. Employees are often proactive and, at a minimum, want to know why they did or did not receive a certain merit increase. Given the importance of merit pay communications, a number of issues that bear on this topic are covered here, including interactional justice, perceived accuracy of performance feedback, pay secrecy, split systems versus combined reviews, and the communication medium.

Interactional Justice

As described above, interactional justice refers to the perceived fairness of the way in which pay is communicated. Two factors appear to contribute to interactional justice. First, pay decisions need to be adequately explained. For example, allocators can and should provide an explanation of the rationale for a particular merit pay increase. Furthermore, recipients must view this explanation as logical and sincere (Greenberg & McCarty, 1990). Second, information must be communicated in a sensitive manner. In terms of merit pay, allocators need to be courteous, honest, timely, and respectful of the rights of the merit pay recipient when they communicate merit pay decisions (Ramaswami & Singh, 2003).

Perceived Accuracy of Performance Feedback

One factor that should influence the recipient's willingness to accept and act upon performance feedback is the perceived accuracy of the performance feedback (Ilgen et al., 1979). A study by Landy et al. (1978) showed, for a sample of professional and managerial employees in a large manufacturing organization, that the perceived accuracy of performance information was greater when performance evaluations were frequent, goals were identified to eliminate performance deficiencies, and the supervisor was knowledgeable about the subordinate's job and performance. When these steps are taken in communicating merit pay decisions, employee perceptions of the accuracy of merit decisions should similarly be increased. In turn, with this perceived accuracy comes a greater likelihood that employees will not only accept decisions but also be willing to act on the decisions because, as suggested in Table 6.1, accuracy is an important component of procedural justice.

The results of the Landy and colleagues (1978) study indicate that the credibility of the source of merit pay communication is an important factor, as well as how pay information is communicated. Allocator credibility is enhanced when the allocator is timely in merit communications, knowledgeable about the true performance of the individual, and sensitive to the recipient's needs to maintain and improve current performance.

As mentioned above, the use of web-based performance appraisal systems has increased (Ullah et al., 2021). While e-performance appraisal plans have eased the process of rating employee performance, they have added complexity and obscurity to employees' understanding and skepticism of the system. Also stated above, Ullah et al. (2021) set out to study these concerns. The results indicate that rater competence and the possibility to challenge performance appraisals judged as unfair or inaccurate highly influence the employees' perception of accuracy of e-performance appraisals. Like the studies above, this study emphasizes rater competence, empathy, and open communication are required for perceptions of accurate feedback.

Pay Transparency

Communication in pay practices exists on a transparency/secrecy continuum. At one extreme, almost all pay practices are transparent to employees and managers. This is also known as an open pay system. Public sector organizations (e.g., state universities, government agencies, primary & secondary education) along with unionized employers operate under an open pay system, where pay practices are known to employees and the public. The former wants transparency because taxpayers pay employee salaries. The latter is required by federal law (The Labor Management Relations Act of 1947) to maintain transparency of union-member pay information. In the private sector, some organizations make pay information available to all employees (Curtius, 1999). At the other extreme, many private employers keep compensation information almost totally confidential. This is known as pay secrecy or a closed pay system. In many organizations, the individual employee's pay level and increase are disclosed only to that individual. Some organizations have policies to discipline employees who violate organizational polices concerning the sharing of salary data with colleagues (Markels & Berton, 1996). An online survey in 2000 found that 68% of 1,830 respondents agreed with the statement that employees should be allowed to discuss their salaries. In contrast, most private-sector employers in the United States utilize some form of pay secrecy policy (Markels & Berton, 1996). Furnham (2003) has argued that too much openness leads to "unhealthy" and "unproductive" social comparisons.

In the last decade, an interest in pay transparency has gained traction with various goals in mind, such as pay fairness, a reduction (if not elimination) of pay disparity and discrimination between men and women, and between different races. Federal and State laws have been enacted to support this social movement. A similar movement has also occurred in Europe. In the US, Executive Order 13665 mandates that Federal Contractors remain open about their compensation practices. California enacted Senate Bill 1162, requiring employers with 15 or more employees to include a pay scale in job postings and to provide pay scale information to current employees upon request.

Pay transparency is more than merely addressing efforts to restrict employees' rights to discuss each other's paychecks. It deals with all facets of compensation. Scholarly writing shows that pay information falls into four broad dimensions of compensation practices (Arnold & Fulmer, 2019; Fulmer & Arnold, 2020; Fulmer et al., 2023). The first involves revealing information about pay *outcomes*. Examples include disclosing an employee's pay or job level or publishing a list of employees' pay. The second focuses on providing information about *how* pay is determined. Examples include bonus formula, merit pay criteria, or salary determination process. In the third, formal or informal policies about whether employees can discuss pay among themselves. The *fourth* looks at different channels or methods to communicate pay information.

A question to ponder is how much pay information do companies share with employees? A WorldatWork (2020) survey examined pay transparency-related policies and practices in 485 US organizations. The study gives us some idea how much transparency companies provide:

- Sixty-seven percent of organizations view pay transparency at an increasing level of importance, while only 14% of organizations have approached pay transparency beyond a "moderate" level highlighting individual pay rates, range and how pay is determined.
- More than 60% of organizations cite that managers are not trained to effectively deliver pay communications.
- Internal opportunities are correlated to pay equity: 94% of companies cite a transparent internal job posting system, but only 79% of companies cite that employees have an awareness of advancement opportunities.
- Forty-two percent of employers do not share information about how jobs are valued and compensated within the company; however, 16% of employers provide ongoing access to all salary ranges for all positions.
- Pay equity information is often shared with senior leaders, but not with people leaders who make and influence decisions.
- Senior leaders with line-of-sight to company strategy and policies get more intentional communication about pay than others.

Pay transparency is more prevalent and complex today than it was a decade ago. As long as social pressure and legal support for pay transparency continue, it probably will remain popular for some time. A review of the Internet identifies several sources (e.g., HR consultants, employment lawyers) citing both the advantages and disadvantages of pay transparency policies. Advantages may include increased employee satisfaction with pay, job, and management; improved employee motivation and performance; less intent to leave the company; and less pay disparity and pay discrimination. Disadvantages may include overpaid employees and pay inequity for employees not receiving a pay increase; increased pressure on management to justify pay increases; and discomfort for employees over concerns of privacy and feeling valued by the company. While these claims have merit, they are conjectural and must be empirically verified. To that end, we now turn to empirical studies to address the validity of these theoretical notions.

Earlier empirical research on pay transparency/secrecy was reviewed by several authors (H. Heneman, 1985; Lawler, 1972, 1981; Leventhal, 1976). In general, this research indicates that pay secrecy is likely to produce a greater differentiation in performance ratings and merit increases by allocators. That is, there are larger differences in the performance ratings and merit increases between high and low performers when pay is closed rather than open (Leventhal et al., 1972; Peters & Atkin, 1980). Under open systems, allocators may be fearful of creating interpersonal conflict among employees by differentiating too much (Leventhal, 1976; Leventhal et al., 1972). One reading of this might be that, from a motivational perspective, a "secret" merit pay plan would be desirable, as it would make it possible to create a stronger link between pay and performance through greater reward differentiation.

The research on the impact of pay transparency/secrecy on employee satisfaction was less clear. Lawler (1972, 1981) argued that empirical studies indicate that employees are more satisfied with open than closed pay plans. Perhaps employees overestimate the pay of other employees under a closed system. H. Heneman (1985) argued that the evidence is more mixed and pointed to several studies where pay secrecy had no impact on pay satisfaction (e.g., Fossum, 1976).

Recent studies have shed more light on this relationship, as well as others, which are described below. Scheller and Harris (2018) examined the degree to which pay transparency affected pay satisfaction (a component of employee satisfaction). A sample of 293 full-time employees provided data from an online survey. Results showed that higher levels of pay transparency indeed led to greater levels of pay satisfaction among the employees. In another study, Futtrell and Jenkins (2018) used a before-after with control group experimental design to show empirically that the amount of disclosed pay information indeed had a major impact on salesmen's job satisfaction.

Finally, Načinović Braje and Kuvač (2022) investigated the effect of sector employers (private vs. public) on pay transparency. The results showed that public sector employees favor pay transparency more than private sector employees. Also, for the public sector employees, pay transparency positively and statistically related to overall job satisfaction.

It would seem that many organizations "hedge their bets" when it comes to pay transparency/secrecy and merit increases by being more closed than open, but not totally closed. Under this partially closed system, an individual employee's merit increase is known only to that employee. The employee is also told the range of increases granted to others, but not the actual amounts. This approach allows employees to better view their position within the merit pay plan.

Some research has recommended a contingency point of view in determining the amount of information to be released under a merit pay plan. For example, Konrad and Pfeffer (1990) provided evidence that some close-knit work groups may favor rather than oppose reward-based differentiations among group members. Hence, the degree of transparency may depend on the social norms of the group. The degree of transparency may also depend on the needs of the allocator. Bartol and Martin (1989) found that open pay systems may be needed when the allocator is highly dependent on the recipient, so that the recipient can verify the amount received relative to other recipients. Balkin and Gomez-Mejia (1990) found that open pay systems were judged to be more effective than closed systems in organizations whose business strategies favored the growth of a single product line, rather than the maintenance of a diversified product line. The former firms were more likely than the latter firms to use innovative approaches to pay like open systems, rather than more traditional pay practices like closed systems. Finally, the impact of transparency seems to be more pronounced in nonunionized than unionized organizations (Kleiner & Boullion, 1988).

The contingency view indicates that openness is more likely to work when satisfaction is more of a concern than is motivation, when the supervisor is dependent on his or her subordinates, when the social norms of the group support openness, and when the organization has innovative pay practices. It should be noted that this perspective is based on research that looks at the impact of pay on the individual employee. When a broader perspective is taken, as with the Kleiner and Boullion (1988) study, the overall influence of the degree of openness on measures of organizational effectiveness is not large. Hence, in administering merit pay plans, managers must direct attention to a variety of other issues beyond the openness of the pay plan.

As mentioned above, the recent popularity of pay transparency has spawned additional research dealing with associated individual and organizational outcomes. We will look at several examples that appear to dominate the popular business press and scholarly writing. They are motivation, performance, intent to leave the organization, and pay fairness (for more detail, we refer the reader to Alterman et al., 2018; Avdul et al., 2023; Stofberg et al., 2022).

Individual motivation and performance are two such outcomes. Several studies have shown that open pay systems increase motivation and performance based on self-assessment measures (Bamberger & Beloglowski, 2010; Belogolowski & Bamburger, 2014; Futtrell & Jenkins, 2018; Načinović Braje and Kuvač, 2022; Obloj & Zenger, 2022; Scheller & Harris, 2018). Other research shows that if employees think they are underpaid, they will not be as productive or perform to their potential (Obloj & Zenzer, 2022). A couple of observations should be noted. An interesting question arises from these studies: Does pay transparency also increase actual performance? We are not aware of any studies that have examined this relationship. Additionally, empirical studies on this topic also can be extended to observe merit-pay effectiveness.

Another outcome deals with *intent to leave the organization*. Scott et al. (2023) investigated pay transparency from an employee perspective. Using an online survey, a sample of 261 full-time employees responded to a series of items regarding their intent to leave the organization and other organizational outcomes (e.g., pay fairness and trust in management). The results showed that respondents who showed high levels of pay transparency were less likely to leave the organization. In addition, the same group also revealed high levels of salary fairness and trust in management. In contrast, respondents who revealed low levels of pay transparency showed the opposite responses. Other research seems to support these findings (Futtrell & Jenkins, 2018; Nacinovic & Kuvac, 2022).

Pay fairness is another frequently seen outcome. Obloj and Zeneger (2022) investigated the relationship between pay transparency and pay fairness and pay equity. The authors compiled a large database with performance, demographic, and salary data for approximately 100,000 US academics between 1997 and 2017. Using multiple regression, they found that pay transparency was significantly related to increases in compensation fairness and equity. Other researchers found similar results (Kacinovic & Kuvac, 2022; Scott et al., 2023).

From a legal standpoint, in the United States, this whole discussion of the extent to which organizations should utilize an open versus closed system, must be considered in light of the National Labor Relations Act, or NLRA (discussed later in this chapter). The NLRA gives all private-sector employees the right to engage in activity for their "mutual aid and protection." The right to act collectively or organize is available to employees whether they are represented by a labor union or not. Segal (2004, p. 113) writes that the National Labor Relations Board, or NLRB, has consistently held that this includes the "right to discuss the terms and conditions of their employment among themselves. This includes, for example, the right to talk about what they are paid. Accordingly, employers cannot prohibit employees from discussing their wages. A rule prohibiting discussions about pay is unlawful, even if the employer does not strictly enforce it." We recognize that this is very different from how many organizations typically handle pay secrecy issues. We urge affected readers to seek legal counsel concerning the implications of this Act on organizational policies and practices concerning pay secrecy.

WorldatWork sponsored a research study of over 6,000 managers and employees in the United States and Canada (Mulvey et al., 2002; see Krattenmaker, 2002, for a summary). In this study, more openness and better communication concerning pay issues was associated with increased satisfaction with pay, greater organizational commitment, and increased trust in management. Mulvey and colleagues (2002) recommend greater transparency in pay structures. Finally, for a fascinating case study on the pay secrecy versus openness debate, see Case (2001).

The prevalence of pay transparency has led individual states to enact their own laws. As of January 1, 2025, 14 states have created such laws: California, Colorado, Connecticut, Hawaii, Illinois, Maryland, Nevada, New York, Rhode Island, and Washington. In addition, the following States also are considering such a law. As of January 1, 2025, they include Alaska, District of Columbia, Kentucky, Massachusetts, Maine, Michigan, Missouri, Montana, New Jersey, Oregon, South Dakota, Vermont, Virginia, and West Virginia.

In summary, pay transparency is a hot topic in the US and abroad (McMullen & Aladag, 2023). Social movement and the wheels of legal justice will most likely keep this topic relevant and focused on our collective consciousness. In the last decade, the prevalence and complexity of this topic has yielded new laws and scholarly research. It will be interesting to see if pay transparency remains equally popular for another decade.

Split Roles versus Combined Reviews

A series of significant studies was conducted at the General Electric Company in the 1960s (Meyer et al., 1965). One important outcome of these studies was the suggested use of split roles in performance reviews. With split roles, the developmental function of performance appraisal is separated from the administrative function. Two reasons were offered for this split (Prince & Lawler, 1986). First, if the two functions of appraisal are combined, the supervisor is required to be a helper and judge at the same time. Second, if self-appraisals are used, they are likely to be more positive than supervisory appraisals, and subordinates may become defensive when supervisors justify their salary actions.

This logic of split roles has led to the use of two separate performance review sessions by some organizations. One session is to discuss performance for purposes of development, and the other session is to communicate salary increase actions on the basis of performance. One survey suggested that a sizable number of organizations used split roles in performance appraisal (Hall et al., 1989). Coens and Jenkins (2000) have advocated the decoupling of the various functions of performance appraisal, including separating the coaching and feedback aspects from more administrative purposes for appraisal.

Subsequent research has not shown the superiority of split roles over combined reviews. If anything, the data seem to indicate that there may be more desirable outcomes with combined reviews (Boswell & Boudreau, 2002; Dorfman et al., 1986; Giles & Mossholder, 1990; Lawler et al., 1984; Prince & Lawler, 1986). Interestingly, Lawler and colleagues (1984) returned to General Electric and found that employees were not supportive of split roles. The authors found that employees wanted pay discussed in their performance reviews and felt that this was not done enough. Two other studies showed that a discussion of salary did lead to increased satisfaction, but did not produce a change in motivation or performance (Dorfman et al., 1986; Prince & Lawler, 1986). Prince and Lawler (1986) found that employee participation and involvement in performance planning subsequently increased when salary was discussed in the development review. Giles and Mossholder (1990) reported increased employee satisfaction in the performance appraisal system when a discussion of salary was included in the performance review.

This research cast serious doubts on assertions that the split role method is superior to a combined review. Looking back to the research discussed in Chapter 2, however, this conclusion is not entirely unexpected. Reinforcement theory would clearly suggest the futility of measuring performance at one point in time, and granting rewards at another point in time. Before a definitive statement can be made as to the superiority of one method over another, a better test of the models should be conducted, in which split roles and combined reviews are directly compared to one another.

Two studies completed a direct comparison of the two approaches. The first was conducted by Boswell and Boudreau (2002). Employees in a large manufacturing plant had traditionally taken part in combined reviews that were conducted by their immediate supervisors. A "treatment" group started receiving developmental feedback only from their immediate supervisors, with the administrative/evaluative appraisal now coming from a supervisor-once-removed. Although the researchers expected that employees in the separated appraisal condition would have higher scores on several attitudinal measures, there were no significant differences between the conditions on three measures. Reverse of their prediction, employees in the control condition actually scored higher on their intent to use developmental feedback in the future (Boswell & Boudreau, 2002). While the results from one organizational setting are certainly not definitive, these findings do not support the claims of those advocating split reviews. Unless stronger research evidence is found, we agree with Prince and Lawler's (1986) recommendation that a discussion of salary should not be restricted or outlawed in appraisal meetings.

The second study was conducted by Milanowski (2005). New teachers hired in a Midwestern school district were assigned to either a split-role group or a combined review group. In the first group, developmental reviews with feedback were provided by a peer mentor, while administrative reviews were completed by managers and peer evaluators. The second group consisted of integrating both developmental reviews (and feedback) with administrative evaluations completed by peers. Using multiple regression, data were analyzed on three outcome measures: (a) reactions of teachers using interviews and a survey, (b) teacher performance ratings and (c) turnover. The results showed no meaningful and statistical differences between the groups regarding quality of communication, reception and acceptance of performance feedback, stress, potential and/or actual turnover, or performance improvement. The results suggest that providing developmental assistance during a combined review is preferred over the use of a split role evaluation.

Two practical issues arise in putting either split role reviews or combined reviews into practice. First, if performance reviews are split, the door is opened to the possibility that an employee will receive conflicting performance reviews. An employee's performance may be rated as acceptable for purposes of the developmental review, but rated unacceptable in terms of a merit increase. How could this happen? The supervisor conducting the reviews may find it more expedient or more comfortable to tell the employee that his or her performance is acceptable than to spend the time and emotional energy to try to redirect unacceptable performance. However, at the end of the fiscal year, under the pressure of a merit budget, the supervisor may be forced to tell the employee the real story, namely, that his or her performance is unacceptable. The point is that the split review system, if used, needs to be closely monitored to make sure that conflicting decisions are not reached. Better yet is the use of a combined review, which should lessen the chances of conflicting assessments of performance.

Second, when using a combined review, some experience problems with too much discussion of the merit increase amount, at the expense of a discussion of the performance that led to the merit increase. Some years ago, one of us (Robert Heneman) was training first-level supervisors in an organization where combined reviews were seen by the supervisors as a problem. The supervisors were required by policy to use a one-page form with performance ratings at the top and middle of the form, and the size of the percentage increase at the bottom of the form.

During discussions of performance and merit pay at the annual review, employees focused attention solely on the bottom of the page. It was nearly impossible for the supervisors to direct the employees' attention to the behaviors at the middle and top of the form. To deal with this situation, the following solution was agreed upon. In the long run, an attempt would be made to change the policy of the organization so that a new form would be created with the merit increase information on a separate page. In the short term, supervisors would put a blank sheet of paper over the form during the discussion, moving it down the page on a line-by-line basis to focus the discussion on each aspect of performance before getting to the size of the merit increase.

Communication Media

A variety of different media or vehicles are used to communicate pay information in organizations. In the 1980s, a national survey reported that organizations made use of the following approaches: one-on-one meetings (66%), group meetings (59%), company newsletters (32%), brochures/ pamphlets (26%), and the grapevine (20%; Sibson and Company, 1989). Another survey again found a heavy reliance on company manuals, handbooks, and large staff meetings to inform employees about pay issues (Mulvey et al., 2002). In 2019, WorldatWork published a report showing an eight-year trend (2010–2018) of media used to communicate pay information. The types of vehicles included individual discussions with supervisor, memos or emails, compensation statements, company website, individual discussions with HR (compensation department), employee meetings, employee handbook or orientation manual, and no pay communications. The frequency of each media remained relatively constant during the 8-year stretch. Except for individual discussions with supervisor, the percentage use of other communication methods ranged from 18 to 48%. Communication with supervisor was 81%. This suggests that employees feel more comfortable discussing compensation-related topics with their supervisors. A recent report from WorldatWork (2024) emphasized the use of various computerized media that are available and easily accessible to employees. They include emails, webinars or online modules, self-service information in an employee portal. While this report is not empirically based, it certainly speaks to the use of current technology that maximizes communication of pay information and likely reduced issues associated with disseminating compensation matters.

Little research has been conducted on the effectiveness of these approaches. One exception is a merit pay newsletter that was developed, used, and evaluated at McDonnell Douglas Corporation (now a part of Boeing; Handshear, 1988, 1989). This newsletter was issued on a periodic basis to all supervisors, and included information on the merit budget, divisional allocations, changes in rate ranges, and distribution guidelines. To evaluate the effectiveness of the newsletter, a survey was conducted of users inside the company. A survey was also conducted of American Compensation Association (WorldatWork) members' reactions to it. Both surveys indicated a positive overall reaction to the newsletter (Handshear, 1988, 1989). The most frequent use of the newsletter was to "explain issues to subordinates," and readers stated that they frequently sought additional detail on merit pay guidelines. As a result of these positive evaluations, the newsletter was expanded to include other compensation topics as well (Handshear, 1989).

Today, a sizeable portion of organizational communications concerning employee compensation and benefits has shifted to computerized information systems, organizational intranets (Allard & Holsapple, 2002), or web-based computerized systems (WorldatWork, 2024). This has been recommended as a way to increase employee self-service (Holtz, 1997), reduce errors (Allard & Holsapple, 2002), reduce publication costs (Wen & Anandarajan, 1998), and increase organizational productivity (Piszczalski, 2002; Wittman, 2003).

According to Michael Munro from Cisco Systems, an organizational intranet must be "positioned within the overall communications strategy of the organization" (cited in White, 2004, p. 41). Wittman (2003, p. 49) describes the "Managers Dashboard" at Cisco, which allows managers to "give salary increases, decide annual cash incentive payout amounts, decide on stock option share amounts, pay spot bonuses, assess employees' skills, and document corrective action." Wittman argues that the Cisco system has led to large productivity gains, a quick recoupment of their initial capital investment, as well as improved communication and a more aligned workforce. More formal research efforts are obviously required concerning communicating about compensation issues electronically. In the Mulvey and colleagues (2002) study, for example, respondents generally found all forms of mass communications to be only modestly effective (both paper and electronic)—unless these were also accompanied by one-on-one contact with one's supervisor. As stated by consultant Bruce Lawson, "When it comes to communicating pay information, people really like personal contact" (cited in Krattenmaker, 2002, p. 4).

Summary of Communications Issues

In summary, an important component in the administration of merit pay plans is the communication of merit pay information. To be effective, the available research suggests that the message needs to be consistent with interactional justice principles and the source needs to be perceived as credible. Although the evidence is mixed, it is generally recommended that compensation systems be more open and transparent than closed and secretive (Alterman et al., 2018; Avdul et al., 2023; Mulvey et al., 2002; Stofberg et al., 2022). Although split roles are sometimes advocated, there is no clear-cut superiority of this policy over combined reviews. Finally, effective communications concerning merit pay issues appear to require a combination of paper and electronic communications, combined with personal contact from supervisors (Krattenmaker, 2002).

Role of the Allocator

Another major area of concern in the administration of merit pay plans is the role of the allocator. As the one most responsible for implementing the merit pay policy, the allocator has a critical role. To ensure that allocators are carrying out the policy as it was intended, allocators must be given the knowledge, skills, and motivation to do so in an effective manner. These three areas are discussed next.

Knowledge

Allocators need to be sensitized to the fact that merit decisions may be influenced by factors other than the intent of the merit pay policy. These other factors include the characteristics of both the merit pay recipient and the allocator. As shown in one study, recipient characteristics accounted for 24% of the variation in merit increases, while allocator characteristics accounted for 11% (R. Heneman & Cohen, 1988). Some of these characteristics, which may not immediately come to the mind of the allocator, are as follows.

Impression Management

You might expect that attempts by the recipient to manage the allocator's impressions of the recipient would influence the size of the merit increase (Ferris et al., 1989). This does not, however, appear to be the case for at least one method of impression management; namely, ingratiation by the recipient. In two studies, ingratiation by the recipient did not lead to larger merit increases (Gould & Penley, 1984; Martin, 1987). A flattery tactic may have backfired because the allocators may have reasoned that they would have the support of the recipient regardless of the merit increase granted

(Martin, 1987). It should be noted that ingratiation is only one of many impression management tactics (Ferris et al., 1989). Impression management techniques may have a bigger impact on the boss when the boss is dependent on the merit pay recipient. Bartol and Martin (1990) found that demands for higher pay by threat of appeal to upper-level management did work when the recipient had a known and credible political connection to upper-level management.

Equity Off the Job

Freedman (1978) looked at the influence of equity for recipients off the job. In particular, she found in a laboratory study that allocators granted larger pay increases to those employees whose homes had burned down than to those employees where such information was not available to the allocator!

Allocator Values, Grades, Board Scores, and idiosyncratic deals (i-deals)

Bass (1968) appears to have conducted the first study on allocator characteristics as they relate to merit pay, and the results of his study are among the most interesting of all merit pay studies conducted. Two results are notable. First, the personal values of the allocator influenced the size of the merit increase allocated to the recipient. In particular, allocators recommended larger merit increases when the allocators held stronger social and service values than theoretical and economic values. Similarly, Vecchio and Terborg (1987) found that allocators high in moral maturity granted larger increases than those low in moral maturity. Interestingly, Wexley and Youtz (1985) found that raters with altruistic beliefs tend to be less accurate raters of performance. It may be the case that more altruistic allocators are more lenient in performance ratings, which in turn leads to larger merit increases.

Second, Bass (1968) reported that merit increases were smaller when allocators had high board scores on the Admissions Test for Graduate Schools of Business and a high undergraduate grade point average. One interpretation of these results is that allocators who have excelled in school may have higher standards of performance than those who have not excelled in school. As a result of these higher standards, allocated increases may be smaller (R. Heneman, 1990).

Finally, researchers recently have investigated the application of idiosyncratic deals (i-deals) with performance-based pay. i-deals constitute personalized arrangements between employees and their supervisors (allocators) that benefit both parties (Rosen et al., 2013). Typically, they are negotiated at the time the employee is hired. Previous research has identified five major types: training i-deals (personalized development opportunities), task i-deals (individually desirable tasks), scheduling flexibility i-deals (customized work schedules), location flexibility i-deals (Rousseau et al., 2006). Now, performance-based pay i-deals can be added to that list. Abdulsalam et al. (2021) and Maltarich et al. (2017) discovered when allocators (supervisors) agreed to an employee's request for a performance-based pay i-deal, employees perceived his/her supervisor to be fair in dispersing pay based on performance. In contrast, the absence of a performance-based pay i-deal resulted in the opposite outcome. The findings here imply that (a) pay transparency can positively affect this type of i-deal and (b) allocator training is highly recommended.

In- and Out-Group Membership

Preferential reward treatment is given to recipients whose relationship with the allocator can be characterized as in-group rather than out-group status (Green & Liden, 1980). In-group members have a relationship with the allocator characterized by a higher degree of trust, interaction, support, and rewards, whereas out-group members have a relationship with the allocator characterized by a lower degree of trust interaction, support, and rewards (Dansereau et al., 1975; Dienesch & Liden, 1986). Preferential reward treatment of in-group over out-group members seems to take place regardless of true performance. R. Heneman et al. (1989) reported that ineffective performance was attributed to unfavorable conditions for in-group but not out-group members. On the other hand, effective performance was attributed to the person for in-group but not out-group members.

These attributions took place even when the level of actual performance was controlled for in the study. Hence, no matter what the true level of performance, causality of performance seems to be assigned in a way to favor in-group rather than out-group members. As outlined by Bannister and Balkin (1990), compensation decisions are unlikely to be accepted and acted upon by employees if employees are not treated consistently in the assignment of performance attributions.

A word of caution is in order at this point. The allocator characteristics just reported should be treated as suggestive of factors other than performance used by allocators to make merit decisions. Given the research methodology used in some of these studies, the results are not always conclusive. Some of these studies used students in the role of managers. Whether students' merit decisions in a prescribed role are similar to actual managers' merit pay decisions is questionable.

Similarly, the use of "paper people" can be problematic. That is, in some of these studies, the manager was asked to give merit increases to a hypothetical employee described on a sheet of paper. The extent to which this person described on paper is treated similarly to an actual employee with these characteristics is again open to question. Both of these concerns relate to the concept of external validity, which is reviewed in detail in Chapter 7. For now, it is important to simply recognize that these concerns make the results tentative and suggest areas for additional research.

Training to Improve Allocator Skills

The importance of training to the measurement of performance was discussed in Chapter 4. Training programs designed to improve the measurement of performance were also reviewed in that chapter. Training is also needed, however, to support the making of merit pay decisions after performance has been measured (Krattenmaker, 2002). According to a survey by the Wyatt Company (1989), lack of training was seen as the "major impediment to success in managing pay for performance." Strategies that can be used to improve the allocators' merit pay decision-making skills are reviewed below.

As shown in a review of the empirical research by Balzer et al. (1989), an excellent approach to the improvement of accuracy in decision making is to provide individuals with cognitive feedback or knowledge about relations among variables. Three particular approaches discussed by Balzer and colleagues seem to be relevant to merit pay decisions and can be used to set the framework for a merit pay training program. It is recommended that the cognitive feedback upon which merit pay training is based consists of three elements: guide chart orientation, policy capturing, and feedback on actual decisions.

Guide Chart Orientation

One component of cognitive feedback is known as *task information.* Essentially, this refers to information cues available for decision making. In the context of merit pay, this task information is essentially the merit pay guide chart (see Chapter 5 for a review of guide charts). A key element of a merit pay training program would be a discussion of the merit pay guide chart to show managers how the pay-for-performance policy is supposed to work. Also, a discussion of this policy may help to shift the frame of reference from egalitarianism (see Chapter 3 for a discussion of pay philosophies) to pay-for-performance for those managers whose reward strategies differ from the desired policy (Kroeck et al., 1987).

Policy Capturing

A second component of feedback is called *cognitive information* and refers to individuals' judgments in relation to cues they pick up in the environment. Cognitive information is a form of feedback that can be given to managers to help them improve the decisions they are required to make. From the perspective of merit pay, this cognitive information is the actual allocation decisions versus those decisions *intended* by policy. One way to build this component into merit pay training is to use a research method known as policy capturing, which has been used to model the decisions used in performance appraisal (Hobson et al., 1981) and merit pay (Sherer et al., 1987).

Policy capturing can be used to provide cognitive information to managers by taking three steps. First, information potentially used to make merit pay decisions would be collected. Actual information could be obtained from personnel files, or vignettes could be used to simulate the information available for a merit pay decision. An example of simulated merit pay information is shown in Table 6.2.

Second, the data collected in the first step would then be analyzed, using various statistical techniques (cf. Hobson et al., 1981), to come up with the actual weights used by managers in making actual or simulated merit pay policies. An example of the weights used by managers in making merit pay decisions in a hospital setting is shown in Table 6.3. The larger the entry shown in each cell of Table 6.3, the greater the weight placed on that variable by the managers in making merit pay decisions.

Third, managers would be given feedback by other managers and trainers on the extent to which their decisions (shown by actual weights) correspond to the weights specified in the organization's desired (or actual) policy. Discussion could take place regarding methods to use to ensure that decisions are as closely in line with desired merit pay policy as possible.

Feedback on Actual Merit Decisions

A third component of feedback is based on the concept known as *functional validity information*. This information consists of the relations among decisions and outcomes. In terms of merit pay, it refers to the link between merit increases allocated and subsequent performance by the recipients. This information should also be provided in merit pay training.

Functional validity can be assessed only after enough time has passed to accurately evaluate changes in performance resulting from merit increases. Once these data have been collected, however, an additional training session should be held to give allocators feedback on the outcomes of their decisions. This feedback would effectively reinforce the guide chart orientation and policy capturing phases of training, as well as lead to discussion on additional ways to tie performance to pay.

Table 6.2.

Merit Increase Exercise

You are a consultant who has been called in by the chairman of the board to make recommendations on handling the merit budget for 2026. The company experienced a drop in profits of 22% in 2024 and 10% in 2025 from the 2022 and 2023 levels. The company is in a cash squeeze, so the merit budget program, which had been fairly generous in past years, is very tight this year. The chairman is concerned about the top people in the company, i.e., those who report to him and to the president (the chief operating officer).

The company has a formal job evaluation program. Salary ranges are set by competitive survey and the salary structure is in good shape. Jobs were evaluated and regraded and the structure was revised only a few months ago. The company does not have a bonus plan and is not in a position to establish one in the near future. So the salary structure is essentially a total compensation structure, which must match competition that, in some cases, uses bonuses.

The chair has decided that he will not get a raise this year, but he wants your recommendations on which of his key executives should receive increases and on the size of those increases, considering the difficult circumstances facing the industry and the company. The economic environment is one of cautionary recovery in the midst of moderate inflation. The current unemployment rate is 4.0% and has ranged between our and five percent for the past year. The inflation rate has been 2.8% for the past 12 months.

The chair's basic objectives are to provide the maximum motivation possible through the merit program under difficult circumstances. He does not want to lose any of his key people. Traditionally, all top executive increases have at least exceeded the inflation rate, but that may not be possible this year.

The chair gives you brief data on salary grade, age, years of service with the company, years in the present job, base salary, compa-ratio, performance, potential, and exposure ratings, as well as an indication of whether there is a qualified backup for each executive. Performance ratings were completed recently on all the key people. An A-B-C-D coding system is used. A is the highest performance rating (Perf.), the highest potential rating (Pot) and the highest level of exposure (Exposure) to the possibility of the individual's being attracted away from the company; B is a good rating, and C is considered adequate. Anyone who receives a D rating must bring it up at the next rating period or face termination or demotion. The company has few special fringe benefits and is not in a position to inaugurate any new ones at this time, if costs are involved.

There is a stock option program, but it has been relatively ineffective in recent years because of the drop in the company's stock price. Few shares are available for grant under the plan and management cannot go to the shareholders for more shares for two years. So the option program offers little opportunity for augmenting the merit program for this year.

The chair informs you that the maximum amount of merit money you can spend is **$110,000** (this represents 3.0% of the payroll for the executive group, excluding the chair). Finally, the chair tells you that no promotions or retirements are expected in this group. The only rule that you have to contend with in allotting the raises is that there can be no increases to pay levels above the maximum of the range.

(Continued)

Table 6.2. (Continued)

Salary Structure			
Grade	**Min.**	**Mid. ($000)**	**Max.**
20	680	799	870
19	544	646	748
18	394	490	610
17	204	286	367
16	177	252	326
15	163	231	299
14	143	204	265
13	122	177	231

Table 6.2. (Continued)

Name	Title	Salary Grade	Age	Years Service	No. of Employees Supv.	In This Job	Base Salary	Compa Ratio	Perf.	Pot	Exposure	Back-Up
Walnut	Chair	20	62	24	20,000	5	826,000	103.3	—	—	—	—
Prexy	President	18	57	8	20,000	7	598,000	119.1	B	B+	B–	Yes*
Numbers	Controller	13	42	3	40	1	199,000	101.0	A	A–	A	No
Money	C.F.O.	17	48	12	15	4	319,900	104.5	B	B–	B	No
Peoples	V.P. H.R.	13	51	17	25	7	190,000	96.4	A	C+	B+	Yes
Press	V.P. P.R.	13	46	6	7	2	203,600	103.4	C+	C	B	Yes
Laws	V.P. Legal	17	45	5	10	5	348,400	113.9	B	B+	A–	No
Maker	V.P. Mfg.	16	59	20	15	6	278,400	102.4	B	B–	B–	Yes
Sellers	V.P. Mktg.	13	54	13	10	3	184,200	93.5	A	B	A–	Yes
Thinker	V.P. R&D	17	50	14	10	8	319,200	104.3	B	C	B	Yes
Nuts	Group V.P.	16	42	4	5,500	4	258,000	94.9	A	A	A	No
Bolts	Group V.P.	15	46	10	4,000	3	251,000	108.7	B+	B+	A	No
Washer	Group V.P.	16	59	19	7,400	11	278,400	102.4	B	B–	B–	No
Hooks	Group V.P.	15	49	15	2,900	8	238,600	95.1	C	C	C	Yes
Total (Excluding Chair) 3,666,700												

Source: Adapted from K. Foster & K. V. Lynn (1978). Adapted with permission from *HR Magazine* (formerly *Personnel Administrator)*, published by the Society for Human Resource Management, Alexandria, VA.

**Nuts*

Table 6.3.

Weights Used by Allocators in a Hospital[a]

	Independent Variables					
Participant[b]	Performance	Tenure	Salary	Perf. Consist.	Job Offer	R2
1	18**	47**	−28**	11	53**	62
2	78**	10**	−16**	14*	14*	69
3	84**	06	00	45*	−01	92
4	62**	28**	−11	37*	−05	62
5	86**	08	−30**	−08	02	86
6	74**	09	−13	04	−01	58
7	96**	−07	00	03	−01	93
8	77**	−01	−10	36*	03	74
9	65**	16**	−11**	53**	23**	80
10	63**	09*	−04	00	62**	79
11	92**	06	−09**	−23**	05	91
r^2	57	03	02	08	04	

Source: Sherer et al. (1987). Reprinted with permission.

Notes: Participant refers to allocator.
Performance consistency refers to the stability of performance over time. Job offer refers to an offer of a job with another company at a higher salary.
$*p < 0.05$.
$**p < 0.01$.
[a]Decimals omitted.
[b]$n = 96$ for each participant.

Increasing Motivation of the Allocator

In Chapter 4, we recommended that there be consequences for the rater to improve the validity of ratings. Similarly, there need to be consequences for allocators to motivate them to make their merit pay decisions consistent with merit pay policy. One consequence for the allocator would be accountability for merit pay decisions (Pulakos et al., 2023).

Accountability can be enforced by insisting that allocators provide face-to-face feedback on merit pay decisions to the recipients. However, in and of itself, this strategy is probably not very effective. Klimoski and Inks (1990) found that raters tended to inflate their ratings when they had to give face-to-face feedback, as compared to when ratings were kept anonymous or no feedback was provided. More effective ways to hold raters accountable may be those outlined below.

First, the signature of the allocator's immediate supervisor can be required as an approval of the ratings given by the allocator. The Human Resource department can ensure that approval signatures are made prior to the distribution of merit increases. A signature of approval by immediate supervisors increases the accountability of allocators for their merit pay decisions.

Second, organizations can evaluate allocators on the basis of how well they conduct merit pay reviews. That is, performance *as an allocator* becomes a performance standard used to evaluate the allocator. According to a survey of *Fortune* 100 firms by Bretz and Milkovich (1989), only about 22% of these firms took such an approach for performance appraisal. The number is probably even less for merit pay.

Although not widely practiced, there are two case study examples where allocators were rated on how well they conducted merit reviews. This practice was undertaken in the city of Scottsdale, Arizona ("Merit pay systems," 1984) and at Pratt and Whitney (Schneier, 1989a). To facilitate the process, standards for conducting merit reviews were developed at Pratt and Whitney. These standards (shown in Box 6.3) are what allocators are rated against in their own annual reviews.

Third, allocator decisions can be audited or reviewed by a third party such as the Human Resource department. This practice is also followed by the city of Scottsdale *(Management Review,* 1984). An empirical study by Rozelle and Baxter (1981) indicated that when ratings are reviewed by a committee, the reliability of these ratings is increased. Hence, there is some empirical support for this practice.

Fourth, recipients can appeal allocators' decisions to a third party (e.g., Human Resource department) to increase allocator accountability. This is yet another practice followed by the city of Scottsdale. Although it seems that this practice, like face to-face feedback, could lead to inflated ratings, other procedures designed to hold raters accountable would suppress this effect. That is, inflated ratings would be detected in the review of the allocator's performance as an allocator. Considering this, it may be desirable to use all three forms of accountability, as is the practice in Scottsdale.

Box 6.3 Merit Pay Standards for Allocators at Pratt and Whitney

Exceptional Manager

Is a leader in drawing high performance from employees and recognizing them for it. Is aware of each employee's level of contribution and supports continued growth through many forms of recognition.

Fully Competent Manager

Assesses accurately the accomplishments of employees, differentiates between performance levels, and communicates candidly regarding performance. Makes compensation decisions that reflect clear distinctions between levels of performance achieved. Spends time in the work area interacting with employees, inquiring about day-to-day activities, and providing specific, timely performance feedback. Effectively uses formal and informal recognition actions. Maintains group performance. When warranted, takes appropriate action with poor performers through corrective action plans, firing employee when necessary.

Developing Manager

Is becoming more aware of the importance of employee recognition and feedback, and is increasing in ability to be involved in the accomplishments of employees on a regular basis.

Source: Schneier, "Capitalizing on Performance Management, Recognition, and Rewards Systems." Reprinted, by permission of the publisher, from *Compensation and Benefits Review,* March/April 1989,© 1989 American Management Association, New York. All rights reserved.

Laws and Regulations

In the 1980s, General Motors Corporation shifted its compensation policies from automatic cost-of-living adjustments to merit pay for roughly 125,000 employees (Kanter, 1987; Schlesinger, 1988). This generated considerable attention in the popular press due to a class-action lawsuit filed against General Motors by four African American salaried employees on behalf of 10,000 such employees in Michigan, Ohio, and Indiana ("Minority employees," 1989). The dispute arose over allegations concerning the performance appraisal system used for salary increase and promotion decisions (Vines, 1989). General Motors did not admit any discrimination and reached a preliminary agreement out of court (Molloy, 1989). The estimated cost of the settlement ranged from 3 (Vines, 1989) to 40 ("Minority employees," 1989) million dollars. Included in the settlement were adjustments in pay for current and former employees (Molloy, 1989) and a computer-based monitoring system ("Minority employees," 1989; Vines, 1989).

This is just one example of the type of litigation that is likely in the area of merit pay. Other pay cases are described by Martin and colleagues (2000). The potential for litigation should serve as an important reminder to employers to comply with relevant laws and regulations concerning compensation issues (Nobile, 1996). Legal compliance was mentioned earlier as one means of promoting procedural justice in organizations (Miceli & Lane, 1991). Interestingly, the due process framework was brought into the performance appraisal literature from the legal literature (Folger et al., 1993; Forkosch, 1958). It was then applied back to the research on performance appraisal court cases to emphasize the procedural aspects of appraisals that can help organizations to be more likely to prevail in legal disputes (Werner & Bolino, 1997). Relevant laws and regulations include the 1964 and 1991 Civil Rights Acts, the Equal Pay Act, Age Discrimination in Employment Act, National Labor Relations Act, the Civil Service Reform Act, and the Merit Pay Reform Act. Each of these acts are briefly reviewed.

The 1964 and 1991 Civil Rights Acts

These Acts prohibit discrimination in virtually all human resource decisions, including merit pay, on the basis of race, color, religion, gender, and national origin. Title VII of the 1964 Act is the section dealing with employment issues. The Acts are enforced by the Equal Employment Opportunity Commission (EEOC). Comprehensive narrative reviews of court cases involving performance appraisal decisions have been conducted (Martin & Bartol; 1991; Martin et al., 2000; Nathan & Cascio, 1986). Empirical analyses of such court cases have also been conducted (Field & Holley, 1982; Lee et al., 2004; Werner & Bolino, 1997). Malos (1998) provides a valuable summary of the recommendations from this literature, which is shown in Box 6.4.

Reviews of Title VII as it relates to merit pay decisions have been conducted, but are more limited, because of the smaller number of cases reviewed (Martin et al., 1987; Sovereign, 1989). Although the reviews are based on small numbers of cases, the results of the merit pay cases are consistent with the larger number of performance appraisal cases (Martin et al., 2000). These reviews suggest that a number of actions could be taken by employers to defend their merit pay practices from allegations of discrimination. These actions are as follows:

- Performance standards should be based on a thorough job analysis. These standards also should be updated to reflect changes in job content. The use of broad employee traits as performance standards is discouraged, as it is difficult to show the job relatedness of these standards.

Box 6.4 Procedural Recommendations for Legally Sound Performance Appraisals.

Appraisal procedures should:

1. *be standardized and uniform for all employees within a job group*
2. *be formally communicated to employees*
3. *provide notice of performance deficiencies and of opportunities to correct them*
4. *provide access for employees to review appraisal results*
5. *provide formal appeal mechanisms that allow for employee input*
6. *use multiple, diverse, and unbiased raters*
7. *provide written instructions and training for raters*
8. *require thorough and consistent documentation across raters that includes specific examples of performance based on personal knowledge*
9. *establish a system to detect potentially discriminatory effects or abuses of the system overall*

Source: Malos, S. B. (1998). Current legal issues in performance appraisal. In J. W. Smither (Ed.), *Performance appraisal: State of the art in practice* (pp. 49–94). Jossey-Bass. Reprinted with permission.

- There should be a demonstrable relationship between pay increases and performance levels. Otherwise, the plan may not be seen as a bona fide merit pay plan.
- The merit pay plan should be clearly communicated to all employees. Information should be provided for both allocators and recipients. This information should be made available *before* the merit pay review.
- Care must be taken to ensure that bias is not present in performance ratings or merit increases. Rater and merit pay training should be provided to allocators. An appeals procedure should be made available to recipients.

The overlap of these recommendations with those made by Malos (1998) is quite apparent. It should be noted that equal employment laws are not written to *require* the above actions by employers, but to prohibit discrimination. These actions are simply employer practices found in written summaries of court cases. They also parallel the types of recommended "best practices" for performance management often found in the human resource management literature (H. Heneman & Judge, 2003; Werner, 1998). These practices are generally persuasive in courts of law as evidence that the employer did not illegally discriminate (Werner & Bolino, 1997).

Concerning discrimination in merit pay decisions, a review by R. Heneman (1990) found little evidence of a relationship between protected-class status and merit pay decisions. Martin and colleagues (2000) reviewed two federal court cases where racial discrimination was alleged in a pay dispute. In both cases, the employer prevailed, as their appraisal and compensation practices were deemed as credible. More recently, Mun and Kodama (2022) found a gender gap in bonus pay for employees in large Japanese companies, which was unexpectedly greater in workplaces that had a merit-based system in place.

Equal Pay Act

The Equal Pay Act prohibits discrimination on the basis of gender in pay decisions. Men and women must be paid the same for jobs requiring "substantially similar" skill, effort, responsibility, and working conditions. Pay differentials between men and women are permissible for men and women performing the same job—but only if the differential is due to seniority, merit, production, or any factor other than sex. As with Title VII, the EEOC is the enforcement agency for the Equal Pay Act.

The Act suggests that different pay increases are permissible for men and women performing the same job if a bona fide merit pay plan is in place and where there is a demonstrable relationship between pay increases and performance. Along with this demonstrable relationship, there should be no relationship between merit increases and gender. The gap between overall pay for males and females in the United States has narrowed from 1982 to 2024, but was estimated at 85% in 2024 (Buckman & Jackson, 2021; Fry & Aragão, 2025; Williams & Werner, 2022). Further research is needed concerning the relationship between gender and merit increases (R. Heneman, 1990; Mun & Kodama, 2022).

Age Discrimination in Employment Act

This Act prohibits discrimination on the basis of age. In essence, the statute makes age a protected class along with race, color, religion, gender, and national origin. The Act provides protection to those over age 40 and is enforced by the EEOC. As an example, a discharged 53-year-old bank vice-president sued his employer for age discrimination. As evidence, he pointed to two younger vice-presidents who received salary increases and bonuses not granted to him, despite their having lower performance evaluation ratings than he did. A jury decided generally in favor of the plaintiff, awarding him over $100,000 (cited in Martin et al., 2000).

Almost no research has been conducted on age effects in merit pay. In one study, however, R. Heneman and Cohen (1988) reported that older employees received smaller merit increases. Given the aging population in the United States, you can expect to see increasing litigation in this area

(Bates, 2003b; Werner, 1998; Wiscombe, 2003). It is an area where employers need to pay strict attention in auditing merit pay plans for compliance to laws and regulations.

National Labor Relations Act

The National Labor Relations Act (or Wagner Act) of 1935 grants employees the broad right to form and join labor unions. The NLRB enforces the Act. Once a labor union is legally recognized, management must bargain with labor over wages, hours, and working conditions. One aspect of wages that may be a negotiable issue is the use of merit pay. One aspect of working conditions is employee participation in the development of a merit pay plan. Merit pay is found in some unionized organizations (as explained in Chapter 3). In those unionized settings where merit pay is present, the collective bargaining agreement between labor and management may spell out the conditions of the merit pay plan, as well as grievance procedures for employees who do not feel the plan is being administered according to the contract (Milkovich & Newman, 2002; Rubin & Elkouri, 2004).

Under the grievance procedure, disputed merit increases are sometimes reviewed by an independent arbitrator when labor and management cannot come to an agreement. In general, merit pay decisions are not subject to successful challenge unless they are shown to be unfair, arbitrary, or discriminatory (Rubin & Elkouri, 2004). When so charged, management's defense is, in general, to show that the decisions are reasonable, demonstrable, and objective (Rubin & Elkouri, 2004). Given the fact that arbitrators can only make judgments under the merit procedures previously agreed upon by labor and management, at least one arbitrator urges the parties to develop a detailed set of procedures in advance of plan usage (Barkin, 1970).

As was mentioned above in our discussion of pay secrecy, the NLRA has been interpreted by the NLRB and many courts to mean that no employer—whether unionized or not—may prohibit employees from discussing their wages with one another (Segal, 2004). This was substantiated in a ruling of the Sixth Circuit of the US Courts of Appeals in *NLRB v. Main Street Terrace Care Center (2000).* Managers at this Ohio nursing home had told workers that they could not discuss their wages with one another. A worker named Mary Craig had sought to rectify disputed pay matters concerning herself, her daughter, and another coworker. At one point, a supervisor overheard her saying, "If we had a union, they would not treat any of us this way" (Palmer & Dodge, 2001). Four days later, Ms. Craig was fired. She filed an unfair labor practice charge against her employer, despite the fact that there was no union involved at the facility. Her claim was that her employer had violated the NLRA by promulgating a rule prohibiting employees from discussing wages amongst themselves, and by discharging her for engaging in "protected concerted activity." This argument was accepted by the NLRB, and then affirmed by a panel of judges from the Sixth Circuit. Precedents for such a decision were cited from the First, Second, Third, and Eighth Circuits (Palmer & Dodge, 2001). Employers would be well advised to drop any oral or written policies that prohibit employees from discussing wage issues amongst themselves (Hatch, 2000; Segal, 2004).

Civil Service Reform Act/Merit Pay Reform Act

The Civil Service Reform Act of 1978 covers most employees working in the federal government. Chapter 4 of the Act established a merit pay plan that was required for some federal government supervisors and managers. In essence, the Act shifted pay increases from a seniority basis to a performance basis as well. The Act went into effect in 1981. In 1983, the Act was changed to the Merit Pay Reform Act. This Act revised the merit pay procedures from the Civil Service Reform Act because of the disappointing results of the original plan in the early 1980s (Holliman, 1983).

The details of these two Acts will not be reviewed here. They led to the establishment of a Performance Management and Recognition System to administer federal merit pay beginning in 1984 (Risher, 2002). Amidst on-going controversies over the administration of this system, the federal Office of Personnel Management (OPM) commissioned and received a report by the National Research Council (1991). This project was conducted by a blue-ribbon commission known as the Committee on Performance Appraisal for Merit Pay, and was used for discussions at congressional hearings on the reauthorization of the federal merit pay system. The report reviewed the literature on merit pay and performance appraisal, and made many policy recommendations for the federal government. These included the following:

- A well-developed performance appraisal system will not automatically lead to desired merit pay outcomes.
- The context in which performance ratings take place must be considered. For example, there must be incentives for managers to do what is expected with performance appraisals.
- Appraisals and merit pay decisions should be decentralized within a centralized set of policy guidelines.
- Merit pay plans should be pilot tested before full-scale implementation.
- While policy guidelines are needed to ensure fairness in merit pay decisions, too many guidelines may prevent a clear link between pay and performance.

Many of these recommendations are relevant for both public- and private-sector employees. Unfortunately, the problems associated with the federal government's merit pay efforts were so severe that the Performance Management and Recognition System was abandoned in 1993 (Kellough & Seldon, 1997). Risher (2002, p. 318) argues that the idea of pay-for-performance was "all but forgotten" until a white paper was produced, once again by the Office OPM (James, 2002). The following extract from this document gives a sense of how provocative it was:

> In the current Federal white-collar pay system, performance does not matter very much. The way the Government delivers pay increases—and the relative value of those pay increases—reinforces the message that performance is secondary at best. In any given year, Federal employees receive more pay increases for remaining on the rolls than for meeting or exceeding performance expectations. The dominance of these performance-insensitive pay increases can make performance-oriented tools appear trivial. As recent events have shown all too clearly, Government performance is critically important, and system improvements may be needed so that agencies can recognize and value the competencies and contributions of their employees better. To be truly results-oriented, the Government would require a compensation system where performance truly makes a difference. (James, 2002, p. 17)

This OPM white paper sought to begin a dialogue within the federal government concerning ways to increase the linkage between individual performance and rewards. Risher (2002) provided guidance concerning how this might take place (many of his recommendations parallel points made throughout this chapter). Risher argued that a focus on results and accountability in the public sector provides an opening for a healthy reappraisal of individual pay-for-performance for federal employees. In effect, the US government's various attempts at merit pay can be seen as a large-scale social experiment. Further developments in this area should be closely monitored to see to what extent they contribute to desirable merit pay outcomes. For example, in 2025, many challenges have been raised concerning the rights and protections of civil service employees, including from within the US executive branch itself (Devine et al., 2023; Fisk, 2025). The use of merit principles, and merit pay, for federal employees is likely to remain controversial in the coming years.

In summary, merit pay decisions, like most human resource decisions, are subject to a number of laws and regulations. To ensure compliance with these laws and regulations, the auditing of merit pay decisions should be a routine practice in organizations. The audit should consist of an investigation as to the degree to which actual merit pay decisions correspond with the provisions of the law. The auditing of merit pay decisions should be fully integrated into other legal compliance-review procedures in the organization. This integration step is necessary to convey to employees that managers are just as accountable for merit pay decisions under the law as they are for other business decisions.

Summary of Major Points

1. *Distributive, procedural, and interactional justice.* The effectiveness of a merit pay plan depends on the perceived fairness of the procedures used to establish and communicate merit increases, as well as the amounts allocated to merit increases. Rules that foster perceptions of procedural and interactional justice include consistent allocations, bias suppression, accurate decisions, correctable decisions, representation by the recipient, and ethical treatment.
2. *Appeals procedure.* One concrete method for establishing procedural justice is to provide an appeals procedure for those employees concerned with their merit increase. While often recommended by legal scholars (Malos, 1998), more widespread implementation of formal appeals mechanisms would likely benefit both employers and employees alike.
3. *Communications.* For merit pay communications to be effective, they need to be made consistent with the principles of interactional justice and come from a credible source. One promising medium for communicating merit pay information is an organizational human resource information system (HRIS), intranet, or web-based system although employees still want human interaction as well (Mulvey et al., 2002).
4. *Pay transparency.* For legal purposes, a more transparent pay plan is generally recommended over a secret or closed plan. A concern with an open plan, however, is that reward differentiation that is tied to performance may be less likely to occur. Another concern stems from employees who receive lower merit increases and/or have salaries less than a newly hired one may reduce their productivity.
5. *Split roles.* The available research does *not* favor the use of split roles over combined reviews. In our view, discussions of salary should not be prohibited during developmental reviews.
6. *Role of the allocator.* The allocator of merit pay has the central role in merit decisions. Steps must be taken by the organization to ensure that allocators have the knowledge, skills, and motivation to make solid merit pay decisions. Training and accountability should help to achieve this objective.
7. *Laws and regulations.* Merit pay decisions must be made in accordance with laws and regulations, as well as company policy

and ethical guidelines. Major laws and regulations that have a bearing on merit pay are set forth in the following acts: the 1964 and 1991 Civil Rights Acts, Equal Pay Act, Age Discrimination in Employment Act, National Labor Relations Act, and Civil Service Reform Act. This is especially challenging in recent years, given a general retrenchment or moving away from long-standing ways of addressing discrimination in the workplace in the United States (McCormick, 2023).

Conclusions

It has been emphasized throughout the book that the relationship between pay and performance must be *perceived* as well as documented if merit pay is to be successful. The key element in ensuring that employees perceive the relationship between pay and performance is the administration of the merit pay plan. More than any other part of the merit pay process, the administration of the merit pay plan has a bearing on the perceived relationship between pay and performance. For there to be a perceived relationship between pay and performance, three events must take place.

First, the merit pay plan must be made highly visible to employees. For example, policies regarding merit pay can be communicated electronically, via paper documentation, or both. Merit pay should be discussed during the appraisal of employee performance. Information that should be communicated includes the possible range of merit increases, the actual range and average merit increase, and the individual's particular merit increase. The individual increases granted to other employees should typically not be communicated.

This recommendation of less-than-complete openness in merit pay decisions may seem to contradict a major theme of the book, namely that the perceived link between pay and performance is as important as the actual link. One could argue that merit decisions must be totally open or public for the perceived link to be clear to employees. Most certainly, as shown in Chapter 2, there is a large body of motivational theory to substantiate the argument that merit pay decisions should be open. However, while an open system is a worthy goal to pursue, in most organizations, it remains premature to put a totally open merit system into operation.

Both research and practice suggest that the current state of affairs in most organizations is not yet conducive to completely open merit pay decisions. In many organizations, rating errors such as those described in Chapter 4 continue to occur. As a result, employees often get very similar merit increases, regardless of actual performance levels. Under these circumstances, making public the merit increases of all employees may well diminish rather than enhance the perception that pay is based on performance. In short, performance must be adequately measured *before* a fully open merit system can be effectively used.

Second, the merit pay system needs to be seen as a fair one. Steps that can be taken to ensure fairness are creating an appeals procedure, training raters, using valid performance measures, following all relevant laws, regulations, and ethical guidelines, and encouraging participation by employees in the development of the merit pay plan.

Third, supervisors must be equipped to make the actual link between performance and pay. At a minimum, supervisors need to be trained in the merit pay process and be held accountable for clearly establishing a link between pay and performance for their subordinates. Unfortunately, training and accountability still have not been as widely implemented by organizations as suggested by theory, research, and case law. To state it plainly, these procedures need to be used more frequently. Merit pay plans will not be as effective as they could be until organizations commit the time and financial resources needed to train supervisors and hold them accountable for merit pay decisions.

To improve current administrative practices, the following priority ordering of activities seems reasonable. The most immediate concern should be the development of performance standards with sound validity properties and a corresponding merit pay system that is perceived to be fair. The next concern should be the proper use of these standards and systems by supervisors. Finally, and only after the preceding steps have been taken, organizations should take steps toward a more open system of merit pay decisions. If the previous two steps have been taken, open merit systems have the potential to strengthen the perceived link between pay and performance. If the previous two steps have not been taken, an open pay system may actually weaken the perceived relationship between pay and performance. In the final chapter, we discuss the evaluation of the outcomes of merit pay plans.

Study Questions

1. Describe three components comprising organizational justice. Are justice and fairness the same? Explain.
2. What are the best methods for communicating pay policies and practices? Give examples for each method.
3. Compare and contrast split role and combined reviews. What practical issues are associated with both techniques?
4. How can organizations ensure allocators best carry out their assignments? Compare and contrast these assignments.

5. Briefly describe the laws and regulations that relate to merit pay.
6. Pay transparency has become popular in the last decade. What are some important points a compensation director should know about pay policies and practices, especially in merit pay administration?
7. Looking at the Merit Increase Exercise (Table 6.2), how would you recommend that the available amount ($110,000) be divided amongst the 13 executives (excluding the Chair)? What is the basis for your recommendations?

PART III

EVALUATION OF RELEVANT OUTCOMES

CHAPTER 7

EVALUATING MERIT PAY OUTCOMES

This final chapter of the book focuses on the second stage of the merit pay process, as we depicted it back in Figure 1.1 (Chapter 1). This stage consists of the relationship between merit increases and *subsequent* outcomes such as performance and satisfaction. You would expect to find that if a merit pay plan has been carefully developed and administered, merit increases allocated under the plan would lead to desirable outcomes. That is, if pay increases are linked to previous performance, then pay increases will lead to improved subsequent performance as well as other desirable outcomes.

The reason that the evaluation stage is so important is that it provides feedback to the organization on the extent to which merit pay is indeed producing desirable outcomes (Chen et al., 2023; St-Onge, 2000). If it is not, the evaluation process should reveal why and what needs to be done to correct the problem. Wallace (1990) found that one distinguishing characteristic of organizations with successful, as opposed to unsuccessful, incentive pay plans is evaluation of the outcomes associated with the plan. Organizations with successful plans devote resources toward evaluating actual outcomes, rather than taking the results of the plan on "blind faith." Simply put, evaluation is a key step in managing the merit pay process (Gomez-Mejia et al., 2014; R. Heneman, 2001a). Without taking this step, it is doubtful that an organization can successfully manage the merit pay process. As we have mentioned before, it is critical than an organization's merit pay and performance appraisal/performance management processes be linked to business goals and strategies (Larkin, 2019; Martocchio, 2023;

Merit Pay, pages 253–304

doi:10.1108/978-1-80686-701-120263007

R. Heneman, 2001a, 2002). This cannot be done without a thorough and complete evaluation process.

In evaluating the results, or outcomes, of a merit pay plan, two issues are of primary importance and are covered first in this chapter. The first issue is defining and measuring favorable outcomes. The second is developing procedures that will be used to collect data on merit pay outcomes. Following a discussion of these two issues, a summary of the existing evaluation research is presented, organized by procedures and outcomes. This final section provides a more detailed answer to the question posed in the first chapter: "Are merit pay plans successful?"

Outcomes

A criterion model for evaluating merit pay plans is shown in Figure 7.1. As shown in this figure, there are a variety of outcomes for merit pay systems, and these outcomes can be grouped along two dimensions. One dimension is the level at which the desired outcome takes place—individual or business unit. You would expect that a well-developed and administered plan would have a positive impact on individuals in the organization, as well as on business units or collections of individuals in the organization.

Figure 7.1

Criterion Model for Evaluating Merit Pay Plans.

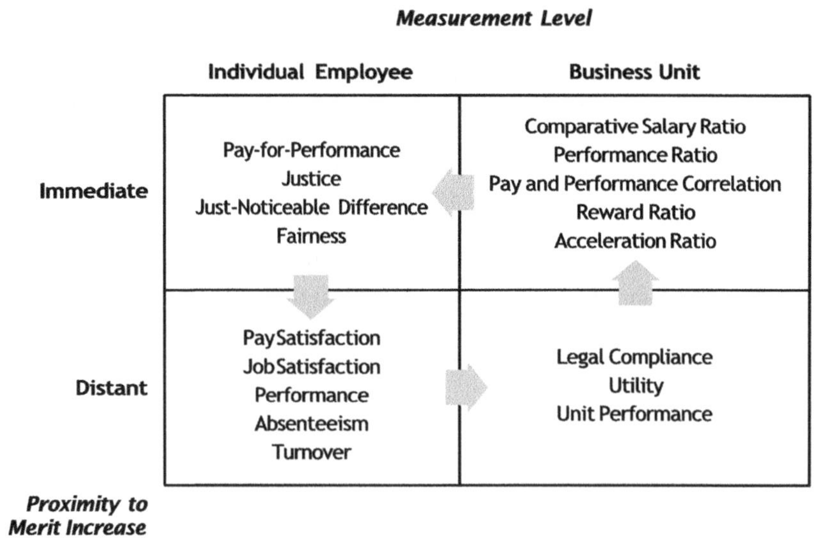

Source: R. Heneman (1991). Reprinted with permission.

Another dimension is the proximity of the outcome to the merit pay increase. While some outcomes would occur close in time to the merit pay increase, others may be more distant, taking place at a later point in time. These dimensions can be used to sort the various outcomes associated with merit pay into four categories.

Immediate Business Unit Outcomes

Merit pay plans are likely to have an immediate impact on two areas of compensation in organizational business units—position and movement of employees within the pay range. Outcomes in each of these areas can be assessed with a variety of indicators, as shown in Figure 7.1.

Comparative Salary Ratio

The position of employees within the pay range is captured in what is called the comparative salary ratio, or "compa-ratio." It is simply the average salary for employees in the business unit, divided by the midpoint. The midpoint is usually established around the market average. Merit increases, if rolled into base salaries, will increase average salaries and therefore increase the compa-ratio. In turn, if maximum salary levels are not adjusted upward, the higher the compa-ratio, the less merit pay will be available for performance in the next round of merit increases, as discussed in Chapter 5. As a result, if compa-ratios are very high in an organization, it may be difficult to motivate future performance using merit pay alone because employees are "maxed out," that is, close to or at the top of the pay range. In a sense, the compa-ratio may serve as an upper boundary to performance as an outcome, because it limits the size of increases (Gobat, 1995; see Chapter 6 for a complete discussion of compa-ratios, and the Merit Increase Exercise in Table 6.2).

Performance Ratio

Another ratio that goes along with the compa-ratio in evaluating merit pay plans is the performance ratio (Goodale & Mouser, 1981). It is the average performance rating divided by the midpoint performance rating. The performance ratio can be used to see whether the value of the compa-ratio reflects actual employee performance. If pay increases in an organization are indeed based on performance, there should be a strong positive relationship between performance ratios and compa-ratios in business units. If you find instead a business unit where the performance ratio is high but the compa-ratio is low, employees may not be receiving all the pay they deserve based on their performance. This discrepancy may be due to a variety of reasons, including low maximums for the pay range or artificially deflated increases given by the allocator. Like compa-ratios, performance ratios send a signal as to the actual tie between pay and performance.

Pay and Performance Correlations

Perhaps the most straightforward way to assess whether merit pay practice follows merit pay policy is to calculate the actual correlation between pay and performance for each business unit. The stronger the correlation between merit increases and performance ratings, the stronger the actual link between pay and performance. Whether this corresponds to employees' *perceptions* of the link between pay and performance is another matter, as we discussed in Chapter 2.

Reward Ratio

The concept of a reward ratio comes from Hunter and Silverman (1980). It refers to a ratio found in many merit pay guide charts that can be compared across business units. The ratio is the largest merit increase granted for excellent performance divided by the lowest merit increase for average or satisfactory performance. Stronger links between pay and performance can be inferred in those business units with larger reward ratios. Some organizations define acceptable reward ratios. For example, at one time the federal Office of Personnel Management (OPM) defined acceptable reward ratios as falling in the range from 2 to 1 through 4 to 1 for the highest performance level over the average or satisfactory level (Hunter & Silverman, 1980). Hence, the OPM could audit federal agencies for compliance with this desired ratio in setting up guide charts and allocating increases.

Acceleration Ratio

An acceleration ratio (Hunter & Silverman, 1980) is the merit increase that can be granted for employees in the highest portion of the pay range (e.g., fourth quartile), divided by the merit increase for employees in the lowest portion of the pay range (e.g., first quartile). The larger the ratio is, the longer it will take employees to progress or accelerate through the pay grade. A large or small ratio may or may not be desirable, depending on the tradeoff between reward and cost orientation for organizations, as discussed in Chapter 5.

Immediate Individual Employee Outcomes

Another set of criteria is also fairly immediate, but is measured at the level of the individual employee, rather than at the level of the business unit.

These criteria primarily relate to employees' perceptions of the merit pay plan.

Pay-for-Performance Perceptions

As stated throughout the book, the perceived relationship between pay and performance can be as important as the actual relationship between these two variables (Park & Sturman, 2022). To measure these perceptions, a multiple-item measure was developed by Heneman et al. (1988), based on the work of Perry and Pearce (1983). This measure of pay-for performance perceptions is shown in Table 7.1. In a study of hospital employees, this measure had modest reliability (R. Heneman et al., 1988). However, a study of hospital employees by Shaw et al. (2003) found a high reliability estimate for this measure ($r = 0.89$). A scale that was adapted from this measure by St-Onge (2000) also had high reliability ($r = 0.88$) with a sample of manufacturing employees.

Justice Perceptions

Included here are measures of distributive, procedural, and interactional justice (discussed in Chapter 6). Distributive justice focuses on the fairness of the reward allocation. Procedural justice focuses on the fairness of procedures used to determine reward allocation (Greenberg, 1986, 1987b).

Table 7.1

Measure of Pay-for-Performance Perceptions

	Strongly Disagree	Disagree	Neutral	Agree	Strongly Agree
If I perform especially well on my job, it is likely that I would get a pay raise	1	2	3	4	5
The best workers in the hospital get the highest pay raises	1	2	3	4	5
The pay raises that I receive on my job make me work harder	1	2	3	4	5
High performers and low performers seem to get the same pay raises	1	2	3	4	5

Source: R. Heneman, Greenberger, and Strasser (1988). Reprinted with permission.

Note: Item 4 is reverse scored to 1 = 5, 2 = 4, 3 = 3, 4 = 2, 5 = 1.

Interactional justice focuses on the manner in which individuals are treated. Folger and Konovsky (1989) developed measures of distributive and procedural justice with good internal consistency reliability for a study of manufacturing employees. The procedural justice measure was multidimensional, consisting of questionnaire items for feedback, planning, recourse, and observation. Moorman (1991) found strong reliability estimates for measures of distributive, procedural, and interactional justice, as did Ramaswami and Singh (2003) and Fong and Shaffer (2003). Research by Jason Colquitt and colleagues suggests splitting the interactional justice dimension into two parts, that is, interpersonal and informational justice dimensions (Colquitt, 2001; Colquitt et al., 2001). These two scales have also demonstrated strong reliability estimates. Recently, a study by Deepak and S (2021a, 2021b) examined professional women's perceptions of fairness in organizations, based on Colquitt's (2001) four dimensions of organizational justice: distributive, procedural, interpersonal, and informational. Deepak and S (2021a, 2021b) found differing results among the four justice dimensions. For distributive justices, women perceived a certain degree of fairness in their organizations. For procedural justice, the same group felt unfairly treated, resulting in perceived gender discrimination. For interpersonal justice, women perceived their treatment to be respectful and dignified. For informational justice, the respondents perceived information sharing to be favorable, but disingenuous at times. There are two research implications to be noted. A replication of this study comparing different groups (e.g., gender, race) is recommended. Second, a replication in other countries or cultures also is suggested, e.g., a recent study of procedural fairness perceptions of teachers in England and Wales (Marsden & Sezer, 2024). Both suggestions would strengthen the external validity of these findings.

Just-Noticeable Differences (JND)

A JND refers to the size of a pay increase that is needed to "make a difference" in influencing employee attitudes and behaviors (H. Heneman & Ellis, 1982). This concept is described in greater detail in Chapter 5. Over the years, a variety of one-item measures have been created to tap this concept. Unfortunately, when one-item measures are used, internal consistency reliability cannot be assessed. A multiple-item measure, which may allow for assessment of internal consistency reliability, was developed by Hinrichs (1969) and is reported in detail in an appendix to Rambo and Pinto (1989). Research by Mitra et al. (1997) used a procedure called "successive categories" to capture responses to the magnitude of pay, as well as affect and behavioral intent. This produced stable results in line with their hypotheses.

Pay Fairness

Many years ago, Belcher (1979) made the distinction between pay fairness and pay satisfaction. Fairness refers to an individual's reaction to his or her pay increase relative to the amount received by others. Satisfaction refers to an individual's reaction to the amount received relative to what he/she believed the amount should have been. Scarpello (1988) developed a measure that focuses on the perceived fairness of pay outcomes and reported that, for a sample of manufacturing employees, perceptions of fairness and satisfaction were strongly related under some, but not all, circumstances. Hence, organizations may wish to measure both pay satisfaction and pay fairness. Jones (1998) studied county government workers, and found the Scarpello (1988) measure to be highly reliable, and also distinct from a four-factor measure of the perceived fairness of pay procedures (highlighting the distinction between the distributive and procedural aspects of fairness; see also Jones, Scarpello, & Bergmann, 1999).

As mentioned above, Colquitt (2001) developed and construct validated a measure (20 items) of organizational justice, from which four items assess pay fairness (distributive justice) (Abuelhassan & AlGassim, 2022; Colquitt, 2001; Mathur & Padmakumari, 2013; Meng & Wu, 2015; Omar et al., 2018; Padmakumari, 2013). Here are examples of the items: [a] My pay reflects the effort I have put into your work; [b] My pay is appropriate for the work I have completed; [c] My pay reflects what I have contributed to the organization; [d] My pay is justified, given my performance. Based on these statements employees respond to a 5-point Likert scale, where 1 = strongly agree, 2 = agree, 3 = neutral, 4 = disagree, 5 = strongly disagree. Typically, responses are reversed scored, so that an overall fairness score can be calculated, ranging from 4 points (lowest) to 20 points (highest).

The original instrument has shown strong psychometric properties (Abuelhassan & AlGassim, 2022; Colquitt, 2001; Omar et al., 2018). Likewise, the pay-fairness scale demonstrates high reliability (Cronbach alpha) based on several studies using them. Mathur and Padmakumari (2013) investigated the effects of organizational Justice on organizational citizenship behavior among store executives of a single retail chain. The pay fairness scale showed a Cronbach alpha (reliability) of 0.84. In another study, Meng and Wu (2015) found a reliability of 0.88 for the 4-item scale when investigating the degree to which perceived fairness of merit pay influences leader-member exchange and in turn influences job engagement. Omar et al. (2018) compared the psychometric properties of Colquitt's organizational justice scale in Argentine workers. The distributive justice (pay fairness) scale revealed an alpha of 0.84. Another study, Abuelhassan and AlGassim (2021) examined how organizational justice in the hospitality industry influences proactive customer service performance. The four-item scale applied to measure distributive justice showed a reliability of 0.85. In summary, while several empirical studies have shown that Colquitt's organizational justice scale is a reliable and valid instrument, its distributive dimension also shows strong psychometric characteristics for measuring pay fairness.

Distant Individual Employee Outcomes

Other outcomes are also at the individual level of measurement, but are more distant than the individual's immediate perceptions of the merit pay system. These more distant criteria include affective and behavioral reactions to the merit pay plan.

Job Performance

One obvious distant individual employee outcome is job performance. Job performance can be viewed as a behavioral reaction to merit pay. As discussed throughout the book, an increase in performance is a major goal of merit pay plans. The measurement of job performance was covered in Chapter 4. In addition, we also direct the reader to review the relationship between merit pay levels and job performance later in this chapter and in Chapter 2.

Along with an increase in the *level* of performance, another desirable merit pay outcome is an increase in the *consistency* of performance over time (Kirk & Brown, 2003). Depending on the person (Henry & Hulin, 1987) and the job (Rambo, Chomiak, & Price, 1983), you would expect an incentive pay plan, such as merit pay, to lead to more stable performance over time (Rothe, 1978). In a 6-year study of chippers and grinders in a foundry, Vinchur, Schippman, Smalley, and Rothe (1991) found evidence that performance was fairly stable over time under a piece-rate incentive plan. This line of argument suggests that for a merit pay plan to be considered successful, it should produce not only a one-time increase in performance but should sustain performance at an increased level over time. To assess the degree to which this takes place, performance needs to be assessed on a repeated, regular basis. This desirable outcome was studied by Nyberg, Pieper, Jenna, and Trevor (2016). The authors postulated and empirically tested the effect of pay-for-performance (merit pay and pay bonus) on job performance over a five-year period. The results showed that both performance-based pay systems indeed related to performance over five years, but more so for merit pay than bonus pay. It appears the compounding affect of merit pay has an advantage in employees "seeing" the pay to reward relationship over time.

Job Satisfaction

One affective reaction to work is known as job satisfaction. This reaction comes from the employee's assessment of what *is* versus what *should be* vis-à-vis the conditions surrounding work and the work itself (Locke, 1976). Although there are many measures of job satisfaction, two have stood the test of time and have sound reliability properties. Because they have been used extensively by organizations, these measures have produced normative data, available for comparison purposes. One of the conditions of work assessed by each of the two measures is pay. The two measures are the Minnesota Satisfaction Questionnaire, or MSQ (Weiss, Davis, England, & Lofquist, 1967) and the Job Descriptive Index, or JDI (Smith, Kendall, & Hulin, 1969). If a measure of overall satisfaction is desired, the JDI and MSQ, which target specific components of work, need to be supplemented with an overall measure of job satisfaction. An overall measure of job satisfaction and its relationship to the MSQ is described in Scarpello and Campbell (1983). For more detail on job satisfaction measures and their psychometric properties, see van Saane, Sluiter, Verbeek, and Frings-Dresen (2003) for a systematic review of the reliability and validity of instruments measuring job satisfaction.

Pay Satisfaction

One specific condition implicit in work is pay, and a questionnaire has been developed to measure satisfaction with pay. This questionnaire is known as the Pay Satisfaction Questionnaire (PSQ) and was developed by H. Heneman and Schwab (1985). It is a measure of employees' affective reactions to pay. The PSQ is shown in Box 7.1. As shown in the questionnaire, pay satisfaction can be viewed as having four dimensions. Satisfaction with *pay level* is the perceived satisfaction with direct wages and salaries. Satisfaction with *pay raises* refers to the perceived satisfaction with changes in pay level. Satisfaction with *structure/administration* is defined as the perceived satisfaction with the internal pay hierarchy and the methods used to distribute pay. Satisfaction with *benefits* concerns perceived satisfaction with indirect payments to employees.

Considerable research has been conducted on the PSQ (Carraher, 1991; R. Heneman, Greenberger, & Strasser, 1988; Judge, 1993; Judge & Welbourne, 1994; see also H. Heneman & Judge, 2000, 2003). In general, it has been found to have excellent reliability properties. It is targeted directly at pay, rather than other facets of work (Scarpello, Huber, & Vanderberg, 1988). Miceli and Mulvey (2000) proposed and tested a more general measure of *pay system* satisfaction, which may be useful, especially in unionized settings. R. Heneman, Greenberger, and Fox (2002) also developed a

Box 7.1 The Modified Pay Satisfaction Questionnaire (PSQ)

The statements below describe various aspects of your pay. For each statement decide how satisfied or dissatisfied you feel about your pay, and put the number in the corresponding blank that best indicates your feeling. To do this, use the following scale:

1	2	3	4	5
Very Dissatisfied	Dissatisfied	Neither Satisfied Nor Dissatisfied	Satisfied	Very Satisfied

1.	My take-home pay.	L
2.	My benefit package.	B
3.	My most recent raise.	R
4.	Influence my supervisor has on my pay.	R
5.	My current salary.	L
6.	Amount the company pays toward my benefits.	B
7.	The raises I have typically received in the past.	R
8.	The company's pay structure.	S/A
9.	Information the company gives about pay issues of concern to me.	S/A
10.	My overall level of pay.	L
11.	The value of my benefits.	B
12.	Pay of other jobs in the company.	S/A
13.	Consistency of the company's pay policies.	S/A
14.	Size of my current salary.	L
15.	The number of benefits I receive.	B
16.	How my raises are determined.	R
17.	Differences in pay among jobs in the company.	S/A
18.	How the company administers pay.	S/A

Source: H. Heneman (1985). Copyright © Herbert G. Heneman, III and Donald P. Schwab, 1983. Reprinted with permission.
Note: L, level; B, benefits; R, raise; S/A, structure/administration.

measure of pay raise satisfaction, one specific dimension of the PSQ, based on the changing nature of work and rewards since development of the PSQ. However, the PSQ remains the most widely used measure of pay satisfaction.

Sturman and Short (2000) presented a four-item scale concerning lump-sum bonus satisfaction. As we indicated in Chapters 3 and 5, lump-sum bonuses are an increasingly popular form of variable pay. The Sturman and

Short scale was meant to supplement the four factors/scales in the PSQ. The items ask each employee to rate the extent to which they are satisfied with:

1. My most recent bonus
2. The influence that others have on my bonus
3. The bonuses I have typically received in the past
4. How my bonuses are determined.

Sturman and Short (2000) collected data from 416 employees in five organizations, and found support for a five-factor structure (i.e., the four PSQ factors, plus their hypothesized lump-sum bonus satisfaction factor). All reliability estimates were strong (i.e., above 0.90), and other supporting analyses indicate that, for organizations using lump-sum bonuses, this might be a useful addition to the PSQ. Finally, other studies have investigated the generalizability of the PSQ to other countries and cultures—*Belgium* (De Gieter et al., 2006), *Cyprus* (Lievens, Anseel, Harris, & Eisenberg, 2007), *Egypt* (Mohamed, Mohamad, & Awad, 2017), In all cases, the results show a 4-factor structure in pay satisfaction and comparable psychometric properties as in the original American instrument.

Absenteeism

Absenteeism may decrease with merit pay because it is typically one aspect of performance that is monitored by organizations. Normally, the less absent an employee is from work, the better his or her performance. The better his or her performance, the larger the merit increase. In turn, this larger merit increase should continue to motivate reduced absenteeism in the future. For example, Pouliakas and Theodoropoulos (2010) found that merit pay using performance ratings indeed was significantly related to lower absenteeism, but incentive pay with objective outcomes had no effect.

A wide variety of measures have been used to assess the incidence of absence from work, including measures of magnitude, frequency, and duration. These measures and others are summarized in Rhodes and Steers (1990). Perhaps the best known and most widely used measure of absence came from the Bureau of National Affairs (BNA, 1983; Mincer, 1977), now a part of Bloomberg. The formula is as follows:

$$\frac{\text{Number of employee days lost through job absence during month}}{(\text{Average number of employees}) \times (\text{Number of workdays})} \times 100$$

Comparative data on absence by industry, age, and gender can be found at the U.S. Department of Labor website (see the Bureau of Labor Statistics, Current Population Survey, Absences from work).

Turnover

Another behavioral reaction to merit pay, along with performance and absenteeism, is turnover, or people leaving the organization. Turnover may be reduced with merit pay because people may be more satisfied with their pay. For example, Froese, Peltokorpi, Varma, and Hitotsuyanagi-Hansel (2018) found that job satisfaction moderated the inverse relationship between merit pay and voluntary turnover. Turnover, like absenteeism, can be measured in a number of ways. These measures were summarized by Mobley (1982). A well-known measure of turnover is shown in the following formula (Mincer, 1977):

$$\frac{\text{Number of separations during month}}{\text{Average number of employees on payroll during month}} \times 100$$

The U.S. Department of Labor provides turnover data online through their Job Openings and Labor Turnover Survey (JOLTS) series (https://www.bls.gov/jlt/).

Distant Business Unit Outcomes

A final category of outcomes is that of distant outcomes related to the business unit level, rather than the individual employee level. These outcomes are assessed using measures of compliance with the law, as well as more financially oriented measures of business unit success.

Legal Compliance

One important standard that must be met in a merit pay plan is compliance with the laws and regulations, especially those covered in Chapter 6. To monitor compliance, merit pay plans can be periodically audited at the business unit level. Such an audit could include correlating performance ratings and merit increases with the protected-class categories such as age, race, sex, color, religion, and national origin to ensure that differences in merit increases are not due to protected-class status. As we have mentioned before, there have been court cases dealing with merit pay and other compensation plans seeking to link pay to individual performance (cf. Martin et al., 2000). We say more about proactive auditing procedures below.

Utility

Another standard that can be used at the business unit level is known as utility, or the financial return on performance increases linked to merit pay.

Landy, Farr, and Jacobs (1982) presented a utility formula that can be applied to merit pay decisions (R. Heneman, 1990). In essence, financial returns on merit pay dollars are calculated by comparing the dollar value of the subsequent performance of those who receive versus those who do not receive merit increases, after the costs of merit pay have been subtracted out. Utility represents the dollar value of a merit pay plan to an organization based on the performance of employees after merit pay has been implemented. Caution should be taken, however, in using the utility standard, as it has not been widely used for merit pay.

Sterling (1990) conducted a utility analysis on the monetary returns associated with a merit pay plan for a set of data used by Schwab and Olson (1990). This data set consisted of data for 157 employees in a simulated organization. To estimate the dollar value of a merit pay program, he used the following formula from Schmidt, Hunter, and Pearlman (1982):

$\Delta U = T \cdot N \cdot d_t \cdot SDy - N \cdot C$

ΔU = the dollar value of the merit pay program

T = the number of years duration of the effect of merit pay on subsequent performance

N = the number of individuals who received merit pay

d_t = the true difference in job performance between the average employee who received merit pay and the average employee who did not receive merit pay in standard deviation units

SDy = the standard deviation of job performance in dollars of the group not receiving merit pay

C = the cost of the merit pay program per employee

Based on estimates of these parameters from Schwab and Olson (1990) and Schmidt et al. (1982), Sterling (1990) found that the dollar value of a merit pay program was slightly over $3 million, or approximately $1 million a year, assuming that the value of T (time in years) is 3 years.

This figure may be an overestimate, as C (cost) was estimated to be zero. Sterling assumed that there were no costs to the program because merit pay represents a more efficient use of the costs associated with existing pay programs. Even if this is the case, there may be some administrative costs in shifting from a traditional pay plan with across-the-board increases to a merit pay plan. As shown throughout the book, there are costs associated with the design, implementation, and evaluation of a merit pay plan, above and beyond the costs of merit pay increases. Hence, the $3 million figure may need to be adjusted downward for a more accurate estimate.

It should also be noted that the data used to derive this estimate of the expected utility of a merit pay plan were simulated in a Monte Carlo study (Schwab & Olson, 1990). We see the Sterling (1990) study as a good beginning. Some additional work linking utility analysis to compensation issues in general is encouraging (Hantula, Rajala, Kellerman, & Bragger, 2001; Klaas & McClendon, 1996; Williams & Dreher, 1992). In particular, a simulation study by Sturman et al. (2003) suggests that an organization that made greater differentiation between employees in awarding pay raises over a 4-year period (based on individual performance ratings) would have substantial net gain over an approach where all employees received "across-the-board" pay raises. The Sturman et al. (2003) study was based on a hypothetical large organization (over 5,000 employees), and utilized realistic assumptions concerning pay, turnover, and the estimates needed to calculate utility. More research along these lines is needed. It would be valuable to see utility analysis linked to merit pay plans used in actual organizations (Fulmer et al., 2023).

Unit Performance

Another set of standards has to do with the effectiveness of the business unit. Several cost-accounting measures could be used to assess the impact of merit increases on the financial performance of business units. Rock (1983) reviewed three financial measures of performance. The first measure comes from a standard profit-and-loss statement (i.e., *earnings per share*, or EPS). A second measure is *return on equity* (ROE), which can be obtained from profit-and-loss statements as well as balance sheets. Both these measures can be tracked over time, or in relation to other companies. Hence, they could be compared before and after the introduction of a merit pay plan, or compared to similar companies without a merit pay plan. According to Rock, advantages to using EPS and ROE as standards is that they are fairly easy to measure and communicate. They are also widely understood by business decision-makers.

A major disadvantage of EPS and ROE is that they do not adequately capture performance during periods of high interest charges, high replacement costs, and high inflation. In effect, measures of earnings such as EPS and ROE may be illusory during these periods because they fail to show how "real" the earnings are (Rock, 1983). Another disadvantage with using EPS and ROE as standards is that they are difficult to assess at the operating-unit level (as opposed to the corporate level).

Given these disadvantages, some organizations are using cash flow indicators of business unit performance instead. Although more difficult to measure and communicate, they can account for economic influences outside the control of the organization, such as inflation, and also can be measured at both the corporate and operating-unit level (Rock, 1983). Examples of this approach come from Ubelhart (1990).

One cash flow indicator is *cash flow return on investment* (CFROI), which is the ratio of cash flow over time to cash investment. Another cash flow indicator is *business value*, which is CFROI-adjusted for the growth or contraction of assets. It should be noted that these cash flow indicators and others need to be carefully reviewed with financial specialists before use, because there are no established formats and procedures for their use (Ubelhart, 1990).

Another method of assessing business units effectiveness is *economic value added* (EVA). The EVA model was promoted (and registered) by consultants Stern Stewart and Company. In essence, this measure of organizational value looks at the return to capital relative to alternative investments that could be made with this capital. Many large organizations have made use of EVA accounting methods, including Coca- Cola, Eli Lilly, Herman Miller, Monsanto, and Whirlpool (McCowan, Bowen, Huselid, & Becker, 1999; Stern Stewart, 2004). A case study on the use of EVA at a pharmaceutical manufacturer is available (Simons & Reinbergs, 2000), as is a book on the subject (Young & O'Byrne, 2001). Earlier research had been mixed concerning the use of this approach to measuring organizational performance, for example, authors such as Kleiman (1999) and Wallace (1997) have argued in favor of it, while Abdeen and Haight (2002) and Malmi and Ikäheimo (2003) have argued against its usage.

Later studies have offered more insight on EVA's potential for measuring organizational effectiveness. For example, Mamun and Mansor (2012) found support for claims that EVA is superior than traditional economic metrics for measuring business units and organizations overall performance in Malaysia. In another study, Subedi and Farazmand (2020) tested the degree to which the metric properties of EVA motivated administrators to increase the performance of public organizations in China. The results confirmed that EVA, as a performance evaluation metric, indeed incentivizes public administrators, which in turn increased overall organizational performance. Goel and Oswal (2020) examined claims that EVA is a superior performance metric than the traditional performance indicators like ROCE, NOPAT, and EPS. The results of multiple regression analyses reveled that claims of EVA's superiority were false. Instead, EVA was inferior to traditional measures of organizational performance in India. Finally, Tripathi, Ghalke, and Kashiramka (2024) discovered that EVA is more reliable than other traditional measurement systems for evaluating a company's financial performance over all lifecycle stages.

In summary, while early research on EVA accounting methods showed mixed results, recent research has shown that EVA models seem to be more effective now than in the past, especially in developing markets (i.e., India). It is not our intent to cover an in-depth discussion on EVA. Instead, we refer the reader to Tripathi et al. (2023).

Relations Among Outcomes and the Need for Multiple Outcomes

The arrows drawn in Figure 7.1 suggest that the categories of outcomes are related to one another in a logical manner. Immediate business unit outcomes should lead to immediate individual employee outcomes. For example, an individual's perceptions of pay, such as pay-for-performance, are likely to be influenced by his or her position in the pay grade and potential for merit increases, as indicated by reward and acceleration ratios. Immediate individual employee outcomes should, in turn, lead to distant individual employee outcomes. That is, individuals' perceptions of the merit pay plan will influence their affective reactions to the plan (e.g., pay satisfaction), as well as their behaviors at work (e.g., performance). Distant individual employee outcomes should then contribute to distant business unit outcomes. Performance, for example, would be expected to have an impact on the financial success of the business unit. Distant business unit outcomes should in turn influence immediate business unit performance. Reward ratios, for example, may be larger when the business unit has greater financial success. These relationships among the categories suggest the importance of using multiple outcomes in assessing merit pay plans.

More specifically, there are two reasons to evaluate merit pay plans with multiple criteria. First, the outcomes of a merit pay plan are unlikely to be all positive or negative. A more likely scenario is that a merit pay plan may be successful along some lines and not others. Multiple criteria will differentiate between areas of success and weakness. For example, Gomez-Mejia and Balkin (1989) reported on a merit pay plan that had a positive effect on performance measured at the business unit level, but did not have an effect on performance measured at the individual level.

Second, multiple criteria can be used to show or diagnose *why* merit pay leads to desirable or undesirable results. For example, a correlation between merit increases and perceptions of pay fairness is interesting, but not terribly useful. It would be useful, however, to see that perceptions of pay fairness are the result of the acceleration ratio and, in turn, pay fairness perceptions have led to lower levels of absenteeism, contributing to the bottom-line performance of the business unit.

Form of the Relationship Between Merit Pay and Outcomes

It is sometimes implicitly assumed that there is a linear or one-for-one return on merit pay increases. Most statistical tests of the relationship between satisfaction (pay or job) and merit increases are based on a linear model. As pointed out by Porter et al. (1990), however, there are several reasons to expect that the relationship between merit increases and satisfaction measures may be nonlinear. These alternatives are summarized in Figure 7.2.

Figure 7.2.

Theorized Relationships: Pay Satisfaction to Actual Pay, (a) Linear, (b) Logarithmic, (c) Power Function, (d) Matthew Effect, (e) Equity.

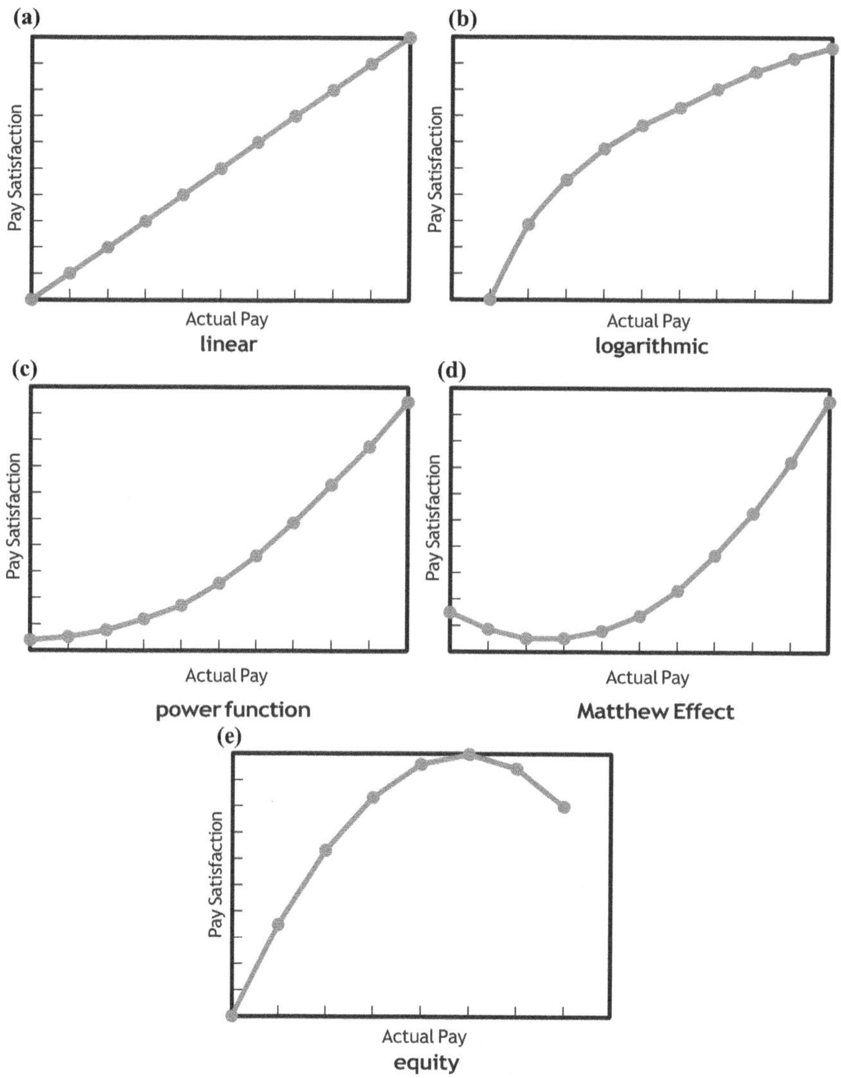

Source: Porter, Greenberger, and R. Heneman (1990). Reprinted with permission.

As shown in Graph B, there may be diminishing marginal returns (Bernoulli, 1984). That is, each additional dollar spent on merit pay may mean less of an increase in satisfaction because each additional dollar contributes less and less to the total available for consumption. Alternatively, based on the work in psychophysics by Stevens (1959), each additional dollar of a merit increase may contribute to greater amounts of satisfaction, as shown in Graph C. The reason for increasing amounts of satisfaction in Graph C is that each additional dollar results in a feeling of increased recognition and status from the organization.

As shown in Graphs D and E, satisfaction may be greater for some merit increases than others. In Graph D, the "Matthew Effect" is represented (Gabris & Mitchell, 1988) and suggests that satisfaction is lowest when an average merit increase is granted, because the employee is likely to feel that pay is being taken from him or her to go to better performers (see Chapter 2 for additional information on the Matthew Effect). In Graph E, an equity effect is depicted (Adams, 1965) in which perceptions of overreward may produce decreased satisfaction with increasing levels of merit pay.

In a limited test of these models, Porter et al. (1990) found that one of the nonlinear models (Graph E) better explained satisfaction than did the linear model (Graph A). The authors concluded that in evaluating merit pay plans using satisfaction as the outcome, care should be taken to examine the form of the relationship for nonlinear as well as linear relationships. The possibility of nonlinear relationships should be explored when other outcomes are used to evaluate merit pay plans as well. In a study of hospital workers, the relationship between pay level and pay satisfaction was best captured using a power function (similar to Graph C), rather than as a linear function (R. Heneman, Porter, Greenberger, & Strasser, 1997).

In a different line of research, Dorsey and Coovert (2003) conducted a interesting study of simulated merit pay decisions. Ten experienced compensation professionals made hypothetical merit pay decisions for a large number of employee profiles. These profiles differed in terms of the extent to which the "employees" varied in terms of five variables, i.e., individual performance, their work unit's performance, their rated importance to accomplishing the organization's goals, their tenure, and the importance to accomplishing the organization's goals, their tenure, and their current salary. In analyses using linear regression, Dorsey and Coovert found that these five variables explained a sizeable portion of the merit pay decisions made by these raters (multiple correlations ranged from 0.74–0.98). However, for six of the 10 raters, nonlinear regression analyses did even better at predicting merit pay decisions. More work along these lines is encouraged.

Data Collection Procedures

Along with outcomes, attention should be given to the procedures that will be used to collect the data needed to assess outcomes. In particular, attention should be given to audit issues, as well as internal and external validity.

Audit Issues

One way to evaluate a merit pay plan is to wait until a problem occurs, then measure outcomes of the plan. This is a reactive approach to evaluation. The problem with a reactive approach is that by the time you evaluate, it may be too late to correct a very large problem. Another approach, which is much more proactive, is to conduct regular, formal audits or reviews of the outcomes associated with merit pay on a periodic basis. Audit data are then fed back to employees and decision-makers in the organization to improve negative outcomes and maintain or improve positive outcomes. Organizations are increasingly seeking to make their human resource management practices more strategic (i.e., more clearly linked to the goals and outcomes of value to the organization). Bargerstock (2000) provides an example of an HRM effectiveness audit that he has utilized in a number of public-sector organizations. Compensation issues are included as one portion of this audit instrument.

An example of proactive auditing procedures concerning a merit pay plan is from Blue Cross of Southern California (Cowan, 1978). To audit the effectiveness of its plan, a task force was organized. This task force consisted of 50% line management and 50% human resource staff. Task force members gathered data on behavioral outcomes associated with the plan. Based on these data, they developed a list of possible problems, both long and short term, and possible solutions. This information was then fed back to line managers and used to develop action plans to resolve the potential problems revealed. Part of the action plan included steps to be taken by individual managers to audit the effectiveness of the merit pay plan in their business unit.

Having employee representation as well as management and human resource representation on the audit task force is desirable. It is especially important when employees' affective reactions to the plan are measured as a part of the audit. Surveying employees' attitudes may heighten their expectations concerning the merit pay plan. Having employee representation on the audit task force creates a channel to give employees feedback on their concerns and to communicate what can be done in response to these concerns, what additional information needs to be gathered, or why nothing can be done about a particular issue.

Study Design Considerations

It is one thing to show that there is a *relationship* between merit increases and outcomes, but this is not the same as showing that the measured outcomes are the *result* of merit increases, and that we are likely to find the same results in other settings. Attention must be given to the concepts of *internal* and *external validity* when collecting outcome data to have confidence in the results. The greater the internal and external validity of a study, the greater the confidence we can place in the results that are obtained.

Internal Validity

In evaluating a merit pay plan, the objective is to see to what extent merit pay caused a change in the outcome variables of interest. In the context of merit pay, internal validity refers to the extent to which merit pay rather than other factors caused a change in outcomes. Probably the most frequently used method to assess this can be called a *one-shot case study* in which outcomes are measured only after merit pay is implemented. Although this method is better than no evaluation at all, it is far from ideal. A one-shot case study fails to answer the question, "Did a change in outcomes take place?" High or low outcome scores after merit increases may be due to the fact that outcomes were already high or low before merit increases were granted.

To see if a change in outcomes took place, a better method of data collection is a *pretest–posttest design,* signifying before and after an intervention. Here, the outcomes of interest are measured both before (pretest) and after (posttest) merit increases. We should make clear that the term "test" does *not* mean that this device has to be a written measure capturing how much an employee knows. A pretest or posttest can measure anything that would be meaningful to evaluate the success of the merit pay system (e.g., attitudes, behaviors, as well as financial or other "hard" measures). By using a pretest and posttest, it is possible to assess whether a change in outcomes actually took place, or whether outcomes remained the same as before, regardless of merit increases. Although a pretest–posttest design is better than a one-shot case study, it is not without problems. In particular, while this design answers the question of whether a change took place, it does not answer the question of whether the change was due to merit pay or to something else.

A variety of factors other than merit pay could be responsible for the change in outcomes from the pretest to posttest. These rival explanations for the change (or lack thereof) are detailed in Shadish, Cook, and Campbell (2002). These other factors are known as "threats" to internal validity, where internal validity refers to the question, "To what extent does merit pay cause certain outcomes?" Threats to internal validity include issues such as history, maturation, and instrumentation (Shadish et al., 2002). These factors or others may be responsible for changes in outcomes, rather than merit pay. *History* refers to events in addition to merit pay that took place between the pretest and posttest. Examples might include changes in technology, human resource practices, or supervision. *Maturation* refers to changes in the employees under study. For example, with the passage of time, employees may become more mature or better at managing impressions. *Instrumentation* refers to changes in the measuring instruments or persons using them. Examples might include using different raters or different standards of performance for the pretest and posttest.

One way to minimize these threats is to use a *control group*. What this means is that in evaluating merit pay, two groups are used. An experimental or treatment group receives merit pay, while a control group does not. A comparison can be made between the experimental and control group to see the extent to which a change in outcomes is due to merit pay. This method is known as a *pretest–posttest control group design*. The only difference between the experimental and control group is that merit pay is given to the experimental group. Hence, any differences in outcomes should be attributable to merit pay.

To ensure that the comparison between experimental and control group is meaningful, employees should, if at all possible, be randomly assigned to each group. Random assignment is another way to minimize threats to internal validity. Each employee has the same chance of being in the experimental and control group, which minimizes differences in employees as the explanation for differences in outcomes.

From an administrative standpoint, there are two obvious problems with the pretest–posttest control group design. First, it is difficult if not impossible to allow some employees to be eligible for a merit increase while others are not eligible. Second, random assignment may not be possible. To illustrate these two problems, imagine how you would feel if your boss came up to you and a coworker and told you that you would not be eligible for a merit increase but your coworker would be. It is doubtful that you would feel much better if your boss then told you that it was simply a random decision for purposes of research and that you shouldn't take the decision personally!

There are two other designs that can be used to minimize these administrative problems. However, they do not minimize the threats to internal validity as well as a pretest–posttest control group design with random assignment to the experimental and control groups.

One alternative design is a *nonequivalent control group design*. With this design, a pretest and posttest is administered to an experimental and control group. Employees are not, however, assigned on a random basis. Instead, intact work groups are assigned as experimental and control groups.

For example, division A of an organization would receive a new merit pay plan, while division B would not receive the new plan until later when the evaluation is completed. The problem with this design is that the groups are not equivalent and, hence, differences in outcomes may be due to differences in the groups. To minimize this possibility, the groups in the evaluation study could be "matched" as well as possible to increase the possibility of equivalence. Employees in the studied sample would be matched along characteristics believed to influence merit pay outcomes. For example, there may be reason to expect that seniority is related to performance. To control for the effects of seniority, an equivalent number of employees with various seniority levels could be included in the studied experimental and control groups. It should be noted that although matching help to minimize differences between groups, it is impossible to perfectly match groups along all variables likely to have an impact on outcomes.

A second design that can be used to minimize administrative problems is called a *time-series design.* With a time-series design, a control group is not used. Instead, multiple pretests and multiple posttests are used. In effect, the experimental group also serves as the control through the use of multiple measures. You could more strongly infer that merit pay led to specific outcomes when the only change in outcomes took place after the introduction of merit pay rather than before, during, and after merit pay. While it may be advantageous from an administrative standpoint to use a time-series design, it is not possible to totally rule out history as an explanation for the change. A more robust design is the *multiple time-series design* (Werner, 2022). With this approach, both the experimental and the control groups receive multiple pretests and posttests, but only the experimental group receives the merit pay intervention. If positive changes are seen after the merit pay intervention—but only for the experimental group—this is a pretty strong indication that the change was due to the change in merit pay.

External Validity

In addition to concerns about internal validity, attention also needs to be directed toward external validity in conducting an evaluation of merit pay. External validity raises the question, "To what extent can we generalize the results of the evaluation to other employee groups, settings, and merit pay plans?" In other words, just because a merit pay plan has a specific set of outcomes under one set of circumstances does not automatically mean it will have the same outcomes under another set of circumstances.

There are also threats to external validity that, when minimized, allow us to generalize the results of the evaluation to other circumstances. This generalizability is an important aspect of evaluation, as it allows organizations to predict outcomes across business units. Also, it is important because it allows organizations to assess the extent to which the results of merit pay studies at other organizations are relevant to their own organizations.

Shadish, Cook, and Campbell (2002) provide a detailed description of threats to external validity. First, the selection of employees to be evaluated is a concern. A merit pay plan that works well for managers, for example, may not work well for lower-level employees. If merit pay is to be used for multiple employee groups, then representatives from each group may need to be included in the evaluation study.

Second, merit pay plans may coincide with other new programs. That is, merit pay may be introduced to the organization at the same time as another human resource intervention, such as training, performance management, or an increased use of teams. As a result, it may be difficult to know if outcomes are attributable to merit pay or to other changes (such as training). Whenever possible, merit pay should be evaluated independently of other interventions. Also, it should not be automatically assumed that the results of one type of merit plan (e.g., lump-sum bonuses, as described in Chapter 5) will generalize to settings with another type of plan (e.g., a traditional merit pay plan).

Third, employee outcomes may have more to do with the fact that employees are being studied than the fact that they are receiving merit pay. That is, employees may be reacting to the novel setting rather than to the merit increases received. To guard against this possibility, multiple posttests can be conducted. You would expect that if the outcomes were due to the novelty of the situation, the novelty would diminish over time. When multiple tests are used, however, another problem may arise. Employees in the evaluation study may become sensitized to what is expected by the organization and respond accordingly.

In summary, when designing a study to evaluate the effectiveness of merit pay, data collection procedures need to account for both internal and external threats to validity. Consideration must be given to using a pretest, control group, random or matched assignment, a representative sample, and multiple posttests. Although there are risks to using these methods in evaluating merit pay, the study results are more usable than when these methods are not used, as in a one-shot case study design.

A Practical Illustration

When reading about study design considerations such as we have just discussed, you may walk away feeling overwhelmed by the technical jargon. There is indeed a fair amount of it. The technical language has been included in this book, however, because the reader may encounter this jargon when reading merit pay studies or interacting with people who conduct evaluation studies on merit pay. Although the labels and phrases can be cumbersome, they are very relevant in terms of applicability. Perhaps the best way to demonstrate the applicability of study design considerations is to put yourself in the role of an executive who is charged with deciding whether to use a merit pay plan for the first time.

As a first step, you may read previous merit pay studies, as suggested in Chapter 1. Also, you may be approached by consultants who would like you to try their particular approach to merit pay. The first question you should ask about the studies you are reviewing and of the consultants is, "What evidence is there that the merit pay plan leads to improved performance?" At this point, you may read or be told: "Productivity was 120% after the introduction of the merit pay plan." At first blush, this seems encouraging. Upon careful consideration of study design issues, however, you conclude that this statement is meaningless. Why? Because if there is no indication that a pretest of productivity was conducted before the plan was implemented, the study results cannot support the claim. For all you know, based on this statement, productivity may have declined from a productivity level of 150% that existed prior to the merit pay plan.

Next, you may turn to yet another study that shows a substantial increase in productivity from the pretest to the posttest. The use of a pretest gives you a greater sense of confidence in this merit pay plan than in the previous one. A careful reading shows, however, that along with the implementation of a merit pay plan, during the period of time from the pretest to the posttest, a new training program was also implemented. You now correctly conclude that while a productivity increase did occur, you cannot be confident that the change in productivity was actually due to merit pay rather than training. Why? There was no control group for comparing a group of similarly trained employees that did not receive merit pay to the experimental group.

In yet another study, you find a similar increase in productivity from pretest to posttest. This time, however, a control group was used. One group received merit pay, and the other did not. Hence, you can feel much more confident in the results found for this merit pay plan. You are still rightfully troubled, however, by the fact that more senior-level people were in the merit pay experimental group than in the control group. That is, there was no random assignment of employees. How might seniority be a problem? Senior people in organizations tend to receive higher salaries, and the higher salaries may have caused a productivity increase rather than merit pay. On the plus side, you are pleased to see that employees in the studied organization are similar to the ones in your own organization, and that productivity was tracked for an extended period of time after an initial merit increase was granted to employees. Hence, a representative sample was studied, and the results were not from a one-time-only evaluation.

Overall, this final study probably would give you the greatest level of confidence of the three described. You may decide to use this plan as the basis for setting up a merit pay plan for your organization. The next steps to take would be to make sure the plan is feasible, adapt it to your circumstances, and implement it. But before you implement it, you may again want to consider study design issues. In particular, you can replicate the pretest/posttest with control group evaluation design in your organization. Moreover, you can carefully match employees by seniority in the experimental and control groups by levels of seniority to eliminate your major concern with the previous study. If possible, you may wish to include multiple pretest and posttest measures as well. As can be seen from this example, study design considerations are critical to sound business decisions concerning evaluation.

Review of Empirical Studies Evaluating Merit Pay Plans

In Chapter 1, an initial attempt was made to answer the question, "Are merit pay plans successful?" The answer was a tentative and qualified "yes." Next, as shown in Tables 2.1 and 2.2, it is possible to tie pay to previous performance. This has been demonstrated in diverse organizations. The extent to which this link then leads to favorable outcomes is less certain. As will be shown in this final section of the book, there is a great deal of variance in the success of merit pay plans when gauged by outcomes subsequent to merit pay. This should not come as a surprise, given the care that must be taken in the assessment of the desirability and feasibility of merit pay, the development and administration of a merit pay plan, and the evaluation of a merit pay plan.

A summary of the empirical studies evaluating outcomes associated with merit pay is shown in Table 7.2. This table is also supplemented by a summary of empirical studies that have evaluated merit pay in the federal government, as shown in Tables 7.3 and 7.4. Finally, Table 7.5 presents a meta-analytic study evaluating the effect of merit pay on various outcomes featured in this chapter (Williams, 2010). In reviewing these summary tables, several aspects of the procedures used and outcomes reported stand out.

Procedures

One notable procedural feature is the heavy reliance placed on managerial employees in the public sector. Managers have been studied in school districts, transit agencies, states, cities, counties, municipalities, and

Table 7.2

Summary of Studies Evaluating Outcomes of Merit Pay Plans

Authors	Participants	Organizations	Criteria	Procedure	Results[a]
Alan and Rosenberg (1986)	2,230 managers	New York City government	Performance ratings	Performance measured far 3 consecutive years after implementation of plan	Performance ratings increased over a 3 year period (at an unspecified level of signif-icance)
Barclay and York (2003)	3 Merit Committee members	Business School at a large, research-oriented public university	Measuring actual weight given to teaching, research, and service in determining merit raises for 36 faculty members	Policy capturing used to determine weights	Merit increases were determined 80% by research, 19% by teaching, and 1% by service
Benson & Brown (2000)	Australia: 294 business units in 1990; 201 business units in 1995 Japan: 253 business units in 1991; 172 business units in 1995	Australia: private manufacturing organizations with 100 or more employees Japan: private manufacturing organizations in Kansai region	Impact of performance-related pay (both piece-rate and merit pay) on productivity, labor costs, absenteeism, turnover, and quality	OLS regression and probit analyses used to predict impact of performance-related pay on the five dependent variables	Performance-related pay was negatively related to turnover, but only for the 1995 Japan sample. All other outcomes were not statistically significant

Authors	Participants	Organizations	Criteria	Procedure	Results[a]
Brown (2001)	3,335 employees	Large, Australian public-sector research organization	Support for merit pay	Surveys mailed to employees	Perceptions of procedural justice had the strongest relationship with support for merit pay, followed by market comparability, job security, and supervisory appraisal rating
Bullock (1983)	380 employees	Engineering division of a southeastern public utility	Pay satisfaction and job satisfaction	Pay and job satisfaction measured before and after implementation of merit pay plan	Merit award statue did not significantly predict changes in pay satisfaction, but did significantly predict increases in job satisfaction
Cherrington, Reitz, and Scott (1971)	90 undergraduate business student volunteers	Academic institution	Relationship between satisfaction and performance perceptions	Comparison of three pay plans: random rewards, positively contingent rewards, and negatively contingent rewards	Positive relationship between satisfaction and performance for positively contingent rewards, and negative relationship for negatively contingent rewards

(Continued)

Table 7.2. (Continued)

Authors	Participants	Organizations	Criteria	Procedure	Results[a]
Daley (1987)	315 mid-level managers and senior executives	Federal government	Motivation as defined by items measuring equity, intrinsic satisfaction, and per-ceived performance-reward relationship	Comparison of employees that received and did not receive merit pay	Intrinsic satisfaction and equity the same for both groups; perceived performance-reward relationship significantly greater for recipients of merit pay
Deadrick and Scott (1987)	222 transit directors	Urban Mass Transportation Administration	Employee motivation	Employee motivation measured at varying years after implementa-tion of merit pay plans	Increased employee motivation was the most frequently mentioned benefit of merit pay programs
Fox (1989)	378 employees in professional or managerial positions	States, counties, and municipalities	Organizational commitment	Comparison of experimental group who received merit pay increases versus matched control group who received other forms of increases	Stronger positive correlation between merit pay and commitment for the experimental than the control group
Gabris and Ihrke (2000; 2003)	125 professional employees	Midwestern county government	Perceptions of procedural justice, distributive justice, and appraisal instrument validity	Data collected before and after the implementation of a new appraisal system	Leadership credibility was significantly related to all three outcomes; however, there was considerable disagreement that the new system would make a "noticeable difference" in take-home pay

Authors	Participants	Organizations	Criteria	Procedure	Results[a]
Gaertner, Gaertner, and Akinnusi (1984)	213 management employees	Five sites of the Environmental Protection Agency and the Mine Safety and Health Administration	Implementation of a merit pay plan	Organizations with "organic" and "mechanistic" structures	The managers in the organic organization were significantly less positive than managers in the mechanistic organization
Giles and Barrett (1971)	157 professional level personnel	Medium-sized eastern electronics company	Satisfaction with merit increase	Perceived merit increase and satisfaction measured at same time	Satisfaction increased as a power function of perceived merit increase
Gomez-;Mejia and Balkin (1989)	175 scientists and engineers	Research and development laboratories in the Boston area	Pay satisfaction, withdrawal cognition, pro-ject performance, individual performance	Participants responded to questionnaire about characteristics and effectiveness of pay system	Merit pay had a significant positive impact on group, but not individual performance
Greene (1973)	62 first-line managers	Marketing and financial divisions of a large manufacturing company	Job satisfaction and performance	Organization had a merit pay plan. All criteria measured at two different time periods	Performance causes merit pay. Job satisfaction does not cause performance. Merit pay and performance cause job satisfaction

(Continued)

Table 7.2. (Continued)

Authors	Participants	Organizations	Criteria	Procedure	Results[a]
Greene and Podsakoff (1978)	Plant 1: 456 line employees and 37 first-line managers. Plant 2:592 employees and 45 first-line supervisors	Two paper mill plants of a large manufacturer	Performance and satisfaction	Comparison of plant 1 (pay based on seniority) and plant 2 (pay based on merit) before and after merit pay was removed at plant 1. Participants matched by personal and job characteristics	Performance decreased and satisfaction increased in plant 1 compared to plant 2
H. Heneman and Young (1988)	96 school administrators	Public school district in medium-sized Midwestern city	Reactions to performance appraisal process, reactions to merit plan, and motivation	Criteria measured before and after implementation of merit plan	Above-average reactions to appraisal process before and after plan implementation. Reactions to plan and motivation below average before and after plan implementation
R. Heneman, Greenberger, and Strasser (1988)	104 nursing, technical, professional, and mana-gerial employees	Midwest hospital	Pay-for-performance perceptions, and pay satisfaction	Criteria measured in hospital with an information merit plan	Positive relationship between pay-for-performance perceptions and pay satisfaction

Authors	Participants	Organizations	Criteria	Procedure	Results[a]
Hills, Scott, and Markham (1988); M. Vest, Scott, J. Vest, and Markham (2000)	About 673 nonunion office employees in managerial, professional, technical and clerical positions	Mass transit organization	Pay increase satisfaction and pay-for-performance correlations	Criteria were measured before and after implementation of a new guidechart emphasizing pay-for-performance philosophy	Correlations between pay and performance increased as a result of new guidechart. Pay increase satisfaction was significantly lower for those employees who received the lowest performance ratings and were highest in their pay grade
Jenkins and Lawler (1981)	58 skilled machinists	Small manufacturer of tool and die equipment	Job satisfaction, pay satisfaction, performance, and pay-for-performance perceptions	Criteria measured before and after implementation of merit plan	Job satisfaction and pay satisfaction increased
Kahn and Sharer (1990)	92 middle to upper level managers	Corporate offices and main production facility in a moderate size pro-duction firm	Performance ratings	Performance measured before and after merit increase	No significant increase in performance
Kopelman (1976)	210 design and development engineers	Three large technology based companies	Motivation, performance, satisfaction, and relationship between pay and performance	All three plants had merit pay system. All criteria were measured at two different time periods	Motivation, performance, and satisfaction were positively related to the pay-per-performance relationship

(Continued)

Table 7.2. (Continued)

Authors	Participants	Organizations	Criteria	Procedure	Results[a]
Kopelman and Reinharth (1982)	1,165 white-collar employees with non-supervisory responsibilities	Ten branches of a large financial institution	Performance of organizational subunits, range of salary increases, and the tie between performance and rewards.	Ten subunits evaluated. Same (unspecified) type of merit plan was used in each branch. Performance was measured at two different time periods.	Positive relationship between the range of salary increases and subunit performance. Performance re-ward relationship was more strongly related to subsequent levels of subunit performance than to -current levels of performance.
Miceli and Near (1988)	About 2000 middle managers and executives	22 departments and agencies of the federal government	Correlations between reception of merit award and motivation and satisfaction with employer, pay level, and pay system	Criteria measured ap-proximately 2 years after implementation of merit pay plan	Positive correlations for merit with motivation, satisfaction with employer, and satis-faction with pay system. Negative correlation between merit and pay level
Nyberg, Pieper, Trevor (2016)	11,939 employees over five years	U.S.-based insurance company.	Relationship between merit pay and future performance	Integrated contextual characteristics (employee, job, pay system, pay system experience) in a PFP system. Tested relationship between merit pay and future performance	Merit pay relates to performance over a five year period within the contextual characteristics.

Authors	Participants	Organizations	Criteria	Procedure	Results[a]
Park & Sturman (2012)	739 employees	Service-related business	Relationship between PFP and job performance	PFP data (merit pay, bonus pay, and long-term incentive) and supervisory ratings were collected over 2 years	Merit pay showed the strongest relationship with job performance over two years. Both incentive pay and long-term incentives positively related to job performance
Park & Sturman (2016)	635 employees	Technology service company	Relationship between PFP and job performance	PFP data (merit pay, bonus pay, and long-term incentive) and supervisory ratings were collected over 2 years	Merit pay and bonus pay related to job performance over two years. Long-term incentive pay did not relate to job performance
Peace, Stevenson, and Perry (1985)	Ranged from 12 to 73 employees and managers	20 local and branch social security administration offices	Four objective meas-ures of office level productivity	Monthly time series data collected for about 98 months. Three interven-tions: (1) merit pay orientation and training (2) merit plan imple-mented (3) merit pay awarded	No significant increase in performance for any of the performance measures after any of the interventions

(Continued)

Table 7.2. (Continued)

Authors	Participants	Organizations	Criteria	Procedure	Results[a]
Ramaswami and Singh (2003)	165 salespeople	Large industrial organization	Self-rated organizational commitment, supervisor-rated performance ratings and opportunistic (dysfunctional) behavior	Surveys completed by salespeople and their supervisors	Merit pay perceptions were significantly related to distributive, procedural, and interactional fairness. Interactional fairness predicted job satisfaction and trust in supervisor. Trust in supervisor was positively correlated with organizational commitment, and strongly and negatively correlated with opportunistic behaviors. Performance ratings were linked to distributive justice and the completion of a performance improvement plan by the supervisor
Schaubroeck, Shaw, Duffy, & Mitra (2008)	140 employees	University hospital	Relationship between merit pay raises and employee reactions	Data collected on merit pay expectations before merit raises and employee reactions to actual merit increases	Pay-for-performance perceptions significantly related to personal reactions - pay raise happiness, pay-level satisfaction, and turnover intentions

Authors	Participants	Organizations	Criteria	Procedure	Results[a]
Schneider and Olson (1970)	148 registered nurses	Two Midwestern hospitals	Effort, pay satisfac-tion, relationship be-tween effort and in-trinsic rewards	Comparison of hospital 1 (pay based on effort and performance) and hospital 2 (pay based on service)	Effort was greater in hospi-tal 1 than in hospital 2. Effort was positively re-lated to intrinsic rewards in hospital 1, but not in hospital 2. The positive relationship between pay satisfaction and effort was greater in hospital 1 than in hospital 2
Schwab and Olson (2000)	640 simulated labor forces	Hypothetical professional and managerial employees	Link between performance and pay	10 time periods used in the simulation; comparisons made between merit pay added to base salary versus as an annual lump-sum bonus	The pay-performance correlation was stronger after 10 periods for the merit pay simulations (0.56) than for the lump-sum bonus simulations (0.39)
Scott, Hills, Markham, and Vest (1987)	Approximately 800 employees eligible for a merit pay plan	Large transit authority on the west coast	Performance ratings and satisfaction	Performance measured for 3 consecutive years; satisfaction measured once; merit pay plan in place for an unspecified period of time	Performance ratings increased over 3 year time period; majority of partici-pants dissatisfied with their last pay raise

(Continued)

Table 7.2. (Continued)

Authors	Participants	Organizations	Criteria	Procedure	Results[a]
Shaw, Duffy, Mitra, Lockhart, and Bowler (2003)	157 employees	Midwestern university hospital	Pay level satisfaction, pay raise affect, and pay raise behavioral intentions	Data collected four months before and four months after merit increases were awarded	Merit increases were significantly related to pay level satisfaction, pay raise affect, and pay raise behavioral intentions; however, an interaction effect demonstrated that this was primarily for employees with low positive affect
St-Onge (2000)	406 employees	Large manufacturing organization	Pay-for-performance perceptions	Survey data linked with employee file data concerning appraisal ratings and merit increases	Pay-for-performance perceptions were significantly predicted by actual merit increase, perceptions of procedural justice, outcome satisfaction, and trust in decision makers (perceived procedural justice had the strongest effect)

Authors	Participants	Organizations	Criteria	Procedure	Results[a]
Taylor and Pierce (1999)	218 professional and managerial employees	New Zealand regional environmental council	Organizational commitment, satisfaction with supervision, and cooperation with supervision	Survey data collected before change, after goals set, after appraisals were conducted, and as a follow-up measure.	All variables went up after the goal setting phase, but then declined after appraisals were conducted and merit increases were granted
Wisdom and Patzig (1987)	26 public sectors managers, 1,130 private sector managers	Respondents to National Survey of Supervisory Management Practices	Employee performance	Comparison of private and public sector man-ager's perceptions	Perceptions of employee performance were higher for private- than public- sector managers

[a]Only statistically significant results ($p < .05$) are reported, unless otherwise specified.

Table 7.3

Summary of Empirical Studies on the Federal Merit Pay System (FMPS)

	Intended Outcomes			
Source	**To Relate Pay to Performance**	**To Provide Flexibility in Recognizing Good Performance with Cash Awards**	**To Motivate Merit Pay Employees**	**To Improve Productivity, Timeliness, and Quality of Work**
Daley (1987). "Merit Pay Enters with a Whimper: The Initial Federal Civil Service Reform Experience"			Merit pay did not heighten sur vey measures of motivation	Merit pay recipients perceived their agency to be no more responsive or effective than nonrecipients
Gaertner & Gaertner (1984). "Performance Evaluation and Merit Pay: Results in the Environmental Protection Agency and the Mine Safety and Health Administration"	Merit pay is not perceived as equitable; raises are too small		Improvement in accuracy of performance standards and overall appraisal	No positive impact on per ceived agency effectiveness or employee work behavior
Gaertner & Gaertner (1984). "Performance Contingent Pay for Federal Managers"	Not perceived to be rewarding people fairly with significant raises		Performance standards and appraisal improve work plan ning and accomplishment	No positive impact on per ceived agency effectiveness or employee work behavior
O'Toole & Churchill (1982). "Implementing Pay-for-Performance: Initial Experiences"	Subjectivity and lack of resources undermine pay-for-performance relationship		Enhances communication on goals and job expectations	Inconclusive

	Intended Outcomes			
Source	**To Relate Pay to Performance**	**To Provide Flexibility in Recognizing Good Performance with Cash Awards**	**To Motivate Merit Pay Employees**	**To Improve Productivity, Timeliness, and Quality of Work**
Pagano (1985). "An Exploratory Evaluation of the Civil Service Reform Act's Merit Pay System for the GS 13–15s"	Small sample of pool managers complained the monetary reward was not worth the amount of paperwork and energy expended			
Pearce & Perry (1983). "Federal Merit Pay: A Longitudinal Analysis"	No improvement in the pay-for-performance con tingency after merit pay		Performance criteria were clearer, but may not reflect agency effectiveness	
Pearce & Porter (1986). "Employee Responses to Formal Performance Appraisal Feedback"			Relatively low (satisfactory) ratings caused a significant drop in organizational commitment	
Pearce, Stevenson, & Perry (1985). "Managerial Compensation Based on Organizational Performance: A Time-Series Analysis of the Impact of Merit Pay"				No significant effect on organi zational performance

(Continued)

Table 7.3. (Continued)

	Intended Outcomes			
Source	**To Relate Pay to Performance**	**To Provide Flexibility in Recognizing Good Performance with Cash Awards**	**To Motivate Merit Pay Employees**	**To Improve Productivity, Timeliness, and Quality of Work**
Perry, Hanzlik, & Pearce (1982). "Effectiveness of Merit-Pay-Pool Management"	Modification of appraisal ratings to achieve agency merit pay goals reduced credibility of the system.			
U.S. General Accounting Office (1984). A 2-Year Appraisal of Merit Pay in Three Agencies	Nonperformance factors influenced size of merit increases more than necessary	Provision of cash awards highly variable across agencies	Standards perceived to be fair, job related, and consistent with organizational goals	
U.S. General Accounting Office (1981). Serious Problems Need to Be Corrected Before Federal Merit Pay Goes Into Effect			Performance appraisals have limitations, including overly quantitative standards and lack of pretesting	OPM method for computing merit pay would exceed former costs by $58 to $74 million
U.S. Merit Systems Protection Board (1981). Status Report on Performance Appraisal and Merit Pay Among Mid-Level Employees	Half of all employees perceived a moderate to strong effect on perfor mance.		Employees perceived ratings as fair and accurate, but not very helpful	

Source: Perry (1988). Reprinted with permission.

Table 7.4.

Assessment of the Performance Management and Recognition System (PMRS)

Source	Intended Outcomes			
	To Relate Pay to Performance	To Provide Flexibility in Recognizing Good Performance with Cash Awards	To Motivate Merit Pay Employees	To Improve Productivity, Timeliness, and Quality of Work
Brudney & Condrey (1993)			Managers who reported higher levels of motivation from the PMRS also scored significantly higher in their attitudes toward merit pay in general, had higher organizational trust, placed a higher importance on monetary rewards, and per ceived higher accuracy and fairness in the system than did managers reporting lower lev els of motivation	
Perry & Petrakis (1987). "Can Merit Pay Improve Performance in Government?"	Employees who achieved high monetary rewards in 1985 were more likely to perform at high levels in the next rating period	About 2/3 of the sample received performance awards		Rewards were poor discrimina tors between "stayers" and "leavers"
Perry, Petrakis, & Miller (1989) "Federal Merit Pay, Round II: An Analysis of the Performance Management and Recognition System"	Lagged monetary rewards were positively and signifi cantly related to perfor mance ratings in 1986 but not 1987	About 2/3 of the sample received performance awards		

(Continued)

Table 7.4. (Continued)

	Intended Outcomes			
Source	**To Relate Pay to Performance**	**To Provide Flexibility in Recognizing Good Performance with Cash Awards**	**To Motivate Merit Pay Employees**	**To Improve Productivity, Timeliness, and Quality of Work**
U.S. General Accounting Office (1987). Pay for Performance: Implemen tation of the Performance Management and Recognition System	Nonperformance factors that caused inequities under merit pay continue to exist in PMRS	Fifty percent of respondents found the amounts of perfor mance awards inadequate	Performance standards for many employees were issued more than 30 days into the appraisal period	
U.S. Merit Systems Protection Board (1987). Performance Management and Recognition System: Linking Pay to Performance	Slightly less than half of employees perceived bet ter performance leading to more pay		Performance standards were perceived to be fair and accurate	
U.S. Merit Systems Protection Board (1988). Toward Effective Performance Management in the Federal Government	Same as MSPB (1987)		Same as MSPB (1987)	Higher turnover rates for employees rated "unacceptable" and "minimally successful"
U.S. Office of Personnel Management (1987). Performance Management and Recognition System	Agencies reported reinforcement of linkage between pay and perfor mance	Size and amount of finding for performance awards increased	Quality of performance stan dards a problem; not stated in measurable terms and did not differentiate between perfor mance levels	
U.S. Office of Personnel Management (1988). Performance Management and Recognition System: FY 1986 Performance Cycle	Performance ratings were inflated and average rating levels increased with grade level	Performance awards were granted to most employees		

Source: Adapted from Perry (1988). Reprinted with permission.

Table 7.5

Williams (2010) Meta-Analysis of Merit Pay Effectiveness

Study	Performance Measure	Study Setting	Participants	Study	Point-Biserial Correlation	95% Confidence Interval
Green & Podsakoff (1978)	Ratings of overall performance	F	operatives	1,048	0.30	0.24–0.35
Green & Podsakoff (1978)	Ratings of overall performance	F	managers	83	0.21	−0.01–0.41
Latham et al. (1978)	Ratings of critical job behaviors	F	engineers, scientists	48	0.52	0.28–0.70
Salvermini & Reilly (1993)	Ratings of motivation	F	students	101	0.40	0.22–0.55
Schneider & Olson (1970)	Ratings of effort behavior	F	nurses	146	0.35	0.20–0.48
Terborg & Miller (1978)	Ratings of quality behavior	L	students	60	−0.13	−0.37–0.13
Terborg & Miller (1978)	Ratings of quality results	L	students	60	−0.05	−0.03–0.21
Terborg & Miller (1978)	Ratings of effort behavior	L	students	60	0.31	0.06–0.51
Terborg (1976)	Ratings of effort behavior	L	students	55	0.33	0.07–0.55
Wimperis & Farr (1979)	Ratings of quality performance	L	students	48	0.12	−17–0.39

especially in federal government agencies. The plus side of relying so heavily on this one type of participant is that it allows an in-depth look at how merit pay plans operate and affect individuals. The downside, however, is concerns over external validity. The results may not generalize to other employee groups or to other sectors of the economy. In reviewing these summaries, also keep in mind that the less than optimal results obtained with merit pay in the federal government may not necessarily generalize to private-sector organizations.

A second notable procedural feature is how little attention has been given to evaluating merit pay against business unit outcomes. Most of the evaluation studies have instead concentrated on individual outcomes. While these outcomes are important, they provide an incomplete look at the overall effectiveness of merit pay plans. More research is needed on the effects of merit pay on business unit outcomes.

A third notable feature is the relative lack of controls in the research designs that have been used. In only 13 of the studies shown in Table 7.2 were attempts made to control for extraneous factors. In five studies, a nonequivalent control group was used (Daley, 1987; Fox, 1989; Greene & Podsakoff, 1978; Schay, 1988; Schneider & Olson, 1970). In another ten studies, a time-series design was used (Allan & Rosenberg, 1986; Gabris & Ihrke, 2000; Kopelman & Reinharth, 1982; Nyberg et al., 2016; Park & Sturman, 2012; Park & Sturman, 2016; Pearce et al., 1985; Scott et al., 1987; Schaubroeck et al., 2008; Taylor & Pierce, 1999). An attempt was made to statistically control for extraneous factors in one study (Jenkins & Lawler, 1981). Given the lack of control over extraneous factors, it is not possible to assign strict causality to merit pay for the outcomes reported. Threats to internal validity need to be kept in mind in reviewing many of these evaluation studies.

Outcomes

The outcomes reported for merit pay in these evaluation studies do little to alter the conclusion reached in Chapter 1, namely that merit pay plans are, overall, moderately effective. Merit pay seems to be consistently related to positive attitudes, but has not been consistently shown to be related to improved subsequent performance. Given the potential problems with internal and external validity in many of these studies, the conclusion that merit pay plans are moderately effective should remain a tentative conclusion.

As just noted, merit pay outcomes have been fairly favorable for employee attitudes, with the notable exception of the federal government. Merit pay plans have been shown to be related to actual and perceived correlations between pay and performance (Daley, 1987; Kopelman, 1976; Kopelman &

Reinharth, 1982; Schay, 1988; St-Onge, 2000; Taylor & Pierce, 1999; Vest et al., 2000). Positive relationships for pay-for-performance perceptions with pay satisfaction (R. Heneman et al., 1988; Shaw et al., 2003; Schaubroeck et al., 2008; St-Onge, 2000) and job satisfaction (Kopelman, 1976; Ramaswami & Singh, 2003) have been reported. That is, the stronger the perception that pay is related to performance, the higher the level of pay and job satisfaction. Merit pay plans have also been shown to be related to measures of job and pay satisfaction (Bullock, 1983; Giles & Barrett, 1971; Greene & Podsakoff, 1978; Jenkins & Lawler, 1981; Miceli & Near, 1988; Schay, 1988) and commitment (Fox, 1989).

The results to date on the relationship between merit pay and subsequent motivation and performance are, unfortunately, not terribly encouraging. This is seen especially in the results reported in Tables 7.3 and 7.4 for the federal government. Disappointing results have been reported in other organizational settings as well (e.g., H. Heneman & Young, 1988; Kahn & Sherer, 1990). It should be noted, however, that not all of the results have been disappointing. Improved performance at the group level has been associated with merit pay (Gomez-Mejia & Balkin, 1989; Kopelman & Reinharth, 1982), as have perceptions of improved motivation (Deadrick & Scott, 1987; Miceli & Near, 1988). Pay-for-performance perceptions have also been found to be strongly related to satisfaction with a group incentive plan (Fong & Shaffer, 2003). While the goal is to be able to pinpoint which characteristics of merit pay plans are associated with which desirable behavioral or attitudinal outcomes, it is not possible to do so at this stage. As discussed previously (e.g., R. Heneman, 1990), a shortfall in current merit pay research is the limited information about the actual characteristics of the merit pay plan in the reporting of merit pay studies.

An important omission in the research on outcomes associated with merit pay is the relationship between merit pay and absenteeism and turnover. Almost no research has been conducted on the impact of merit pay on absenteeism and turnover, yet there is ample reason to believe that merit pay would lead to reduced levels of absence and turnover. The reason for this belief is shown in Figure 7.3.

In most cases, merit pay is not a one-time bonus, but is instead an addition to base pay. As a result, merit pay increases show a positive relationship with pay levels (H. Heneman, 1973). In other words, a merit increase in one year contributes to a larger base salary in the next year. The impact of merit pay on pay level has been overlooked in much of the merit pay research since 1973. However, it has been consistently reported in the pay satisfaction literature that, as would be expected, pay satisfaction is greater when pay level is larger (H. Heneman, 1985). When pay satisfaction is high, it has also been shown in the pay satisfaction literature that absenteeism and turnover are both decreased. What these results suggest is that if absenteeism and

Figure 7.3

Impact of Merit Pay on Absenteeism and Turnover.

turnover had been included more often as outcomes in merit pay evaluation studies, the results of these merit pay studies may have been more favorable than the results presented in Table 7.2, where absenteeism was not studied and only one study showed an indirect relationship between merit pay and turnover intent (Schaubroeck et al., 2008). Some research suggests that employees who do not perceive a link between their job performance and desirable outcomes (i.e., low instrumentality) have higher absenteeism (Hirschfeld, Schmitt, & Bedeian, 2002). Other research suggests that the perceived fairness of pay procedures is related to voluntary turnover (Jones, 1998), and that satisfaction with contingent pay is related to reduced intentions to withdraw from the organization (Deckop, Merriman, & Blau, 2004; Scott et al., 2024). This line of research should be linked to the study of merit pay plans in particular.

Outcomes Based on Meta-Analysis

In addition to the above results of one-shot studies of merit pay outcomes, we also include the results of a meta-analytic study on the same topic (Williams, 2010). As the reader may remember, meta-analysis aggregates a collection of individual research studies of a common topic, calculates an average common metric or statistic across said studies. A common metric in determining the effectiveness of merit pay on outcomes (e.g., job performance) is a statistic based on a group comparison design, usually a treatment group compared to a control group. This design was described earlier in this chapter. Two common statistics (metrics) for this purpose is a *d statistic* and a *point-biserial correlation*, a special form of a *Pearson product-moment correlation* used in Chapter 2. Schmidt and Hunter (2004, 2015) recommend a point-biserial correlation because it is easier to interpret than the d-statistic. It has a range of −1.00 to +1.00, where positive values imply the treatment condition exceeded the control condition. In addition, a value closer to +1.00 suggests a larger difference between both groups and a greater treatment effect on the outcome. A zero figure means that no meaningful difference exists between the treatment and control group. A negative value implies the control group exceeded the treatment group. Note that all individual studies in this meta-analysis had a treatment and control group.

Table 7.5 is a summary of studies included in the meta-analysis that shows the effectiveness of merit pay increases on various outcomes. The first column shows authors and date of each study in the analysis. Each citation can be used to find the full reference for the study in the reference section at the end of the book. In the second column, the type of performance outcome is listed. In every case, supervisory ratings were used to evaluate outcome results. The third column illustrates the study setting—laboratory and field—of the study. The fourth column specifies general job classifications of participants in the study. In the fifth column, the size of each sample is shown. The effect-size statistics (point-biserial correlations) shown in sixth column indicate the strength of merit pay increases on outcome measures. The seventh column reveals 95% confidence intervals (CI) for sample effects. The reader is referred to Chapter 2 for a detailed description on the interpretation of CI.

The *average* effect size (point-biserial correlation) across 10 studies (1,709 individuals) is 0.28 with a standard deviation of 0.12. The 95% confidence interval of the average ES is 0.21–0.49 and excludes zero, implying that, on average, merit increases indeed positively affected stated outcomes beyond chance. While the use of meta-analysis over one-shot studies increases our confidence that merit pay indeed affects stated outcomes, we cannot say merit pay *caused* an increase or improvement. Other unwanted influences on this relationship (internal validity) would have to be ruled out. In their seminal article, Velghe et al. (2024) provide suggestions for designing future meta-analytic studies on the effectiveness of merit pay plans. They spend a good deal of time exploring methods to reduce threats to internal and external validity. However, the greatest challenge facing meta-analysts is the need for well-designed individual studies on merit pay effectiveness.

Conclusion Concerning the Evaluation of Outcomes for Merit Pay

The major conclusion from this review of empirical studies evaluating merit pay outcomes is that organizations should evaluate the results of their merit pay plans, rather than relying solely on the results of these reviewed studies. The studies reviewed here (both single studies and meta-analytic studies) are suggestive of probable results, but are limited in number, show inconsistent findings, and include potential threats to internal and external validity. Given the constraints of this current research, organizations are well advised to conduct their own evaluation studies. We conclude this section by repeating a statement made before:

> It is an embarrassment to our profession how few well-designed empirical studies have ever been conducted to assess the impact of merit pay, given the overwhelming number of companies that use merit pay and the huge direct and indirect costs involved. At an absolute minimum, companies should routinely collect data on the attitudinal impact of merit pay. Standardized measures of employees' attitudes towards pay, with sound reliability and validity properties, are easily accessible from the research literature (R. Heneman, Eskew, & Fox, 1998). Better yet, employers might assess using controlled designs to measure the impact of merit pay on performance and productivity. Unfortunately, the number of studies of this type can literally be counted on one hand. (R. Heneman, 2001b, p. 458)

We think that the results displayed in Tables 7.2 and 7.5 demonstrate that there has been improvement since the above words were first written. However, the number of well-controlled studies focusing on the *outcomes* of merit pay plans can probably still be counted on two hands. It is our hope that this volume will stimulate further research along the lines recommended in this chapter.

Summary of Major Points

1. *Merit pay outcomes.* A variety of merit pay outcomes can be used to evaluate the results of a merit pay plan. These outcomes can be categorized as immediate versus distant to the merit increase, and can be measured at the individual as well as the business unit level.
2. *Relations among outcomes and need for multiple outcomes.* Merit pay outcomes are not independent of one another. Instead, they exert an influence on one another. Multiple outcomes should be used in evaluating merit pay in an effort to show *how* and *why* merit pay plans are successful or not successful.
3. *Possible nonlinear relationships between merit pay and outcomes.* A one-for-one return on merit pay outcomes for each dollar of merit increases should not be automatically assumed. Instead, tests are recommended to explore the possibility of nonlinear forms of the relationship between merit increases and outcomes.
4. *Proactive versus reactive audits.* Audits of the results of merit pay plans should be conducted proactively, on an ongoing basis. If a reactive approach is taken, and merit pay plans are only audited when a problem arises, it may be too late to correct the problem. The legal

costs and consequences of unaddressed issues can be extremely high (Calluso & Devetag, 2024; Martin et al., 2000; Werner, 1998).

5. *Validity of evaluation research.* The most common approach to evaluating merit pay plans is a one-shot case study. While we can definitely learn from individual case studies, this research approach is limited by threats to internal and external validity. To minimize these threats, consideration should be given to using a pretest, a control group, random or matched assignment, representative samples, and multiple pretests and posttests. The use of meta-analysis is a step in the right direction.
6. *Empirical studies on outcomes.* Overall, merit pay plans can be viewed as moderately successful, as merit pay is consistently related to favorable employee attitudes and less consistently related to improved performance. Interestingly, the average point-biserial correlation of 0.28 found in the Williams (2010) meta-analysis supports this claim. This overall assessment remains tentative, however, given the threats to internal and external validity in this body of research. Again, the use of meta-analysis can reduce these threats.

Conclusions

The most disappointing aspect of merit pay is that relatively few evaluation studies have been conducted to tell us how effective these plans are to organizations. This is amplified when the reader sees that only four studies of this type have been added to the third edition. Many organizations have merit plans, and the majority of them seem to operate on "blind faith" that their plans are working. We strongly recommend that organizations conduct regular evaluation studies on the effectiveness of their merit pay plans.

Another disappointing aspect of merit pay is the limitations inherent in the existing evaluation research, which make interpretation of the results difficult. There is a need for more research, and a need for *better* research as well. Better evaluation research would broaden the evaluated outcomes to include outcomes at the business-unit level, as well as at the individual level. Such research would also use better research designs to minimize the threats to internal and external validity, which are too often present in existing evaluation efforts. In addition, extra effort in well-designed research in one-shot studies will help enormously with meta-analytic research.

On a more positive note, the evaluation research that has been conducted does show that merit pay *can* be an effective method of incentive pay. Merit pay almost always appears to be related to pay and job satisfaction, and sometimes is associated with improved performance. Note the average correlation of 0.28 between merit pay and various outcomes that was obtained in the meta-analysis by Williams (2010), and highlighted above.

This record can be improved with a better understanding of how merit pay works. As pointed out throughout the book, to better understand merit pay you need to recognize that (1) the merit pay process must be carefully managed, (2) a balance must be struck between organizational performance and cost considerations, (3) the link between individual past performance and pay is a necessary but insufficient condition to establish a link between pay and improved future performance, and (4) the relationship between pay and performance must be perceived by employees, as well as documented.

Merit pay plans continue to be widely used (Shaw et al., 2003; Velghe et al., 2024). However, much more can and should be done with these plans from both research and practice perspectives. From a research perspective, greater attention needs to be given to the institutional arrangements that govern merit pay decisions. Many have now researched the relationship between pay and performance. Some are now examining the informal arrangements in the work environment that influence the relationship between pay and performance. Certainly, this new direction in research, focusing on more informal arrangements, is important and should continue. An example is the attention given to organizational politics as this relates to merit increases (Salimäki & Jämsén, 2010). We undoubtedly need more research on this fact of organizational life. What is still missing in merit pay research, however, is a more thorough investigation of formal institutional arrangements that also influence the pay and performance relationship. Using again the example of politics, formal political actions taken by institutions also have a bearing on performance management and merit pay and deserve greater attention (Rosen et al., 2017). The use of meta-analysis can be beneficial here.

As discussed elsewhere in this book, the formal procedures specified for merit pay by the federal government have had a large impact on merit pay decisions and the reactions of federal government employees (Risher, 2002). Institutional arrangements such as these can be found in many other organizations as well (see Chapter 3). For example, concerning merit pay guide charts, we know little about what factors are considered by policymakers in setting up these guide charts and to what extent they are actually followed by managers.

In terms of merit pay practice, more remains to be done with merit pay plans as well. First and foremost, as emphasized in this chapter, we must conduct better evaluation studies. Along with the need for more evaluation, there is also a need for more creativity and experimentation with merit pay plans. For example, merit pay could be used as a short-term, as well as a long-term, reward strategy. For example, to reinforce the application of materials learned in training, merit pay could be allocated in increments as employees get closer to the desired behavior back on the job. This type of arrangement would presumably have advantages over a one-time cash bonus granted for a single instance of effective behavior after training. Short-term merit pay could, in effect, be made contingent on a performance management plan for one part of a job. This is just one example of an innovative use of merit pay. Organizations may become more willing to experiment with variations on traditional merit pay plans as they come to view the evaluation of merit pay as an integral part of the merit pay process, and an effective tool in managing the process.

In summary, there are many potential problems and pitfalls in designing, implementing, and evaluating merit pay plans (Adamovic, 2023; Bartol, 2023; Campbell et al., 1998; Fulmer et al., 2023; LeBlanc & Mulvey, 1998; Lowery et al., 1996; Velghe et al., 2024). We have tried to address these honestly throughout this book. Nevertheless, given the continued widespread use of such plans in both the private and public sectors, it is imperative that organizations pursue every option available to make their plans effective. Among other things, this means that merit pay should not be viewed as a "standalone" program, that is, as the major or sole form of individual reward offered to employees (Eskew & R. Heneman, 1996). Instead, merit pay needs to be viewed in the context of the "total compensation" package provided by the organization (Martocchio, 2023; R. Heneman, 2001b). Organizations also need to look at the "total rewards" package they offer, which includes total pay, individual growth, a compelling organizational future, and a positive workplace climate (Fulmer & Li, 2022; Zingheim & Schuster, 2000).

As we have stated throughout the book, merit pay needs to be clearly linked to the organization's business strategy (R. Heneman, 2001a, 2002). From a strategic HR management perspective, merit pay should be clearly aligned with other human resource practices, including recruitment, selection, appraisal, and training (Bartel, 2004; R. Heneman, 2001b; Huselid, 1995; Lawler & Mohrman, 2003; Mello, 2002; Werner, 2021). We also think it is important to link merit pay to the broader topic of "performance management" (Gerhart, Trevor, & Scott, 2023; Lawler & McDermott, 2003; O'Neill & Holsinger, 2003; Rheem, 1995; Taylor & Pierce, 1999). With such an approach, goal setting, appraisal, training, and rewards are all linked together in a coherent fashion. It is our hope that the next decade will see further progress in producing compensation and reward systems where merit pay is one part of an integrated management system (Lawler, 2003).

Many important questions have been raised concerning the effectiveness of merit pay (Fox, 2003; Webb, Glover, & Roberts, 2024). Merit pay must be approached carefully, strategically, and proactively (Bates, 2003c; Fulmer, Gerhart, & Kim, 2023; Varma, Budhwar, & DeNisi, 2023; Werner, 2021).

There are plenty of things that can go wrong when pay issues (including merit pay) are not approached in this manner. Hopefully, this volume will contribute to the growing literature concerning "what can go right" when strategic merit pay is effectively implemented.

Study Questions

1. What is the relationship between past performance and merit pay increases in Chapter 2? What is the relationship between merit increases and merit pay outcomes in Chapter 7? In your opinion, is one relationship more important than the other? Or, are they equally important? Explain.
2. Explain the criterion model of merit pay outcomes. Give examples of each outcome.
3. What are the relationships among outcomes and the need for multiple outcomes.
4. What do the measurement properties of reliability and construct validity mean for merit pay outcomes? Why are these important?
5. Describe the different study design considerations. How do these relate to threats to internal and external validity?
6. Briefly summarize the state of merit pay effectiveness research. Why is this important to practitioners? What are the future implications for research and practice?

REFERENCES

Abd Razak, M. R., Ali, E., Kolandan, S., & Abd Razak, A. Z. A. (2025). Evaluating the effectiveness of performance-based pay management on perceived procedural justice in Malaysian government-linked companies. *International Journal of Research and Innovation in Social Science, 8*(19), 153–166. https://doi.org/10.47772/IJRISS.2024.ICAME2412

Abdeen, A. M., & Haight, G. T. (2002). A fresh look at economic value added: Empirical study of the fortune 500 companies. *Journal of Applied Business Research, 18*(2), 27–36.

Abdulsalam, D., Maltarich, M. A., Nyberg, A. J., Reilly, G., & Martin, M. (2021). Individualized pay-for-performance arrangements: Peer reactions and consequences. *Journal of Applied Psychology, 106*(8), 1202–1223. https://doi.org/10.1037/apl0000820

Abuelhassan, A. E., & AlGassim, A. (2022). How organizational justice in the hospitality industry influences proactive customer service performance through general self-efficacy. *International Journal of Contemporary Hospitality Management, 34*(7), 2579–2596. https://doi.org/10.1108/IJCHM-10-2021-1238

Adamovic, M. (2023). The cultural influence on employees' preferences for reward allocation rules: A two-wave survey study in 28 countries. *Human Resource Management Journal, 33*(4), 889–921. https://doi.org/10.1111/1748-8583.12486

Adams, J. S. (1965). Inequity in social exchange. In L. R. Berkowitz (Ed.), *Advances in experimental social psychology* (Vol. 2, pp. 267–299). Academic Press.

Adams, R., & Turner, S. (2024). Aligning performance and compensation: A 2024 survey of HR leaders. *Journal of Human Resource Management, 45*(2), 125–142.

Adler, S., Campion, M., Colquitt, A., Grubb, A., Murphy, K., Ollander-Krane, R., & Pulakos, E. D. (2016). Getting rid of performance ratings: Genius or folly? A debate. *Industrial and Organizational Psychology, 9*(2), 219–252. https://doi.org/10.1017/iop.2015.106

Aiken, L. R. (1980). Content validity and reliability of single items on questionnaires. *Educational and Psychological Measurement, 40*, 950–959.

Akhtar, T., & Khattak, S. (2013). Employee acceptability of performance appraisals: Issues of fairness and justice. *World Applied Sciences Journal, 24*(4), 507–518. https://idosi.org/wasj/wasj24(4)13/15.pdf

Allard, S., & Holsapple, C. W. (2002). Knowledge management as a key for e-business competitiveness: From the knowledge chain to KM Audits. *Journal of Computer Information Systems, 42*(5), 19–25.

Alexander, R. A., & Barrett, G. A. (1982). Equitable salary increase judgments based upon merit and nonmerit considerations: A crossnational comparison. *International Review of Applied Psychology, 31*, 443–454.

Allan, P., & Rosenberg, S. (1986). An assessment of merit pay administration under New York City's managerial performance evaluation system: Three years of experience. *Public Personnel Management, 15*, 297–309.

Allen, T. D., & Rush, M. C. (1998). The effects of organizational citizenship behavior on performance judgments: A field study and a laboratory experiment. *Journal of Applied Psychology, 83*, 247–260.

Alloy, J. L. (1988, August 1). A move to pay workers the old-fashioned way. *Business First Magazine, 4*(45), 4–5.

Ambrose, M. L., & Kulik, C. T. (1999). Old friends, new faces: Motivation research in the 1990s. *Journal of Management, 25*(3), 231–292.

Arapovic-Johansson, B., Jensen, I., Wåhlin, C., Björklund, C., & Kwak, L. (2020). Process evaluation of a participative organizational intervention as a stress preventive intervention for employees in Swedish primary health care. *International Journal of Environmental Research and Public Health, 17*(19), 72–85.

Archer, J. (2000, July 12). NEA delegates take hard line against pay for performance. *Education Week, 19*(42), 21–22.

Arnold, A., & Fulmer, I. S. (2019). Pay transparency. In S. J. Perkins (Ed.), *The Routledge companion to reward management* (pp. 87–96). Routledge. https://www.routledge.com/The-Routledge-Companion-to-Reward-Management/Perkins/p/book/9781032338736

Arnold, A., Fulmer, I., Shaw, J. D., Alterman, V., Bamberger, P., Belogolovsky, E., Montag-Smit, T., Park, T., Shi, J., Smit, B. & Woehler, M. L. (2018). Pay transparency: Advancing theory and empirical knowledge. *Academy of Management Annual Meeting Proceedings* 2018(1). 10346. https://doi.org/10.5465/AMBPP.2018.10346symposium

Arribas-Aguila, D., Castaño, G., & Martínez-Arias, R. (2024). A systematic review of evidence-based general competency models: Development of a general competencies taxonomy. *Journal of Work and Organizational Psychology, 40*(2), 61–76.

Arvey, R. D., & Murphy, K. R. (1998). Performance evaluation in work settings. *Annual Review of Psychology, 49*, 141–168.

Aryee, S., Budhwar, P. S., & Chen, Z. X. (2002). Trust as a mediator of the relationship between organizational justice and work outcomes: Test of a social exchange model. *Journal of Organizational Behavior, 23*(3), 267–285.

Ashford, S. J., De Stobbeleir, K., & Nujella, M. (2016). To seek or not to seek: Is that the only question? Recent developments in feedback-seeking literature. *Annual Review of Organizational Psychology and Organizational Behavior, 3*, 213–239.

Avdul, D. N., Martin, W. M., & Lopez, Y. P. (2023). Pay transparency: Why it is important to be thoughtful and strategic. *Compensation & Benefits Review, 56*(2), 103–116. https://doi.org/10.1177/08863687231181454

Balkin, D. B. (1989). Union influences on pay policy: A survey. *Journal of Labor Research, 10*, 299–307.

Balkin, D. B., & Gomez-Mejia, L. R. (1984). Determinants of R and D compensation in the high tech industry. *Personnel Psychology, 37*, 635–650.

Balkin, D. B., & Gomez-Mejia, L. R. (1987). The strategic use of short-term and long-term pay incentives in the high technology industry. In D. B. Balkin & L. R. Gomez-Mejia (Eds.), *New perspectives on compensation* (pp. 237–246). Prentice Hall.

Balkin, D. B., & Gomez-Mejia, L. R. (1990). Matching compensation and organizational strategies. *Strategic Management Journal, 4*, 153–169.

Balkin, D. B., Markman, G. D., & Gomez-Mejia, L. R. (2000). Is CEO pay in high-technology firms related to innovation? *Academy of Management Journal, 43*, 1118–1129.

Balkin, D. B., & Werner, S. (2023). Theorizing the relationship between discretionary employee benefits and individual performance. *Human Resource Management Review, 33*(1), 100901. https://doi.org/10.1016/j.hrmr.2022.100901

Ball, S. A., & Heneman, R. L. (1988). Accurate performance ratings: There is hope. In Paper presented at the Annual Conference of the Human Resource Management and Organizational Behavior Conference, Long Beach, CA.

Balzer, W. K., Doherty, M. E., & O'Connor, R. J. (1989). Effects of cognitive feedback on performance. *Psychological Bulletin, 106*, 410–433.

Bamberger, P., & Belogolovsky, E. (2010). The impact of pay secrecy on individual task performance. *Personnel Psychology, 63*(4), 965–996. https://doi.org/10.1111/j.1744-6570.2010.01194.x

BambooHR.com. (2024, December 12). *The great pay divide: Compensation trends for 2025*. https://www.bamboohr.com/resources/data-at-work/data-stories/2025-compensation-trends#half-of-employees-are-talking-about-salary-transparencyregardless-of-policy

Bandura, A., & Locke, E. A. (2003). Negative self-efficacy and goal effects revisited. *Journal of Applied Psychology, 88*, 87–99.

Banks, C. G., & Roberson, L. (1985). Performance appraisers as test developers. *Academy of Management Review, 88*, 87–99.

Bannister, B. D., & Balkin, D. B. (1990). Performance evaluation and compensation feedback messages: An integrated model. *Journal of Occupational Psychology, 63*, 97–111.

Barclay, L. A., & York, K. M. (2003). Clear logic and fuzzy guidance: A policy capturing study of merit increase decisions. *Public Personnel Management, 32*, 287–299.

Bargerstock, A. S. (2000). The HRM effectiveness audit: A tool for managing accountability in HRM. *Public Personnel Management, 29*, 517–527.

Barkin, S. (1948). Labor's attitude toward wage incentive plans. *Industrial and Labor Relations Review, 1*, 553–572.

Barkin, S. (1970). Wage incentive problems in arbitration. *Labor Law Journal, 21*(1), 22–27.

Barksdale, K., & Werner, J. M. (2001). Managerial ratings of in-role behaviors, organizational citizenship behaviors, and overall performance: Testing different models of their relationship. *Journal of Business Research, 51*, 145–155.

Barney, J. (1997). *Gaining and sustaining competitive advantage*. Addison-Wesley.

Baron, J. N., Dobbin, F. R., & Jennings, P. D. (1986). War and peace: The evolution of modern personnel administration in U.S. industry. *American Journal of Sociology, 92*, 350–383.

Bartel, A. P. (2004). Human resource management and organizational performance: Evidence from retail banking. *Industrial and Labor Relations Review, 57*, 181–203.

Bartlett, C. J. (1983). What's the difference between valid and invalid halo? Forced choice measurement without forcing a choice. *Journal of Applied Psychology, 68*, 218–226.

Bartol, K. M. (2023). Pay for performance. In C. L. Pearce & E. A. Locke (Eds.), *Principles of organizational behavior: The handbook of evidence-based management* (3rd ed., pp. 137–160). Wiley.

Bartol, K. M., & Martin, D. C. (1989). Effects of dependence, dependency threats, and pay secrecy on managerial pay allocations. *Journal of Applied Psychology, 74*, 105–113.

Bartol, K. M., & Martin, D. C. (1990). When politics pays: Factors influencing managerial compensation decisions. *Personnel Psychology, 43*, 599–610.

Basnight, T. A. (1980). Designing master or "ideal" pay-performance matrices. *Compensation Review, 12*(4), 44–50.

Bass, B. M. (1968). Ability, values, and concepts of equitable salary increases in exercise compensation. *Journal of Applied Psychology, 52*, 299–303.

Bates, S. (2003a, March). Benefit packages nearing 40 percent of payroll. *HR Magazine, 48*, 36–38.

Bates, S. (2003b, June). Forced ranking. *HR Magazine, 48*, 63–68.

Bates, S. (2003c, January). Top pay for best performance. *HR Magazine, 48*, 30–38.

Bauwens, R., Audenaert, M., & Decramer, A. (2024). Performance management systems, innovative work behavior and the role of transformational leadership: An experimental approach. *Journal of Organizational Effectiveness: People and Performance, 11*(1), 178–195. https://doi.org/10.1108/JOEPP-03-2022-0066

Bayo-Moriones, A., Galdon-Sanchez, J. E., & Martinez-de-Morentin, S. (2020). Performance appraisal: Dimensions and determinants. *The International Journal of Human Resource Management, 31*(15), 1984–2015.

Becker, B. E., & Huselid, M. A. (1998). High performance work systems and firm performance: A synthesis of research and managerial implications. In G. Ferris (Ed.), *Research in personnel and human resource management* (Vol. 16, pp. 53–101). JAI Press.

Becker, B. E., Huselid, M. A., & Ulrich, D. (2001). *The HR scorecard: Linking people, strategy, and performance*. Harvard Business School Press.

Beer, M., & Gery, G. J. (1972). Individual and organizational correlates of pay system preferences. In H. L. Tosi, R. J. House, & M. D. Dunnette (Eds.), *Managerial motivation and compensation* (pp. 325–349). MSU Business Studies.

Belcher, D. W. (1979). Pay equity or pay fairness? *Compensation Review, 11*(2), 31–37.

Belcher, D. W. (1980). Pay and performance. *Compensation Review, 12*(3), 14–20.

Belcher, D. W., & Atchison, T. J. (1987). *Compensation administration*. Prentice-Hall.

Bell, L. A., & Neumark, D. (1993). Lump-sum payments and profit-sharing plans in the union sector of the United States economy. *Economic Journal, 103*, 602–619.

Bellavari, J. R., & Allen, R. W. (1995). Rewarding performance: The role of variable pay. *Journal of Interdisciplinary Studies, 8*, 85–92.

Belliveau, M. A. (2012). Engendering inequity? How social accounts create vs. merely explain unfavorable pay outcomes for women. *Organization Science, 23*(4), 1154–1174.

Belogolovsky, E., & Bamberger, P. A. (2014). Signaling in secret: Pay for performance and the incentive and sorting effects of pay secrecy. *Academy of Management Journal, 57*(6), 1706–1733. https://doi.org/10.5465/amj.2012.0937

Benson, J., & Brown, M. (2000). Individual performance related pay and enterprise outcomes in Australia and Japan. *International Journal of Employment Studies, 8*(2), 1–26.

Berger, C. J., & Schwab, D. P. (1980). Pay incentives and pay satisfaction. *Industrial Relations, 19,* 206–210.

Bergmann, T. J., & Scarpello, V. G. (2001). *Compensation decision making* (4th ed.). South-Western.

Bernardin, H. J., & Matt, L. A. (1985). Managerial appraisal systems: Has practice caught up to the state of the art? *The Personnel Administrator, 30*(11), 71–86.

Bernoulli, D. (1984). Exposition of a new theory on the measurement of risk. *Econometrica, 22,* 23–36.

Bernstein, A. (1991, July 15). Joe Sixpack's grip on corporate America. *Business Week,* 108–109.

Bies, R. J. (2001). Interactional (in)justice: The sacred and the profane. In J. Greenberg & R. Cropanzano (Eds.), *Advances in organizational justice* (pp. 89–118). Stanford University Press.

Binning, J. P., & Barrett, G. V. (1989). Validity of personnel decisions: A conceptual analysis of the inferential and evidential bases. *Journal of Applied Psychology, 74,* 478–494.

Birnbaum, M. H. (1983). Perceived equity of salary policies. *Journal of Applied Psychology, 68,* 48–59.

Bishop, J. (1987). The recognition and reward of employee performance. *Journal of Labor Economics, 5,* 36–56.

Blassingame, K. M. (2003, March). Workplace wellness participation lowers health risks, reduces premiums. *Employee Benefit News, 17,* 52–53.

Bommer, W. H., Johnson, J. L., Rich, G. A., Podsakoff, P. M., & McKenzie, S. B. (1995). On the interchangeability of objective and subjective measures of employee performance: A meta-analysis. *Personnel Psychology, 48,* 587–605.

Bond, A. M., Schpero, W. L., Casalino, L. P., Zhang, M., & Khullar, D. (2022). Association between individual primary care physician merit-based incentive payment system score and measures of process and patient outcomes. *JAMA, 328*(21), 2136–2146. https://doi.org/10.1001/jama.2022.20619

Borman, W. C. (1978). Exploring upper limits of reliability and validity in job performance ratings. *Journal of Applied Psychology, 63,* 135–144.

Borman, W. C. (1987). Personal constructs, performance schemata, and "folk theories" of subordinate effectiveness: Explanations in an army officer sample. *Organizational Behavior and Human Decision Processes, 40,* 307–322.

Borman, W. C., & Dunnette, M. D. (1975). Behavior based versus trait-oriented performance ratings: An empirical study. *Journal of Applied Psychology, 60,* 561–565.

Boswell, W. R., & Boudreau, J. W. (2002). Separating the developmental and evaluative performance appraisal uses. *Journal of Business and Psychology, 16,* 391–412.

Boudreau, K. J., Lacetera, N., & Lakhani, K. R. (2011). Incentives and problem uncertainty in innovation contests: An empirical analysis. *Management Science, 57,* 843–863.

Bouvé College of Health Sciences Merit Policy, Northeastern University. (2001, June 14). http://www.bouve.neu.edu/merit.html. Accessed on March 25, 2004.

Bowman, J. S. (1999). Performance appraisal: Verisimilitude trumps veracity. *Public Personnel Management, 28,* 557–576.

Brennan, E. J. (1985). The myth and the reality of pay for performance. *Personnel Journal, 64*(3), 73–75.

Brenner, O. C., & Bertsch, T. M. (1983). Do assertive people prefer merit pay? *Psychological Reports, 52,* 595–598.

Bretzy, R. D. Jr., & Milkovich, G. T. (1989). *Performance appraisal in large organizations: Practice and research implications.* Working Paper No. 89-17. Center for Advanced Human Resource Studies, School of Industrial and Labor Relations, Cornell University.

Brinkerhoff, R. (2015). Using evaluation to build organizational performance and learning capability: A strategy and a method. *Performance Improvement, 41*(6), 14–21.

Brinkerhoff, R. O., & Dressler, D. E. (1990). *Productivity measurement: A guide for managers and evaluators.* Sage.

Brockner, J. (1988). *Self-esteem at work.* Lexington Books.

Brogden, H. E., & Taylor, E. K. (1950). A theory and classification of criterion bias. *Educational and Psychological Measurement, 10,* 159–186.

Brown, C. (1990). Firms choice of method of pay. *Industrial and Labor Relations Review, 43*(3, Special Issue), 165S–182S.

Brown, M. (2001). Merit pay preferences among public sector employees. *Human Resource Management Journal, 11,* 38–54.

Brown, M. & Heywood, J. S. (Eds.). (2002). *Paying for performance: An international comparison.* M.E. Sharpe.

Brown, M. P., Sturman, M. C., & Simmering, M. J. (2003). Compensation policy and organizational performance: The efficiency, operational, and financial implications of pay levels and pay structure. *Academy of Management Journal, 46,* 752–762.

Brown, T. C., O'Kane, P., Mazumdar, B., & McCracken, M. (2019). Performance management: A scoping review of the literature and an agenda for future research. *Human Resource Development Review, 18*(1), 47–82. https://doi.org/10.1177/1534484318798533

Brudney, J. L., & Condrey, S. E. (1993). Pay for performance: Explaining the differences in managerial motivation. *Public Productivity & Management Review, 17,* 129–144.

Brunker, G. P. (1982). The potential for performance-based benefit plans. *Compensation Review, 14*(3), 23–32.

Buckman, D. G., & Jackson, T. E. (2021). Addressing the gender pay gap. *Journal of Education Finance, 47*(1), 71–91.

Bullock, R. J. (1983). Participation and pay. *Group and Organization Studies, 8,* 127–136.

Bureau of National Affairs. (1983). *Performance appraisal programs.* Personnel Policies Forum Survey No. 135. Author.

Bureau of National Affairs. (1988). Changing pay practices: New developments in employee compensation. *Labor Relations Week, 2*(24), 1–200.

Burnkrant, S. R. (2002). Linking merit pay to motivation, organizational commitment, turnover intention, and performance. In Paper presented at the Society for Industrial and Organizational Psychology Conference, Toronto.

Cabanas, S., Proença, T., & Carozzo-Todaro, M. (2020). Pay for individual performance: Aiding or harming sustainable intrinsic motivation? *Sustainability, 12*(16), 6322. https://doi.org/10.3390/su12166322

Cable, D. M., & Judge, T. A. (1994). Pay preferences and job search decisions: A person-organization fit perspective. *Personnel Psychology, 47*, 317–348.

Calluso, C., & Devetag, M. G. (2024). Discrimination in the hiring process–state of the art and implications for policymakers. *Equality, Diversity and Inclusion: An International Journal, 43*(9), 103–121. https://doi.org/10.1108/EDI-10-2023-0340

Campbell, D. J., Campbell, K. M., & Chia, H.-B. (1998). Merit pay, performance appraisal, and individual motivation: An analysis and alternative. *Human Resource Management, 37*, 131–146.

Campbell, D. T., & Fiske, D. W. (1959). Convergent and discriminant validation by the multitrait-multimethod matrix. *Psychological Bulletin, 56*, 81–105.

Campbell, J. P. (1990). Modeling the performance prediction problem in industrial and organizational psychology. In M. D. Dunnette & L. M. Hough (Eds.), *Handbook of industrial and organizational psychology* (2nd ed., Vol. 1, pp. 687–732). Consulting Psychologists.

Campbell, J. P., McCloy, R. A., Oppler, S. H., & Sager, C. E. (1993). A theory of performance. In N. Schmitt & W. C. Borman (Eds.), *Personnel selection in organizations* (pp. 35–70). Jossey-Bass.

Carrell, M. R., & Dittrich, J. E. (1978). Equity theory: The recent literature, methodological considerations, and new directions. *Academy of Management Review, 3*, 202–210.

Carnevale, A. P. (1991). *America and the new economy*. American Society for Training and Development and U.S. Department of Labor.

Carraher, S. M. (1991). On the dimensionality of the pay satisfaction questionnaire. *Psychological Reports, 69*, 887–890.

Carroll, S. J. (1987). Business strategies and compensation systems. In D. B. Balkin & L. R. Gomez-Mejia (Eds.), *New perspectives on compensation* (pp. 343-355). Prentice Hall.

Carstensen, L. L., & Hershfield, H. E. (2021). Beyond stereotypes: Using socioemotional selectivity theory to improve messaging to older adults. *Current Directions in Psychological Science, 30*(4), 327–334. https://doi.org/10.1177/09637214211011468

Case, J. (2001, May). When salaries aren't secret. *Harvard Business Review, 79*(5), 37–49.

Castilla, E. J., & Benard, S. (2010). The paradox of meritocracy in organizations. *Administrative Science Quarterly, 55*, 543–576.

Caza, A., McCarter, M. W., & Northcraft, G. B. (2015). Performance benefits of reward choice: A procedural justice perspective. *Human Resource Management Journal, 25*(2), 184–199. https://doi.org/10.1111/1748-8583.12073

Cerasoli, C. P., Nicklin, J. M., & Ford, M. T. (2014). Intrinsic motivation and extrinsic incentives jointly predict performance: A 40-year meta-analysis. *Psychological Bulletin, 140*(4), 980–1008. https://doi.org/10.1037/a0035661

Chamberlin, R., Wragg, T., Haynes, G., & Wragg, C. (2002). Performance-related pay and the teaching profession: A review of the literature. *Research Papers in Education, 17*(1), 31–49.

Chen, P., & Edin, P.-A. (2002). Efficiency wages and industry wage differentials: A comparison across methods of pay. *Review of Economics and Statistics, 84*, 617–631.

Chen, Y., Zhang, Z., Zhou, J., Liu, C., Zhang, X., & Yu, T. (2023). A cognitive evaluation and equity-based perspective of pay for performance on job performance: A meta-analysis and path model. *Frontiers in Psychology: Section in Organizational Psychology, 13*, 1039375. https://doi.org/10.3389/fpsyg.2022.1039375

Cherrington, D. J., Reitz, H. J., & Scott, W. E. Jr. (1971). Effects of contingent and noncontingent rewards on the relationship between satisfaction and task performance. *Journal of Applied Psychology, 55*, 531–536.

Chien, M. S., Lawler, J. S., & Uen, J. F. (2010). Performance-based pay, procedural justice and job performance for R&D professionals: Evidence from the Taiwanese high-tech sector. *The International Journal of Human Resource Management, 21*(12), 2234–2248. https://doi.org/10.1080/09585192.2010.509626

Choi, S. (2011). Organizational justice and employee work attitudes: The federal case. *The American Review of Public Administration, 41*(2), 185–204. https://doi.org/10.1177/0275074010373275

Ciavarella, M. A. (2001). Linking high involvement environments to the organizational life cycle: A descriptive and prescriptive approach. In *Academy of management proceedings, organization development and change* (pp. C1–C6).

Cimini, M. H. (1990). Developments in industrial relations. *Monthly Labor Review, 113*(3), 63–66.

Cimini, M. H. (1991). Developments in industrial relations. *Monthly Labor Review, 114*(5), 43–47.

Clark, J. B. (1889). The possibility of a scientific law of wages. *Publications of the American Economic Association, 4*, 39–69.

Clark, K. (2003, January 13). Judgment day. *U.S. News & World Report*, 31–32.

Clark, R. E., Feldon, D., van Merriënboer, J., Yates, K., & Early, S. (2008). Cognitive task analysis. In J. M. Spector, M. D. Merrill, J. J. van Merriënboer, & M. P. Driscoll (Eds.), *Handbook of research on educational communications and technology* (3rd ed.). Lawrence Erlbaum Associates.

Clark, T. B., & Wachtel, M. (1988, June). The quiet crisis goes public. *Government Executive*, 14–21.

Cleveland, J. N., Murphy, K. R., & Williams, R. E. (1989). Multiple uses of performance appraisal: Prevalence and correlates. *Journal of Applied Psychology, 74*, 130–135.

Clugston, M., & Howell, J. P. (2000). Dispositional influences on pay preferences. *Journal of Business & Psychology, 15*, 311–320.

Coens, T., & Jenkins, M. (2000). *Abolishing performance appraisal: Why they backfire and what to do instead*. Berrett-Koehler.

Cohen, D., & Murname, R. J. (1980). The merits of merit pay. *Public Interest, 80*, 3–30.

Colquitt, J. A. (2001). On the dimensionality of organizational justice: A construct validation of a measure. *Journal of Applied Psychology, 86*, 386–400.

Colquitt, J. A., Conlon, D. E., Wesson, M. J., Porter, C. O. L. H., & Ng, K. Y. (2001). Justice at the millennium: A meta-analytic review of 25 years of organizational justice research. *Journal of Applied Psychology, 86*, 415–445.

Connelly, B. L., Tihanyi, L., Crook, T. R., & Gangloff, K. A. (2014). Tournament theory: Thirty years of contests and competitions. *Journal of Management, 40*(1), 16–47. https://doi.org/10.1177/0149206313498902

Conroy, S. A., Roumpi, D., Delery, J. E., & Gupta, N. (2022). Pay volatility and employee turnover in the trucking industry. *Journal of Management, 48*(3), 605–629.

Cook, F. W. (1987). Rethinking compensation practices in light of economic conditions. *Personnel, 27*(1), 46–51.

Cooper, W. H. (1981). Conceptual similarity as a source of illusory halo in job performance ratings. *Journal of Applied Psychology, 66*, 302–307.

Cotton, J. L., & Cook, M. S. (1982). Meta-analyses and the effects of various reward systems: Some different conclusions from Johnson et al. *Psychological Bulletin, 92*, 176–183.

Cowan, P. (1978). How Blue Cross put pay-for-performance to work. *Personnel Journal, 57*(5), 250–269.

Cropanzano, R., & Mitchell, M. S. (2005). Social exchange theory: An interdisciplinary review. *Journal of Management, 31*(6), 874–900.

Cropanzano, R., Rupp, D. E., Mohler, C. J., & Schminke, M. (2001). Three roads to organizational justice. *Research in Personnel and Human Resource Management, 20*, 1–113.

Cubrich, M., & Petruzzelli, A. (2020). Advancing our understanding of successful aging at work: A socioemotional selectivity theory perspective. *Industrial and Organizational Psychology, 13*(3), 369–373. https://doi.org/10.1017/iop.2020.71

Curtius, M. (1999, June 7). Trust your boss? Checking pay; Most bosses keep the salary scale hidden from rank-and-file, but one company leaves its books open. *Los Angeles Times*, 3.

Daley, D. (1987). Merit pay enters with whimper: The initial federal civil service reform experience. *Review of Public Personnel Administration, 7*(2), 72–79.

Dansereau, F., Graen, G., & Haga, W. J. (1975). A vertical dyad-linkage approach to leadership within formal organizations. *Organizational Behavior and Human Performance, 13*, 46–78.

Davis, B. (2002). Public Service Credit Union focuses on individual incentives using online tracking. In *Three innovative searches for better incentive programs* (pp. 21–28). Filene Research Institute.

Day, D. V., & Sulsky, L. M. (1995). Effects of frame-of-reference training and information configuration on memory organization and rating accuracy. *Journal of Applied Psychology, 80*, 158–167.

de Bara, D., & Test, L. (Febuary, 2024). Pay-for-performance: How to motivate and reward your people. https://lattice.com/library/should-compensation-and-performance-be-linked.

De Gieter, S., De Cooman, R., Pepermans, R., Caers, R., du bois, C., & Jegers, M. (2006). Dimensionality of the pay satisfaction questionnaire: A validation study in Belgium. *Psychological Reports, 98*, 640–650. https://doi.org/10.2466/PR0.98.3.640-650

Deadrick, D. L., & Scott, K. D. (1987). Employee incentives in the public sector: A national survey of urban mass transit authorities. *Public Personnel Management, 16*, 135–143.

Deci, E. L. (1972). The effects of contingent and noncontingent rewards and controls on intrinsic motivation. *Organizational Behavior and Human Performance, 8*, 217–229.

Deckop, J. R., Merriman, K. K., & Blau, G. (2004). Impact of variable risk preferences on the effectiveness of control by pay. *Journal of Occupational and Organizational Psychology, 77*, 63–80.

Deepak, S. (2021a). Perceptions of organization justice: An empirical study of working women from Bangalore. *Journal of International Women's Studies, 22*(6), 84–100. https://vc.bridgew.edu/jiws/vol22/iss6/10

Deepak, S. (2021b). Perceptions of organization justice: An empirical study of working women from Bangalore. *Journal of International Women's Studies, 22*(6), 84–100. https://vc.bridgew.edu/jiws/vol22/iss6/10

Deming, W. E. (1986). *Out of the crisis*. MIT Center for Advanced Engineering Study.

Deming, W. E. (1994). *The new economics* (2nd ed.). MIT Center for Advanced Engineering Study.

DeNisi, A. S., Cafferty, T. P., & Meglino, B. M. (1984). A cognitive view of the performance appraisal process: A model and research propositions. *Organizational Behavior and Human Performance, 33*, 360–396.

DeNisi, A., Murphy, K., Varma, A., & Budhwar, P. (2021). Performance management systems and multinational enterprises: Where we are and where we should go. *Human Resource Management, 60*(5), 707–713.

DeNisi, A. S., & Peters, L. H. (1996). Organization of information in memory and the performance appraisal process: Evidence from the field. *Journal of Applied Psychology, 81*, 717–737.

DeNisi, A. S., Robbins, T., & Cafferty, T. P. (1989). Organization of information used for performance appraisals: Role of diary keeping. *Journal of Applied Psychology, 74*, 124–129.

Denrell, J., Zeijen, A., Romagnoli, M., & Marengo, L. (2025). Absolute, average-based, and rank-based aspirations. *Strategic Management Journal*. https://doi.org/10.1002/smj.3715

DeVaro, J. (2006). Strategic promotion tournaments and worker performance. *Strategic Management Journal, 27*, 721–740.

Devine, D., Kirk, D. D., & Dans, P. (2023). Central personnel agencies: Managing the bureaucracy. In P. Pans & S. Groves (Eds.), *Madate for leadership: The conservative promise. Project 2025, presidential transition project* (pp. 69–85).

Dienesch, R. M., & Liden, R. C. (1986). Leader-member exchange model of leadership: A critique and further development. *Academy of Management Review, 11*, 618–634.

Distefano, M. X., Pryer, M. O. W., & Erllineyer, R. C. (1983). Application of content validity methods to the development of a job-related performance rating criterion. *Personnel Psychology, 36*, 621–631.

Dorfman, P. W., Stephen, W. G., & Loveland, J. (1986). Performance appraisal behaviors: Supervisor perceptions and subordinate reactions. *Personnel Psychology, 39*, 579–598.

Dorsey, D. W., & Coovert, M. D. (2003). Mathematical modeling of decision making: A soft and fuzzy approach to capturing hard decisions. *Human Factors, 45*, 117–135.

Dossett, D. L. (1989). Dimensional characteristics of behaviorally based performance ratings. *Journal of Management Systems, 1*, 51–66.

Downs, C. W., & Moscinski, P. (1979). A survey of appraisal processes and training in large corporations. In Paper presented at the Annual Academy of Management Meetings, Atlanta, GA.

Dreher, G. F. (1981). Predicting the salary satisfaction of exempt employees. *Personnel Psychology, 34*, 579–589.

Duckwall, J. M. (1986). *An analysis of a faculty merit pay allocation system in a College of Education.* Unpublished dissertation, Florida State University.

Dyer, L. D., & Parker, D. F. (1975). Classifying outcomes in work motivation research: An examination of the intrinsic–extrinsic dichotomy. *Journal of Applied Psychology, 60*, 455–458.

Dyer, L. D., & Theriault, R. (1976). The determinants of pay satisfaction. *Journal of Applied Psychology, 61*, 596–604.

Eisenberg, D. (2001, June 18). Where people are never let go. *Time, 157*(24), 40.

Eisenberger, R., & Cameron, J. (1996). Detrimental effects of reward: Reality or myth? *American Psychologist, 51*, 1153–1166.

Elsner Twesme, E., Werner, J. M., & Simha, A. (2021). Can we talk? Improving employee contextual performance using motivating language and feedback orientation. *International Journal of Business Communication, 62*(2), 326–346. https://doi.org/10.1177/23294884211038745

Engler, H., & Mason, C. (2016). Enabling new levels of performance at Sears Holdings Corp. *WorldatWork Journal, 25*(2), 35–46.

Eskew, D., & Heneman, R. L. (1996). A survey of merit pay plan effectiveness. *Human Resource Planning, 19*(2), 12–19.

Eubanks, B. (2018). *Artificial intelligence for HR: Use AI to support and develop a successful workforce.* Kogan Page. https://ecommons.cornell.edu/bitstream/handle/1813/72363/Sturman43_How_and_what_you_pay_matters_The_relative_effectiveness_of_merit_pay__bonuses__and_long_term_incentives_on_future_job_performance.pdf?sequence=1

Evans, W. A. (1970). Pay for performance: Fact or fable? *Personnel Journal, 49*(9), 726–731.

Ewing, B. T., & Payne, J. T. (1999). The trade-off between supervision and wages: Evidence of efficiency wages from the NLSY. *Southern Economic Journal, 66*, 424–432.

Farh, J. L., & Dobbins, G. H. (1989). Effects of comparative performance information on the accuracy of self-ratings and agreement between self- and supervisory ratings. *Journal of Applied Psychology, 74*, 606–610.

Farmer, C. R. (1978). Merit pay: Viable? *Personnel, 16*(5), 57–63.

Fay, C. H. (1972). Salary budgeting and planning: Enhancing the process through the use of the computer. In M. Rock (Ed.), *Handbook of wage and salary administration* (pp. 448–464). McGraw-Hill.

Feldman, J. M. (1981). Beyond attribution theory: Cognitive processes in performance appraisal. *Journal of Applied Psychology, 66*, 127–148.

Felix, G. H., & Riggs, J. L. (1983). Productivity measurement by objectives. *National Productivity Review, 2*(4), 386–393.

Ferrin, D. L., & Dirks, K. T. (2003). The use of rewards to increase and decrease trust: Mediating processes and differential effects. *Organization Science, 14*, 18–31.

Ferris, G. R., Russ, G. S., & Fandt, P. M. (1989). Politics in organizations. In R. A. Giacalone & P. Rosenfeld (Eds.), *Impression management in the organization* (pp. 143–170). Erlbaum.

Field, H. S., & Holley, W. H. (1982). The relationship of performance appraisal system characteristics to verdicts in selected employment discrimination cases. *Academy of Management Journal, 25*, 392–406.

Fisk, C. L. (2025). Democracy and a nonpartisan civil service. *UC Berkeley Public Law Research Paper.* https://doi.org/10.2139/ssrn.5124299

Flanagan, J. L. (1954). The critical incident technique. *Psychological Bulletin, 51*, 327–358.

Florida Power Corporation: Focus on performance. (1985). *Training, 22*(11), 57–60.

Folger, R., & Konovsky, M. A. (1989). Effects of procedural and distributive justice on reactions to pay raise decisions. *Academy of Management Journal, 32*, 115–130.

Folger, R., Konovsky, M. A., & Cropanzano, R. (1993). A due process metaphor for performance appraisal. In B. Staw & L. Cummings (Eds.), *Research in organizational behavior* (Vol. 14, pp. 129–177). JAI Press.

Fong, S. C. L., & Shaffer, M. A. (2003). The dimensionality and determinants of pay satisfaction: A cross-cultural investigation of a group incentive plan. *International Journal of Human Resource Management, 14*, 559–580.

Forkosch, M. D. (1958). American democracy and procedural due process. *Brooklyn Law Review, 24*, 173–253.

Fossum, J. A. (1976). Publicity or secrecy: Pay and performance effects on satisfaction. In *Proceedings of the academy of management* (pp. 270–272).

Fossum, J. A., & Fitch, M. K. (1985). The effects of individual and contextual attributes on the size of recommended salary increases. *Personnel Psychology, 38*, 587–603.

Foster, K., & Lynn, K. V. (1978). Dividing up the "merit" increase pie for management. *Personnel Administrator, 23*(5), 42–48.

Fox, A. (2003). Is merit pay dead? *HR Magazine, 48*(1), 12.

Fox, S. F. (1989). Intergenerational differences, merit pay, and loyalty in a state and local government. *Review of Public Personnel Administration, 9*(2), 15–27.

Frank, R. H. (1984). Are workers paid their marginal products? *The American Economic Review, 74*, 549–571.

Franz, W., & Pfeiffer, F. (2003). The rationale for wage rigidity: Employers' viewpoint. *Jahrbücher für Nationalökonomie und Statistik, 223*(1), 23–57.

Freedman, S. M. (1978). Some determinants of compensation decisions. *Academy of Management Journal, 21*, 397–409.

Freedman, S. M., & Montanari, J. R. (1980). An integrative model of managerial reward allocation. *Academy of Management Review, 5*, 381–390.

Freeman, R. B. (1982). Union wage practices and wage dispersion within establishments. *Industrial and Labor Relations Review, 36*, 3–21.

Friedman, B. A., & Cornelius, E. T. III (1976). Effect of rater participation in scale construction on the psychometric characteristics of two rating scale formats. *Journal of Applied Psychology, 61*, 210–216.

Froese, F., Peltokorpi, V., Varma, A., & Hitotsuyanagi-Hansel, A. (2018). Merit-based rewards, job satisfaction and voluntary turnover: Moderating effects of employee demographic characteristics: Employee demographic characteristics. *British Journal of Management, 30.* https://doi.org/10.1111/1467-8551.12283

Fry, R., & Aragão, C. (2025, March 4). *Gender pay gap in U.S. has narrowed slightly over 2 decades.* Pew Research Center. https://www.pewresearch.org/short-reads/2025/03/04/gender-pay-gap-in-us-has-narrowed-slightly-over-2-decades/

Fuller, J. J., & Tinkham, R. (2002, September). Making the most of scarce reward dollars: Why differentiation makes a difference. *Employee Benefits Journal, 27*(3), 3–7.

Fulmer, I. S., & Arnold, A. (2020). Pay communication: A global look at practices and preferences. *Journal of Total Rewards, 29*(4), 25–35.

Fulmer, I. S., Gerhart, B., & Kim, J. H. (2023). Compensation and performance: A review and recommendations for the future. *Personnel Psychology, 76*(2), 687–718.

Fulmer, I. S., & Li, J. (2022). Compensation, benefits, and total rewards: A bird's-eye (re)view. *Annual Review of Organizational Psychology and Organizational Behavior, 9*(1), 147–169. https://doi.org/10.1146/annurev-orgpsych-012420-055903

Furnham, A. (2003, January/February). The case for secrecy. *Across the Board, 40*(1), 7–8.

Futrell, C. M., & Jenkins, O. C. (2018). Pay secrecy versus pay disclosure for salesmen: A longitudinal study. *Journal of Marketing Research, 15*(2), 214–219. https://doi.org/10.1177/002224377801500204

Gabor, A. (1989, June 5). Catch a falling star system. *U.S. News & World Report,* 43–44.

Gabris, G. T., & Ihrke, D. M. (2000). Improving employee acceptance toward performance appraisal and merit pay systems: The role of leadership credibility. *Review of Public Personnel Administration, 20,* 41–53.

Gabris, G. T., & Ihrke, D. M. (2003). Unanticipated failures of well-intentioned reforms: Some lessons from federal and local governments. *International Journal of Organization Theory and Behavior, 6,* 195–225.

Gabris, G. T., & Mitchell, K. (1988). The impact of merit raise scores on employee attitudes: The Matthew effect of performance appraisal. *Public Personnel Management, 17,* 369–382.

Gabris, G. T., Mitchell, K., & McLemore, R. (1985). Rewarding individual and team productivity: The Biloxi merit bonus plan. *Public Personnel Management, 14,* 231–244.

Gaertner, G. H., Gaertner, K. H., & Akinnusi, D. M. (1984). Environment, strategy, and the implementation of administrative change: The case of civil service reform. *Academy of Management Journal, 27,* 525–543.

Gaertner, K. H., & Gaertner, G. H. (1984). Performance evaluation and merit pay: Results in the environmental protection agency and health administration. In P. I. Ingraham & C. Ban (Eds.), *Legislating bureaucratic change: The Civil Service Reform Act of 1978* (pp. 87–111). State University of New York.

Gaga, U. A., & Kaz, M. S. (1996, November–December). The post-privatization period: A look at personal motivation systems for Russian enterprises. *American Compensation Association News,* 8–11.

Gagné, M., & Deci, E. L. (2005). Self-determination theory and work motivation. *Journal of Organizational Behavior, 26*(4), 331–362.

Gagné, M., & Forest, J. (2008). The study of compensation systems through the lens of self-determination theory: Reconciling 35 years of debate. *Canadian Psychology/Psychologie Canadienne, 49*(3), 225–232.

Gallup. (2024). *Hybrid work trends.* Gallup, Inc.

Garbers, Y., & Conradt, S. (2014). Performance-based pay and employees' motivation: A meta-analysis. *Journal of Economic Psychology, 41*, 245–261.

García-Buades, M. E., Peiró, J. M., Montañez-Juan, M. I., Kozusznik, M. W., & Ortiz-Bonnín, S. (2019, December). Happy-productive teams and work units: A systematic review of the 'happy-productive worker thesis'. *International Journal of Environmental Resources Public Health, 7*(1), 69. https://doi.org/10.3390/ijerph17010069

Gardner, J. W. (1961). *Excellence.* Harper.

Garland, H. (1973). The effects of piece-rate underpayment and overpayment on job performance: A test of equity theory with a new induction procedure. *Journal of Applied Social Psychology, 3*, 325–334.

Gary, L. (2001). The controversial practice of forced ranking. *Harvard Management Update, 6*(10).

George, L., & Holbein, J. (2016). Engaging employees to transform performance management at Cardinal Health. *World at Work Journal, 25*(2), 47–59.

Georgopoulos, B. S., Mahoney, G. M., & Jones, N. W. (1957). A path–goal approach to productivity. *Journal of Applied Psychology, 41*, 345–353.

Gephart, M. (1995, June). The road to high performance. *Training & Development,49*(6) pp. 29–38.

Gerhart, B. (2023). *Compensation* (14th ed.). McGraw-Hill.

Gerhart, B., & Fang, M. (2014). Pay for (individual) performance: Issues, claims, evidence and the role of sorting effects. *Human Resource Management Review, 24*(1), 41–52.

Gerhart, B., Rynes, S. L., & Fulmer, I. S. (2009). Pay and performance: Individuals, groups, and executives. *Academy of Management Annals, 3*(1), 251–315.

Gerhart, B., Trevor, C., & Scott, D. (2023). Merit pay. In A. Varma, P. S. Budhwar, & A. DeNisi (Eds.), *Performance management systems* (pp. 83–104). Routledge.

Gerhart, B. A., & Milkovich, G. J. (1989). Salaries, salary growth, and promotions of men and women in a large, private firm. In R. Michael, H. Hartman, & B. O'Farrell (Eds.), *Pay equity: Empirical inquiries* (pp. 23–43). National Academy Press.

Gerhart, B. A., & Rynes, S. L. (2003). *Compensation: Theory, evidence, and strategic implications.* Sage.

Gettel, C. J., Han, C. R., Canavan, M. E., Bernheim, S. M., Drye, E. E., Duseja, R., & Venkatesh, A. K. (2022, February). The 2018 merit-based incentive payment system: Participation, performance, and payment across specialties. *Medical Care, 60*(2), 156–163.

Ghiselli, E. E., Campbell, J. P., & Zedeck, S. (1981). *Measurement theory for the behavioral sciences.* W. H. Freeman.

Giles, B. A., & Barrett, G. V. (1971). Utility of merit increases. *Journal of Applied Psychology, 55*, 103–109.

Giles, W. F., & Mossholder, K. W. (1990). Employee reactions to contextual and session components of performance appraisal. *Journal of Applied Psychology, 75*, 371–377.

Gilliland, S. W., & Langdon, J. C. (1998). Creating performance management systems that promote perceptions of fairness. In J. W. Smither (Ed.), *Performance appraisal: State of the art in practice* (pp. 209–243). Jossey-Bass.

Glueck, W. F. (1976). *Business policy: Strategy formulation and management action*. McGraw-Hill.

Gobat, P. E. (1995). Measuring the internal equity of executive pay. *Journal of Compensation and Benefits, 10*(5), 40–42.

Goel, K., & Oswal, S. (2020). EVA-based financial performance measurement: An evidential study of selected emerging country companies. *Corporate Ownership and Control, 18*, 179–195. https://doi.org/10.22495/cocv18i1art14

Goffin, R. D., Gellatly, I. R., Paunonen, S. V., Jackson, D. N., & Meyer, J. A. (1996). Criterion validation of two approaches to performance appraisal: The behavioral observation scale and the relative percentile method. *Journal of Business and Psychology, 11*, 23–33.

Goffin, R. D., Jelley, R. B., & Wagner, S. H. (2003). Is halo helpful? Effects of inducing halo on performance rating accuracy. *Social Behavior and Personality: An International Journal, 31*(6), 625–636.

Gomez-Mejia, L. R., & Balkin, D. B. (1989). Effectiveness of individual and aggregate compensation strategies. *Industrial Relations, 28*, 431–445.

Gomez-Mejia, L. R., Balkin, D. B., & Milkovich, G. T. (1990). Rethinking rewards for technical employees. *Organizational Dynamics, 18*, 62–75.

Gomez-Mejia, L. R., Berrone, P., & Franco-Santos, M. (2014). *Compensation and organizational performance: Theory, research, and practice*. Routledge.

Gomez-Mejia, L., Trevino, L. J., & Mixon, F. G. (2009). Winning the tournament for named professorships in management. *International Journal of Human Resource Management, 20*, 1843–1863.

Goodale, J. G., & Mouser, M. W. (1981). Developing and auditing a merit pay system. *Personnel Journal, 60*(5), 391–397.

Goodman, P. S. (1975). Effect of perceived inequity on salary allocation decisions. *Journal of Applied Psychology, 60*, 372–375.

Gordon, D. F. (1974). A neo-classical theory of Keynsian unemployment. *Economic Inquiry, 12*(4), 431–459.

Gordon, M. E., & Johnson, W. A. (1982). Seniority: A review of its legal and scientific standing. *Personnel Psychology, 35*, 255–280.

Gorman, C. A., Jackson, D. J., Meriac, J. P., Himmler, J. R., & Contreras, T. F. (2024). Beyond rating accuracy: Unpacking frame-of-reference assessor training effectiveness. *Industrial and Organizational Psychology, 17*(2), 206–219. https://doi.org/10.1017/iop.2024.6

Gosselin, A., Werner, J. M., & Hallé, N. (1997). Ratee preferences concerning performance management and appraisal. *Human Resource Development Quarterly, 8*, 315–333.

Gould, S., & Penley, L. E. (1984). Career strategies and salary progression: A study of their relationships in a municipal bureaucracy. *Organizational Behavior and Human Performance, 34*, 244–265.

Green, E., Peterson, K., Markiewicz, K., O'Brien, J., & Gerring, N. (2017, November). The impact of a merit-based incentive payment system on quality of healthcare: A framed field experiment. https://ssrn.com/abstract=3066257

Green, S. G., & Liden, R. C. (1980). Contextual and attributional influences on control decisions. *Journal of Applied Psychology, 65*, 453–458.

Greenberg, J. (1986). Determinants of perceived fairness of performance evaluations. *Journal of Applied Psychology, 71*, 340–342.

Greenberg, J. (1987a). Reactions to procedural justice in payment distributions: Do the means justify the ends? *Journal of Applied Psychology, 72*, 55–61.

Greenberg, J. (1987b). A taxonomy of organizational justice theories. *Academy of Management Review, 12*, 9–22.

Greenberg, J. (1990). Organizational justice: Yesterday, today, and tomorrow. *Journal of Management, 16*, 399–432.

Greenberg, J. (2001). Setting the justice agenda: Seven unanswered questions about "what, why, and how". *Journal of Vocational Behavior, 58*, 210–219.

Greenberg, J., & McCarty, C. L. (1990). The interpersonal aspects of procedural justice: A new perspective on pay fairness. In Paper presented at the Spring Meeting of the Industrial Relations Research Association, Buffalo, NY.

Greene, C. N. (1973). Causal connections among managers' merit pay, job satisfaction, and performance. *Journal of Applied Psychology, 58*, 95–100.

Greene, C. N., & Podsakoff, P. M. (1978). Effects of removal of a pay incentive: A field experiment. *Academy of Management Proceedings, 38*, 206–210.

Greenhouse, S. (2000, January 28). Unions call merit pay proposal unacceptable. *New York Times, 149*, B6.

Greiner, J. W., Bell, L., & Hatry, H. P. (1975). *Employee incentives to improve state and local government in productivity*. National Commission on Productivity and Work Quality.

Gupta, N., Conroy, S. A., & Delery, J. E. (2012). The many faces of pay variation. *Human Resource Management Review, 22*, 100–115.

Gupta, V., & Dev, V. (2020). When is pay-for performance effective? *Journal of Total Rewards, 29*(2), 48–61.

Gupta, V., Mittal, S., Ilavarasan, P. V., & Budhwar, P. (2024). Pay-for-performance, procedural justice, OCB and job performance: A sequential mediation model. *Personnel Review, 53*(1), 136–154. https://doi.org/10.1108/PR-11-2021-0782

Guzzo, R. A., & Bondy, J. S. (1983). *A guide to worker productivity experiments in the United States: 1976–1981*. Work in America Institute.

Guzzo, R. A., Jette, R. D., & Katzell, R. A. (1985). The effects of psychologically based intervention programs on worker productivity: A meta-analysis. *Personnel Psychology, 38*(2), 275–291.

Haire, M., Ghiselli, E. E., & Gordon, M. E. (1967). A psychological study of pay. *Journal of Applied Psychology Monograph, 51*(Whole No. 636).

Hall, J. L., Posner, B. Z., & Harder, J. W. (1989). Performance appraisal systems: Matching practice with theory. *Group and Organization Studies, 14*, 51–69.

Hamner, C., Luthans, F., & Krietner, R. (2015). Operant behavior and organizational behavior modification. In J. B. Miner (Ed.), *Organizational behavior 1: Essential theories of motivation and leadership* (pp. 114–133). Routledge.

Hamner, W. C. (1975). How to ruin motivation with pay. *Compensation Review, 7*(4), 17–27.

Handshear, N. A. (1988). News preferred over mystery-members favor merit review news. *American Compensation Association News, 31*(5), 10.

Handshear, N. A. (1989). *Personal communication*.

Hansen, F. (2002, December). The perils of cutting merit pay. *Workforce, 81*(13), 19.

Hansen, W. L. (1988). Merit pay in structured and unstructured salary systems. *Academe, 74*(6), 10–13.

Hantula, D. A., Rajala, A. K., Kellerman, E. G. B., & Bragger, J. L. D. (2001). The value of workplace safety: A time-based utility analysis model. *Journal of Organizational Behavior Management, 21*, 79–98.

Harris, B. R., Huselid, M. A., & Becker, B. E. (1999). Strategic human resource management at Praxair. *Human Resource Management, 38,* 315–320.

Harris, M. M. (1994). Rater motivation in the performance appraisal context: A theoretical framework. *Journal of Management, 20,* 737–756.

Harris, M. M., Gilbreath, B., & Sunday, J. A. (1998). A longitudinal examination of a merit pay system: Relationships among performance ratings, merit increases, and total pay increases. *Journal of Applied Psychology, 83,* 825–831.

Harris, M. M., Gilbreath, B., & Sunday, J. A. (2002). Why are women paid less than men, but given higher raises? *Journal of Business and Psychology, 16,* 499–514.

Hatch, D. D. (2000). Employers may not bar pay discussions. *Workforce, 79*(10), 124.

Hauenstein, N. M. A. (1998). Training raters to increase the accuracy of appraisals and the usefulness of feedback. In J. W. Smither (Ed.), *Performance appraisal: State of the art in practice* (pp. 404–442). Jossey-Bass.

Hausknecht, J. P., Rodda, J., & Howard, M. J. (2009). Targeted employee retention: Performance-based and job-related differences in reported reasons for staying. *Human Resource Management, 48*(2), 269–288.

Henderson, A. D., & Fredrickson, J. W. (2001). TMT coordination needs and the CEO pay gap: A competitive test of economic and behavioral views. *Academy of Management Journal, 44,* 96–117.

Henderson, R. (1980). *Performance appraisal: Theory to practice.* Prentice Hall.

Heneman, H. G. III (1973). Impact of performance on managerial pay levels and pay changes. *Journal of Applied Psychology, 58,* 128–130.

Heneman, H. G. III (1985). Pay satisfaction. In K. N. Rowland & G. R. Ferris (Eds.), *Research in personnel and human resources management* (Vol. 3, pp. 115–139). JAI Press.

Heneman, H. G. III, & Ellis, R. A. (1982). Correlates of just-noticeable differences in pay increases. *Labor Law Journal, 34,* 533–538.

Heneman, H. G. III, & Judge, T. A. (2000). Compensation attitudes: A review and recommendations for future research. In S. L. Rynes & B. Gerhart (Eds.), *Compensation in organizations: Current research and practice* (pp. 61–103). Pfeiffer/Jossey-Bass.

Heneman, H. G. III, & Judge, T. A. (2003). *Staffing organizations* (4th ed.). Mendota House.

Heneman, H. G. III, & Schwab, D. P. (1979). Work and rewards theory. In D. Yoder & H. G. HenemanJr. (Eds.), *ASPA handbook of personnel and industrial relations* (pp. 6-1–6-22). Bureau of National Affairs.

Heneman, H. G. III, & Schwab, D. P. (1985). Pay satisfaction: Its multidimensional nature and measurement. *International Journal of Psychology, 20,* 129–141.

Heneman, H. G. III, Schwab, D. P., Fossum, J. A., & Dyer, L. D. (1989). *Personnel/human resource management.* Irwin.

Heneman, H. G. III, Schwab, D. S., Standal, J. T., & Peterson, R. B. (1978). Pay comparisons: Dimensionality and predictability. *Academy of Management Proceedings, 38,* 211–215.

Heneman, H. G. III, & Young, I. P. (1988). Evaluation of school district administrator's reactions to a merit pay program. In Paper presented at the National Academy of Management Meetings, Anaheim, CA.

Heneman, R. L. (1984a). *The effects of rating format and rater training on performance rating accuracy and the motivation to rate accurately.* Unpublished doctoral dissertation. Michigan State University.

Heneman, R. L. (1984b). *Pay for performance: Exploring the merit system.* Work in America Institute/Studies in Productivity #38. Pergamon.

Heneman, R. L. (1986). The relationship between supervisory ratings and results-oriented measures of performance: A meta-analysis. *Personnel Psychology, 39,* 811–826.

Heneman, R. L. (1988). Traits, behaviors, and rater training: Some unexpected results. *Human Performance, 1,* 85–98.

Heneman, R. L. (1990). Merit pay research. In G. R. Ferris & K. M. Rowland (Eds.), *Research in personnel and human resources management* (Vol. 8, pp. 203–262). JAI Press.

Heneman, R. L. (1991). Evaluating the effectiveness of merit pay: A criterion model. In *Proceedings of the 34th annual meeting of the Midwest academy of management* (Vol. 34, pp. 121–126).

Heneman, R. L. (2001a). *Business-driven compensation policies: Integrating compensation systems with corporate strategies.* AMACOM.

Heneman, R. L. (2001b). Merit pay. In C. Fay (Ed.), *The executive handbook of compensation* (pp. 447–464). Free Press.

Heneman, R. L. (Ed.). (2002). *Strategic reward management: Design, implementation, and evaluation.* Information Age.

Heneman, R. L., & Cohen, D. J. (1988). Supervisory and employee characteristics as correlates of employee salary increases. *Personnel Psychology, 41,* 345–360.

Heneman, R. L., Eskew, D., & Fox, J. (1998). Using survey data to evaluate the effectiveness of a profit sharing and performance management system in a high technology firm. *Compensation and Benefits Review, 30*(1), 40–44.

Heneman, R. L., Fay, C. H., & Wang, Z.-M. (2002). Compensation systems in the global context. In N. Anderson, D. S. Ones, H. K. Sinangil, & C. Viswesvaran (Eds.), *Handbook of industrial, work & organizational psychology* (Vol. 2, pp. 77–92). Sage.

Heneman, R. L., Greenberger, D. B., & Anonyuo, C. (1989). Attributions and exchanges: The effects of interpersonal factors on the diagnosis of employee performance. *Academy of Management Journal, 32,* 466–476.

Heneman, R. L., Greenberger, D. B., & Fox, J. A. (2002). A reconceptualization of pay raise satisfaction based on changes in work and pay practices. *Human Resource Management Review, 11,* 1–12.

Heneman, R. L., Greenberger, D. B., & Strasser, S. (1988). The relationship between pay-for-performance perceptions and pay satisfaction. *Personnel Psychology, 41,* 745–759.

Heneman, R. L., & Gresham, M. T. (1998). Performance-based pay plans. In J. W. Smither (Ed.), *Performance appraisal: State-of-the-art methods for performance management* (pp. 496–536). Jossey-Bass.

Heneman, R. L., Porter, G., Greenberger, D. B., & Strasser, S. (1997). Modeling the relationship between pay level and pay satisfaction. *Journal of Business and Psychology, 12,* 147–158.

Heneman, R. L., & Schutt, W. (2003). Total reward management. In S. Chowdhury (Ed.), *Organization 21C: Someday all organizations will lead this way* (pp. 125–134). Financial Times Prentice-Hall.

Heneman, R. L., & von Hippel, C. (1996). The assessment of job performance: Focusing attention on context, process and group issues. In D. Lewin, D. J. B. Mitchell, & M. A. Zaidi (Eds.), *Handbook of human resource management* (pp. 587–617). JAI Press.

Heneman, R. L., von Hippel, C., Eskew, D. E., & Greenberger, D. B. (1997, Summer). Alternative rewards in unionized environments. *American Compensation Association Journal,* 42–55.

Heneman, R. L., & Werner, J. M. (2005). *Merit pay: Linking pay to performance in a changing world* (2nd ed.). IAP.

Heneman, R. L., & Wexley, K. N. (1983). The effects of time delay in rating and amount of information observed on performance rating accuracy. *Academy of Management Journal, 26,* 677–686.

Heneman, R. L., Wexley, K. N., & Moore, M. L. (1987). Performance-rating accuracy: A critical review. *Journal of Business Research, 15,* 431–448.

Henry, R. A., & Hulin, C. L. (1987). Stability of skilled performance across time: Some generalizations and limitations on utilities. *Journal of Applied Psychology, 72,* 457–462.

Herman, J. B. (1973). Are situational contingencies limiting job attitude-job performance relationships? *Organizational Behavior and Human Performance, 10,* 208–224.

Herrnstein, R. J. (1990). Behaviors, reinforcement, and utility. *Psychological Science, 1,* 217–224.

Hewitt Associates. (2002). *U.S. salary increase survey report for 2002.* Author.

Hewitt Associates. (2003). *U.S. salary increase survey; Survey highlights 2003 and 2004.* Hewitt Associates.

Hills, F. S., Scott, D. K., & Markham, S. E. (1988, August). Pay system structure as a moderator of the pay-performance relationship and employee pay increase satisfaction. In Paper presented at the Academy of Management, Anaheim, CA.

Hinkin, T. R., Podsakoff, P. M., & Schriesheim, C. A. (1987). The mediation of performance-contingent "compensation" by supervisors in work organizations: A reinforcement perspective. In D. B. Balkin & L. R. Gomez-Mejia (Eds.), *New perspectives on compensation* (pp. 196–210). Prentice Hall.

Hinrichs, J. R. (1969). Correlates of employee evaluations of pay increases. *Journal of Applied Psychology, 53,* 481–489.

Hirschfeld, R. R., Schmitt, L. P., & Bedeian, A. G. (2002). Job-content perceptions, performance–reward expectancies, and absenteeism among low-wage public-sector clerical employees. *Journal of Business and Psychology, 16,* 553–564.

Hobson, C. J., Mendel, R. M., & Gibson, F. W. (1981). Clarifying performance appraisal criteria. *Organizational Behavior and Human Performance, 28,* 164–188.

Holliman, S. D. (1983). *Merit pay: The federal government's pay-for-performance experience.* Unpublished master's thesis. Naval Postgraduate School.

Holmstrom, B. (1999). Managerial incentive problems: A dynamic perspective. *Review of Economic Studies, 66,* 169–182.

Holtz, S. (1997). Strategizing a human resources presence on the internet. *Compensation & Benefits Management, 13*(4), 31–37.

Honeywell-Johnson, J. A., & Dickinson, A. M. (1999). Small group incentives: A review of the literature. *Journal of Organizational Behavior Management, 19,* 89–120.

How one company has taken pay for performance to the max: Performance based benefits. (1989). *Compensation and Benefits Managers Report (Prentice Hall Professional Newsletter), 3*(20), 149–151.

Hox, J., Moerbeek, M., & Van de Schoot, R. (2017). *Multilevel analysis: Techniques and applications* (3rd ed.). Routledge.

HR Focus. (2001, April). Incentive pay plans: Which ones work... and why. *HR Focus, 78,* 3–4.

HR Focus. (2003, October). Average '04 merit pay raises won't top 4%. *HR Focus, 80,* 12.

Huber, V. L., Neale, M. A., & Northcraft, G. B. (1987). Judgment by heuristics: Effects of ratee and rater characteristics and performance standards on performance-related standards. *Organizational Behavior and Human Decision Processes, 40,* 149–169.

Hui, C., & Triandis, H. C. (2021). Individualism-collectivism and reward allocation preferences: A cross-cultural comparison. *Journal of Cross-Cultural Psychology, 52*(6), 523–540.

Hulin, C. L. (1982). Some reflections on general performance dimensions and halo rating error. *Journal of Applied Psychology, 67,* 165–170.

Hunter, J. E., & Schmidt, F. L. (1990). *Methods of meta-analysis: Correcting error and bias in research findings.* Sage.

Hunter, J. E., & Schmidt, F. L. (2004). *Methods of meta-analysis: Correcting error and bias in research findings* (2nd ed.). Sage.

Hunter, R. W., & Silverman, B. R. S. (1980). Merit. Pay in the federal government. *Personnel Journal, 59,* 1003–1007.

Hurwich, A. C. (1986). Strategic compensation designs that link pay to performance. *Journal of Business Strategy,* 7(3), 79–83.

Huselid, M. A. (1995). The impact of human resource management practices on turnover, productivity, and corporate financial performance. *Academy of Management Journal, 38,* 635–672.

Huseman, R. C., Hatfield, J. D., & Miles, E. W. (1987). A new perspective on equity theory: The equity sensitivity construct. *Academy of Management Review, 12*(2), 222–234.

Hyde, A. C. (1988). The new environment for compensation and performance in the public sector. *Public Personnel Management, 17,* 351–357.

Ilgen, D. R., Fisher, P. D., & Taylor, M. S. (1979). Consequences of individual feedback on behavior in organizations. *Journal of Applied Psychology, 64,* 349–371.

Ingersoll, R. M. (2000). Merit pay for teachers: A historical perspective. *Educational Policy, 14*(3), 153–172.

IOMA. (2003, November). *Three studies predict historically low merit raises for '04. IOMA's pay for performance report* (pp. 1–13).

IOMA. (2006). *Cost reduction and control best practices: The best ways for a financial manager to save money.* John Wiley & Sons.

Ivancevich, J. M. (1983). Contrast effects in performance evaluations and reward practices. *Academy of Management Journal, 26,* 465–476.

Jackson, S. E., & Schuler, R. S. (1995). Understanding human resource management in the context of organizations and their environments. *Annual Review of Psychology, 46,* 237–264.

Jackson, S. E., Schuler, R. S., & Rivero, J. C. (1989). Organizational characteristics as predictors of personnel practices. *Personnel Psychology, 42,* 727–786.

James, K. C. (2002, April). *A fresh start for federal pay: The case for modernization.* U.S. Office of Personnel Management. https://ourpublicservice.org/wp-content/uploads/2002/04/ea4746e133b5f93e4f4086c873bd0bd9-1414080224.pdf

James, L. R. (1973). Criterion models and construct validity for criteria. *Psychological Bulletin, 80,* 75–83.

Jelley, R. B., & Goffin, R. D. (2001). Can performance-feedback accuracy be improved? Effects of rater priming and rating-scale format on rating accuracy. *Journal of Applied Psychology, 86*(1), 134–144.

Jenkins, D. G. Jr. (1986). Financial incentives. In E. A. Locke (Ed.), *Generalizing from laboratory to field settings* (pp. 167–180). D. C. Heath.

Jenkins, D. G. Jr., & Lawler, E. E. III (1981). Impact of employee participation in pay plan development. *Organizational Behavior and Human Performance, 28,* 111–128.

Jenkins, D. G. Jr., Mitra, A., Gupta, N., & Shaw, J. D. (1998). Are financial incentives related to performance? A meta-analytic review of empirical research. *Journal of Applied Psychology, 83,* 777–787.

Jick, T. D. (1979). Mixing qualitative and quantitative methods: Triangulation in action. *Administrative Science Quarterly, 24,* 602–611.

Johnson, D. E., Erez, A., Kiker, D. S., & Motowidlo, S. J. (2002). Liking and attributions of motives as mediators of the relationships between individuals' reputations, helpful behaviors, and raters' reward decisions. *Journal of Applied Psychology, 87,* 808–815.

Johnson, D. W., Maruyama, G., Johnson, R., Nelson, D., & Skon, L. (1981). Effects of cooperative, competitive, and individualistic goal structures on achievement: A meta-analysis. *Psychological Bulletin, 89,* 47–62.

Johnson, M., & Kasten, K. (1983). Meritorious work and faculty rewards: An empirical test of the relationship. *Research in Higher Education, 19,* 49–71.

Johnson, M. D., Narayanan, A., & Sawaya, W. J. III (2021). Rewarding teaching excellence in higher education: An analysis of an incentive program at a tier I research institute and a prescription for future teaching incentive programs. *International Journal of Public Sector Performance Management,* 7(3), 314–336.

Johnson, N. B. (2026). *Personal communication.* Accessed on January 8, 2026.

Jones, F. F. (1998). Pay procedures and voluntary turnover: Does procedural justice matter? *Psychological Reports, 83,* 475–482.

Jones, F. F., Scarpello, V., & Bergmann, T. (1999). Pay procedures—What makes them fair? *Journal of Occupational and Organizational Psychology, 72,* 129–145.

Jones, F. F., & Skarlicki, D. P. (2003). The relationship between perceptions of fairness and voluntary turnover among retail employees. *Journal of Applied Social Psychology, 33*(6), 1226–1243.

Judge, T. A. (1993). Validity of the dimensions of the pay satisfaction questionnaire: Evidence of differential prediction. *Personnel Psychology, 46,* 485–519.

Judge, T. A., & Welbourne, T. M. (1994). A confirmatory investigation of the dimensionality of the pay satisfaction questionnaire. *Journal of Applied Psychology, 79,* 461–466.

Kahn, L. M., & Sherer, P. D. (1990). Contingent pay and managerial performance. *Industrial and Labor Relations Review, 43*(3 Special Issue), 107S–120S.

Kanter, R. M. (1987). From status to contribution: Some organizational implications of the changing basis for pay. *Personnel, 17*(1), 12–37.

Kaplan, R. S., & Norton, D. P. (1996). *The balanced scorecard.* Harvard Business School Press.

Karambir, K., Ashutosh, M., & Palika, C. (2024). An amalgamation of cognitive aspects in software engineering: A content analysis. *Expert Systems with Applications, 246,* 122968.

Katkowski, D. A., Medsker, G. J., & Pritchard, K. H. (2002). Literature review of "acceptable" or "just noticeably different" pay increases. In Paper presented at the Society for Industrial and Organizational Psychology, Toronto.

Katz, L. F. (1986). Efficiency wage theories: A partial evaluation. In S. Fischer (Ed.), *National Bureau of Economics Research macroeconomics annual* (pp. 235–276). MIT Press.

Katzell, R. A., Beinstock, P., & Faerstein, P. (1977). *A guide to worker productivity experiments in the United States: 1971–1975.* Work in America Institute.

Katzenbach, J. R., & Smith, D. K. (1993). *The wisdom of teams: Creating the high-performance organization.* Harvard Business Review Press.

Kaufman, B. E. (1989). Models of man in industrial relations research. *Industrial and Labor Relations Review, 43,* 72–88.

Kaun, D. E. (1984). Faculty advancement in a nontraditional university environment. *Industrial and Labor Relations Review, 37,* 592–606.

Kavanaugh, M. J., Mackinney, A. L., & Wolins, L. (1971). Issues in a managerial performance: Multitrait-multimethod analyses of ratings. *Psychological Bulletin, 75,* 34–39.

Keely, M. (1978). A contingency framework for performance evaluation. *Academy of Management Review, 3,* 428–438.

Kellough, J. E., & Nigro, L. G. (2002). Pay for performance in Georgia state government. *Review of Public Personnel Administration, 22,* 146–166.

Kellough, J. E., & Selden, S. C. (1997). Pay-for-performance systems in state government. *Review of Public Personnel Administration, 17,* 5–21.

Kellough, J. E., & Selden, S. C. (2003). The reinvention of public personnel administration: An analysis of the diffusion of personnel management reforms in the states. *Public Administration Review, 63,* 165–176.

Kennedy, C. W., Fossum, J. A., & White, B. J. (1983). Empirical comparison of within-subjects expectancy theory models. *Organizational Behavior and Human Performance, 20,* 124–143.

Keown-Gerrard, J. L., & Sulsky, L. M. (2001). The effects of task information training and frame-of-reference training with situational constraints on rating accuracy. *Human Performance, 14,* 305–320.

Khoshsoroor, S., Liang, D., Salami, G., & Chitsaz, E. (2019). Team cohesion: A double-edged sword in the relationship between rival estimation and escalation of commitment. *Social Behavior and Personality, 47,* 1–12.

Khtatbeh, M. M., Mahomed, A. S., Rahman, S. A., & Mohamed, R. (2020). The mediating role of procedural justice on the relationship between job analysis and employee performance in Jordan Industrial Estates. *Heliyon, 6*(10), e04973. https://doi.org/10.1016/j.heliyon.2020.e04973

Kidder, L., Bellettirie, G., & Cohn, E. S. (1977). The effects of anonymity on reward allocations made by women and men. *Journal of Experimental Social Psychology, 13,* 70–80.

Kiker, D. S., & Motowidlo, S. J. (1999). Main and interaction effects of task and contextual performance on supervisory reward decisions. *Journal of Applied Psychology, 84,* 602–609.

Kim, J. H. (2025). Experimental examination of the incentive and sorting effects of pay-for-performance on creative performance. *Journal of Applied Psychology, 110*(4), 598–617. https://doi.org/10.1037/apl0001245

King, J. & Langdon, P. (Eds.). (2002). *CRS and the business of architecture.* Texas A&M University Press.

King, L. M., Hunter, J. E., & Schmidt, F. L. (1980). Halo in a multidimensional, forced-choice performance evaluation scale. *Journal of Applied Psychology, 65,* 507–516.

Kirk, A. K., & Brown, D. F. (2003). Latent constructs of proximal and distal motivation predicting performance under maximum test conditions. *Journal of Applied Psychology, 88,* 40–49.

Klaas, B. S. (1999). Containing compensation costs: Why firms differ in their willingness to reduce pay. *Journal of Management, 25,* 829–850.

Klaas, B. S., & McClendon, J. A. (1996). To lead, lag, or match: Estimating the financial impact of pay level policies. *Personnel Psychology, 49,* 121–141.

Klaas, B. S., & Ullman, J. C. (1995). Sticky wages revisited: Organizational responses to a declining market-clearing wage. *Academy of Management Review, 20,* 281–310.

Kleiman, R. (1999). Some evidence on EVA companies. *Journal of Applied Corporate Finance, 12,* 80–91.

Klein, H. J., Wesson, M. J., Hollenbeck, J. R., & Alge, B. J. (1999). Goal commitment and the goal-setting process: Conceptual clarification and empirical synthesis. *Journal of Applied Psychology, 84,* 885–896.

Kleiner, M. M., & Bouillon, M. L. (1988). Providing business information to production workers: Correlates of compensation and profitability. *Industrial and Labor Relations Review, 41,* 605–617.

Klimoski, R., & Inks, L. (1990). Accountability forces in performance appraisal. *Organizational Behavior and Human Decision Processes, 45,* 194–208.

Kline, R. B. (2023). *Principles and practice of structural equation modeling* (5th ed.). Guilford Press.

Kniffin, K. M., Narayanan, J., Anseel, F., Antonakis, J., Ashford, S. P., Bakker, A. B., Bamberger, P., Bapuji, H., Bhave, D. P., Choi, V. K., & Creary, S. J. (2021). COVID-19 and the workplace: Implications, issues, and insights for future research and action. *American Psychologist, 76*(1), 63–77. https://doi.org/10.1037/amp0000716

Knouse, S. B. (1995). *The reward and recognition process in total quality management.* ASQC Quality Press.

Koch, J. V., & Chizmar, J. F. (1973). The influence of teaching and other factors upon absolute, salaries and salary increases at Illinois State University. *Journal of Economic Education, 5*, 27–34.

Kohn, A. (1993a). *Punished by rewards*. Houghton Mifflin.

Kohn, A. (1993b, September-October). Why incentive plans cannot work. *Harvard Business Review*, 54–63.

Komald, J. (1986). Applied behavior analysis and organizational behavior: Reciprocal influence of the two fields. In B. Staw & L. L. Cummings (Eds.), *Research in organizational behavior* (Vol. 8, pp. 297–334). JAI Press.

Konrad, A. M., & Pfeffer, J. (1990). Do you get what you deserve? Factors affecting the relationship between productivity and pay. *Administrative Science Quarterly, 35*, 258–285.

Kopelman, R. E. (1976). Organizational control system responsiveness, expectancy theory constructs, and work motivation: Some interrelations and causal connections. *Personnel Psychology, 29*, 205–220.

Kopelman, R. E., & Reinharth, L. (1982). Research results: The effect of merit-pay practices on white collar performance. *Compensation Review, 14*(4), 30–40.

Koys, D. J., Keaveny, T. J., & Allen, R. E. (1989). Demographic and attitudinal predictors of preferences for alternative pay increase policies. In *Proceedings of the thirty-second annual meeting of the Midwest academy of management* (Vol. 32, pp. 159–163).

Kozlowski, S. W., & Bradford, S. (2013). Work groups and teams in organizations: Review update. In *The handbook of psychology* (2nd ed., Vol. 12). Wiley Online. Organizational Psychology. https://doi.org/10.1002/9781118133880

Kozlowski, S. W. J., Chao, G. T., & Morrison, R. F. (1998). Games raters play: Politics, strategies, and impression management in performance appraisal. In J. W. Smither (Ed.), *Performance appraisal: State of the art in practice* (pp. 163–205). Jossey-Bass.

Kozlowski, S. W. J., Chao, G. T., Smith, E. M., & Hedlund, J. (1993). Organizational downsizing: Strategies, interventions, and research implications. *International Review of Industrial and Organizational Psychology, 8*, 263–332.

Krattenmaker, T. (2002, October). *Compensation: What's the big secret? Harvard management communication letter*. Harvard Business School Press.

Krefting, L. A., & Mahoney, T. A. (1977). Determining the size of a meaningful pay increase. *Industrial Relations, 16*, 83–93.

Krefting, L. A., Newman, J. M., & Krzystofiak, F. (1987). What is a meaningful pay increase? In D. B. Balkin & L. R. Gomez-Meiia (Eds.), *New perspectives on compensation* (pp. 135–140). Prentice Hall.

Kroeck, M. G., Avolio, B. J., Small, R. L., & Einstein, W. O. (1987). Shifts in resource allocation preference following panel discussion. *Journal of Management, 13*, 713–724.

Kronberg, K. A. (2020). Workplace gender pay gaps: Does gender matter less the longer employees stay? *Work and Occupations, 47*(1), 3–43.

Krueger, A. B., & Summers, L. H. (1988). Efficiency wages and interindustry wage structure. *Econometrica, 56*, 259–293.

Kruglanski, A. W. (1989). The psychology of being "right": The problem of accuracy in social perception and cognition. *Psychological Bulletin, 106*, 395–409.

Kuvaas, B., & Ding, H. (2025). Pay for performance and employee outcomes: The mediating roles of controlling and informational perceptions of pay. *Journal of Occupational & Organizational Psychology, 98*(3), e70055. https://doi.org/10.1111/joop.70055

Kuvaas, B., Shore, L. M., Buch, R., & Dysvik, A. (2020). Social and economic exchange relationships and performance contingency: Differential effects of variable pay and base pay. *International Journal of Human Resource Management, 31*(3), 408–431.

Kwon, S. H. (2024, March). Analyzing the impact of team-building interventions on team cohesion in sports teams: A meta-analysis study. *Frontier Psychology, 15,* 1353944. https://doi.org/10.3389/fpsyg.2024.1353944

La Police, C. C. (2002). Pay for performance: A five-year evaluation of a contribution-based compensation system. In Paper presented at the Society for industrial and organizational psychology conference, Toronto.

Lacey, K. J. (2021). Teacher pay for performance: Historical trends and contemporary debates. *Journal of Policy Analysis and Management, 40*(2), 345–368.

Laguerre, R. A. (2022). Minding employee pay equality policy perceptions. *Industrial and Organizational Psychology, 15*(1), 73–75.

Landau, S. B., & Leventhal, G. S. (1976). A simulation study of administrator's behavior toward employees who receive job offers. *Journal of Applied Social Psychology, 6,* 291–306.

Landry, A. T., Gagné, M., Forest, J., Guerrero, S., Séguin, M., & Papachristopoulos, K. (2017). The relation between financial incentives, motivation, and performance. *Journal of Personnel Psychology, 16*(2), 61–76. https://doi.org/10.1027/1866-5888/a000182

Landy, F. J. (1986). Stamp collecting versus science: Validation as hypothesis testing. *American Psychologist, 41,* 1183–1192.

Landy, F. J., Barnes, J. L., & Murphy, K. R. (1978). Correlates of perceived fairness and accuracy of performance evaluations. *Journal of Applied Psychology, 63,* 751–754.

Landy, F. J., & Farr, J. L. (1980). Performance rating. *Psychological Bulletin, 87,* 72–107.

Landy, F. J., Farr, J. L., & Jacobs, R. R. (1982). Utility concepts in performance measurement. *Organizational Behavior and Human Performance, 30,* 15–40.

Landy, F. J., Vance, R. J., Barnes-Farrell, J. L., & Steele, J. W. (1980). Statistical control of halo error in performance ratings. *Journal of Applied Psychology, 65,* 501–506.

Larkin, I. (2019). Strategic compensation: A critique and research agenda. In A. J. Nyberg & T. P. Moliterno (Eds.), *Handbook of research on strategic human capital resources* (pp. 403–424). Edward Elgar.

Latham, G. P., & Seijts, G. H. (1997). The effect of appraisal instrument on managerial perceptions of fairness and satisfaction with appraisals from their peers. *Canadian Journal of Behavior Science, 29,* 275–282.

Latham, G. P., & Wexley, K. N. (1994). *Increasing productivity through performance appraisal* (2nd ed.). Addison-Wesley.

Lattice. (2023). *2023 state of people strategy report: How HR drives results in a times of change* (pp. 1–28). Lattice.com.

Lawler, E. E. III (1965). Manager's perceptions of their subordinates' pay and of their superiors' pay. *Personnel Psychology, 18,* 413–422.

Lawler, E. E. III (1971). *Pay and organizational effectiveness: A psychological view.* McGraw-Hill.

Lawler, E. E. III (1972). Secrecy and the need to know. In H. L. Tosi, R. J. House, & M. D. Dunnette (Eds.), *Managerial motivation and compensation* (pp. 455–476). MSU Business Studies.

Lawler, E. E. III (1976). Comments on Herbert H. Meyer's "the pay for performance dilemma". *Organizational Dynamics, 4*(1), 73–75.

Lawler, E. E. III (1981). *Pay and organization development.* Addison-Wesley.

Lawler, E. E. III (2003). Reward practices and performance management system effectiveness. *Organizational Dynamics, 32,* 396–404.

Lawler, E. E. III, & Hackman, J. R. (1969). Impact of employee participation in the development of pay incentives plans: A field experiment. *Journal of Applied Psychology, 53,* 467–471.

Lawler, E. E. III, & McDermott, M. (2003, Second Quarter). Current performance management practices: Examining the varying impacts. *WorldatWork Journal,* 49–60.

Lawler, E. E. III, & Mohrman, S. A. (2003). *Creating a strategic human resources organization: Trends and new directions.* Stanford University Press.

Lawler, E. E. III, Mohrman, A. M. Jr., & Resnick, S. M. (1984). Performance appraisal revisited. *Organizational Dynamics, 12,* 20–35.

Lawshe, C. H. (1975). A quantitative approach to content validity. *Personnel Psychology, 28,* 563–575.

Lawther, W. C., Bernardin, H. J., Traynham, E., & Jennings, K. (1989). Implications of salary structure and merit pay in the fifty American states. *Review of Public Personnel Administration, 9*(2), 1–14.

Lazear, E., & Rosen, S. (1981). Rank order tournaments as an optimum labor contract. *Journal of Political Economy, 89,* 841–864.

Lazear, E. P. (1986). Salaries and piece rates. *Journal of Business, 59*(3), 405–431.

LeBlanc, P. V., & Mulvey, P. W. (1998). How American workers see the rewards of work. *Compensation and Benefits Review, 30,* 24–28.

Ledford, G. E., Benson, G., & Lawler, E. E. (2016a). A study of cutting-edge performance management practices: Ongoing feedback, ratingless reviews and crowdsourced feedback. *WorldatWork Journal, 25*(2), 8–24.

Ledford, G. E., Benson, G., & Lawler, E. E. (2016b). *Cutting-edge performance management: 244 organizations report on ongoing feedback, ratingless reviews and crowdsourced feedback.* WorldatWork.

Ledford, G. E. Jr., & Benson, G. (2019). *Ratingless performance reviews: A quasi-experiment.* https://ceo.usc.edu/wp-content/uploads/2019/11/Ratingless-Performance-Reviews-G19-04-695.pdf

Lee, C., Lin, Y., Huan, H., Huang, W., & Teng, H. (2015). The effects of task interdependence, team cooperation, and team conflict on job performance. *Social Behavior and Personality: An International Journal, 43*(4), 529–536.

Lee, J. A., Havighurst, L. C., & Rassel, G. (2004). Factors related to court references to performance appraisal fairness and validity. *Public Personnel Management, 33,* 61–77.

Lerner, M. J. (1982). The justice motive in human relations and the economic model of man: A radical analysis of facts and fictions. In V. Derlega & J. Grezlak (Eds.),

Cooperation and helping behavior: Theories and research (pp. 121–145). Academic Press.

Leventhal, G. S. (1976). The distribution of rewards and resources in groups and organizations. In L. Berkowitz & E. Walster (Eds.), *Equity theory: Toward a general theory of social interaction, Advances in experimental social psychology* (Vol. 9, pp. 92–131). Academic Press.

Leventhal, G. S., Karuza, J., & Fry, W. R. (1980). Beyond fairness: A theory of allocation preferences. In J. Mikula (Ed.), *Justice and social interaction* (pp. 167–218). Springer-Verlag.

Leventhal, G. S., Michaels, J. W., & Sanford, C. (1972). Inequity and interpersonal conflict: Reward allocation and secrecy about reward as methods of preventing conflict. *Journal of Personality and Social Psychology, 23*, 88–102.

Levine, D. (1989). Efficiency wages in Weitzman's share economy. *Industrial Relations, 28*, 321–333.

Levine, E. L., Ash, R. A., Hall, H., & Sistrunk, F. (1983). Evaluation of job analysis methods by experienced job analysts. *Academy of Management Journal, 26*, 339–347.

Lewin, D. (2003). Incentive compensation in the public sector: Evidence and potential. *Journal of Labor Research, 24*, 597–619.

Lievens, F., Anseel, F., Harris, M., & Eisenberg, J. (2007). Measurement invariance of the pay satisfaction questionnaire across three countries. *Educational and Psychological Measurement, 67*(6), 1042–1051. https://ink.library.smu.edu.sg/lkcsb_research/5654

Lincoln, J. F. (1951). *Incentive management.* The Lincoln Electric Company.

Locher, A. H., & Teel, K. S. (1988, September). Assessment: Appraisal trends. *Personnel Journal, 67*, 139–145.

Locke, E. A. (1968). Towards a theory of task motivation and incentives. *Organizational Behavior and Human Performance, 3*, 157–189.

Locke, E. A. (1976). The nature and causes of job satisfaction. In M. D. Dunnette (Ed.), *Handbook of industrial and organizational psychology* (pp. 297–349). Rand McNally.

Locke, E. A., Bryan, J. F., & Kendall, L. M. (1968). Goals and intentions as mediators of the effects of monetary incentives on behavior. *Journal of Applied Psychology, 52*, 104–121.

Locke, E. A., Feren, D. B., McCaleb, V. M., Shaw, K. N., & Denny, A. J. (1980). The relative effectiveness of motivating employee performance. In K. D. Duncan, M. M. Gruneberg, & D. Wallis (Eds.), *Changes in working life* (pp. 363–388). Wiley.

Locke, E. A., & Latham, G. P. (1990). *A theory of goal-setting and task performance.* Prentice Hall.

Locke, E. A., & Latham, G. P. (2002). Building a practically useful theory of goal setting and task motivation: A 35-year odyssey. *American Psychologist, 57*, 705–717.

Locker, C., & Teague, J. (2024). Assessing the role of generational conflict in the performance appraisal process. *Journal of Behavioral and Applied Management, 24*(1), 3–13. https://jbam.scholasticahq.com/

Longenecker, C. O., & Nykodym, N. (1996). Public sector performance appraisal effectiveness: A case study. *Public Personnel Management, 25*, 151–164.

Longenecker, C. O., Sims, H. P. Jr., & Gioia, D. A. (1987). Behind the mask: The politics of employee appraisal. *Academy of Management Executive, 1*, 183–193.

Lowery, C. M., Beadles, N. A. II, Petty, M. M., Amsler, G. M., & Thompson, J. W. (2002). An empirical examination of a merit bonus plan. *Journal of Managerial Issues, 14*, 100–117.

Lowery, C. M., Petty, M. M., & Thompson, J. W. (1996). Assessing the merits of merit pay: Employee reactions to performance-based pay. *Human Resource Planning, 19*, 26–37.

Lump-sum salary increases. (1983). *Small Business Report, 8*(6), 9–10.

Luthans, F., & Kreitner, R. (1975). *Organizational behavior modification*. Scott, Foresman.

Luthans, F., & Kreitner, R. (1985). *Organization behavior modification and beyond*. Scott, Foresman.

Luthans, F., & Stajkovic, A. D. (1999). Reinforce for performance: The need to go beyond pay and even rewards. *Academy of Management Executive, 13*, 49–57.

Magnusen, K. O. (1987). Faculty evaluation, performance, and pay—Application and issues. *Journal of Higher Education, 58*, 516–529.

Mahoney, T. A. (1964). Compensation preferences of managers. *Industrial Relations, 3*, 135–144.

Majors, B. (1988). Gender, justice, and the psychology of entitlement. *Review of Personality and Social Psychology, 7*, 124–148.

Maley, J. F., Dabic, M., & Moeller, M. (2021). Employee performance management: Charting the field from 1998 to 2018. *International Journal of Manpower, 42*(1), 131–149. https://doi.org/10.1108/IJM-10-2019-0483

Malmi, T., & Ikäheimo, S. (2003). Value-based management practices—Some evidence from the field. *Management Accounting Review, 14*, 235–254.

Malos, S. B. (1998). Current legal issues in performance appraisal. In J. W. Smither (Ed.), *Performance appraisal: State of the art in practice* (pp. 49–94). Jossey-Bass.

Maltarich, M. A., Nyberg, A. J., Reilly, G., Abdulsalam, D. D., & Martin, M. (2017). Pay-for-performance, sometimes: An inter-disciplinary approach to integrating economic rationality with psychological emotion to predict individual performance. *Academy of Management Journal, 60*(6), 2155–2174. https://doi.org/10.5465/amj.2015.0737

Mamun, A., & Mansor, S. (2012). EVA as superior performance measurement tool. *Modern Economy, 3*, 310–318. https://doi.org/10.4236/me.2012.33041

Mani, B. G. (2002). Performance appraisal systems, productivity, and motivation: A case study. *Public Personnel Management, 31*, 141–159.

March, J. G., & Olson, J. P. (1983). Organizing political life: What administrative organization tells us about government. *American Political Science Review, 77*(6), 281–296.

Markels, A., & Berton, L. (1996, April 11). Executive pay: Something to talk about. *Wall Street Journal*. Eastern Edition, R10.

Markham, S. E. (1988). Pay-for-performance dilemma revisited: Empirical example of the importance of group effects. *Journal of Applied Psychology, 73*, 172–180.

Marriott, R. (1962). An exploratory study of merit rating payment systems in three factories. *Occupational Psychology, 36*, 179–214.

Marsden, D., & Sezer, L. A. (2024). Appraisal process, merit pay and performance: Evidence from a longitudinal survey of school teachers in England and Wales. *British Journal of Industrial Relations*. https://doi.org/10.1111/bjir.12869

Martin, D. C. (1987). Factors influencing pay decisions: Balancing managerial vulnerabilities. *Human Relations, 40,* 417–430.

Martin, D. C., & Bartol, K. M. (1991). The legal ramifications of performance appraisal: An update. *Employee Relations Law Journal, 17,* 257–286.

Martin, D. C., Bartol, K. M., & Kehoe, P. E. (2000). The legal ramifications of performance appraisal: The growing significance. *Public Personnel Management, 29,* 379–406.

Martin, D. C., Bartol, K. M., & Levine, M. J. (1987). The legal ramifications of performance appraisal. *Employment Relations Law Journal, 26,* 12–16.

Martinez, M. N. (1994, August). Lump-sum payments may replace merit increases. *HR Magazine, 39,* 20–24.

Martocchio, J. J. (2023). *Strategic compensation: A human resource management approach* (7th ed.). Pearson Prentice-Hall.

Mathur, S., & Padmakumari, P. (2013). Organizational justice and organizational citizenship behavior among store executives. *Human Resource Management Research, 3*(4), 124–149. https://doi.org/10.5923/j.hrmr.20130304.02

McBriarty, M. A. (1988). Performance appraisal: Some unintended consequences. *Public Personnel Management, 17,* 421–433.

McCormick, M. (2023). Promoting change in the face of retrenchment. *FIU Law Review, 17,* 807–832. https://doi.org/10.25148/lawrev.17.4.9

McCowen, R. A., Bowen, U., Huselid, M. A., & Becker, B. E. (1999). Strategic human resource management at Herman Miller. *Human Resource Management, 38,* 303–308.

Mcdonald, D., & Smith, A. (1995). A proven connection: Performance management and business results. *Compensation & Benefits Review, 27*(1), 59–64.

McDonnell Douglas Corporation. (1987). *Merit review notes.* Author.

McKinsey, R. (2025, July 21). *How to tackle merit increases when part of your workforce is maxed out.* Workspan Daily, WorldatWork. https://worldatwork.org/publications/workspan-daily/how-to-tackle-merit-increases-when-part-of-your-workforce-is-maxed-out

McMullen, T., & Aladag, S. (2023, October 19). Pay transparency: A closer look at the risks, rewards and regulations. *WorldatWork.* https://worldatwork.org/publications/workspan-daily/pay-transparency-a-closer-look-at-the-risks-rewards-and-regulations

Medoff, J. L., & Abraham, M. G. (1980). Experience, performance, and earnings. *Quarterly Journal of Economics, 95,* 703–736.

Medoff, J. L., & Abraham, K. G. (1981). Are those paid more really more productive? The case of experience. *Journal of Human Resources, 16,* 186–216.

Meindl, J. R. (1989). Managing to be fair: An exploration of values, motives, and leadership. *Administrative Science Quarterly, 34,* 252–276.

Meisler, A. (2003, July). Dead man's curve. *Workforce Management,* 44–49.

Mello, J. A. (2002). *Strategic human resource management.* South-Western.

Meng, F., & Wu, J. (2015). Merit pay fairness, leader-member exchange, and job engagement: Evidence from Mainland China. *Review of Public Personnel Administration, 35*(1), 47–69.

Mento, A. J., Steel, R. P., & Karren, R. J. (1987). A meta-analytic study of goal setting on task performance: 1966–1984. *Organizational Behavior and Human Decision Processes, 39,* 52–83.

Mercer. (2003). *U.S. compensation planning survey.* Mercer Human Resource Consulting.

Merit pay systems in the public sector: A tale of two cities (1984). *Management Review, 73*(10), 46–47.

Meyer, H. H. (1975). The pay-for-performance dilemma. *Organizational Dynamics, 3*(1), 55–61.

Meyer, H. H. (1987). How can we implement a pay-for-performance policy successfully? In D. B. Balkin & L. R. Gomez-Meija (Eds.), *New perspectives on compensation* (pp. 179–186). Prentice Hall.

Meyer, H. H., Kay, E., & French, J. R. P. (1965). Split roles in performance appraisal. *Harvard Business Review, 43*, 123–129.

Meyer, H. H., & Walker, W. B. (1961). Need for achievement and risk preference as they relate to attitudes toward reward systems and performance appraisal in an industrial setting. *Journal of Applied Psychology, 51*, 251–256.

Meyers, L. S., Gamst, G., & Guarino, A. J. (2016). *Applied multivariate research: Design and interpretation* (3rd ed.). Sage.

Miceli, M. P., & Lane, M. C. (1991). Antecedents of pay satisfaction: A review and extension. In K. M. Rowland & G. R. Ferris (Eds.), *Research in personnel and human resources management* (Vol. 9, pp. 235–309). JAI Press.

Miceli, M. P., & Mulvey, P. W. (2000). Consequences of satisfaction with pay systems: Two field studies. *Industrial Relations, 39*(1), 62–87.

Miceli, M. P., & Near, J. P. (1988). Correlates of satisfaction with pay level and pay system in pay-for-performance plans. In Paper presented at the National Academy of Management meetings, Anaheim, CA.

Milanowski, A. T. (2005). Split roles in performance evaluation—A field study involving new teachers. *Journal of Personnel Evaluation in Education, 18*, 153–169. https://doi.org/10.1007/s11092-006-9017-0

Miles, E. W., Hatfield, J. B., & Huseman, R. C. (1994). Equity sensitivity and outcome importance. *Journal of Organizational Behavior, 15*(7), 585–596.

Miles, R. E., & Snow, C. C. (1978). *Organizational strategy, structure, and process.* McGraw-Hill.

Milkovich, G. T. (1987). Compensation systems in high-technology companies. In D. B. Balkin & L. R. Gomez-Meija (Eds.), *New perspectives on compensation* (pp. 269–277). Prentice Hall.

Milkovich, G. T., & Newman, J. M. (2002). *Compensation* (7th ed.). McGraw-Hill/Irwin.

Miller, D., & Friesen, P. H. (1984). A longitudinal study of the corporate life cycle. *Management Science, 30*, 1161–1183.

Miller, E. C. (1979). Pay for performance. *Personnel, 15*(7), 4–11.

Miller, J. S. (2003). High tech and high performance: Managing appraisal in the information age. *Journal of Labor Research, 24*, 409–424.

Miller, R. A. (2001). Firms' cost functions: A reconstruction. *Review of Industrial Organization, 18*, 183–200.

Mincer, M. G. (1977). Job absence and turnover: A new source of data. *Monthly Labor Review, 100*(10), 24–31.

Miner, J. B. (1980). *Theories of organizational behavior.* Dryden.

Minken, S. L. (1988). Does lump-sum pay merit attention? *Personnel Journal, 67*(6), 77–83.

Minority employees call for GM boycott. (1989, June 26). *The Ohio State Lantern,* 2.

Mitchell, D. J. B. (1989). *Human resource management: An economic approach.* PWS-KENT.
Mitchell, D. J. B., Lewin, D., & Lawler, E. E. III (1990). Alternative pay systems, firm performance, and productivity. In A. S. Blinder (Ed.), *Paying for Productivity. A look at the evidence* (pp. 15–94). The Brookings Institution.
Mitchell, T. R. (1974). Expectancy models of job satisfaction, occupational preference, and effort: A theoretical, methodological, and empirical appraisal. *Psychological Bulletin, 81,* 1053–1077.
Mitra, A., Gupta, N., & Jenkins, Jr., G. D. (1997). A drop in the bucket: When is a pay raise a pay raise? *Journal of Organizational Behavior, 18,* 117–137.
Mitra, A., Tenhiälä, A., & Shaw, J. D. (2015). Smallest meaningful pay increases: Field test, constructive replication, and extension. *Human Resource Management, 55*(1), 69–81.
Mobley, W. H. (1982). *Employee turnover: Causes, consequences, and control.* Addison-Wesley.
Mohamed, A. A., Mohamad, M. S., & Awad, A. E. (2017). The relationship between pay satisfaction and turnover intention in Egypt. *Journal of Competitiveness Studies, 25*(1), 65–79.
Mohrman, A. J. Jr., Resnick-West, S. M., & Lawler, E. E. III (1989). *Designing performance appraisal systems.* Jossey-Bass.
Molloy, P. J. (1989). *Press release.* General Motors Corporation.
Montemayer, E. F. (1994, Winter). Aligning pay systems with market strategies. *ACA Journal,* 44–53.
Montemayor, E. F. (2003). Decisional and interactional fairness: Supervisor influence on merit pay satisfaction. *Management Research, 1*(2), 145–160.
Moore, M. L., & Heneman, R. L. (1983). *Performance assessment and critical skills model for the rehabilitation management system.* Office of Management Practices, Department of Management and Budget, State of Michigan.
Moran, P. F. (1986). Equitable salary administration in high-tech companies. *Compensation and Benefits Review, 18*(5), 31–40.
Morgeson, F., Brannick, M. T., & Levine, E. L. (2020). *Job and work analysis: Methods, research and applications for human resource management.* Sage.
Morin, D., Murphy, K. R., & Larocque, A. (1999). The relationship between performance appraisal and indulgence in the evaluation process. *Industrial Relations, 54,* 694–726.
Morris, D. (2016). Adobe reinvents its customer service. *MIT Sloan Management Review.* May 3. https://sloanreview.mit.edu/article/adobe-reinvents-its-customer-experience/
Mount, M. K. (1987). Coordinating salary action and performance appraisal. In D. B. Balkin & L. R. Gomez-Mejia (Eds.), *New perspectives on compensation* (pp. 187–195). Prentice Hall.
Mowday, R. T. (1979). Equity theory predictions of behavior in organizations. In R. M. Steers & L. W. Porter (Eds.), *Motivation and work behavior* (2nd ed., pp. 124–146). McGraw-Hill.
Mueller-Hanson, R. (2020). Driving organizational strategy through performance management. In E. D. Pulakos & M. Battista (Eds.), *Performance management transformation: Lessons learned and next steps* (pp. 289–317).
Mulvey, P. W. (1991). *Pay system satisfaction: An exploration of the construct and predictors.* Unpublished doctoral dissertation. Ohio State University.

Mulvey, P. W., LeBlanc, P. V., Heneman, R. L., & McInerney, M. (2002). *The knowledge of pay study: E-mails from the frontline.* WorldatWork.
Mun, E., & Kodama, N. (2022). Meritocracy at work? Merit-based reward systems and gender wage inequality. *Social Forces, 100*(4), 1561–1591.
Murdock, K. (2002). Intrinsic motivation and optimal incentive contracts. *The RAND Journal of Economics, 33*, 650–671.
Murphy, K. R. (2021). Life after COVID-19: What if we never go back to the office? *The Irish Journal of Management, 40*(2), 78–85.
Murphy, K. R., & Balzer, W. K. (1989). Rater errors and rating accuracy. *Journal of Applied Psychology, 74*, 619–624.
Murphy, K. R., & Cleveland, J. N. (1991). *Performance appraisal: An organization's perspective.* Allyn & Bacon.
Murphy, K. R., & Cleveland, J. N. (1999). *Understanding performance appraisal: Social, organizational, and goal-based perspectives.* Sage.
Murphy, K. R., Cleveland, J. N., & Hanscom, M. (2019). *Performance appraisal and management.* Sage.
Murphy, K. R., Garcia, M., Kerkar, S., Martin, C., & Balzer, W. K. (1982). Relationship between observational accuracy and accuracy in evaluating performance. *Journal of Applied Psychology, 67*, 320–325.
Načinović Braje, I., & Kuvač, A. (2022). Pay transparency and its effects: A comparative analysis of public and private sector. *Revija za socijalnu politiku, 29*(1), 35–50.
Nadler, D. A. (1998, March 15). Ten steps to a happy merger. *New York Times*, 3–14.
Nalbantian, H. R. (1987). Incentive compensation in perspective. In H. R. Nalbantian (Ed.), *Incentives, cooperation, and risk sharing* (pp. 3–43). Rowman & Littlefield.
Napier, N. K., & Latham, G. P. (1986). Outcome expectancies of people who conduct performance appraisals. *Personnel Psychology, 39*, 827–837.
Nathan, B. R., & Cascio, W. F. (1986). Technical and legal standards. In R. A. Berk (Ed.), *Performance assessment* (pp. 1–50). Johns Hopkins Press.
Nathan, B. R., & Tippins, N. (1990). The consequences of halo "error" in performance ratings: A field study of the moderating effect of halo on test validation results. *Journal of Applied Psychology, 75*, 290–296.
National Research Council. (1991). *Pay-for-performance: Evaluating performance appraisal and merit pay.* National Academy Press.
Naughton, I. L. (1990, August 31). Chrysler's merit raises rile UAW. *Detroit News*, 1.
Nigro, L. G. (1981). Attitudes of federal employees toward performance appraisal and merit pay: Implications for CSRA implementation. *Public Administration Review, 41*, 84–86.
NLRB v. Main Street Terrace Care Center. (2000). *218 F.3d 531 (Sixth Circuit).*
Nobile, R. J. (1996). How discrimination laws affect compensation. *Compensation & Benefits Review, 28*(4), 38–42.
Noonan, L. E., & Sulksy, L. M. (2001). Impact of frame-of-reference and behavioral observation training on alternative training effectiveness criteria in a Canadian military sample. *Human Performance, 14*, 3–26.
Nunnally, J. C., & Bernstein, I. H. (1994). *Psychometric theory* (3rd ed.). McGraw-Hill.
Nyberg, A. (2010). Retaining your high performers: Moderators of the performance–job satisfaction–voluntary turnover relationship. *Journal of Applied Psychology, 95*(3), 440–453. https://doi.org/10.1037/a0018869

Nyberg, A. J., Pieper, J. R., & Trevor, C. O. (2016). Pay-for-performance's effect on future employee performance: Integrating psychological and economic principles toward a contingency perspective. *Journal of Management, 42*(7), 1753–1783. https://doi.org/https://doi-org.libproxy.uww.edu/10.1177/0149206313515520

O'Dell, C. O. (1987). *Major findings from people, performance, and pay*. American Productivity Center and American Compensation Association.

O'Hara, K., Johnson, C. M., & Baehr, T. A. (1985). Organizational behavior management in the private sector: A review of empirical research and recommendations for further investigation. *Academy of Management Review, 10*, 848–864.

O'Toole, D. E., & Churchill, J. R. (1982). Implementing pay-for-performance: Initial experiences. *Review of Public Personnel Administration, 2*(3), 13–28.

Obloj, T., & Zenger, T. (2022). The influence of pay transparency on (gender) inequity, inequality and the performance basis of pay. *Nature Human Behaviour, 6*(5), 646–655. https://doi.org/10.1038/s41562-022-01288-9

Ockenfels, A., Sliwka, D., & Werner, P. (2024). *Multi-rater performance evaluations and incentives*. IZA Discussion Paper No. 16812. https://doi.org/10.2139/ssrn.4736397

Omar, A., Salessib, S., Vaamonde, J. D., & Urteaga, F. (2018). Psychometric properties of Colquitt's organizational justice scale in Argentine workers. *Liberabit. Revista Peruana de Psicología, 24*(1). https://doi.org/10.24265/liberabit.2018.v24n1.05

O'Neill, C., & Holsinger, L. (2003, Second Quarter). Effective performance management systems: 10 key design principles. *WorldatWork Journal*, 61–67.

Orben, A. (2020). The Sisyphean cycle of technology panics. *Perspectives on Psychological Sciences, 15*(5), 1143–1157.

Ordine, B. (1990, October 29). QB ratings confounding, controversial. *Columbus Dispatch*, 4C.

O'Reilly, C. A., Main, B. G., & Crystal, G. S. (1988). CEO compensation as tournament and social comparison: A tale of two theories. *Administrative Science Quarterly, 33*(2), 257–274. https://doi.org/10.2307/2393058

Organ, D. W. (1988). *Organizational citizenship behavior: The good soldier syndrome*. D. C. Heath.

Organ, D. W. (1997). Organizational citizenship behavior: It's construct clean-up time. *Human Performance, 10*, 85–97.

Osburn, H. G., Timmreck, C., & Bigby, D. (1981). Effect of dimensional relevance on accuracy of hiring decisions by employment interviewers. *Journal of Applied Psychology, 67*, 320–325.

Ott, J. S. (1989). *The organizational culture perspective*. Dorsey Press.

Overstreet, J. S. (1985). The case for merit bonuses. *Business Horizons, 15*(3), 53–58.

Pacific Gas & Electric Co. (1989). *The 1989 management incentive program and information on the 1989 merit plan and the performance recognition program*. Author.

Padgett, M. Y., & Ilgen, D. R. (1989). The impact of ratee performance characteristics on rater cognitive processes and alternative measures of rater accuracy. *Organizational Behavior and Human Decision Processes, 44*, 232–260.

Pagano, M. A. (1985). An exploratory evaluation of the Civil Service Reform Act's merit pay system for GS 13-158: A case study of the U.S. Department of Health and Human Services. In D. H. Rosenbloom (Ed.), *Public personnel policy: The politics of civil service* (pp. 161–182). Associated Academic Press.

Palley, T. I. (2001). The stock market and investment: Another look at the microfoundations of q theory. *Cambridge Journal of Economics, 25*, 657–667.

Palmer & Dodge LLC. (2001, Winter). Employers cannot prohibit employees from discussing wages. *Labor and Employment Review*. http://www.palmerdodge.com/dspSingleArticle.cfm?ArticleID=340#3

Parco, J. E., Rapoport, A., & Stein, W. E. (2002). Effects of financial incentives on the breakdown of mutual trust. *Psychological Science, 13*, 292–297.

Park, S., & Sturman, M. C. (2012). How and what you pay matters: The relative effectiveness of merit pay, bonuses and long-term incentives on future job performance. *Compensation & Benefits Review, 44*(2), 80–85. https://doi.org/10.1177/0886368712450391

Park, S., & Sturman, M. C. (2016). Evaluating form and functionality of pay-for-performance plans: The relative incentive and sorting effects of merit pay, bonuses, and long-term incentives. *Humam Resource Management, 55*, 697–719. https://doi.org/10.1002/hrm.21740

Park, S., & Sturman, M. C. (2022). When perception is reality, there is more than one reality: The formation and effects of pay-for-performance perceptions. *Personnel Psychology, 75*(3), 529–555. https://doi.org/10.1111/peps.12466

Pasteur, R. D., & David, J. A. (2017). Evaluation of quarterbacks and kickers. In *Handbook of statistical methods and analyses in sports* (pp. 181–198). Chapman and Hall/CRC.

Patten, T. H. Jr. (1976). Linking financial rewards to employee performance: The roles of OD and MBO. *Human Resource Management, 15*(1), 2–17.

Patten, T. H. Jr. (1977). Pay for performance or placation? *The Personnel Administrator, 22*(9), 26–29.

Pearce, J. L. (1987). Why merit pay doesn't work: Implications from organization theory. In D. B. Balkin & L. R. Gomez-Mejia (Eds.), *New perspectives on compensation* (pp. 169–178). Prentice Hall.

Pearce, J. L., & Perry, J. L. (1983). Federal merit pay: A longitudinal analysis. *Public Administration Review, 43*, 315–325.

Pearce, J. L., & Porter, L. W. (1986). Employee responses to formal performance appraisal feedback. *Journal of Applied Psychology, 71*, 211–218.

Pearce, J. L., Stevenson, W. B., & Perry, J. L. (1985). Managerial compensation based on organizational performance: A time series analysis of the effects of merit pay. *Academy of Management Journal, 28*, 261–278.

Pearsall, M., Christian, M., & Ellis, P. (2010). Motivating independent teams: Individual rewards, shared rewards, or something in between? *Journal of Applied Psychology, 95*(1), 183–191.

Peck, C. (1984). *Pay and performance; the interaction of compensation and performance appraisal*. Research Bulletin No. 155. The Conference Board.

Perkins, S. J., & Jones, S. (2020). *Reward management: Alternatives, consequences and contexts*. Kogan Page Publishers.

Perry, J. L. (1986). Merit pay in the public sector: The case for a failure of theory. *Review of Public Personnel Administration, 7*(1), 57–69.

Perry, J. L. (1988). Making policy by trial and error: Merit pay in the federal service. *Policy Studies Journal, 17*(2), 389–405.

Perry, J. L., Hanzlik, M. C., & Pearce, J. L. (1982). Effectiveness of merit pay-pool management. *Review of Public Personnel Administration, 2*(3), 5–12.

Perry, J. L., & Pearce, J. L. (1983). Initial reactions to federal merit pay. *Personnel Journal, 62*(3), 230–237.

Perry, J. L., & Pearce, J. L. (1985). Civil service reform and the politics of performance appraisal. In D. H. Rosenbloom (Ed.), *Public personnel policy: The politics of civil service* (pp. 146–160). Associated Academic Press.

Perry, J. L., & Petrakis, B. A. (1987). Can merit pay improve performance in government? In Paper presented at the Annual Research Conference of the Association for Public Policy Analysis and Management.

Perry, J. L., & Petrakis, B. A. (1988). Can pay for performance succeed in government? *Public Personnel Management, 17,* 359–366.

Perry, J. L., Petrakis, B. A., & Miller, T. K. (1989). Federal merit pay, Round II: An analysis of the performance management and review system. *Public Administration Review, 49,* 29–37.

Perry, T. A. (1990). Staying within the basics. *HR Magazine, 35*(11), 73–76.

Personiak, M. E. (1984). White-collar pay determination under range-of-rate systems. *Monthly-Labor Review, 107*(12), 25–30.

Personnel Policies Forum. (1981). *Wage and salary administration.* PPF Survey No. 131. Bureau of National Affairs.

Peters, R., & Atkin, R. (1980). The effects of open pay systems on allocation of salary increases. *Academy of Management Proceedings, 40,* 293–297.

Pettijohn, L. S., Parker, R. S., Pettijohn, C. E., & Kent, J. L. (2001). Performance appraisals: Usage, criteria and observations. *Journal of Management Development, 20*(9/10), 754–771.

Pfeffer, J. (1998). Six dangerous myths about pay. *Harvard Business Review, 76,* 108–120.

Pfeffer, J., & Langton, N. (1993). The effect of wage dispersion on satisfaction, productivity, and working collaboratively: Evidence from college and university faculty. *Administrative Science Quarterly, 38,* 382–407.

Pham, L. D., Nguyen, T. D., & Springer, M. G. (2021). Teacher merit pay: A meta-analysis. *American Educational Research Journal, 58*(3), 527–566. https://doi.org/10.3102/0002831220905580

Pierce, J. L., Gardner, D. G., Cummings, L. L., & Dunham, R. B. (1989). Organization-based self-esteem: Construct definition, measurement, and validation. *Academy of Management Journal, 32*(3), 622–648.

Piszczalski, M. (2002). GM's smart new portal. *Automotive Design & Production, 114*(2), 14–15.

Ployhart, R. E., Lim, B. C., & Chan, K. Y. (2001). Exploring relations between typical and maximum performance ratings and the five-factor model of personality. *Personnel Psychology, 54,* 809–843.

Podolske, A. (1996). Tools for defending pay-for-performance against the skeptics. In *Pay-for-performance report* (pp. 1, 12–14). Institute for Management and Administration.

Podsakoff, N. P., Whiting, S. W., Podsakoff, P. M., & Blume, B. D. (2009). Individual- and organizational-level consequences of organizational citizenship behaviors: A meta-analysis. *Journal of Applied Psychology, 94*(1), 122–141.

Pollack, A. (1993, October 2). Japanese starting to link pay to performance. *New York Times*, A1.

Poole, M., & Jenkins, G. (1998). Human resource management and the theory of rewards: Evidence from a national survey. *British Journal of Industrial Relations, 36*, 227–247.

Porter, L. W., & Lawler, E. E. III (1968). *Managerial attitudes and behavior.* Irwin.

Porter, G., Greenberger, D. B., & Heneman, R. L. (1990). Pay and pay satisfaction: A comparison of economic, political, psychological, and psychophysical predictions. *Academy of Management Best Paper Proceedings, 50*, 289–293.

Porter, M. E. (1980). *Competitive strategy.* Free Press.

Posthuma, R. A., Campion, M. C., & Campion, M. A. (2018). A taxonomic foundation for evidence-based research on employee performance management. *European Journal of Work and Organizational Psychology, 27*(2), 168–187. https://doi.org/10.1080/1359432X.2018.1438411

Pouliakas, K., & Theodoropoulos, N. (2010). *Variety of performance pay and firm performance: Effect of financial incentives on worker absence and productivity.* MPRA Paper No. 18820. https://mpra.ub.uni-muenchen.de/18820/

Powell, D., & Lorenz, R. (2019, September). The effect of team size on the performance of continuous improvement teams: Is seven really the magic number? In *IFIP international conference on advances in production management systems (APMS), Austin, TX, United States* (pp. 69–76). https://doi.org/10.1007/978-3-030-30000-5_9

Prince, J. B., & Lawler, E. E. III (1986). Does salary discussion hurt the developmental performance appraisal? *Organizational Behavior and Human Decision Processes, 37*, 357–375.

Pritchard, R. D. (1990). *Measuring and improving organizational productivity: A practical guide.* Praeger.

Pritchard, R. D., Jones, S. D., Roth, P. L., Stubing, K. K., & Ekeberg, S. E. (1989). The evaluation of an integrated approach to measuring organizational productivity. *Personnel Psychology, 42*, 69–115.

Pulakos, E. D., & Battista, M. (Eds.). (2020). *Performance management transformation: Lessons learned and next steps.* Oxford University Press.

Pulakos, E. D., Mueller-Hanson, R., & Arad, S. (2019). The evolution of performance management: Searching for value. *Annual Review of Organizational Psychology and Organizational Behavior, 6*, 249–271.

Pulakos, E., Mueller-Hanson, R. A., & O'Leary, R. S. (2023). Performance management in the United States. In *Performance management systems* (pp. 123–147). Routledge.

Pulakos, E. D., & O'Leary, R. S. (2011). Why is performance management broken? *Industrial and Organizational Psychology, 4*(2), 146–164. https://doi.org/10.1111/j.1754-9434.2011.01315.x

Pulakos, E. D., Schmitt, N., & Ostroff, C. (1986). A warning about the use of a standard deviation across dimensions within ratees to measure halo. *Journal of Applied Psychology, 71*, 29–32.

Quinn, J. B. (1991, June 3). The hard new facts of pay. *Newsweek*, 44.

Quiñones, M. A., Ford, J. K., & Teachout, M. S. (1995). The relationship between work experience and job performance: A conceptual and meta-analytic review. *Personnel Psychology, 48*, 887–910.

Raff, D. M. G., & Summers, L. H. (1987). Did Henry Ford pay efficiency wages? *Journal of Labor Economics, 5*, 557–586.

Rainey, H. G. (1979). Perceptions of incentives in business and government: Implications for civil service reform. *Public Administration Review, 39*, 440–448.

Ramaswami, S. N., & Singh, J. (2003). Antecedents and consequences of merit pay fairness for industrial salespeople. *Journal of Marketing, 67*, 46–66.

Rambo, W. W., Chomiak, A. M., & Price, J. M. (1983). Consistency of performance under stable conditions at work. *Journal of Applied Psychology, 68*, 78–87.

Rambo, W. W., & Pinto, J. N. (1989). Employees' perceptions of pay increases. *Journal of Occupational Psychology, 62*, 135–145.

Rees, A. (1992). The tournament as a model for executive compensation. *Journal of Post Keynesian Economics, 14*(4), 567–571. https://doi.org/10.1080/01603477.1992.11489918

Rheem, H. (1995, May/June). Performance management: A progress report. *Harvard Business Review, 73*(3), 11–12.

Rhodes, S. R., & Steers, R. M. (1990). *Managing employee absenteeism.* Addison-Wesley.

Risher, H. (1992). Paying employees for quality. In *Perspectives in total compensation.* American Compensation Association.

Risher, H. (1997). The search for a new model for salary management: Is there support for private sector practices? *Public Personnel Management, 26*, 431–0439.

Risher, H. (1999a). Are public employees ready for a "new pay" program? *Public Personnel Management, 28*, 323–343.

Risher, H. (1999b). Merit pay can be a hard sell. *Public Management, 81*(7), 8–13.

Risher, H. (2000). Compensating today's technical professional. *Resource Technology Management, 43*, 50–56.

Risher, H. (2002). Pay-for-performance: The keys to making it work. *Public Personnel Management, 31*, 317–332.

Roberts, G. E. (1996). A case study in performance appraisal system development: Lessons from a municipal police department. *American Review of Public Administration, 26*, 361–385.

Rock, R. H. (1983). Pay for performance: A concept in search of standards. *Directors and Boards, 7*(3), 15–17.

Rock, R. H. (1988). Performance management: Chasing the right bottom line. In R. L. Rock (Ed.), *Handbook of wage and salary administration* (pp. 311–322). McGraw-Hill.

Rosen, C. C., Kacmar, K. M., Harris, K. J., Gavin, M. B., & Hochwarter, W. A. (2017). Workplace politics and performance appraisal: A two-study, multilevel field investigation. *Journal of Leadership & Organizational Studies, 24*(1), 20–38. https://doi.org/10.1177/1548051816661480

Rosen, C. C., Slater, D. J., Chang, C. H., & Johnson, R. E. (2013). Let's make a deal: Development and validation of the ex post i-deals scale. *Journal of Management, 39*(3), 709–742.

Rosen, S. (1985). Implicit contracts: A survey. *Journal of Economic Literature, 23*, 1144–1175.

Rothe, H. F. (1946). Output rates among butter wrappers: I. Work curves and their stability. *Journal of Applied Psychology, 30*, 199–211.

Rothe, H. F. (1978). Output rates among industrial workers. *Journal of Applied Psychology, 63*, 40–46.

Rothstein, H. R. (1990). Interrater reliability of job performance ratings: Growth to asymptote level with increasing opportunity to observe. *Journal of Applied Psychology, 75*, 322–327.

Rousseau, D. M., & Ho, V. T. (2000). Psychological contract issues in compensation. In S. L. Rynes & B. Gerhart (Eds.), *Compensation in organizations: Current research and practice* (pp. 273–310). Jossey-Bass.

Rousseau, D., Ho, V., & Greenberg, J. (2006). I-deals: Idiosyncratic terms in employment relationships. *Academy of Management Review, 31*, 977–993. https://doi.org/10.5465/AMR.2006.22527470

Rozelle, R. M., & Baxter, J. C. (1981). Influence of role pressures on the perceiver: Judgments of videotaped interviews varying judge accountability and responsibility. *Journal of Applied Psychology, 66*, 437–441.

Rubin, A. M., & Elkouri, F. (2004). *Elkouri & Elkouri: How arbitration works* (6th ed.). BNA Books.

Ruffini, R., Modarelli, G., Sferrazzo, R., Turri, M., & Bisogno, M. (2020). Is merit pay changing ethos in public administration? *Cogent Business & Management, 7*(1), 1–17. https://doi.org/10.1080/23311975.2020.1724703

Saal, F. E., Downey, R. G., & Lahey, M. A. (1980). Rating the ratings: Assessing the psychometric quality of rating data. *Psychological Bulletin, 88*, 413–428.

Sackett, P. R., Zedeck, S., & Fogli, L. (1988). Relations between measures of typical and maximum job performance. *Journal of Applied Psychology, 73*, 482–486.

Salamin, A., & Hom, P. W. (2005). In search of the elusive U-shaped performance-turnover relationship: Are high performing Swiss bankers more liable to quit? *Journal of Applied Psychology, 90*(6), 1204–1216.

Salimäki, A., & Jämsén, S. (2010). Perceptions of politics and fairness in merit pay. *Journal of Managerial Psychology, 25*(3), 229–251. https://doi.org/10.1108/02683941011023721

Salop, S. C. (1979). A model of the natural rate of unemployment. *American Economic Review, 69*, 117–125.

Salvemini, N. J., Reilly, R. R., & Smither, J. W. (1993). The influence of rater motivation on assimilation effects and accuracy in performance ratings. *Organizational Behavior and Human Decision Processes, 55*(1), 41–60.

Sanchez, J. I., & Levine, E. L. (2009). What is (or should be) the difference between competency modeling and traditional job analysis? *Human Resource Management Review, 19*(2), 53–63.

Sauley, K. S., & Bedeian, A. G. (2000). Equity sensitivity: Construction of a measure and examination of its psychometric properties. *Journal of Management, 26*(5), 885–1010.

Scarpello, V. (1988). Pay satisfaction and pay fairness: Are they the same? In Paper presented at the Third Annual Conference of the Society for Industrial and Organizational Psychology (Division 14 of the American Psychological Association), Dallas, TX.

Scarpello, V., & Campbell, J. P. (1983). Job satisfaction: Are all the parts there? *Personnel Psychology, 36*, 577–600.

Scarpello, V., Huber, V., & Vandenberg, R. J. (1988). Compensation satisfaction: Its measurement and dimensionality. *Journal of Applied Psychology, 73*, 163–171.

Scarpello, V., & Jones, F. F. (1996). Why justice matters in compensation decision making. *Journal of Organizational Behavior, 17*(3), 285–299.

Schaubroeck, J., Shaw, J., Duffy, M., & Mitra, A. (2008). An under-met and over-met expectations model of employee reactions to merit raises. *Journal of Applied Psychology, 93*, 424–434. https://doi.org/10.1037/0021-9010.93.2.424

Schay, B. W. (1988). Effects of performance-contingent pay on employee attitudes. *Public Personnel Management, 17*(2), 237–250.

Schay, B. W. (2002). The history of merit pay experiments and their evaluation in the federal government. In Paper presented at the Society for Industrial and Organizational Psychology Conference, Toronto.

Scheele, A. (1991, January). How to get the raise you want (no matter what the boss says at first). *Working Woman, 71*.

Scheller, E. M., & Harrison, W. (2018). Ignorance is bliss, or is it? The effects of pay transparency, informational justice and distributive justice on pay satisfaction and affective commitment. *Compensation & Benefits Review, 50*(2), 65–81. https://doi.org/10.1177/0886368719833215

Schellhardt, T. D. (1996, November 19). It's time to evaluate your work, and all involved are groaning. *Wall Street Journal*, A1.

Schermling, D., & Scaduto, A. (2016). Use the best; leave the rest: The productivity measurement and enhancement system (ProMES) for performance ratings. *Industrial and Organizational Psychology, 9*(2), 305–309.

Scheulen, K. C., Lawler, E. E. III, & Hackman, J. R. (1971). Long-term impact of employee participation in the development of pay incentive plans: A field experiment revisited. *Journal of Applied Psychology, 55*, 182–186.

Schleicher, D. J., & Day, D. V. (1998). A cognitive evaluation of frame-of-reference rater training: Content and process issues. *Organizational Behavior and Human Decision Processes, 73*, 76–101.

Schlesinger, J. M. (1988, January 26). GM's new compensation plan reflects general trend tying pay to performance. *Wall Street Journal*, 1.

Schmidt, F. L., & Hunter, J. E. (2015). *Methods of meta-analysis*. Sage.

Schmidt, F. L., Hunter, J. E., Outerbridge, A. N., & Goff, S. (1988). Joint relation of experience and ability with job performance: Test of three hypotheses. *Journal of Applied Psychology, 73*, 46–57.

Schmidt, F. L., Hunter, J. E., & Pearlman, K. (1982). Assessing the economic impact of personnel programs on workforce productivity. *Personnel Psychology, 35*, 333–346.

Schmitt, N. W., & Klimoski, R. J. (1991). *Research methods in human resource management*. South-Western.

Schmitt, N. W., & Stults, D. M. (1986). Methodology review: Analysis of multitrait-multimethod matrices. *Applied Psychological Measurement, 10*, 1–22.

Schneider, B., & Olson, L. K. (1970). Effort as a correlate of organizational reward system and individual values. *Personnel Psychology, 23*, 313–326.

Schneier, C. E. (1974). Behavior modification: A review and critique. *Academy of Management Journal, 17*, 528–548.

Schneier, C. E. (1989a). Implementing performance management and recognition and rewards (PMRR) systems at the strategic level: A line management-driven effort. *Human Resource Planning, 12*(3), 205–220.

Schneier, C. E. (1989b). Capitalizing on performance management, recognition, and reward systems. *Compensation and Benefits Review, 22*(2), 20–30.

Scholl, R. W., Cooper, E. A., & McKenna, J. F. (1987). Referent selection in determining equity perceptions: Differential effects on behavioral and attitudinal outcomes. *Personnel Psychology, 40*, 113–124.

Schrøder-Hansen, K., & Hansen, A. (2023). Performance management trends–reflections on the redesigns big companies have been doing lately. *International Journal of Productivity and Performance Management, 72*(5), 1201–1220.

Schuster, J. R., Colletti, J. A., & Knowles, L. Jr. (1973). The relationship between perceptions concerning magnitudes of pay and the perceived utility of pay: Public and private organizations compared. *Organizational Behavior and Human Performance, 9*, 110–119.

Schwab, D. P. (1980). Construct validity in organizational behavior. In L. L. Cummings & B. M. Staw (Eds.), *Research in organizational behavior* (Vol. 2, pp. 1–37). JAI Press.

Schwab, D. P. (1988). Predicting salary levels and salary increments: An examination of merit system inequities. In D. P. Schwab (Chair) (Ed.), *Determinants and consequences of merit pay programs: Interorganizational illustrations.* (Symposium conducted at the Annual Academy of Management Meetings, Anaheim, CA).

Schwab, D. P., Olian-Gottlieb, J., & Heneman, H. G. III (1979). Between subjects expectancy theory research. *Psychological Bulletin, 86*, 139–147.

Schwab, D. P., & Olson, C. A. (1990). Merit pay practices: Implications for pay performance relationships. *Industrial and Labor Relations Review, 43*(3 Special Issue), 2375–2565.

Schwab, D. P., & Olson, C. A. (2000). Simulating effects of pay-for-performance systems on pay–performance relationships. In D. R. Ilgen & C. L. Hulin (Eds.), *Computational modeling of behavior in organizations: The third scientific discipline* (pp. 115–127). American Psychological Association.

Schwadel, F. (1990, July 5). Chain finds incentives a hard sell. *Wall Street Journal*, Bl–B4.

Schweyer, A. (2021, September). *Academic research in action: Individual or team-based incentives?* Incentive Research Foundation Report (pp. 1–8). https://theirf.org/research_post/academic-research-in-action-individual-or-team-based-incentives/

Scott, D., Tenhiälä, A., Karaeminogullari, A., & Varma, A. (2023). The employee perspective on pay transparency. *The Journal of Total Rewards, 32*(3), 28–39.

Scott, D. W., Hills, F. S., Markham, S. E., & Vest, M. J. (1987). Evaluating a pay-for-performance program at a transit authority. In Paper presented at the National Academy of Management Meetings, New Orleans, LA.

Scott, K. D., Markham, S. E., & Vest, M. J. (1996). The influence of a merit pay guide chart on employee attitudes toward pay at a transit authority. *Public Personnel Management, 25*, 103–117.

Scott, K. L., Shaw, J. D., & Duffy, M. K. (2008). Merit pay raises and organization-based self-esteem. *Journal of Organizational Behavior, 29*(7), 967–980.

Scott, W. E. Jr., Farh, J. L., & Podsakoff, P. M. (1988). The effects of "intrinsic" and "extrinsic" reinforcement contingencies on task behavior. *Organizational Behavior and Human Decision Processes, 41*, 405–425.

Seals, D. (1984). Making employee pay a strategic issue. *Financial Executive, 52*(10), 40–41.

Seamster, T. L., Redding, R. E., & Kaempf, G. L. (2017). *Applied cognitive task analysis in aviation.* Routledge.

Segal, J. A. (2004, March). Labor pains for union-free employers. *HR Magazine, 49*(3), 113–118.

Seithal, W. W., & Emens, J. S. (1983). Calculating merit increases: A structured approach. *Personnel, 36*(5), 56–68.

Shadish, W. R., Cook, T. D., & Campbell, D. T. (2002). *Experimental and quasi-experimental designs for generalized causal inference.* Houghton Mifflin.

Shaw, J. D., Duffy, M. K., Mitra, A., Lockhart, D. E., & Bowler, M. (2003). Reactions to merit pay increases: A longitudinal test of a signal sensitivity perspective. *Journal of Applied Psychology, 88,* 538–544.

Shaw, J. D., Gupta, N., & Delery, J. E. (2002). Pay dispersion and workforce performance: Moderating effects of incentives and interdependence. *Strategic Management Journal, 23,* 491–512.

Shenoy, A. (2021, December 6). The merit-based incentive payment system: Pearson's chi-square and categorical dependent variable models analyzed for domains-effective clinical care and efficiency/cost reduction. *Journal of Health Economical Outcomes Research, 8*(2), 93–104.

Sherer, P. D., Schwab, D. P., & Heneman, H. G. III (1987). Managerial salary-raise decisions: A policy capturing approach. *Personnel Psychology, 40,* 27–38.

Shields, J. (2002). Performance related pay in Australia. In M. Brown & J. S. Heywood (Eds.), *Paying for performance: An international comparison* (pp. 179–213). M.E. Sharpe.

Shippmann, J. S., Ash, R. A., Battista, M., Carr, L., Eyde, L. D., Hesketh, B., & Sanchez, J. I. (2000). The practice of competency modeling. *Personnel Psychology, 53,* 703–740.

Shorter, A. A. (2002). The effects of performance rating labels in merit pay systems. In Paper presented at the Society for Industrial and Organizational Psychology Conference, Toronto.

Sibson and Company, Inc. (1989). *Compensation planning survey, 1989.* Author.

Silverman, B. R. S. (1981). Developmental pay: Forerunner to merit pay in the federal government. *Compensation Review, 13*(2), 25–36.

Silverman, B. R. S. (1983). Why the merit pay system failed in the federal government. *Personnel Journal, 62*(4), 294–302.

Silverman, S. B., & Wexley, K. N. (1984). Reaction of employees to performance appraisal interviews as a function of their participation in scale development. *Personnel Psychology, 37,* 703–710.

Simons, R., & Reinbergs, I. A. (2000). *Vyaderm pharmaceuticals case.* Harvard Business School Press.

Singh, R., Yoo, S., Park, S., Chaudhuri, S., & Sihag, P. (2024). State of the art on high performance work systems research: A bibliometrics study. *Human Resource Development Review.* https://doi.org/10.1177/15344843241301668

Skinner, B. F. (1953). *Science and human behavior.* McMillan.

Smith, D. E. (1986). Training programs for performance appraisal: A review. *Academy of Management Review, 11,* 22–40.

Smith, M. L., O'Dowd, E. J., & Christ, G. M. (1987). Pay for performance: One company's experience. *Compensation and Benefits Review, 18,* 19–27.

Smith, P. C., & Kendall, L. M. (1963). Retranslation of expectations: An approach to the construction of unambiguous anchors for rating scales. *Journal of Applied Psychology, 47,* 149–155.

Smith, P. C., Kendall, L. M., & Hulin, C. L. (1969). *The measurement of satisfaction in work and retirement.* Rand McNally.

Snell, S. A., & Dean, J. W. Jr. (1992). Integrated manufacturing and human resource management: A human capital approach. *Academy of Management Journal, 35,* 467–504.

Sovereign, K. L. (1989). *Personnel law* (2nd ed.). Prentice Hall.

St-Onge, S. (2000). Variables influencing the perceived relationship between performance and pay in a merit pay environment. *Journal of Business and Psychology, 14,* 459–479.

Stajkovic, A. D., & Luthans, F. (1997). A meta-analysis of the effects of organizational behavior modification on task performance, 1975–95. *Academy of Management Journal, 40,* 1122–1149.

Stajkovic, A. D., & Luthans, F. (2001). Differential effects of incentive motivators on work performance. *Academy of Management Journal, 44,* 580–590.

Stajkovic, A. D., & Luthans, F. (2003). Behavioral management and task performance in organizations: Conceptual background, meta-analysis, and test of alternative models. *Personnel Psychology, 56,* 155–194.

Stayer, R. (1990). How I learned to let my workers lead. *Harvard Business Review, 68*(6), 65–72.

Sterling, C. L. (1990). *A utility analysis framework for merit pay systems.* Unpublished manuscript. Ohio State University.

Stern Stewart & Co. (2004). *About EVA.* http://www.sternstewart.com/evaabout/evacomp.php. Accessed on February 18, 2004.

Stevens, S. S. (1959). Measurement, psychophysics, and utility. In C. W. Churchman & P. Ratoosh (Eds.), *Measurement: Definitions and theories* (pp. 18–63). Wiley.

Stiglitz, J. E. (1987). The design of labor contracts: The economics of incentives and risk sharing. In H. R. Nalbantian (Ed.), *Incentives, cooperation, and risk sharing* (pp. 47–68). Rowman & Littlefield.

Stimel, D. (2009). A statistical analysis of NFL quarterback rating variables. *Journal of Quantitative Analysis in Sports, 5*(2). https://doi.org/10.2202/1559-0410.1166

Stofberg, R., Mabaso, C. M., & Bussin, M. H. R. (2022). Employee responses to pay transparency. *SA Journal of Industrial Psychology, 48*(1), 1–12. https://doi.org/10.4102/sajip.v48i0.1906

Stokes, D. M. (1981). A new mathematical approach to merit-based compensation systems. *Compensation Review, 18*(4), 43–55.

Stonich, P. J. (1984). The performance measurement and reward system: Critical to strategic management. *Organizational Dynamics, 16,* 45–57.

Sturman, M. C. (2003). Searching for the inverted U-shaped relationship between time and performance: Meta-analyses of the experience/performance, tenure/performance, and age/performance relationships. *Journal of Management, 29,* 609–640.

Sturman, M. C., Shao, L., & Katz, J. H. (2012). The effect of culture on the curvilinear relationship between performance and turnover. *Journal of Applied Psychology, 97*(1), 46–62.

Sturman, M. C., & Short, J. C. (2000). Lump-sum bonus satisfaction: Testing the construct validity of a new pay satisfaction dimension. *Personnel Psychology, 53,* 673–700.

Sturman, M. C., Trevor, C. O., Boudreau, J. W., & Gerhart, B. (2003). Is it worth it to win the talent war? Evaluating the utility of performance-based pay. *Personnel Psychology, 56*, 997–1035.

Subedi, M., & Farazmand, A. (2020). Economic value added (EVA) for performance evaluation of public organizations. *Public Organization Review, 20*(4), 613–630. https://doi.org/10.1007/s11115-020-00493-2

Sullivan, J. F. (1988). The future of merit pay programs. *Compensation and Benefits Review, 20*(3), 22–30.

Sulsky, L. M., & Balzer, W. K. (1988). Meaning and measurement of performance rating accuracy: Some methodological and theoretical concerns. *Journal of Applied Psychology, 73*, 497–506.

Sulsky, L. M., Skarlicki, D. P., & Keown, J. L. (2002). Frame-of-reference training: Overcoming the effects of organizational citizenship behavior on performance rating accuracy. *Journal of Applied Social Psychology, 32*, 1224–1240.

Swaby, L., Shu, P., Hind, D., & Sutherland, K. (2022). The use of cognitive task analysis in clinical and health services research - A systematic review. *Pilot Feasibility Studies., 8*(1), 57. https://doi.org/10.1186/s40814-022-01002-6

Sweeney, K. (2003, October). Studies reveal conflicting trends among wages, benefits. *Employee Benefit News*, 11–13.

Tambe, P., Cappelli, P., & Yakubovich, V. (2019). Artificial intelligence in human resource management: Challenges and a path forward. *California Management Review, 61*(4), 15–42.

Tatum, B. C. (2018). *Measuring up: Personnel and organizational assessment.*

Tatum, B. C., & Nebeker, D. M. (2002). A strategic approach to measuring organizational performance: Tools for the consulting psychologist. In R. L. Loman (Ed.), *Handbook of organizational consulting psychology* (pp. 668–691). Jossey-Bass/ John Wiley.

Tatum, B. C., Nebeker, D. M., & De Young, P. H. (1996). *Using performance indexing to measure organizational gains in white collar environments (NPRDC TR-96-27).* Navy Personnel Research and Development Center.

Taylor, P. J., & Pierce, J. L. (1999). Effects of introducing a performance management system on employees' subsequent attitudes and effort. *Public Personnel Management, 28*(3), 423–452.

Teel, M. S. (1986). Are merit raises really based on merit? *Personnel Journal, 64*(3), 88–95.

Tenhiala, A., & Jamsen, S. (2010). Perceptions of politics and fairness in merit pay. *Journal of Managerial Psychology, 25*, 229–251.

Terborg, J. R. (1976). The motivational components of goal setting. *Journal of Applied Psychology, 61*(5), 613–621.

Terborg, J. R., & Miller, H. E. (1978). Motivation, behavior, and performance: A closer examination of goal setting and monetary incentives. *Journal of Applied Psychology, 63*(1), 29–39.

Terry, R. J. (2003, June 25). Strike averted: Sun union accepts labor deal in 319-102 vote. *Baltimore Business Journal.* http://baltimore.bizjournals.com/baltimore/stories/2003/06/23/daily24.html. Accessed on January 13, 2004.

Terwiesch, C., & Ulrich, K. T. (2009). *Innovation tournaments: Creating and selecting exceptional opportunities.* Harvard Business School Press.

Terwiesch, C., & Xu, Y. (2008). Innovation contests, open innovation, and multiagent problem solving. *Management Science, 54*(9), 1529–1543.

Tesluk, P. E., & Jacobs, R. R. (1998). Toward an integrated model of work experience. *Personnel Psychology, 51*, 321–355.

Tetlock, P. E., & Goldgeier, J. M. (2000). Human nature and world politics: Cognition, identity, and influence. *International Journal of Psychology, 35*, 87–96.

Thaler, R. H. (1989). Interindustry wage differentials. *The Journal of Economic Perspectives, 3*(2), 181–193.

Thomas, L., Ambrosini, V., & Hughes, P. (2019). The role of organizational citizenship behaviour and rewards in strategy effectiveness. *The International Journal of Human Resource Management, 30*(18), 2628–2660.

Thomas, S. L., & Bretz, R. D. (1994). Research and practice in performance appraisal: Evaluating employee performance in America's largest companies. *SAM Advanced Management Journal, 59*(2), 28–34.

Thorndike, R. L. (1949). *Personnel selection.* Wiley.

Timp, S., van Foreest, N. D., & van Rhenen, W. (2024). Effect of financial incentives on the cost and duration of sickness absence. *PLoS One, 19*(6). https://doi.org/10.1371/journal.pone.0305235

Tobin, J. (1985). Neoclassical theory in America: J.B. Clark and Fisher. *American Economic Review, 75*(6), 28–38.

Todd, J. T., Thompson, P. H., & Dalton, G. W. (1974). Management control of personnel. *Journal of Accountancy, 137*, 34–40.

Trevor, C. (2017, February 22). *Rethinking the merits of merit pay and other pay-for-performance tools.* Faculty Insights, Wisconsin School of Business.

Tripathi, M., Ghalke, A., & Kashiramka, S. (2024). Exploring value relevance of EVA over different stages of business lifecycle. *International Journal of Organizational Analysis.* https://doi.org/10.1108/IJOA-06-2024-4596

Tripathi, P. M., Chotia, V., Solanki, U., Meena, R., & Khandelwal, V. (2023). Economic value added research: Mapping thematic structure and research trends. *Risks, 11*(1), 9. https://doi.org/10.3390/risks11010009

Tubbs, M. E. (1986). Goal setting: A meta-analytic examination of the empirical evidence. *Journal of Applied Psychology, 71*, 474–483.

Turban, D. B., & Jones, A. P. (1988). Supervisor-subordinate similarity: Types, effects and mechanisms. *Journal of Applied Psychology, 73*, 228–234.

Two automakers resume merit pay increases. (1981). *Monthly Labor Review, 104*(7), 47.

Tziner, A., & Kopelman, R. E. (2002). Is there a preferred performance rating format? A non-psychometric perspective. *Applied Psychology—An International Review, 51*(3), 479–503.

Ubelhart, M. C. (1990). What goes 'round comes 'round:. The emergence of shareholder value measures in executive compensation. *Compensation and Benefits Management, 6*, 313–318.

Ullah, Z., Ahmad, N., Scholz, M., Ahmed, B., Ahmad, I., & Usman, M. (2021). Perceived accuracy of electronic performance appraisal systems: The case of a non-for-profit organization from an emerging economy. *Sustainability, 13*(4), 2109. https://doi.org/10.3390/su13042109

Ungson, G. R., & Steers, R. M. (1984). Motivation and politics in executive compensation. *Academy of Management Review, 9*, 313–323.

University of New Mexico Human Resources Department. (2003). http://www.unm.edu/hr/comp/increase.htm. Accessed on January 15, 2004.

U.S. Congress. (1981, September 11). *Serious problems need to be corrected before federal merit pay goes into effect.* Report of the Comptroller General of the United States. FPCD-81-73. https://www.gao.gov/products/fpcd-81-73

U.S. General Accounting Office. (1981). *Serious problems need to be corrected before federal merit pay goes into effect (FPCD-81-73).* Author.

U.S. General Accounting Office. (1984). *A two-year appraisal of merit pay in three agencies (GGD-84-1).* U.S. Government Printing Office.

U.S. General Accounting Office. (1987). *Pay for performance: Implementation of the performance management and recognition system (GGD-87 28).* U.S. Government Printing Office.

U.S. Merit Systems Protection Board. (1981, June). *Status report on performance appraisal and merit pay among mid-level employees.* Author.

U.S. Merit Systems Protection Board. (1987). *Performance management and recognition system: Linking pay to performance.* Author.

U.S. Merit Systems Protection Board. (1988). *Toward effective performance management in the federal government.* Author.

U.S. Office of Personnel Management. (1987). *Performance management and recognition system.* Author.

U.S. Office of Personnel Management. (1988). *Performance management and recognition system: FY1986 performance cycle.* Author.

Van Adelsberg, H. (1978). Relating performance evaluation to compensation of public-sector employees. *Public Personnel Management,* 7(2), 72–79.

Van Buren, M. E., & Werner, J. M. (1995, October–December). High performance work systems. *Business & Economic Review, 43*(1), 15–23.

Van den Broeck, A., Vansteenkiste, M., De Wittle, H., Soenens, B., & Lens, W. (2010). Capturing autonomy, competence, and relatedness at work: Construction and initial validation of the work-related basic needs satisfaction scale. *Journal of Occupational and Organizational Psychology, 83,* 981–1002.

van Dijke, M., de Cremer, D., Bos, A. E. R., & Schefferlie, P. (2009). Procedural and interpersonal fairness moderate the relationship between outcome fairness and acceptance of merit pay. *European Journal of Work and Organizational Psychology, 18*(1), 8–28. https://doi.org/10.1080/13594320701856699

van Raaij, W. F. (1999). Economic psychology between psychology and economics: An introduction. *Applied Psychology—An International Review, 48*(3), 263–272.

van Saane, J. K., Sluiter, J. H., Verbeek, A. M., & Frings-Dresen, M. H. (2003). Reliability and validity of instruments measuring job satisfaction—A systematic review. *Occupational Medicine, 53,* 191–200. https://doi.org/10.1093/occmed/kqg038

Varadarajan, P., & Futrell, C. (1984). Factors affecting perceptions of smallest meaningful pay increases. *Industrial Relations, 23,* 278–286.

Varma, A., Budhwar, P. S., & DeNisi, A. (Eds.). (2023). *Performance management systems.* Routledge.

Varma, A., DeNisi, A. S., & Peters, L. H. (1996). Interpersonal affect and performance appraisal: A field study. *Personnel Psychology, 49,* 341–360.

Vecchio, R. P., & Terborg, J. R. (1987). Salary increment allocation and individual differences. *Journal of Occupational Behavior, 8*, 37–43.

Velghe, C., McIlquham-Schmidt, A., Celik, P., Storme, M., & Spiegelaere, S. (2024). PROTOCOL: Employee work motivation, effort, and performance under a merit pay system: A systematic review. *Campbell Systematic Reviews-Wiley*. https://doi.org/10.1002/cl2.70001

Vest, M. J., Hills, F. S., & Scott, M. D. (1989). Determinants of instrumentality beliefs in a merit pay system. In Paper presented at the National Academy of Management Meetings, Washington, DC.

Vest, M. J., Scott, K. D., Vest, J. M., & Markham, S. E. (2000). Factors influencing employee beliefs that pay is tied to performance. *Journal of Business and Psychology, 14*, 553–562.

Vinchur, A. J., Schippmann, J. S., Smalley, M. D., & Rothe, H. Y. (1991). Productivity consistency of foundry chippers and grinders: A six year field study. *Journal of Applied Psychology, 7*(6), 134–136.

Vines, L. S. (1989). GM offers $3 million to settle suit. *Human Resource Executive, 3*(3), 8.

Vroom, V. H. (1964). *Work and motivation*. Wiley.

Waldman, S., & Roberts, B. (1988, November 14). Grading merit pay. *Newsweek*, 45–46.

Walker, D. O., & Larson, M. (2025). Leveraging generative artificial intelligence (AI) for human resource management: The AI job description assignment. *Journal of Management Education, 49*(1).

Wallace, J. S. (1997). Adopting residual income-based compensation plans: Do you get what you pay for? *Journal of Accounting and Economics, 24*, 275–300.

Wallace, M. J. (1990). *Rewards and renewal: America's search for competitive advantage through alternative pay strategies*. American Compensation Association.

Wang, M., Burlacu, G., Truxillo, D., James, K., & Yau, X. (2015). Age differences in feedback reactions: The roles of employee feedback orientation on social awareness and utility. *Journal of Applied Psychology, 100*(4), 1296–1308.

Wang, S., & Chen, Y. (2022). Aligning incentives with interdependence: A study of team-based reward systems in collaborative work environments. *Academy of Management Perspectives, 36*(4), 489–505.

Wanous, J. P., Keon, T. L., & Latack, J. C. (1983). Expectancy theory and occupational/organizational choices: A review and test. *Organizational Behavior and Human Performance, 32*, 66–86.

Webb, L., Glover, L., & Roberts, B. (2024, July 19). The great debate: Are merit increases effective or not? *Mercer Blog*. https://www.imercer.com/articleinsights/merit-increases#:~:text=The%20merit%20process%20is%20incredibly,all%2C%20often%20to%20be%20disappointed

Weekly, J. A., & Gier, J. A. (1989). Ceilings in the reliability and validity of performance ratings: The case of expert raters. *Academy of Management Journal, 32*, 213–222.

Weeks, D. A. (1976). *Compensating employees: Lessons from the 1970's (Report No. 707)*. The Conference Board.

Weiner, N. (1980). Determinants and behavioral consequences of pay satisfaction: A comparison of two models. *Personnel Psychology, 33*, 741–757.

Weiss, D. J., Dawis, R. V., England, G. W., & Lofquist, L. H. (1967). Manual for the Minnesota satisfaction questionnaire. *Minneapolis: Minnesota Studies in Vocational Rehabilitation, Bulletin, 45.*

Welbourne, T. M., & Cable, D. M. (1995). Group incentives and pay satisfaction: Understanding the relationship through an identity theory perspective. *Human Relations, 48,* 711–726.

Wen, H. J., & Anandarajan, A. (1998). Intranet: A cost reduction tool for corporate publication. *Industrial Management & Data Systems, 98*(5), 200–204.

Werner, J. M. (1994). Dimensions that make a difference: Examining the impact of in-role and extrarole behaviors on supervisory ratings. *Journal of Applied Psychology, 79,* 98–107.

Werner, J. M. (1998). Employment discrimination cases in U.S. Courts of Appeals: A brief commentary on Mollica. *Employee Rights and Employment Policy Journal, 2*(1), 255–265.

Werner, J. M. (2000). Implications of OCB and contextual performance for human resource management. *Human Resource Management Review, 10,* 3–24.

Werner, J. M. (2021). Chapter 4: Linking pay to performance via merit pay. In D. Cafaro (Ed.), *The WorldatWork handbook of total rewards: A comprehensive guide to compensation, benefits, HR & employee engagement* (2nd ed.). John Wiley & Sons.

Werner, J. M. (2022). *Human resource development/talent development* (8th ed.). Cengage.

Werner, J. M. (2024). The C.A.S.E. for HR: Practices and pillars of human resource management and development. In T. S. Rocco, M. L. Morris, & R. Poell (Eds.), *Handbook of human resource development* (2nd ed., pp. 661–671). Sage.

Werner, J. M., & Bolino, M. C. (1997). Explaining U.S. Courts of Appeals decisions involving performance appraisal: Accuracy, fairness, and validation. *Personnel Psychology, 50,* 1–24.

Wexley, K. N., & Youtz, M. A. (1985). Raters' beliefs about others: Their effects on rating errors and rating accuracy. *Journal of Occupational Psychology, 58,* 265–275.

White, M. (2004, March). Does your intranet have a win–win strategy? *EContent, 27*(3), 41.

Whyte, W. F. (1955). *Money and motivation.* Harper.

Wiersma, U., & Latham, G. P. (1986). The practicality of behavioral observation scales, behavioral expectation scales, and trait scales. *Personnel Psychology, 39,* 619–628.

Wildstrom, S. R. (1986, May 19). Reagan's bombshell for civil servants: Merit pay. *Business Week,* 61.

Wilkinson, J. G. (1993, Summer). Duke power integrates employee rewards and business vision of excellence. *National Productivity Review, 12*(3), 325–335.

Williams, M. L., & Dreher, G. F. (1992). Compensation system attributes and applicant pool characteristics. *Academy of Management Journal, 35,* 571–595.

Williams, S. E. (2010). *A meta-analytic view of performance-based pay systems.* An unpublished doctoral dissertation. Alliant International University.

Williams, S. E., & Werner, J. M. (2022). An examination of similarity between a costume designer and a production designer: Job analysis goes to Hollywood. *Compensation & Benefits Review, 54*(4), 127–139. https://doi.org/10.1177/08863687221077729

Wimperis, B. R., & Farr, J. L. (1979). The effects of task content and reward contingency upon task performance and satisfaction. *Journal of Applied Social Psychology, 9*(3), 229–249.

Wiscombe, J. (2001, August). Can pay for performance really work? *Workforce, 80*(8), 28–34.

Wiscombe, J. (2003, March). The cost of age discrimination. *Workforce, 82*(3), 20.

Wisdom, B., & Patzig, D. (1987). Does your organization have the right climate for merit? *Public Personnel Management, 16*(2), 127–133.

Wittman, B. (2003). Cisco systems puts its HR programs and processes on the line and reaps big productivity gains. *Journal of Organizational Excellence, 23*(1), 43–54.

Woehr, D. J., & Huffcutt, A. I. (1994). Rater training for performance appraisal: A quantitative review. *Journal of Occupational and Organizational Psychology, 67*, 189–205.

Wood, R. E., Atkins, P. W. B., & Bright, J. E. H. (1999). Bonuses, goals, and instrumentality effects. *Journal of Applied Psychology, 84*, 703–720.

WorldatWork. (2005–2024). *2005–2024 salary budget surveys.* WorldatWork, Inc.

WorldatWork. (2019). *2019 compensation programs and practices.* WorldatWork. https://worldatwork.org/media/CDN/dist/CDN2/documents/pdf/resources/research/CompensationProgramsandPractices.pdf

WorldatWork. (2020). *Pay transparency study.* WorldatWork, Inc. https://worldatwork.org/media/CDN/dist/CDN2/documents/pdf/resources/research/Survey-Brief-Pay-Transparency-Survey-Jan.-2020.pdf

WorldatWork. (2024). Could constructive communication combat compensation challenges? *Workspan Daily.* Rebecca McKinsey. WorldatWork, Inc. https://worldatwork.org/publications/workspan-daily/could-constructive-communication-combat-compensation-challenges-

Wright, P. M. (1989). Testing the mediating role of goals in the incentive-performance relationship. *Journal of Applied Psychology, 74*, 699–705.

Wright, P. M., Kacmar, K. M., McMahan, G. C., & DeLeeuw, K. (1995). P=*f*(m x a)–Cognitive ability as a moderator of the relationship between personality and job performance. *Journal of Management, 21*, 1129–1139.

Wyatt Company. (1987). *Salary management practices in the private sector.* U.S. Advisory Committee on Federal Pay in cooperation with the American Compensation Association.

Wyatt Company. (1989, Fourth Quarter). *Results of the 1989 Wyatt performance management survey* (pp. 4–18). The Wyatt Communicator.

Yang, J., Ma, J., & Li, L. (2023). The relationship between performance appraisal interval and employees' proactive working behavior–analysis based on time-gain effect and time-loss effect. *Frontiers in Psychology, 14*, 1213547. https://doi.org/10.3389/fpsyg.2023.1213547

Yoon, Y., & Sengupta, S. (2023). Need to cut or freeze pay of your employees? Providing work–life balancing practices can help if maintaining employee morale is a concern. *Employee Relations, 45*(4), 983–1008. https://doi.org/10.1108/ER-02-2022-0056

Young, S. D., & O'Byrne, S. F. (2001). *EVA® and value-based management: A practical guide to implementation.* McGraw-Hill.

Zedeck, S., & Smith, P. C. (1968). A psychophysical determination of equitable payment. *Journal of Applied Psychology, 52*, 343–347.

Zingheim, P. K., & Schuster, J. R. (2000). *Pay people right! Breakthrough reward strategies to create great companies.* Jossey-Bass.

INDEX

Absenteeism, 263
Absolute standards, 126–129
  behaviors, 127–128
  results, 129
  traits, 126, 126–127
Acceleration ratio, 256–257
Accountability, 240
Accuracy, 144–145
Actual correlation, 256
Actual employee performance, 145
Actual merit
  feedback on actual merit decisions, 234
  pay, 8
Actual pay-for-performance relationship, 181
Actual relationship, 181
  between pay and performance, 50–54
Actual size of merit increases, 177–178
Adequate performance, 123
  importance of adequate performance measures, 123–125
Adjustment system, 93–94
Administrative practices, 165–167
  amount of observation, 166
  diary keeping, 166
  time delay in ratings, 165–166
Age Discrimination in Employment Act, 243–244
Air traffic controllers, 96
Allocator(s), 192–193, 219
  developing manager, 240
  exceptional manager, 240
  feedback on actual merit decisions, 234
  fully competent manager, 240
  guide chart orientation, 233
  increasing motivation of, 239–240
  knowledge, 230–233
  merit increase exercise, 235–237
  policy capturing, 234
  role of, 230–240
  selection, 198
  training to improve allocator skills, 233–234
  values, 231–232
  weights used by allocators in hospital, 238
Alternative measures of performance for merit pay, 133–140
Alternative performance measures, policy guidelines for, 140
Alternatives or additions to merit pay, 108–114

monetary incentive plans, 109–113
nonmonetary rewards, 113–114
promotions, 108–109
Altruistic allocators, 231
American Compensation Association, 228–229
American Express, 193
Attention, 198–199, 209
Audit
data, 271
issues, 271
Australian survey, 9
Autonomous motivation, 38
Average ES, 55–58

"Balanced scorecard" approach, 84
Base pay, 39
Birthright, 93–94
Blue Cross of Southern California, pro-active auditing example, 272
Blue-collar jobs, 104
Boeing Helicopters, 95–96
Bottom-up models, 185–186
Brinkerhoff process, 155–156
Budget, adequacy of, 81–82
Budgeting issues, 184–187
considerations in establishing merit increase budgets, 187
gross *vs.* net costs, 187
overall size of budget, 186–187
top-down *vs.* bottom-up models, 185–186
uniform *vs.* flexible budgets, 185
Budgeting process, 184
Business strategy, 82, 82–84
Business units, 185
strategies, 83

Cash flow return on investment (CFROI), 267
Central tendency, 146
Cisco Systems, 229
Citizenships, 137–138
Civil Rights Acts, 241–243
Civil Service Reform Act, 245–247
Cognitive information, 234
Cognitive task analysis (CTA), 158
Communication, 220, 228
issues, 229–230
media, 228–229
Compa-ratio, 191–192, 255
Comparative salary ratios, 186, 191–192, 255
Compensation administrators, 27–28
Competency modeling, 158–159, 158–161
Competition, 93–94
Comprehensive Employment and Training Act (CETA), 81
Confidence intervals (CI), 299
Conoco, 193
Consistency, 143
Contamination, 147
Content
merit pay, 6
validity, 142, 149
Controlled motivation, 38
Conventional methods, 59–60
Convergent validity, 142–143
Cooperation, merit pay and, 65–66
Correctability, 216–217
Counter clerk, 13
CRS Sirrine, Inc., 179
Customer service, 14

Data collection procedures, 271–277
audit issues, 271
external validity, 274–275
internal validity, 272–274
practical illustration, 275–277
study design considerations, 272–277

Dayton-Hudson Corporation, 204
Defender organization, 82–83
Deficiency, 147
Deflation, 78–79
Diary keeping, 166
Discriminant validity, 142–143
Distant business unit outcomes, 264–267, 268
  legal compliance, 264
  unit performance, 266–267
  utility, 264–266
Distant individual employee outcomes, 260–264
  absenteeism, 263
  job performance, 260
  job satisfaction, 261
  pay satisfaction, 261–263
  turnover, 264
Distant past performance, 140
Distributive justice, 209–210, 257–258, 259–260
Dressler Seven-Step Process, 155–156

Earnings per share (EPS), 266
Economic aspects of merit pay context, 81–82
  budget adequacy, 81–82
  economy-level influences, 78–81
  firm-level influences, 81–82
  government subsidies, 81
  price stability, 78–79
  tax rates, 80–81
  wage/price guidelines, 79–80
Economic conditions, 77
Economic theories, 28, 39–48, 124
  efficiency wage theory, 43–45
  implicit contract theory, 41–43
  marginal productivity theory, 40–41
  sorting effects, 47–48
  tournament theory, 45–47
Economic value added (EVA), 83, 267
Economy, 81–82
Economy-level influences, 78–81
  price stability, 78–79
  tax rates, 80–81
  wage and price guidelines, 79–80
Efficiency wage theory, 40, 45, 48, 43–45, 151
Egalitarianism, 93–94
Employee stock ownership plan (ESOP), 80–81
Employee(s), 30–31, 31, 34, 43, 68–69, 78, 97–98, 105, 124, 128, 130, 135–136, 144, 161, 177–178, 179, 197, 204, 216, 255, 270, 273–274, 297–298
  behavior, 127
  motivation, 29, 107, 218
  outcomes, 275
  participation, 207
  performance, 126, 129, 193–194
  preferences, 102
  representation, 271
  satisfaction, 182–183
  traits, 126–127
  trust, 203–204
Employer(s), 33, 191, 248
  contributions, 179
  practices, 125, 163–164
Enterprise resource planning (ERP), 166–167
Environmental Protection Agency (EPA), 93
Equal Employment Opportunity Commission (EEOC), 244
Equal Pay Act, 243
Equity
  off job, 231
  theory, 33–36, 35–36, 48, 177
Evaluating merit pay outcomes

acceleration ratio, 256
assessment of performance management and recognition system, 293–294
comparative salary ratio, 255
criterion model, 254
data collection procedures, 271–277
distant business unit outcomes, 264–267
distant individual employee outcomes, 260–264
empirical studies on federal merit pay system, 290–292
concerning evaluation of outcomes for merit pay, 299–300
form of relationship between merit pay and outcomes, 268–270
immediate business unit outcomes, 255–256
immediate individual employee outcomes, 256–260
justice perceptions, 257–258
just-noticeable differences, 258
measure of pay-for-performance perceptions, 257
outcomes, 254–270, 296–300
outcomes based on meta-analysis, 298–299
pay and performance correlations, 256
pay fairness, 259–260
pay-for-performance perceptions, 257
performance ratio, 255–256
procedures, 277–296
relations among outcomes and need for multiple outcomes, 268
review of empirical studies evaluating merit pay plans, 277–300
reward ratio, 256
studies evaluating outcomes of merit pay plans, 278–289
Williams meta-analysis of merit pay effectiveness, 295
Evaluation process, 253–254
Evanston, Illinois, school district, 200
Exempt jobs, 98
Expectancy theory, 29, 29–31, 147
External validity, 274–275, 301

Face-to-face feedback, 240
Fair Labor Standards Act, 98
Federal Aviation Administration, 86–89
Federal Fair Labor Standards Act, 98
Federal guidelines, 80
Feedback-seeking behavior, 164
Firm-level influences, 81–82
adequacy of budget, 81–82
government subsidies, 81
Fixed-step systems, 192–193
Flexible budgets, 185
Florida Power Corporation, 199
Forced choice, 169
Forced distribution, 193, 193–194
Forced ranking, 193
Ford Motor Company, 136
Foster conflict, 62
Frame of reference (FOR), 164
Frequency-of-behavior scale, 127
Functional validity information, 239–240

Gender, 105–106
General Electric Company (GE), 66
General Motors Corporation, 9–10

Goal-setting theory, 36–37, 48, 127
Goldman Sachs, 193
Goodyear, and forced ranking, 24
Government subsidies, 81

Halo
  error, 145
  statistical control of, 168–170
Hard work, 7–8
Harley-Davidson, and merit pay, 95–96
Healthcare providers, 158
Hewlett-Packard, forced ranking, 24
Hierarchical linear model, 95
High performance work system, 101
High technology firms, 85
Higher-level salaried employees, 96
Highly-interdependent teams, 111
Highly-interdependent work, 111
Houston-based organization, 179
Human resource (HR), 161
  department, 5
  function, 146
  intervention, 275
  managers, 86
Human resource management (HRM), 1–2
  activities, 100
  practices, 100–101
Human systems, 91–92
Human-resource information system (HRIS), 186
Hybrid team-based financial incentives, 110

Idiosyncratic deals, 231–232
Immediate business unit outcomes, 255–256, 268
Immediate individual employee outcomes, 256–260, 268
Immediate performance, 140
Implicit contracts, 48
  theory, 41–43
Impression management, 230–231
In-group membership, 232–233
Incentive pay, 6, 7
  classification of merit pay and, 15, 16–18
  merit *vs.* forms of, 12–14
Income, 105
Indicator to evaluate performance standards, selecting, 149
Individually-based financial incentives, 110
Inflation, 266
Informational justice, 257–258
Institutional arrangements, 82–101, 302
  business strategy, 82–84
  human resource management practices, 100–101
  job characteristics, 97–99
  labor unions, 95–97
  organizational culture, 93–95
  organizational life-cycle, 91–92
  organizational politics, 99–100
  organizational structure, 92–93
  product or service markets, 84–91
Instrumentality theory, 29
Integrated reward strategy, 13–14
Interactional justice, 209–210, 219, 257–258
  importance of, 210–211
Internal consistency reliability, 143–144
Internal validity, 272–274. 301
Interpersonal justice, 257–258
Interrater reliability, 143–144
Intrinsic motivation, merit pay and, 63–65

Job Descriptive Index (JDI), 261
Job Openings and Labor Turnover Survey (JOLTS), 264

Job Training and Partnership Act (JTPA), 81
Job(s), 97–98, 104, 136
  analysis, 157–158
  characteristics, 97–99
  evaluation, 139, 187–188, 188–189
  level, 102–104, 138–139, 139
  performance, 182–183, 260
  satisfaction, 261
  type, 102–104
Johnsonville Foods of Wisconsin, 65–66
Just-noticeable differences (JNDs), 175, 175–177, 204, 258
Justice perceptions, 257–258

Knowledge, 230–233
  allocator values, grades, board scores, and idiosyncratic deals, 231–232
  equity off job, 231
  impression management, 230–231
  in-and out-group membership, 232–233

Labor Management Relations Act (1947), 220
Labor unions, 95–97
Large teams, 111–113
Larkin Company, 8
Leader-member exchange (LMX), 215
Legal compliance, 264
Leniency error, 145–146
Lincoln Electric, 13–14
Linear regression, 270
Local governments, 9
Locked-step systems, 192–193
Long-term goals, 133
Long-term incentives, 112
Loosely dependent teams, 111
Low technology firms, 85
Lump-sum bonus satisfaction, 182–183
Lump-sum merit pay plans, 182–183
Lump-sum plan, 181, 206

Management by objectives (MBO), 13, 129
Managers, 102
  preferences, 102
Marginal productivity theory, 40–41, 48
Market worth, 136–137
Marxian justice, 93–94
Matrix organizations, 198
Matthew effect, 68–69, 270
Maximum performance, 138
McDonnell Douglas Corporation, 228–229
Media, 228
Merit budgets, 186
Merit increase(s), 135–136, 175–176
  actual size of, 177–178
  earned-out approach, 182
  form of, 178–183
  gender, 105–106
  income and performance, 105
  job level and type, 102–104
  merit pay plan characteristics, 104–105
  motivation, 107
  no-strings approach, 182
  permanence of increase, 180–183
  preferences for, 102–107
  salary-advance approach, 182
  type of, 178–180
Merit may, 139
Merit pay, 1, 5–6, 6, 31, 33, 36, 65, 75, 77, 79, 92, 100, 100–101, 109, 123–124,

135, 156–157, 192–193, 233
alternative measures of performance for, 133–140
alternatives or additions to, 108–114
central themes, 20–21
classification of merit pay and incentive pay plans, 15, 16–18
and cooperation, 65–66
decisions, 160, 251
defined, 6–7
description of, 6–19
economic theories, 39–48
of equity, 68–70
first encounters with, 1–4
framework, 76–77, 77
frequency of use, 8–9
guide chart, 195
history of, 7, 7–8
immediate *vs.* distant past performance, 140
implementing merit pay policy, 198–199
importance of, 8–12
and intrinsic motivation, 63–65
job level, 138–139
as lag system, 199–200
as lead system, 200
market worth, 136–137
Matthew effect, 68–69
merit *vs.* forms of incentive pay, 12–14
normative model of merit pay process, 19, 19–20
organizational citizenship behavior, 137–138
overall effectiveness, 10–12
overreward inequity, 69–70
plan characteristics, 104–105
plan(s), 27–28, 82, 85, 97, 140, 199, 255
policy guidelines for alternative performance measures, 140
potential pitfalls with, 62–70
process, 2
promotions, 134
psychological theories, 28–39
research, 60
and self-esteem, 67, 66–68
seniority, 134–136
symbolic nature of, 9–10
system, 200
theories, 48–49
theories behind, 27–49
tough managerial decisions, 4–6
types of merit pay plans, 14–15
typical *vs.* maximum performance, 138
Merit pay administration
Age Discrimination in Employment Act, 243–244
appeals procedure, 216–218, 218
Civil Rights Acts, 241–243
Civil Service Reform Act/Merit Pay Reform Act, 245–247
communication media, 228–229
communications issues, 229–230
Equal Pay Act, 243
interactional justice, 219
laws and regulations, 240–247
major points, 247–248
merit pay communications, 218–230
National Labor Relations Act, 244–245
organizational justice, 209–216
pay transparency, 220–225
perceived accuracy of performance feedback, 219–220
role of allocator, 230–240
split roles *vs.* combined reviews, 225–228
Merit Pay Reform Act, 245–247

Merit pay settings/situational characteristics
alternatives or additions to merit pay, 108–114
business strategy, 82–84
economic considerations, 77–82
economy-level influences, 78–81
firm-level influences, 81–82
human resource management practices, 100–101
institutional arrangements, 82–101
job characteristics, 97–99
labor unions, 95–97
merit pay framework, 76–77, 77
organizational culture, 93–95
organizational life-cycle, 91–92
organizational politics, 99–100
organizational structure, 92–93
pay plan types, 107–108
preferences for merit increases, 102–107
product or service markets, 84–91
Merit plans, 89–90
Merit system, 6
Merit-based system, 62
Meta-analysis, 54–58, 132
moderator variables in, 58–61
outcomes based on, 298–299
Microsoft, forced ranking, 24
Minnesota Satisfaction Questionnaire (MSQ), 261
Mission statement, 151
Moderator variables, 54
in meta-analysis, 58–61
Monetary incentive plans, 109–113
highly-interdependent teams, 111
large teams, 111–113
loosely dependent teams, 111
small teams, 111
Monetary pay systems, 109
Motivation, 107
Motorola, 13–14
Multiple indicators, 149
Multiple regression, 214, 215, 224, 227

National Football League (NFL), 147
National Labor Relations Act (NLRA), 224–225, 244–245
National Labor Relations Board (NLRB), 224–225
National Research Council, 248–249
National surveys, 8–9
Negative leniency, 145–146
New merit-pay program, 58–59
Nixon administration, 79–80
Non-linear model, 95
Nonlinear regression analyses, 270
Nonlinear relationships, 270
Nonmonetary rewards, 113–114
Normative model of merit pay process, 19, 19–20

Objectives matrix (OMX), 156
Office of Personnel Management (OPM), 248–249, 256
One-shot case study, 272
Organization(s), 179–180, 183, 186, 189, 190–191, 193, 198, 204, 206, 241, 253–254, 259, 266, 271, 273–274
Organizational business units, 255
Organizational citizenship behavior (OCB), 137–138, 216
Organizational commitment, 211
Organizational communications, 229
Organizational culture, 93–95

Organizational decision-makers, 207
Organizational effectiveness, 223
model, 82–83
Organizational justice, 209–216, 257–258, 259
importance of procedural and interactional justice, 210–211
procedural justice and attitudes, 212–214
procedural justice and behavior, 215–216
procedural justice rules applied to merit pay, 212
research, 211–212
rules, 211
theory, 209–210
Organizational life cycle, 82, 91–92
theory, 92
Organizational policy, 195
Organizational politics, 99–100
Organizational recognition, 177
Organizational structure, 92–93
Organizational-based self-esteem (OBSE), 68
Out-group membership, 232–233
Overpayed employee, 69
Overreward inequity, 69–70

Pacific Gas and Electric Company, 72
Participation, 202–203, 204, 207
in plan development, 201–203
in scale development, 161–162
Pay, 27, 34–35, 40, 76, 93–94, 100, 124, 125–126
correlations, 256
fairness, 202–203, 224, 259–260
level theories, 28
levels, 28
pay-for-performance relationship, 49–62
plan types, 107–108
potential pitfalls with merit pay, 63, 62–70
ranges, 189–191, 190
rates, 189
review of theory and research, 27
satisfaction, 202–203, 211, 261–263, 297–298
theories behind merit pay, 27–49
transparency, 221, 222, 220–225, 225,
Pay and performance
actual relationship between, 50–54
perceived relationship between, 61–62
Pay increases
creating merit pay policy, 175–198
employee trust, 203–204
implementing merit pay policy, 198–199
major points, 204–206
merit pay as lag system, 199–200
merit pay as lead system, 200
participation in plan development, 201–203
timing of plan, 199–204
upper-level support, 200–201
Pay Satisfaction Questionnaire (PSQ), 182–183, 261
Pay structures, 189
comparative salary ratios, 191–192
forced distributions, 193–194
issues, 187–194
job evaluation, 188–189
locked or fixed-step systems, 192–193
pay ranges, 189–191
range penetration, 194
salary surveys, 189

Pay-for-performance, 6–7, 76, 268
actual relationship between pay and performance, 50–54
merit pay research, 60
meta-analysis, 54–58
moderator variables in meta-analysis, 58–60
new techniques, mounting evidence, 54–58
perceived relationship between pay and performance, 61–62
perceptions, 61, 61–62, 210–211, 297, 257
relationship, 49–62
Pay-for-performance plan creation issues
actual size of merit increases, 177–178
allocator selection, 198
budgeting issues, 184–187
comparative salary ratios, 191–192
considerations in establishing merit increase budgets, 187
creating merit pay policy, 175–198
earned-out approach, 182
forced distributions, 193–194
form of merit increases, 178–183
gross *vs.* net costs, 187
guide charts, 195–198
job evaluation, 188–189
just-noticeable differences, 175–177
locked or fixed-step systems, 192–193
no-strings approach, 182
overall size of budget, 186–187
pay ranges, 189–191
pay structure issues, 187–194
permanence of increase, 180–183
range penetration, 194
salary surveys, 189
salary-advance approach, 182
simple merit guide chart, 195
timing considerations, 183–184
top-down *vs.* bottom-up models, 185–186
type of merit increase, 178–180
uniform *vs.* flexible budgets, 185
Peanut butter approach, 23
Pearson product-moment correlation, 298–299
Perceptions, 81–82, 124–125
of equity, 68–70
Performance, 27, 76, 105, 124, 253, 268
absolute standards, 126–129
accuracy, 144–145
actual relationship between pay and, 50–54
adequacy of performance measures, 141–149
administrative practices, 165–167
alternative measures of performance for merit pay, 133–140
Brinkerhoff and Dressler Seven-Step Process, 155–156
choosing performance standard, 132–133
competency modeling, 158–159, 158–161
content validity, 142
convergent and discriminant validity, 142–143
correlations, 256
importance of adequate performance measures, 123–125
indexing, 156
job analysis, 157–158

linked to strategic mission, 151
management, 151–157
methods to improve validity of performance standards, 150–170
participation in scale development, 161–162
perceived accuracy of performance feedback, 219–220
perceived relationship between pay and, 61–62
effect of performance evaluation intervals, 59
performance-based benefits, 179–180
performance-related pay, 89–90
ProMES, 156–157
rater motivation, 168
rater training, 162–164
rating errors, 145–146
rating format, 162
ratingless feedback reviews, 131–132
ratings, 125–126
ratio, 255–256
relative comparisons, 129–132
relevance, 147–149
reliability, 143–144
selecting indicator to evaluate performance standards, 149
social comparisons, 167–168
standards, 142
statistical control of Halo, 168–170
types of performance measures, 125–133
understanding generational differences in performance feedback, 164–165
upper boundary of performance rating validity, 149–150
Performance appraisals, 146, 153–155
broader, 151–157
Performance management, 123–124, 153–155
system, 155
Performance Management, Recognition, and Reward System (PMRR), 112
Performance-based pay (PBP), 1–2, 69–70
Piece-rate pay plan, 109
Pilots, 158
Point-biserial correlation, 298–299, 301
Policy
capturing, 234
guidelines for alternative performance measures, 140
Politics, 99
Potential pitfalls with merit pay, 62–70, 63
Potential value, 32
Pratt and Whitney integrated reward strategy, 112
Pretest–posttest control group design, 273
Pretest–posttest design, 272
Price
guidelines, 79–80
stability, 78–79
Private sector, 85–91
organization, 184
Procedural justice, 209–210, 257–258
and attitudes, 212–214
and behavior, 215–216
importance of, 210–211
Product markets, 82, 84–91
high *vs.* low technology, 85
manufacturing *vs.* service, 84–85
public *vs.* private sector, 85–91
Productivity, 276

Productivity Measurement and Enhancement System (ProMES), 156–157
Professional bowler, 138
Professional employees, 86
Promotions, 108–109, 134
Prospector organization, 82–83
Protestant Reformation, 7–8
Psychological process, 42–43
Psychological theories, 28, 28–39, 124
  equity theory, 33–36
  expectancy theory, 29, 29–31
  goal-setting theory, 36–37
  reinforcement theory, 31–33
  self-determination theory, 37–38
  social exchange theory, 38–39
Public administrators, 267
Public sector, 85–91
  employees, 86–89, 125
  managers, 168
  organizations, 184, 214, 220

Random assignment, 273
Range penetration, 194
Ranking, 129–130
Rater motivation, 168
Rater training, 162–164
Rating errors, 145–146
Rating format, 162
Ratingless feedback reviews, 131–132
Reagan, R., 96
Recessionary conditions, 79
Reinforcement theory, 31–33, 33, 195, 226
Reinforcers, 32
Relative comparisons, 129–132
Relative system, 93–94
Relevance, 147–149
  of performance ratings, 99
Reliability, 143–144, 149
Return on equity (ROE), 266
Reward ratio, 256, 268

Salary surveys, 187–188, 189
Salary-advance approach, 182
Sales employees, 204
Satisfaction, 253, 259
Scale development, participation in, 161–162
School districts, 277–296
Scottsdale, Arizona, 300
Self-Determination Theory (SDT), 37–38, 38
Self-esteem, merit pay and, 66–68, 67
Senior executives, 161
Seniority, 134–136
Service markets, 82, 84–91
  different industries, 90–91
  high *vs.* low technology, 85
  manufacturing *vs.* service, 84–85
  public *vs.* private sector, 87, 85–91
Service supervisors, 143
Service-sector organizations, 84–85
Single-rate structure, 189
Skill-based pay, 112
Small teams, 111
Social comparisons, 167–168
Social exchange theory (SET), 38–39
Social movement, 225
Socioemotional selectivity theory (SST), 165
Software engineers, 158
Sophisticated methods, 54
Sorting effects, 47–48
Standard deviation (SD), 102
State governments, 9
Statistical control of Halo, 168–170
Strategic mission, linked to, 151
Strategic performance management, 152
Strictness, 145–146

Structural equation modeling (SEM), 46, 214
"Successive categories", 258
Supervisors, 166, 216, 228

Talent
- acquisition, 6
- development, 6

Task information, 233
Tax
- rates, 80–81
- structure, 80

Team members, 111
Team-based, financial incentives, 110
Team-based incentives, 111
Technical employees, 86
Test–retest reliability, 143–144
Theories of merit pay
- economic theories, 39–48
- efficiency wage theory, 43–45
- equity theory, 33–36
- expectancy theory, 29, 29–31
- goal-setting theory, 36–37
- implicit contract theory, 41–43
- marginal productivity theory, 40–41
- Matthew effect, 68–69
- meta-analysis, 54–58
- overreward inequity, 69–70
- pay-for-performance relationship, 49–62
- potential pitfalls with merit pay, 62–70
- reinforcement theory, 31–33
- self-determination theory, 37–38
- social exchange theory, 38–39
- sorting effects, 47–48
- tournament theory, 45–47

Time delay in ratings, 165–166
Time-series design, 274
Top-down models, 185–186
Total compensation system, 206–207
Tough managerial decisions, 4–6
Tournament theory, 45–47, 46
Traditional merit
- pay plans, 180
- plan, 180

Traditional voting system, 54
Training programs, 233
Traits, 126, 126–127
Turnover, 264
Two-way communication, 212–213
Typical performance, 138

U.S. government, 81
Uniform budgets, 185
Unit performance, 266–267
United States, 4
Unstable conditions, 82–83
Unstructured conditions, 83
Upper boundary of performance rating validity, 149–150
Upper-level support, 200–201
Utility, 264–266
- analysis, 12

Valence theory, 29
Validation, 123
"Variable pay", 6–7, 39, 41
Vehicles, 228

Wage guidelines, 79–80
Wagner Act, 246–247
Welch, J., 24
Westinghouse, 133
White-collar employees, 191
White-collar jobs, 104
WorldatWork, 225, 228

Printed and bound by CPI Group (UK) Ltd, Croydon, CR0 4YY
15/09/2026
14962485-0008